The Political Economy of Gender

Hebatallah Adam · Firdous Ahmad Malik
Editors

The Political Economy of Gender

Power, Patriarchy, and Intersectionality in the Global South

Springer

Editors
Hebatallah Adam
Jindal School of International Affairs
O. P. Jindal Global University
Sonipat, Haryana, India

Firdous Ahmad Malik
Department of Management
University of The People
Pasadena, CA, USA

ISBN 978-981-92-2784-6 ISBN 978-981-92-2785-3 (eBook)
https://doi.org/10.1007/978-981-92-2785-3

This Springer imprint is published by the registered company Springer Nature Singapore Pte Ltd.
The registered company address is: 152 Beach Road, #21-01/04 Gateway East, Singapore 189721, Singapore

Preface

The book was the result of a shared understanding that political economy of gender in the Global South cannot be viewed in a vacuum without references to historical, cultural, and structural pressures that create it. Women and marginalized people are not disproportionately exposed to inequalities; they are inherent to the fabric of capitalism all over the world, patriarchy institutionalized, and stratification of the society. In the Global South, resistance has been raised by literature, grassroots action, and academic dissent against the systems that uphold exclusion.

The concept of this book developed out of continuous debates between scholars, researchers, and practitioners who have been long struggling to understand how gender mingles with politics, economy, and culture in the context of colonial pasts, neoliberal globalization, and authoritarian populism. The outcome of these discussions was to unequivocally highlight that the Global South cannot be regarded as a single group. Instead, it is a multi-space in which other histories and competing identities have defined gendered experiences. These chapters reflect on this heterogeneity, and they include experiences of South Asia, Africa, Southeast Asia, and Latin America.

The book is guided by three primary concepts: power, patriarchy and intersectionality. Power is taken in two senses, one fairing of formal power, another that regards subtle and quotidian processes that uphold imbalances. Patriarchy is discussed as a cultural and institution mechanism of sustaining gender exclusion. Intersectionality offers a framework to understand the interdependence of the analysis of class, caste, race, ethnicity, religion and gender. The combination of these ideas provides us with a new perspective on political economy seen through the perspectives of individuals most excluded by it.

In our role as editors, our intention was to introduce voices of diversity across disciplinary, methodological and geographical borders. The contributors of this volume are scholars and researchers from various countries of the Global South that made it an exclusive perspective at cross-over point between gender and political economy. This volume is addressed to a wide range of readers including scholars and scholars engaged with the intertwined field of gender studies, economics, sociology, and study of development. It can also assist policy makers, practitioners, and activists who might like to create initiatives and policies that would be based on the lives of women and other vulnerable groups. In conclusion, this volume is an important addition to the body of literature on Gender and Global South Studies that is increasingly becoming more within the literature. We hope our readers, can find in coming pages a source of inspiration to render the future just.

Sonipat, India Prof. Dr. Hebatallah Adam

Introduction

In Global South, the political economy of gender must be viewed as an interconnected process involving histories, institutions, and struggles. Furthermore, gender does not exist in a vacuum; rather, it is a powerful pillar that shapes political and economic structures, perpetuates inequality, and allocates resources and opportunities. Colonialism, neoliberal globalization, and authoritarian governance all affect how gender and power are connected. Even though women and other marginalized groups are often left out of the system, they also create chances for subversion, negotiation, and change. This book looks at how power, patriarchy, and intersectionality shape life in the Global South by bringing together several perspectives.

Power is not only exercised through formal political structures; cultural and economic systems, along with quotidian behavior, also contribute. Patriarchy in both the workplace and the home is another reason why women don't work, stay at home, or even not getting involved in politics very often. In terms of intersectionality, which is a way to look at these differences, class, race, caste, religion, and ethnicity all influence them at the same time.

Both strengths and vulnerabilities show how power works in the Global South. Global supply chains and neoliberal economic policies have affected the lives of women who work in low-paying jobs, as well as domestic workers and garment workers. In these systems, women are not just victims; they are also those who come up with strategies to survive and attain their aspirations. Their stories demonstrate how race, class, ethnicity, and other identities always serve as leading factors to inequality, which is universal. Professional women, such as those in academic or administrative roles, encounter similar levels of intersectional barriers. In terms of legitimacy and access to power, they are frequently impacted by their gender in addition to their racial and cultural affinities. These examples demonstrate that intersectionality is both a reality and a theoretical concept.

One of the persistent systems that still affects the Global South is patriarchy. This shows up in cultural practices that limit autonomy as well as in formal structures like financial institutions that lack access to rural women, politics that silences women, and labor markets that confine women to low-wage, unstable jobs. However, patriarchy can still be changed. Resistance takes place in institutional and cultural contexts. Examples of how institutional modalities can be reorganized to recognize the agency of women are changes to laws pertaining to gender equality systems and financial options such as women banks. These examples demonstrate that even in patriarchal systems, there are chances to establish contests and reforms.

The structure of this volume consists of four main sections:

- Part I—Gendered Power and Political Participation reflects on political and economic agency, of women, including feminist foreign policy, political leadership, and structural reforms.
- Part II—Cultural and Institutional Patriarchy sets out to understand how cultural narratives, literature, legal systems, and financial systems continue to control patriarchal authority or challenge it.
- Part III—Resistance, Right-Wing Populism, and Gendered Narratives focuses on how aspects of populist politics, media space, and nationalist rhetoric fashion femininity and the place of women in the Global South.
- Part IV—Voice, Violence, and Visibility highlights ecofeminist movements, gender violence and gender labor vulnerabilities at the core of global capitalism, with emphasis on resilience and survival tactics by women.

All parts elaborate on the principles of power, patriarchy, and intersectionality through various methodologies, including ethnography, discourse analysis, literary criticism, and feminist legal theory. To make progress towards gender equality in the Global South, this volume concludes that we need creative institutions and activism.

The study of intersectionality provides a pathway to address gender inequality in the Global South. It is essential to recognize that the movements for gender justice are fundamentally interconnected with significant struggles against racism, caste oppression, environmental degradation, and economic dependency. Intersectional perspectives enhance the vision of comprehensive social transformation that not only tackles gender injustice but also targets the more profound institutional frameworks that perpetuate gender inequity. This volume contributes to academics, politics, and ethics. It aims to shed light on the intricate dynamics of power, patriarchy, and intersectionality within the Global South, amplifying voices of resistance, reinvention, and reconstruction. It advocates in a concerted effort to create more egalitarian and accommodating futures.

Hebatallah Adam
Professor of Economics
Jindal School of International Affairs
(JSIA)
O.P. Jindal Global University (JGU)
Sonipat, India

Contents

Editors and Contributors

About the Editors

Prof. (Dr.) Hebatallah Adam is a distinguished scholar and academic leader with over two decades of expertise in International Economic Development. She is Full Professor of Economics and Academic Dean at the Jindal School of International Affairs, O.P. Jindal Global University, India, and a recipient of the UAE's Golden Residence Visa for outstanding academic contributions (Geniuses of Talent).

She is the founder of the Jindal Centre for the Global South, the Global South Research Foundation (GSRF), and the Africa Dialogue Forum (ADF), all dedicated to advancing research and policy on development challenges in the Global South. Her academic background spans Ain Shams University, Poitiers University, and the Sorbonne (Paris), and her research focuses on International Development Economics, Global South Studies, Political Economy of Development, Green Economics, and International Trade.

Dr. Adam has published widely in Scopus-indexed journals and with Springer, Routledge, and Palgrave Macmillan. She is a member of the Organization for Women in Science for the Developing World (OWSD), an associate member of the African Studies Centre at Leiden, and serves on the International Editorial Committee of the Journal of Liberty and International Affairs. She is also a peer reviewer and frequent invited speaker at international conferences.

Dr. Firdous Ahmad Malik is Economist and Assistant Professor of Economics at the University of the People, California, USA, and currently a post-doctoral researcher at Amity University, Dubai. He has previously worked as Research Fellow at the National Institute of Public Finance and Policy (NIPFP), New Delhi, and as Senior Research Associate at the Jindal Centre for the Global South, O.P. Jindal Global University. His research focuses on microfinance, financial inclusion, development economics, and public finance.

Dr. Malik has published widely in Scopus-indexed journals and authored more than eight books with leading publishers, including Springer, Routledge, and IGI

Global. His forthcoming book, Gender and Global Economic Stability: Insights and Strategies for Women's Financial Resilience, will be published by Palgrave Macmillan. He has received multiple awards, including the Best Paper Presentation Award from the Jindal Centre for the Global South and the Best Reviewer Award at the AIBPM Malaysian Conference in 2023. An active member of international networks such as the Young Scholars Initiative, Dr. Malik continues to contribute to advancing inclusive finance and global development research.

List of Contributors

Princewill Chukwuma Abakporo Theatre & Media Arts Programme, Bowen University, Iwo, Nigeria

Hebatallah Adam Jindal School of International Affairs (JSIA), Jindal Global University (JGU), Sonipat, India

Abhilash Aggarwal School of Law, CHRIST (Deemed to be University), Bangalore, India

Masroor Ahmad Department of Economics, Central University of Kashmir, Ganderbal, India

Mary-Ann O. Ajayi College of Law, Bowen University, Iwo, Nigeria

Naila Febrina Akmalia Department of Government Studies, Universitas Muhammadiyah Malang, Malang, Indonesia

Anna Bashir School of Law, University of Kashmir, Srinagar, India

Alaya Chhabra Amity School of Economics, Amity University Noida, Noida, India

Sameena Dalwai Jindal Global Law School, OP Jindal Global University, Sonipat, Haryana, India

Sumedh Dalwai University of St Andrews, St Andrews, UK

Muhammad Januar Galang Department of Politics and Government, Universutas Gadjah Mada, Yogyakarta, Indonesia

Tanni Ganguly School of Law, Manav Rachna University, Faridabad, India

Anam Ul Haq Ganie School of Business, Woxsen University, Hyderabad, India

Jacqueline Elisha Gomes Jain (Deemed-to-Be University), Bengaluru, India

Ishika Jaiswal Former Faculty of Economics, Indian Institute of Management Sambalpur, Sambalpur, Odisha, India

Divleen Kaur Amity School of Economics, Amity University Noida, Noida, India

Daisy Mui Hung Kee Universiti Sains Malaysia, Penang, Malaysia

Louis Yong Yu Lee Universiti Sains Malaysia, Penang, Malaysia

Firdous Ahmad Malik Department of Management, University of People California, Pasadena, CA, US

M. Maya Christ University, Bangalore, India

Mehvish Mehraj Department of Business Studies, University of the People, California, USA

Nisha Nair O.P. Jindal Global University, Sonipat, India

Samanvi Narang O.P. Jindal Global University, Sonipat, India

Nitin Narayanan O.P. Jindal Global University, Haryana, India

Caroline C. Netto Christ University, Bangalore, India;
Independent Researcher, Bengaluru, Karnataka, India

Stanley Timeyin Ohenhen Theatre & Media Arts Programme, Bowen University, Iwo, Nigeria;
Theatre & Media Arts Programme, Bowen University, Iwo, Nigeria

Rajdeep Pakanati Jindal School of International Affairs, OP Jindal Global University, Sonipat, Haryana, India

Aaratrika Pandey School of Law, Manav Rachna University, Faridabad, India

Rubina Pradhan Jain (Deemed-to-Be University), Bengaluru, India

Salahudin Department of Government Studies, Universitas Muhammadiyah Malang, Malang, Indonesia

Sakshi Shukla M S Ramaiah University of Applied Sciences, Bengaluru, India

Neeru Sidana Amity School of Economics, Amity University Noida, Noida, India

Iradhad Taqwa Sihidi Department of Government Studies, Universitas Muhammadiyah Malang, Malang, Indonesia

Jyot Shikhar Singh Jindal School of International Affairs (JSIA), Jindal Global University (JGU), Sonipat, India

Vanya Srivastava Department of Languages (English), FOHSS Integral University, Lucknow, India

Poornima Vijaya Kumaraguru College of Liberal Arts and Science, Coimbatore, Tamil Nadu, India

Jamin Kun Peng Xia Universiti Sains Malaysia, Penang, Malaysia

List of Figures

Chapter 8

Chapter 9

Chapter 16

List of Tables

Part I
Gendered Power and Political Participation

Chapter 1
Feminist Foreign Policy as a Strategy for Status-Signalling–The Indian Perspective

Poornima Vijaya and Nitin Narayanan

Abstract The feminist foreign policy (FFP) discourse has undoubtedly gained traction over the last decade, with several states globally championing gender issues, their merits, and efficacy. In this regard, gender equality becomes an important normative ideal that states often use as a token for status signalling. This chapter aims to explore the various aspects of FFP. Using discourse analysis, this study aims to answer critical questions on how it is construed, whether it has been effective, and the interface of gender equality and status-seeking strategies. On paper, India's commitment towards gender equality is impressive. Taking a deeper look at India's relationship with the discourse on FFP and promises for gender equality demonstrates how India's efforts tend to approach the problem on a superficial level. Does this indicate that gender equality is merely an instrument for signalling its rising status? While gaps in policy and implementation are prevalent, signalling a stronger FFP approach could help India better position itself to fulfil its global power pursuit by prioritising gendered issues and human security. Adopting an effective FFP can also help revitalise necessary shifts in India's domestic context. Finally, such an approach would help India foster closer ties and champion the cause of gender equality in the global south.

Keywords Gender equality · Feminist foreign policy · Global south · Status signalling · Indian foreign policy · Moralpolitik · Women's rights

---

P. Vijaya (✉)
Kumaraguru College of Liberal Arts and Science, Coimbatore, Tamil Nadu, India
e-mail: poornima.r.bps@kclas.ac.in

N. Narayanan
O.P. Jindal Global University, Haryana, India
e-mail: nnarayanan@jgu.edu.in

H. Adam and F. A. Malik (eds.), *The Political Economy of Gender*,
https://doi.org/10.1007/978-981-92-2785-3_1

1 Introduction

In International Relations (IR), foreign policy paradigms have evolved to witness the emergence of feminist foreign policy (FFP) as a progressive framework. FFP originated from feminist movements that acquired endurance in the late twentieth century. Feminist researchers and activists advocated for a more inclusive and gender-sensitive approach to policymaking, challenging conventional norms that neglected or overlooked women's experiences in domestic and international environments (Fotaki & Pullen, 2023). While the narratives of feminist foreign policy have gained momentum in the West, they largely exclude feminist thought in non-Global North traditions (García & Castelán, 2023).

At present, many more states, such as Mexico, Libya, Chile, Colombia, Liberia, and South Asian countries like India, have adopted or have strongly indicated the adoption of FFP. This indicates that FFP as a construct is not exclusive to the Western hemisphere. FFP, which has been relegated to the margins for many decades, is slowly gaining much-needed recognition due to the efforts of transnational feminist movements in peace-making, peacebuilding, and peacekeeping (Patel, 2023a). The uptake of FFP is now taking shape in the Global South. While the phenomenon of FFP is new in the West, "feminist traditions and ambitions in have existed in South Asia context for long" (Achilleos-Sarll et al., 2022).

An FFP framework provides a powerful prism through which individuals can challenge detrimental global power systems, such as patriarchy, racism, cultural nationalism, imperialism, and militarism, that keep the vast majority of the population in constant vulnerability and despair (Haastrup, 2024). It places gender issues at the forefront of a nation's diplomatic efforts (Killare, 2023). These developments have far-reaching consequences for women and other marginalized groups who are disempowered by patriarchy and social stratification. As countries rethink the global power structure and form new alliances, gender fairness and inclusion must be central to these transformations (MacArthur et al., 2022). Unfortunately, various governments have done the reverse, staying gender-blind, particularly on traditionally "masculine" policy matters such as trade, foreign policy, and national security (Thomson, 2020).

Moreover, in our case, India, which has seen a gradual transformation in the increase of its regional and global profile, has not realised these great power ambitions with the emergence of a new multipolar world order, also extend greater opportunities for India to champion the cause of FFP (Puri, 2023). Though India has remained somewhat committed to the gender goals, the overall achievements reflect that the progress has been limited (Puri, 2023). Responsibility towards gender issues must be meaningful and progressive rather than symbolic and superficial. Despite limited achievements, many countries, including India, continue to endorse FFP as a future foreign policy direction, yet many a time merely as lip service (Sethi & Rakhra, 2025). A deeper inquiry into this also unravels how countries across the globe, including India, use FFP as a tool or an instrument for status-signalling (Kullar, 2021). However, it must also realise the benefits of adopting an FFP framework to fulfil its global power pursuit better and champion the causes of women's empowerment, development, and sustainable peace (Michalko, 2023). Therefore, India must develop a gender-inclusive lens for policies and institutional structures for balanced growth and development. As a result, the discussion of feminist foreign policy (FFP) in India has remained a work in progress.

In this context, this chapter will continue as follows. Firstly, we will examine the literature in two parts: FFP as a discourse in IR and explore the gaps in the overall adoption and implementation of the FFP, leading to answers on how the FFP framework is used as an instrument for strategic signalling. These aspects would constitute the foundation of our analytical framework. The following section details the aim of this study, and the methodology of discourse analysis used in this study. In the further sections, we examine India as a case study in two parts by analysing India's desire for status and its objectives of FFP and delving into the advantages of FFP for India's overall global standing and signalling its 'moralpolitik'. The final sections end with recommendations and a conclusion.

2 Literature Review

2.1 Feminist Foreign Policy as a Discourse

The early twentieth century saw the emergence of liberalism and international institutions focused on peace and security, allowing non-state actors to participate in international affairs (Devitt, 2021). The emergence of human security as a concept explains the rise of intrastate conflicts and their effects on civilian populations, as well as the growing significance of human rights, which helped to establish personal safety and security as a fundamental component of global peace and security (United Nations, 2009). Along these lines, feminist theories grew in influence as they dislocated the concept of 'State' from the centrality of discipline. Instead, studies were calling attention to individuals and groups that were traditionally marginalised, especially women (Fotaki & Pullen, 2023). Feminist approaches have stressed the importance of inclusivity and intersectionality on several themes, including climate change, health, economic empowerment, development, security, and peace (Baccarini et al., 2019).

Nevertheless, the most oft-cited FFP origins begin with Sweden as the first country to use the characterisation of 'Feminist' in its foreign policy in 2014 (Achilleos-Sarll et al., 2022). Swedish government policy documents highlight that Sweden will "systematically integrate a gender perspective in their foreign policy agenda" (Aggestam et al., 2018; Swedish Ministry of Foreign Affairs, 2018; Rosamond, 2020). Several countries across the Global North and South have adopted or expressed an interest in potentially adopting an FFP, sparking debates for its uptake (Achilleos-Sarll et al., 2022). One noteworthy aspect of this narrative is that FFP is popularly a "thought from the Global North" and, therefore, is exported (Jezierska & Towns, 2018). However, the adoption and implementation by the Global South, such as

Chile, Mexico, Liberia, Colombia, and others, has signalled how the concept and practice of FFP is taking its roots in such regions. (Parashar & D'Costa, 2017).

Five major factors influenced the development of FFP: firstly, works which envisioned a world with no violence, involving numerous feminist thinkers such as Christine de Pizan, Jane Addams, Bertha von Suttner, and others"; secondly, "peace advocacy that promoted new perspectives on international order at the International Women's Congresses in 1915 and 1919″; thirdly, "feminist international relations and its studies on international power systems"; fourthly, "norm entrepreneurs like the former Swedish Foreign Minister, Margot Wallström"; and lastly, "underscoring the importance of integrating of pro-feminist principles in bureaucratic and governments offering positive conditions." (Uspenskaya & Kozlova, 2022; Vogelstein, 2019). Other research has also shown that incorporating pro-feminist norms in governmental and bureaucratic organizations created progressive circumstances for foreign policy (Rosamond, 2020).

Another point of origin is the story of the Swedish delegation's 1915 arrival in The Hague. To advocate for the end of World War I, more than 1,100 female delegates from twelve nations convened here (Patterson, 2014). In addition to establishing the "International Congress of Women (ICW)," which subsequently evolved into the "Women's International League for Peace and Freedom (WILPF)," they also contemplated the use of intervention tactics to end the conflict and eliminate its primary reasons (Confortini, 2012). They emphasized women's vulnerability during wartime, advocated for the "immediate cessation of all warfare, as well as full disarmament and arms control," acknowledged states' rights to self-government, proposed the formation of a conference of nations, and further demanded equal representation for women. (Tickner & True, 2018). As stated by civil society advocacy, these can be seen as the main tenets of FFP (UN Women, n.d.). It is also true that feminist international thought and its underlying assumptions ignore the historical experiences, customs, and particular difficulties in the Global South, even though this narrative may have gained traction. Both feminist practices as well as goals in foreign policy have existed in South Asia. (Parashar & D'Costa, 2017, 28). They challenge epistemic violence by defining FFP as an export of the Global North, as well as practicing and exporting liberal feminism (Das, 2017).

State-centric theories and FFP implementations demonstrate that many states are still formulating a concrete policy stance. So, what does FFP mean for these states? The FFP has been adopted by several countries at varying points, creating a complete framework. A "formal FFP declaration frequently occurs before adopting a policy or clear definition" (Gill-Atkinson et al., 2021, 17). This could be due to newer governments seeking an 'announceable' and administrations wanting to align with FFP issues (Gill-Atkinson et al. 2021, 13). Though FFP relies on international work on women's issues in pre-existing transnational and multilateral mechanisms, states' conceptualisation of FFP and understanding of the f-word is rather novel in depicting their foreign policy through the prism of feminism and gender equality. (Achilleos-Sarll et al., 2022; Zhukova et al., 2021). Therefore, combating issues through the lens of feminism has been reduced to limited engagement and tokenism, also constraining the overall conceptualisation, implementation, and adoption of the feminist discourse in the world, especially in the global south.

2.2 *FFP and Signalling: What Do States Achieve?*

The "three Rs—rights, representation, and resources"—officially sum up the FFP and identify the areas to promote gender equality in foreign policy (Nylund et al., 2022). The FFP is applied "throughout" and "at all levels," according to the foreign ministry, and the three Rs essentially cover various aspects of foreign policy, including trade, aid, and diplomacy (Government Offices of Sweden, 2019). However, Sweden under Ulf Kristersson in 2022, has abandoned the once-groundbreaking FFP policy. In this regard, the foreign affairs Minister, Tobias Billström, stated, "gender equality is an essential principle, but the government is not going to continue FFP since the tag obscures the fact that Swedish foreign policy must be grounded in Swedish values and interests" (Granlund, 2022). While countries are backtracking on labels, multilateral institutions fail to implement strong measures and frameworks on gendered issues within and outside the system (Larson & Shevchenko, 2010). Furthermore, it is important to note that "definitional questions of what they mean by feminist" in their policies or announcements are hardly addressed despite the fact that the nations that have committed to or intend to adopt an FFP have widely differing levels of policy development and reports (Baruah & Bhide, 2022).

Fresh concerns have been raised regarding the efficacy of multilateral groupings. Meanwhile, developing countries are contesting for more equitable representation and influence on the international stage as global economic inequality rises. In the face of volatility, many nations have adopted FFP to tackle these concerns by recognising the intersectionality of several issues. Nonetheless, practising, applying, and strong implementation of FFP is much more complex than merely adopting it (Sikkink & Clapp, 2024). Besides that, countries like Canada and Sweden have been criticised for their inconsistent actions, including sending weapons to nations with a poor record of protecting women's rights (Zhukova et al., 2021). The discrepancy between the domestic women's rights record and the branding of feminist foreign policy is another subject of criticism (Zhukova et al., 2021).

If the implementation is sub-standard, why do countries continue to use the rhetoric of feminism and FFP? Status is a crucial aspect of the interaction between states, just as it is in human society. Status is a collection of accepted beliefs about each country's relative position that dictates who gets what, when, and under what conditions (Wohlforth et al., 2017). The attitudes underpinning status ascription are based on the values assigned to material and ideational traits (Pu, 2017). This list of elements to status is not absolute. Symbols of status evolve over time and take different shapes depending on the culture and geography of the region (Basrur & De Estrada, 2017; Bjarnegård & Zetterberg, 2022). Scholars from multiple schools of political science and international relations (IR) concur that status—"standing or rank in a hierarchy"—is an important feature of international politics (Götz, 2020;

Murray, 2018; Renshon, 2017; 2019). It has three key characteristics: positional, perceptual, and social, which work together to make all actors' status positions a function of higher order. Status is commonly used in a positional sense: standing, rank, or position of a country in a hierarchy (Mattern & Zarakol, 2016; Renshon, 2019). The phrase "status community" refers to a hierarchical structure composed of actors (Renshon, 2017; 2019). Thus, states might employ tangible and ideational elements such as feminism to signal toward improving their international image. In IR, "feminism as a signalling instrument" refers to acts of state or political actor publicly adopting feminist policies or rhetoric to convey a specific message about their commitment to gender equality, often to improve their international status or gain political capital, rather than enacting significant changes that tackle underlying gender inequalities within their society.

3 Aim of the Study

This research examines how intersectionality in FFP can contribute to peace-making, peacekeeping, and overall growth and development in the Global South. Moreover, this chapter aims to analyse the double-edged nature of signalling and how signalling FFP goals in their current iterations have been inadequate in providing rights, representation, and resources. However, if used positively and combined with robust action, it can help states in the Global South signal their priorities in gendered issues, human security, peace, and development.

In this book, our chapter explores how governments in the global south have resorted to feminist interpretations to serve their interests, power, and ambition, thereby using the critical lens of feminist discourse to signal status and policy. At the same time, achievements on this front are somewhat limited.

4 Methodology

In general, the application of qualitative discourse analysis is "to examine information [texts] in a systematic way according to given principles and theoretical frameworks in order to reach conclusions on certain elements of the information" (Mayring and Fenzl 2019). Discourse analysis, which is described as "a particular way of talking about and understanding the world" (Jorgenson & Phillips, 2002, 1), will be used in this study. Discourse analysis relies heavily on knowledge, which can be viewed as "socially produced forms of knowledge" (Bacchi & Goodwin, 2016, 35). Knowledge is not interpreted as the truth but rather as what is considered to be true, thus making it a product of context and culture.

In this case, conclusions will be drawn from the discursive support on policies and implementation of FFP in the global south, especially India. Data on gender gaps, policies, and implementation has been taken from various sources, including UN websites, government data, speeches, and secondary journal articles. This information is used to contextualise the progress, or lack thereof, in the action and implementation of FFP goals worldwide, especially in India.

5 Case Selection

India's position in the world has gradually changed over the past ten years due to its growing regional and international prominence, aspirations to become a great power, and the emergence of a progressive voice on some of the most important contemporary issues. However, it has not yet acknowledged the necessity of applying an inclusionary lens to institutional structures and policies that can result in a more innovative shift in its capacity to influence global politics. (Killare, 2025). Therefore, it is a unique case to study as achieving FFP goals with robust execution of a holistic vision can benefit India in signalling 'moralpolitik' and an inclusivity agenda.

5.1 India's Rising Status Ambitions

Status is an essential element for a state's global standing. Status is the collective recognition that it obtains based on its material and non-material capabilities, which is critical to understanding its actions in its regional environment and on a global scale (Khory, 2022; MacDonald & Parent, 2021). As a rising power, India is a status-conscious state (Kumar, 2024). India's path from the perception of 'Fallen People' to being recognised as a 'rising power' is noteworthy, albeit still evolving (Pardesi, 2015; Paul & Shankar, 2014).

During the Nehru era, leading systemic pressures included power politics and opposing ideologies of capitalism and communism (Chakrabarty, 1992). India prioritised unique liberal democracy with socialist influences over traditional capitalism or socialist economics, rejecting power politics. In the post-Cold War era, global power politics continued, and free enterprise grew unchallenged, simultaneously strengthening the norms of democracy, participation, and representation. India, as a whole, embraced these norms and free market reforms to modernise its material strength further. Over the past two decades, Indian political elites have been emphasising their normative agenda (De Estrada, 2023). United Progressive Alliance (UPA) governments led by Congress Party's PM, Manmohan Singh, from 2004–2014, repeatedly argued for India's leading role in promoting the 'virtues of democracy' and its distinguishing development model in the Global South (Bagchi, 2011). Other Indian leaders and thinkers have advocated for India's role in promoting human rights, disaster relief, and inclusive growth. Bharatiya Janata Party (BJP) government, under the leadership of Narendra Modi, aims to position India as a 'vishwaguru' and a 'leading power' in international relations (De Estrada, 2023). This includes having a clear vision of how international affairs and international institutions should be organised rather than simply accepting the status quo (De Estrada, 2023). Moreover, India's "ability to project itself as a responsible power has helped it gain recognition as a rising power" (Paul et al., 2014; Saran, 2024).

India's actions in the global south are motivated mainly by two goals. One, to strengthen solidarity within the camp, and second, to project its international agenda (Bhatia, 2024). It also underlines the significance of India's growth trajectory and achievements for the Global South and New Delhi's status as an important actor and leader in this region (Ministry of Information and Broadcasting of India, 2024). The repeated efforts to become the voice of the global south are necessary, considering the numerous candidates vying for this position, ranging from China to Brazil to South Africa (Bhatia, 2024). The Foreign Minister, Dr S Jaishankar, rejected the power play by emphasising that the Global South is more of a solidarity camp with countries with similar interests and challenges (Jaishankar, 2024). However, the aspects of power play in the global south are active (Bhatia, 2024).

Many more issues are challenging the global south, such as climate change mitigation, health security, international financial stability, counterterrorism, nuclear non-proliferation, economic development, and trade. Many scholars and economists have categorised these challenges as global public goods potentially affecting many countries. While gender is not spelt separately as an issue faced by the Global South grouping, all the above have a gendered lens to consider for sustainable policies (Al-Ali, 2020). FFP, inspired by feminist principles, offers governments alternative approaches to international relations with states, civil society groups, and other actors, addressing the current polycrisis (Adam & Rena, 2024). Countries, including those in the Global South, have adopted a narrow conceptualisation of the term like security while prioritising their national interests. Agency and power are still implicitly portrayed as masculine spheres with slim chances for women, who are viewed as passive beings (Hogan & Patrick, 2024). Meanwhile, gender mainstreaming remains a work in progress with few to no positive outcomes, giving India immense space and opportunity to step in as a pioneering voice on FFP in the Global South.

However, India, which is desiring its rising international status and leadership role in South Asia and the global south, continues to face severe challenges to gender equality and empowerment in the domestic sphere as well. On paper, India has committed to gender equality, which is impressive. It has reiterated its goals of supporting UN Sustainable Development Goals (UN SDGs) on providing aid and assistance to multilateral programmes on women's empowerment and recently becoming a member of the UN Commission on the Status of Women in 2020 (Tamang, 2024). However, India is one of the countries with the lowest gender equality in global rankings (PTI, 2024). Taking a deeper look at India's relationship with the discourse on FFP and promises for gender equality demonstrates how India's efforts tend to approach the problem on a superficial level. This has drawn several criticisms for being disingenuous (Magan, 2023). Nonetheless, active advocacy and implementation would also help India to utilise FFP frameworks as a 'moralpolitik' to project its rising status and leadership in the Global South (Khullar, 2021; Schottli, 2022).

5.2 FFP in the Indian Context- Signalling 'Moralpolitik'

The discourse of FFP in India is still a work in progress. An uneven sex ratio at birth affects the rising gender imbalance. Moreover, the National Crime Records Bureau of India notes that, on average, 87 rape cases are recorded daily in 2019, with a four-percentage increase in 2023 (Jha, 2024; Patel, 2024). It has also fallen the ranks to 140th position in the World Economic Forum's Gender Gap Report (Joy, 2021). India has also advocated the goals that resonate with the UNSCR 1325 and Women Peace and Security (WPS) agenda ideals at various international forums; however, these efforts are mainly directed under the peacekeeping and development assistance paradigm. It has refrained from adopting the WPS National Action Plan (NAP) to this day (Seth, 2022). It has not yet ratified the Optional Protocols that allow for women to directly petition the CEDAW committee in the event that the domestic state apparatus fails to provide them with justice, even though it ratified the Convention for the Elimination of All Forms of Discrimination Against Women (CEDAW) in 1993 (Shritha, 2022). Lastly, the representation of women in foreign policy positions is declining, with varied degrees of inconsistency. India has so far taken an outward-looking stance in its commitment to a gender-sensitive foreign policy (Rathore, 2021).

The existing gaps between its gender commitments on paper and the reality in the context of India's adoption of FFP can be ascribed to two major reasons. First, India's policy announcements are largely decided by political concerns (Khillare 2023; Patel, 2023a, 2023b). This can be seen when India did not ratify the WPS agenda on the reasons that it was not valid in India's setting despite the presence of several conflict-ridden regions within India (Khullar, 2020). It is also viewed as external interference in domestic matters, explaining the reasons for not ratifying the Optional Protocols of CEDAW (Bhattacharya, 2017). Therefore, in simple words, the idea of FFP and its formulations must be tailored to specific needs, political agendas, and historical and cultural backgrounds of a state. This makes it imperative that India derive its own definition and conceptualisation of the FFP agenda, making implementation and advocacy smooth and consistent (Llacer, 2023). In the Indian context, an FFP would involve dismantling power systems that thrive on various forms of inequality. It would centre on the experiences of people who face persistent impediments to accessing their fundamental human rights. Moreover, the key aspects of FFP in India should indicate its more profound commitment towards securing sustainable peace and accessibility to women's rights, thereby allocating resources specifically aimed at achieving FFP outcomes (Lahiry, 2024).

The interpretation and smooth implementation of FFP goals would enable India to become a crucial actor in international, regional, and domestic affairs. It helps India promote friendlier ties with countries in the Western Hemisphere and the Global South by championing the 'moralpolitik' agenda (Ogden, 2022). The idea of a *vishwaguru* (world leader) is an outward-facing or signalling project of the state with social and political dimensions (De Estrada, 2023; Hall, 2017). Aptly, FFP has both pedagogical and transformative dimensions, providing several avenues for India to convey its agenda and status in the world. The public discourse in India centres on eradicating social, cultural, and institutional impediments that hinder women from engaging in their country's affairs. A gender-oriented foreign policy would be important for both external and internal politics in India. An inclusive foreign service will implement institutional changes to ensure the representation of marginalised groups and areas. A gender-concerned foreign service will endeavour to guarantee that individuals of all genders, not just men, have space in the political system (Devasia, 2022). Therefore, an effective FFP can help India achieve transformational changes in the domestic context on issues ranging from representation, gender parity, empowerment, rights, peace, and security. An Indian FFP will also advance India's ability to engage progressively with any number of local, regional, and global gender challenges, thereby improving its international recognition (Baruah & Bhide, 2022).

India has a history of progressive foreign policy participation. It has emphasised peace-oriented solutions to conflicts, using diplomacy and giving an alternative, such as the Non-Aligned Movement during the Cold War (Dutt, 2013). It is, therefore, crucial to explore the feminist lens to essential sectors of India's Global South Cooperation in humanitarian aid and disaster relief (HADR), economic and development cooperation, institutional governance, global public goods, and climate cooperation. However, India must also walk the talk rather than address the issues superficially, thereby using FFP as a signalling instrument with disingenuity, leading to backlash domestically and internationally.

6 Policy Recommendations

India has some stellar policies helping its women-led growth and development agenda. Several schemes and incentives through Bima Shakti Yojana, Ujjwala Yojana, Mudra Loans, and state government schemes like Ladli Behan Yojanas strongly aim to promote women-led initiatives domestically (Sarkar & Kumar, 2022). However, we recommend that stronger and more grassroots implementation of these schemes in manufacturing will also help women be part of the Make in India initiatives, thereby promoting women-led middle and small enterprises. Such initiatives can be exported as a model for developing smaller countries in the global south to emulate.

Second, the skewed gender ratio reveals the need to revisit abortion laws and implement more decisive measures to prevent female infanticide. Regarding foreign policy, representation is not sufficient as a standalone measure. Addressing international issues such as global health, climate change, education, economic development, peace, and security from a woman-centric outlook would ensure long-lasting solutions.

Third, India's FFP agenda will benefit from intersectionality and must be modelled on its diplomatic values of inclusive growth through the ideals of *vasudhaiva kutumbakam* and interests based on rising as a *vishwaguru*. More profound research is required to envision a framework suitable for the Indian context and challenges.

Fourth, the FFP framework must ensure proper representation, rights, and redressal mechanisms. Moreover, training the diplomatic corps on gender issues and embedding a gender-sensitive perspective across significant areas of India's global engagement will also benefit India on the global high table. FFP would require continual rethinking to address newer challenges and strengthen advocacy in changing and turbulent times.

7 Conclusion

This study demonstrates that adopting FFP can contribute to progressive foreign policy in states. There is a varying degree of adoption of FFP by several countries in the northern hemisphere and the global south countries, including Chile and Mexico, while many other countries, such as India, have openly expressed their intentions to implement an effective FFP. An FFP framework would help India achieve its desired metrics in the domestic sphere and rise in international status and recognition. However, a concrete framework best suited to the Indian context is crucial to realising its effectiveness. This study examined how signalling through rhetoric has garnered criticisms of its superficiality and falsehood.

In this regard, strengthening the FFP framework through indicators such as human rights, social justice, and gender equality can lead to better inclusion, representation, and empowerment of women. Furthermore, women's leadership and engagement in diplomacy would bring a more diversified intellectual perspective to foreign policy while also deconstructing gender and patriarchal prejudices. Margot Wallström once stated, "More women means more peace" (Wallström, 2019). We also find that strong implementation of an FFP helps improve India's domestic policy environment and treatment of women. This will also position India better when signalling moralpolitik by prioritising gendered security issues.

References

Achilleos-Sarll, C., Thomson, J., Haastrup, T., Färber, K., Cohn, C., & Kirby, P. (2022). The past, present, and future(s) of feminist foreign policy. *International Studies Review, 25*(1). https://doi.org/10.1093/isr/viac068

Adam, H., & Rena, R. (2024). Polycrisis and economic development in the global South. *In Routledge eBooks*. https://doi.org/10.4324/9781032694337

Al-Ali, N. (2020). Covid-19 and feminism in the Global South: Challenges, initiatives and dilemmas. *European Journal of Women S Studies, 27*(4), 333–347. https://doi.org/10.1177/1350506820943617

Aggestam, K., Rosamond, A. B., & Kronsell, A. (2018). Theorising feminist foreign policy. *International Relations, 33*(1), 23–39. https://doi.org/10.1177/0047117818811892

Baccarini, M. P. O., Minillo, X. K., & Alves, E. E. C. (2019). Gender issues in the Ivory Tower of Brazilian IR. *Contexto Internacional, 41*(2), 365–396. https://doi.org/10.1590/s0102-8529.2019410200007

Bacchi, C., & Goodwin, S. (2016). Poststructural Policy Analysis. Palgrave Macmillan- New York
Bagchi, I. (2011). A tale of two Manmohan Singhs. *Current History, 110*(735), 131–135. https://doi.org/10.1525/curh.2011.110.735.131
Baruah, N., & Bhide, P. (2022). Applying a feminist lens to India's foreign policy. In *A Compendium of Essays*. The Asia Foundation. https://asiafoundation.org/wp-content/uploads/2022/09/Applying-a-Feminist-Lens-to-Indias-Foreign-Policy.pdf
Basrur, R., & De Estrada, K. S. (2017). Rising India. *In Routledge eBooks*. https://doi.org/10.4324/9781315227825
Bhatia, R. (2024, August 24). *Is India emerging as the voice of Global South?* Deccan Herald. https://www.deccanherald.com/opinion/is-india-emerging-as-the-voice-of-global-south-3162866
Bhattacharya, P. (2017, June 9). India's deepening gender imbalance. *Mint*. https://www.livemint.com/Politics/pfqm3WGSJIIyMqGCbzdNXO/Indias-deepening-gender-imbalance.html
Bjarnegård, E., & Zetterberg, P. (2022). How autocrats weaponise women's rights. *Journal of Democracy, 33*(2), 60–75. https://doi.org/10.1353/jod.2022.0018
Chakrabarty, B. (1992). Jawaharlal Nehru and planning, 1938–41: India at the Crossroads. *Modern Asian Studies, 26*(2), 275–287. (https://doi.org/10.1017/s0026749x00009781
Confortini, C. C. (2012). *Intelligent compassion: Feminist critical methodology in the women's international league for peace and freedom*. Oxford University Press.
Das, D. (2017). What's in a Term: Can feminism look beyond the Global North/Global South geopolitical paradigm? *M/C Journal, 20*(6). https://doi.org/10.5204/mcj.1283
De Estrada, K. S. (2023). What is a vishwaguru? Indian civilisational pedagogy as a transformative global imperative. *International Affairs, 99*(2), 433–455. https://doi.org/10.1093/ia/iiac318
Devasia, A. J. (2022, August 24). *A feminist foreign policy for India?* Economic and Political Weekly. https://www.epw.in/journal/2022/34/special-articles/feminist-foreign-policy-india.html
Devitt, R. (2021, March 29). *Liberal institutionalism: An alternative IR theory or just maintaining the status quo?* E-International Relations. https://www.e-ir.info/2011/09/01/liberal-institutionalism-an-alternative-ir-theory-or-just-maintaining-the-status-quo/
Dutt, S. (2013). India's foreign policy and global politics. In *Manchester University Press eBooks*. https://doi.org/10.7765/9781847792143.00015
Fotaki, M., & Pullen, A. (2023). Feminist theories and activist practices in organisation studies. *Organization Studies, 45*(4), 593–616. https://doi.org/10.1177/01708406231209861
García, A.G., & Castelán, B.R. (2023). Ten years of feminist foreign policy and feminist international development cooperation policy, *In United Nations*, https://repositorio.cepal.org/server/api/core/bitstreams/cf4ca332-203e-4a38-b016-0818dabb74cf/content
Gill-Atkinson, L., Ridge, A., Pradela, J., Tilbury, B., Warambourg, C., & Porras, T. P. (2021). From seeds to roots: Trajectories towards feminist foreign policy. In *International Women's Development Agency (IWDA)*.
Götz, E. (2020). Status matters in world politics. *International Studies Review, 23*(1), 228–247. https://doi.org/10.1093/isr/viaa046
Government Offices of Sweden. (2019). *Sweden's feminist foreign policy*. Government communication 2019/20:17. https://www.regeringen.se/contentassets/8db3c4560ab0466faf82edaa1c209fe0/swedens-feminist-foreign-policy-skr-20192017.pdf
Granlund, J. (2022, October 18). Tobias Billström skrotar den feministiska utrikespolitiken [Tobias Billström scraps feminist foreign policy]. *Aftonbladet*. https://aftonbladet.se/nyheter/a/eJJOMl/tobias-billstrom-skrotar-ud-s-feministiska-utrikespolitik
Haastrup, T. (2024). *Global conflict trends: Planning for the future*. Research Explorer the University of Manchester. https://research.manchester.ac.uk/en/publications/global-conflict-trends-planning-for-the-future
Hall, I. (2017). Narendra Modi and India's normative power. *International Affairs, 93*(1), 113–131. https://doi.org/10.1093/ia/iiw004
Hogan, E., & Patrick, S. (2024). *A closer look at the global South*. Carnegie Endowment for International Peace. https://carnegieendowment.org/research/2024/05/global-south-colonialism-imperialism?lang=en

Jaishankar, Dr. S. (2024). *Transcript of remarks by External Affairs Minister, Dr. S. Jaishankar at the Doha Forum 2024 Opening Panel on 'Conflict Resolution in a New Era.'* Ministry of External Affairs, Government of India. https://www.mea.gov.in/Speeches-Statements.htm?dtl/38739/Transcript_of_remarks_by_External_Affairs_Minister_Dr_S_Jaishankar_at_the_Doha_Forum_2024_Opening_Panel_on_Conflict_Resolution_in_a_New_Era

Jezierska, K., & Towns, A. (2018). Taming feminism? The place of gender equality in the 'Progressive Sweden' brand. *Place Branding and Public Diplomacy, 14*(1), 55–63. https://doi.org/10.1057/s41254-017-0091-5

Jha, R. (2024). *Crime in India: A critical review of data collection and analysis.* Observer Research Foundation. https://www.orfonline.org/public/uploads/posts/pdf/20240517132118.pdf

Joy, S. (2021, March 31). *India slips 28 ranks to 140 in global gender gap index.* Deccan Herald. https://www.deccanherald.com/india/india-slips-28-ranks-to-140-in-global-gender-gap-index-968648.html

Jorgensen, M., & Phillips, L. J. (2002). *Discourse analysis as theory and method*. Sage.

Khory, K. R. (2022). India rising? Opportunities and challenges. In *Edward Elgar Publishing eBooks* (pp. 46–60). https://doi.org/10.4337/9781788977692.00009

Khullar, A. (2021, November 17). *Feminist foreign policy: A new innovation for Indian diplomacy.* South Asian Voices. https://southasianvoices.org/feminist-foreign-policy-a-new-innovation-for-indian-diplomacy/

Khullar, A. (2020, January 23). A lukewarm commitment: India and gender equality in security affairs. *The Diplomat.* https://thediplomat.com/2020/01/a-lukewarm-commitment-india-and-gender-equality-in-security-affairs/

Killare, T. (2023). *The feminist foreign policy agenda: What is it and why should India engage with it?* Heinrich Böll Stiftung. https://in.boell.org/en/feminist-foreign-policy01

Khillare, T. (2025, March 21). *Why India needs a feminist foreign policy, now.* India's World. https://indiasworld.in/why-india-needs-a-feminist-foreign-policy-now/

Kumar, R. (2024). The unfinished quest: India's search for major power status from Nehru to Modi T.V. Paul, *International Relations of the Asia-Pacific*, https://doi.org/10.1093/irap/lcae014

Lahiry, S. (2024). Gender-human security interface: Critical perspectives with special reference to India. *Discover Global Society, 2*(1). https://doi.org/10.1007/s44282-024-00037-9

Larson, D. W., & Shevchenko, A. (2010). Status concerns and multilateral cooperation. In *Cambridge University Press eBooks* (pp. 182–207). https://doi.org/10.1017/cbo9780511761119.010

Llacer, Z. (2023, February 12). *Towards the adoption of a feminist foreign policy in India?* Institut Du Genre En Géopolitique. https://igg-geo.org/en/2023/02/12/towards-the-adoption-of-a-feminist-foreign-policy-in-india/

MacArthur, J., Carrard, N., Davila, F., Grant, M., Megaw, T., Willetts, J., & Winterford, K. (2022). Gender-transformative approaches in international development: A brief history and five uniting principles. *Women S Studies International Forum, 95*, Article 102635. https://doi.org/10.1016/j.wsif.2022.102635

Magan, T. (2023, December 4). *A closer look into feminist foreign policy in India.* orfonline.org. https://www.orfonline.org/expert-speak/a-closer-look-into-feminist-foreign-policy-in-india

Mayring, P., & Fenzl, T. (2019). Qualitative Inhaltsanalyse. In *Springer eBooks* (pp. 633–648). https://doi.org/10.1007/978-3-658-21308-4_42

Mattern, J. B., & Zarakol, A. (2016). *Review essay: Hierarchies in world politics.* University of Cambridge. https://api.repository.cam.ac.uk/server/api/core/bitstreams/0de404c0-0bb9-4964-8776-515c4a470d9d/content

MacDonald, P. K., & Parent, J. M. (2021). The status of status in world politics. *World Politics, 73*(2), 358–391. https://doi.org/10.1017/s0043887120000301

Michalko, J. (2023) *'Where next for feminist foreign policy?' ODI Briefing note.* ODI (https://odi.org/en/publications/where-next-feminist-foreign-policy).

Ministry of Information and Broadcasting. (2024). *India's exceptional growth trajectory: A multi-sectoral overview.* https://pib.gov.in/PressNoteDetails.aspx?NoteId=153213&ModuleId=3&reg=3&lang=1

Murray, M. (2018). The struggle for recognition in international relations. *In Oxford University Press eBooks.* https://doi.org/10.1093/oso/9780190878900.001.0001

Nylund, M., Håkansson, S., & Bjarnegård, E. (2022). The transformative potential of feminist foreign Policy: The case of Sweden. *Journal of Women Politics & Policy, 44*(3), 257–273. https://doi.org/10.1080/1554477x.2022.2113662

Ogden, C. (2022). Global India. *In Routledge eBooks.* https://doi.org/10.4324/9781003305132

Parashar, S., & D'Costa, B. (2017). Feminist foreign policy: The South Asia conundrum. *Disrupted, 1*, 27–30.

Pardesi, M. S. (2015). Is India a great power? Understanding great power status in contemporary international relations. *Asian Security, 11*(1), 1–30. https://doi.org/10.1080/14799855.2015.1005737

Patel, S. (2024). *India struggles with high rape cases, low conviction rates.* Reuters. https://www.reuters.com/world/india/indias-struggles-with-high-rape-cases-low-conviction-rates-2024-08-15/

Patel, V. (2023a, September 23). *Charting a path towards feminist foreign policy: Chair's summary—IMPRI impact and policy research.* IMPRI Impact and Policy Research Institute. https://www.impriindia.com/insights/feminist-foreign-policy-chart-remarks/

Patel, V. (2023b, July 16). *Analysing the impact of feminist foreign policy in India: A critical perspective on South Asia.* Impact and Policy Research Institute (IMPRI). https://www.impriindia.com/insights/analyzing-ffp-impact-india/

Patterson, D. (2014). *Pacifism handbook—1914–1918 (WW1)* Encyclopedia. https://encyclopedia.1914-1918-online.net/article/pacifism/

Paul, T. V., Larson, D. W., & Wohlforth, W. C. (2014). Status in world politics. *In Cambridge University Press eBooks.* https://doi.org/10.1017/cbo9781107444409

Paul, T. V., & Shankar, M. (2014). Status Accommodation through institutional means: India's rise and the global order. In *Cambridge University Press eBooks* (pp. 165–191). https://doi.org/10.1017/cbo9781107444409.011

PTI. (2024, June 12). India ranks 129th on global gender gap index, Iceland on top: WEF. *The Economic Times.* https://economictimes.indiatimes.com/jobs/hr-policies-trends/india-ranks-129th-on-global-gender-gap-index-iceland-on-top-wef/articleshow/110931099.cms?from=mdr

Pu, X. (2017). Ambivalent accommodation: Status signalling of a rising India and China's response. *International Affairs, 93*(1), 147–163. https://doi.org/10.1093/ia/iiw002

Puri, L. (2023, November 5). What's in a name? India's march towards a feminist foreign policy—The Sunday guardian live. The Sunday Guardian Live. https://sundayguardianlive.com/opinion/whats-in-a-name-indias-march-towards-a-feminist-foreign-policy

Rathore, K. S. (2021, August 6). *Opinion—A feminist foreign policy for India: Where to turn?* E-International Relations. https://www.e-ir.info/2021/08/06/opinion-a-feminist-foreign-policy-for-india-where-to-turn/#google_vignette

Renshon, J. (2019). Status in international relations. *International Relations.* https://doi.org/10.1093/obo/9780199743292-0254

Renshon, J. (2017). *Fighting for status.* https://doi.org/10.23943/princeton/9780691174501.001.0001

Rosamond, A. B. (2020). Swedish feminist foreign policy and "Gender Cosmopolitanism." *Foreign Policy Analysis, 16*(2), 217–235. https://doi.org/10.1093/fpa/orz025

Saran, S. (2024, September 10). *As a rising global power, what is India's vision for the world?* World Economic Forum. https://www.weforum.org/stories/2018/08/what-is-indias-vision-for-the-world-modi/

Sarkar, D., & Kumar, S. (2022). *Women-centric Approaches under MUDRA Yojana: Setting G20 priorities for the Indian Presidency.* Observer Research Foundation. https://www.orfonline.org/research/women-centric-approaches-under-mudra-yojana-setting-g20-priorities-for-the-indian-presidency

Schottli, J. (2022). India and the 'great powers': from the Indian Ocean to the Indo-Pacific region, *The Round Table*. https://doi.org/10.1080/00358533.2022.2082743

Seth, S. (2022). *India's inconsistent adherence to the women, peace and security agenda*. Lowy Institute. https://www.lowyinstitute.org/the-interpreter/india-s-inconsistent-adherence-women-peace-security-agenda

Sethi, M., & Rakhra, K. (2025). *Emerging from the Shadows: Essays on disarmament by Indian Women*. Routledge & CRC Press. https://www.routledge.com/Emerging-from-the-Shadows-Essays-on-Disarmament-by-Indian-Women/Sethi-Rakhra/p/book/9781032263007?srsltid=AfmBOoo7u0ZzPrNwiO3KS2FYWppSB2-sJg79-CwdisEw0bhRhdcNPkNf

Shritha, V. (2022). Would the "Optional Protocol" effectuate India's due diligence obligation under the women's convention? *Asian Journal of International Law, 13*(1), 76–96. https://doi.org/10.1017/s204425132200025x

Sikkink, K. A., & Clapp, H. (2024). *How feminist foreign policy enhances gender justice | GJIA*. Georgetown Journal of International Affairs. https://gjia.georgetown.edu/2024/02/18/how-feminist-foreign-policies-work-to-enhance-gender-justice/

Swedish Ministry of Foreign Affairs. (2018). Handbook for Swedish feminist foreign policy. https://www.swedenabroad.se/globalassets/ambassader/zimbabwe-harare/documents/handbook_swedens-feminist-foreign-policy.pdf

Tamang, D. (2024). Feminist foreign policy in India. In *Routledge eBooks* (pp. 146–164). https://doi.org/10.4324/9781003264200-10

Thomson, J. (2020, February 10). *The growth of feminist (?) foreign policy*. E-International Relations. https://www.e-ir.info/2020/02/10/the-growth-of-feminist-foreign-policy/#google_vignette

Tickner, J. A., & True, J. (2018). A century of international relations feminism: From World War I women's peace pragmatism to the women, peace and security agenda. *International Studies Quarterly*. https://doi.org/10.1093/isq/sqx091

United Nations. (2009). *Human security in theory and practice*. Human Security Unit, Office for the Coordination of Humanitarian Affairs, United Nations Development Programme. https://procurement-notices.undp.org/view_file.cfm?doc_id=11983

Uspenskaya, V. I., & Kozlova, N. N. (2022). Feminist foreign policy: Selected issues of conceptualisation and implementation. *RUDN Journal of Political Science, 24*(1), 25–41. https://doi.org/10.22363/2313-1438-2022-24-1-25-41

Vogelstein, R. B. (2019, November 18). Five questions on feminist foreign Policy: Margot Wallström. *Council on Foreign Relations*. https://www.cfr.org/blog/five-questions-feminist-foreign-policy-margot-wallstrom

Wallström, M. (2019, October 7). Feminist foreign policy: A conversation with former Foreign Minister Margot Wallström of Sweden. *Council on Foreign Relations*. https://www.cfr.org/event/feminist-foreign-policy-conversation-former-foreign-minister-margot-wallstrom-sweden-0

Wohlforth, W. C., De Carvalho, B., Leira, H., & Neumann, I. B. (2017). Moral authority and status in international relations: Good states and the social dimension of status seeking. *Review of International Studies, 44*(3), 526–546. https://doi.org/10.1017/s0260210517000560

Zhukova, E., Sundström, M. R., & Elgström, O. (2021). Feminist Foreign Policies (FFPs) as strategic narratives: Norm translation in Sweden, Canada, France, and Mexico. *Review of International Studies, 48*(1), 195–216. https://doi.org/10.1017/s0260210521000413

Dr. Poornima Ravindra Vijaya is currently an Assistant Professor of Political Science at the School of Political Science, Kumaraguru College of Liberal Arts and Science in Tamil Nadu, India. She has completed her Ph.D. in International Relations from the Jindal School of International Affairs (JSIA) at O.P. Jindal Global University. She is a Research Associate at Nehghinpao Kipgen's Centre of Southeast Asian Studies and has worked in independent research projects on ASEAN for Economic Research Institute for ASEAN and East Asia (ERIA), Indonesia.

Her research interests include Asian Studies, Southeast Asia, Indo-Pacific Affairs, middle power geopolitics, and Global IR perspectives.

Nitin Narayanan is a Doctoral Scholar at the Jindal School of International Affairs, O.P. Jindal Global University, India. He graduated with a Masters in Defence and Strategic Studies from Kurukshetra University, India. His research interests include Indian foreign policy, strategic culture, neoclassical realism, grand strategy, and the Arabian/Persian Gulf.

Chapter 2
Strategic Choices in Retaining Political Power: Analysing the Participative Role of Women Leaders in Global South

Jacqueline Elisha Gomes and Rubina Pradhan

Abstract The relationship between 'power' and 'politics' becomes increasingly complex due to the multifaceted nature of the concepts. The layered characteristics of the terms thereby makes it important to address the attributes which are being looked upon for the study. The study therefore relies on politics as a political organization. The attribute of 'power' is, the fluid nature of power which reflects how alternatives and choices of leaders are important for analysing how the power is experienced and exercised. The aspect which aligns these concepts together is 'gender'. While we see the participative role of women in political administration, their decision-making qualities are either overlooked or criticized. Throughout history, there have been instances where women have relied on clothing to create a statement. Women political leaders relying on political clothing remains an arena which requires attention. Besides addressing the problem, the objective of the paper is to highlight on power being analysed not as an authoritative and dominant medium, but as a soft tool, making the population abide by the leaders not due to coercion, but by a sense of collectiveness. Therefore, the study aims to investigate the clothing strategic choices women political leaders in the Global South have relied on to retain power in politics. Based on the review of literature and Michel Foucault's theory of power, the clothing choices of four eminent women leaders of Global South that is Ellen Johnson Sirleaf, Former President of Liberia, Indira Gandhi, Former Prime Minister of India, Sheikha Lubna Al Qasimi, Former Minister of International Cooperation and Development, United Arab Emirates and Cristina Fernandex de Krischner, Former President of Argentina. Analysis of the literature and the theories reveals the possibility that political clothing holds the characteristic of power, as it creates a political discourse by being a tool of communication. However, the underrepresentation of countries, where women leaders rely on clothing to create a political statement remains a concern. Further research, both empirical and theoretical, is required to identify the rationale behind the clothing choices of political leaders in the world.

J. E. Gomes (✉) · R. Pradhan
Jain (Deemed-to-Be University), Bengaluru, India
e-mail: jacquelinegomes215@gmail.com

R. Pradhan
e-mail: rubina.pradhan@jainuniversity.ac.in

H. Adam and F. A. Malik (eds.), *The Political Economy of Gender*,
https://doi.org/10.1007/978-981-92-2785-3_2

Keywords Power · Politics · Women · Choices · Leaders · Clothing · Decision making · Gender · Administration · Global South

1 Introduction

"Power is everywhere and comes from everywhere."

(Foucault, 1998).

The concept of 'power' is believed to be one of the important parameters in the understanding of a society. Besides the omnipresence of the term, a collaborative approach to the term in social science remains difficult. Starting from the intrinsic, in ancient Athens, power have been differentiated between the legitimate and illegitimate, where in the former it has been associated with the practice of law, whereas in the latter, it has been aligned with the purpose of elevating the stature of an individual entity (Haugaard, 2009 In Leviathan, Hobbes highlighted the coercive power exercised by the sovereign (Hobbes, 1968).According to thinkers like Nietzsche, 'power' lied in discovering reality. However, with time, the characteristics of domination and authority which were previously attached with the concept, got replaced by more subtler aspects of control (Haugaard, 2009). Therefore, the term cannot be seen as a single entity but associated with a series of different concepts. The Multiperspectivity of the term can be aligned with Wittgenstein's concept of family resemblance (Kalita, 2020), highlighting the different ideas which overlap simultaneously with 'power' that justifies 'Power' to be a range of social phenomena fundamental for social order.

Similarly, the term 'politics' is known for possessing a plethora of different characteristics. Many would agree 'politics' to be associated with something which we read in newspapers, something we criticize or ridicule or something which we do not prefer to be associated with. Max Weber in his famous lecture titled 'Politics as a Vocation' (Weber, 1946), emphasized on politics being the idea of leadership in practice. Politics is therefore an extension of power distribution. 'Politics' cannot be narrowed down to only government and politicians. 'Politics therefore exists wherever there is struggle for power, with an attempt to maintain or retain leadership (Sinha, 2020). The third concept the paper highlights would be the concept of 'gender'. Theorists have believed that gender has to do more with activity than being born with it. (West & Zimmerman, 1987). While 'gender' and 'sex' are often used as synonyms of each other, 'sex' on one hand is considered to be biological categorization based primarily on reproductive potentiality, 'gender' on the other hand is believed to be a social extension of 'sex'. However, the clear demarcation between 'sex' and 'gender' is not specific, challenging the binaries further. The fact that 'gender' is associated with culture too needs to be highlighted (Arvanitidou & Gasouka, 2011). An extension of this, 'gender' is believed to be existing both at social and individual level. In 'social' level it conveys information in terms of what lives of a gendered individual disseminate, whereas in the individual level it deals with personal form of gendered expression. The most challenging association of gender is when it is considered as a social construct. Under this, socio-cultural and historical parameters influence the discussion rather than psychological and internal processes (Bohan, 1993). Two major components that associate such a believe are anti-essentialism and social categorization. Under this, gender is seen more as an action rather than the aspects which one possesses. In spite of this, one continues to consider itself as gendered (Bohan, 1993). However, gender experiences are felt differently by both men and women, becoming one of the prime reasons for us associating women with 'gender' itself. In a parallel connotation, even if men are considered to be in an advantageous position than women, owing to their experiences and practices, men are too believed to be constrained under the dimensions of gender, just as women (Clarke & Braun, 2009). Women's role in politics, whether in the form of voting or political representation, evolved over a period of time. It was during the twentieth century, when women came to terms with the fact that politics is a man's domain (Chafetz & Dworkin, 1986). While the formal political representation of women has started unfolding, the challenges surrounding descriptive representation continue to exist.

After an individual assessment of the term 'power', 'politics' and 'gender', the consecutive objective for this study would be to analyze the association between the above concepts. In contradiction to its meaning, the similarity between the terms is that all of the contested concepts highlight some characteristics of discussion-however it doesn't capture the full range of perspectives of the concepts. The paper thereby aims to reflect on the association between the terms, reflecting on the affiliation which has been at its initial stages of theorizing. To emphasize further the 'strategic choices' which my title specifies, will refer to the choices women leaders make in terms of their clothing or attire. Clothing under such scenarios acts as a medium of communication which is both interpretive and systematic. The transmission therefore through clothing remains open, often providing the individual the freedom to create their own identity through his/her appearance (Tijana, 2014). In the arena of politics, understanding the strategic choices of the political leaders through their clothing choices, is a parameter which requires further analysis. Though there are countries which profoundly highlight the clothing choices of leaders, there are countries where the acknowledgement hasn't been recorded yet. Power as a characteristic, reflected in the form of clothing by the women political leaders. The objective of the study will be to highlight clothing as a strategic medium to retain political position, an act of communication or an aspect which strengthens the decision-making capabilities. The study will be restricted towards the women political leaders of the global south.

It is important to conceptualize power beyond the traditional notions of discourses attached with the term. In this context, the strategic clothing choices of women political leaders acts as a characteristic of inquiry as their attire raises certain questions regarding the interplay between power, politics and gender, which gets shaped by their clothing practices and public perception.

The next section will further explore the concept of 'power' through the analysis of Foucault, along with its association with clothing of political leaders, followed by the research methodology. The consecutive section will thereby reflect on the discussion, highlighting the case studies of eminent women political leaders. The concluding section of the chapter will analyze the potential global significance of the study, along with a scope of theorizing.

2 Review of Literature

Foucault's analysis of the concept 'power' requires attention. Foucault has mentioned that 'power is everywhere' (Foucault, 1998:63), highlighting its omnipresence. In reality, such an ideology contradicts with our beliefs, because the definition of power which we are acquainted with is the one which deals with laws, rules and authority. In the arena of Political Theory, 'power' is seen as a privilege and ability, which is often associated with the will of the powerful, and therefore occurs at distinct moments. According to Foucault, such an understanding is flawed and incomplete. The primary established method of power comes in the form of Judicial- which is restrictive and centralized. This gets further characterized into a repressive, sovereign and commodity model of power. While repressive views 'power' as an ability to diminish, where human desires are suppressed, sovereign negates decentralization, whereas the commodity model reflects the transmitting features of power (Pillai, 2017). Foucault mentions the need of widening the definition of power, if one had to substantiate the concept. While the theory of power in itself is significant, it requires it to be treated as a tool rather than an outcome. By emphasizing on the critical appreciation of the term can therefore prove to be helpful in understanding the term in a meaningful manner (Foucault, 1982).

Foucault further elaborates on how the idea of power needs to be approached. According to him, power needs to be visualized in an empirical way as doing so will help us to understand its challenges. Secondly, resistance is proportional to power, as the former possesses the ability to shape the dynamics of power. Thirdly, one needs to investigate power not with reasoning and logic, but with strategies of hostility towards it. Fourthly, power needs to be viewed against transversal struggles, where the diversity of these struggles reflects the common aim of highlighting the impacts of power, on the lives of individuals (Foucault, 1982: 781). Foucault continues to specify the need for the institutional shift in power. Such a shift allows power to flow through a network of organisations which engage individuals in shaping their lives, identities and choices. The purpose is not liberation from the State but from any form of individualization which is imposed on oneself by the State, focusing on creating new forms of identity. Power operates through a network of relationships, practices and discourses (Foucault, 1982: 784–785).

Foucault even expands on the strategies to analyze power relationships. According to him, social networks are important as power relations are centred around social communications. One needs to identify cultural, economic and linguistic differentiation in facilitating power, along with investigating different means of exercising power, and assess different parameters of reasoning. Foucault further highlighted that confrontation and resistance forms the true dynamics of power. Foucault through his work had never directly been influenced by the theories of other philosophers, but a similar connotation can always be drawn through his writings (Sarvesh & Tarushikha, 2022). Foucault like Durkheim was inclined in knowing about the typical and unconventional and how these notions changed over the period of time. During his time, many theorists had expressed their admiration towards the existential theory- of how decisions governed the lives of the individuals. He even admired the work of Merleau Ponty, who expressed his displeasure towards scientific theory which he believed prevented the capture of the interpretive experience of individuals (Pillai, 2017).

Besides Foucault, there have been various eminent philosophers who had come with diverse theories of power. According to Max Weber, violence is taken as a characteristic in politics-power relationship. He further emphasizes on achieving the political tasks with the help of violence. Weber therefore defines power as the ability to exercise one's will within the social relationship. (Guzzini, 2017:100). According to Karl Marx, power is a resource, concentrated in the hands of the ruling class and state, emerging mainly from the economic aspects. This analysis thereby becomes responsible in bringing changes in the political economy, which acts as the major proponent of power aligned with various other institutions (Rogers & Murphy, 2014). Another poignant philosopher, Antonio Gramsci's most predominant idea has been the concept of 'hegemony', which deals with the influence of the dominant class over the other classes. Civil society and state, according to Gramsci are the institutions exercising the control. Under this theory, 'hegemony' also deals with the consent of the individuals willing to be governed by the small elite. (Balakrishnan, 2015). Similarly, Nicolo Machiavelli's concept of power was reflected in his work *Prince,* where he emphasized on the idea of political theory being embedded in the belief that human beings are flawed and therefore rulers must be ruthless and pragmatic. His work even focused on the efficiency of the governance rather than on moral perfection, with the sole purpose being on the prosperity and stability of the State. (Hauer, 2017).

One similarity between the above philosophers has not only been the concept of 'power', but also the approach towards it. 'Power' has been viewed as an authoritative figure, which is primarily centralized and is exercised over the masses. In this process, being oppressive appears to be the norm. Under the above theories, the institutions too are considered to be fixed, with the most prominent among them being that of the State. On the contrary to this, Foucault, specified on the fluid nature of Power. More than institutions, power exists in communication and discourses. Confrontations in power relationships give rise to different forms of power dynamics. Foucault's theory of power therefore is a viable choice for this study, solely due to the perspective towards the term 'power'. Considering the fluidity of power- the study will align this idea with the strategic choices made in the form of clothing by the women leaders, in the arena of politics. Such an association will not only be exploratory in nature, but it will even address the complexity of power relations, as specified by Foucault in his theory.

An extension of power which this paper aims to explore is through the aspect of political clothing. Clothing becomes political when it conveys meaning through its portrayal-either in the form of ideology or supporting a cause or particular movement. Many historians consider the discussion towards political clothing nothing new. Political clothing reflected during the time of French Revolution- where statements were made in the form of 'sans- culottes' and 'red cap of liberty'. In France 'clothing' soon shifted from being a characteristic of social status to an aspect of political identities (Wrigley, 2002). In politics, surrounding gender, clothing became a significant tool for women leaders. The term 'power dressing' itself became a movement in the history of women's fashion which stemmed due to the women liberation movement (Karaminas & Geczy, 2024). Women traditionally have been absent from the role of power in huge numbers, while even now it becomes challenging to understand what they could wear which would convey the same amount of power as men in suits do (Morgan, 2024). Often personal and political issues are explicated through one's body- expressed in the form of dressed or undressed (Wikramasinghe, 2003). One aspect which requires attention is the diversity in political clothing of women leaders. Regional and cultural diversity plays an important characteristic behind the choices of political leaders. Often the dominance of institutions too governs the dressing choices of the political leaders (Coghlan & Hackett, 2023). Instances have suggested that the reflection of clothing in power, along with identity and body has been neglected by many social scientists (Entwistle, 2000). The paper therefore aims at understanding the strategic choices which women leaders make towards their political clothing, the power it holds in making a political statement or retaining their political position.

3 Methodology

Conducting a study dealing with non-empirical approach and preliminary explorative data, comes with its own set of challenges. One of the primary factors lies in the fact that the study is predominated with perspectives of theorists or theories, which have been analysed or reviewed at different scenarios. The study is therefore based on review of literature and theorization. Along with this, the study even focuses on the visual observation of images and aligning it with the existing theories. It won't be incorrect therefore to label the study as conceptual in nature. Conceptual framework is believed to be viewed as a 'tentative theory' (Maxwell, 2013, pp. 9) dealing with the integration of elements. Conceptual framework therefore allows the researcher to make analyses and use of disjuncture and overlaps within and between the core concepts used in the study to derive deeper meanings.

Taking the above parameters into consideration, the analysis of it can be applied in the following ways. Firstly, an analysis of the important concepts which will be aligned in the study has been initially viewed in its original setting, followed by a need to explore its diversity with the help of the study. The second part deals with understanding the concept through different cases taken from Global South, making the application of the concept a possibility. The countries which will be referred for this study will be Africa (Liberia), Asia (India), United Arab Emirates and Argentina. The purpose of focusing on the aforementioned countries is to analyze and understand the political attire of women leaders who deserve recognition, whereas, in most developed countries, the political clothing of women leaders has been poignant and has received the necessary acclaim. The review of literature therefore serves as the foundation of the study. However, any development in the course of the chapter will only be aligned with these analyses. The next section deals with discussion, highlighting the aspect of power used as a diplomatic tool.

4 Discussion- Power as a 'Soft Tool'

Global South appears to be one of the most evolving regions in the world currently. The ideology surrounding the rise of the Global South emerged in the year 2000 owing to the fast- paced rise of economies in countries like Latin America, Africa, East and SouthEast Asia. With time, it was even believed that both North and South grew at different rates. It was further deduced that the growth of the global south was due to economic integration and domestic transformation. The progress however of the countries happened at different paces. (UN, 2024). The role of leadership therefore becomes a significant aspect for the region. Strategic leadership thereby plays an important role in encouraging domestic industrialization, structural reforms and economic integration. In addition, an association with gender too becomes paramount in understanding the different methods adopted by leaders to create an impact.

4.1 Ellen Johnson Sirleaf

It was believed that Liberia was already affected by the civil war for a period of 15 years after which Sirleaf became the President in the year 2006. Her being the first female head of State in Africa made her tenure a landmark one (Mikell, 2009). Besides her political accolades, her clothing choices had created an impact and therefore needs to be highlighted. It is said that Sirleaf's ability to win over the critics goes to her clearly crafted personality, representing a grandmother, exuding authority without being discouraging. However, achieving such an image in a society which faces challenges in terms of religion, ethnicity and tribe makes it difficult. Literacy too becomes a major challenge, making the power of clothing significant in conveying ideology. Post her election, Sirleaf started being seen in plainer fabrics, primarily dominated by the wrapper, 'lapas' (Patel & Leslie, 2023). Coming to the strategic choice of Sirleaf, she often preferred being dressed in the traditional Afro-ethnic clothing especially on her visit abroad. It was also analyzed that Sirleaf dressing choices highlighted the national identity of her country. In her election campaign, she earned the title of being called the 'Iron Lady', the characteristics which don't align with her dressing choices. Nevertheless, her clothing did exude meaning and power, highlighting her position and the situation of her country. The colours and the headscarf that she wore reflected simplicity, modesty and cultural relevance. Her head-wraps too added to her physical stature. Example of Sirleaf reflects how the power of clothing can be analysed as a soft tool, going beyond the characteristic of authority and domination. Secondly the strategic clothing choices of Sirleaf has not been intentional but a political statement, relying primarily on the representation of culture. Lastly, the example of Sirleaf explains the significance of understanding political administration and principles of the country through an association between gender-politics-power and clothing.

4.2 Indira Gandhi

Indira Gandhi continues to remain one of the most eminent women leaders of India. Being the only women Prime Minister, the transformation in Indira Gandhi's personality has been analyzed throughout. From being labelled as 'gungi gudiya' (dumb doll) to 'iron lady'(Kumari, 2023), Indira Gandhi's political journey remains remarkable not only for her resilient decisions in administration, but also for her clothing choices. Writer Sagarika Ghose expressed that for Gandhi, saree has always meant power. She even mentioned that Indira Gandhi never wore saree to exude any feminine characteristics, but she used it to create a powerful symbol in the world of politics which is often preferred to be a man's world (Jyoti, 2018). Gandhi's clothing has been taken as a strategic means to communicate information regarding the governance of her country. This analysis can be drawn only after considering the clothing expectations which leaders had pre- and post-Independence. While there hasn't been any strict regiment regarding the clothing choices the leaders must abide by in the Parliament, it still cannot overlook the fact that clothing does create political statements. What the political leaders are expected to wear was discussed briefly even by the Constituent Assembly (Rowchowdhury, 2021). India got its own moment of creating strategic impact through their clothing choices during the twentieth century, when while fighting for nationalism, formed the basis of the Swadeshi movement, making the decision of promoting local weavers and utilising it as a sign of propaganda. Creating a moral obligation of donning Khadi, became a powerful symbolic tool of Mahatma Gandhi.

Post Independence, this strategic takeaway was observed in political leaders as well. Considering the choices of Indira Gandhi in this scenario, she too chose wearing Khadi sarees, through which she not only reflected on the ideology of rural development and self-reliance, but even reaffirmed and reconceptualized the ideals of nationalism. She preferred wearing sarees during international gatherings, as a means to convey messages surrounding the principles of economic independence. Her adoption of traditional attire became a tool for challenging stereotypes and shaping public perception. Her choice of handloom sarees containing understated borders aligned with the ideals of self-reliance and swadeshi, in other words stressing on the characteristic of political clothing (Tripathi, 2024). When Gandhi was serving as the finance minister of India, between the year 1970–71, her clothing choices were defined as 'elitist', when she presented the budget of the year in a plain silk saree and a gray shawl ("Bow tie and pinstripe", 2022). During the time of Emergency, Gandhi's stature as 'India is Indira and Indira is India', reflected in her clothing. She preferred muted colors in white, beige and pastels, symbolising neutrality and minimalism. The colors chosen by her too was an initiative to avoid distraction from the political environment. Saree itself has been viewed as a weapon, owing to its cultural and nationalistic connotations (Bera & Saha, 2024). The clothing of Gandhi throughout her reign helped in reaffirming her policies and ideologies. The attire which Gandhi wore during her assassination, remains immortalised even today at the Teen Murti Bhavan in New Delhi, not only highlighting the commemoratory but it even preserves the visual memory of Gandhi in our mind.

On November 23, 1974, Indira Gandhi delivered a speech at the Indraprastha College, New Delhi, where she mentioned that what we wear is unimportant, but what is important is what we are thinking. Gandhi's choice of donning saree was never to exhibit femininity, but a sense of uncanny power. Her saree resonated with her constituency. Secondly her clothing choices allowed her to appear approachable and formidable to her audience. Lastly, the association between gender-politics and power through the parameters of clothing had recently been witnessed when after more than a decade, in the year 2024, Priyanka Gandhi, decided to don the 'kasavu' saree of her grandmother, Indira Gandhi, during her oath taking ceremony in the Parliament. The decision was not only in memory of the former Prime Minister, but also to create a sense of identification, symbolism and allegiance with the leader.

4.3 Sheikha Lubna Al Qasimi

After taking the ministerial post in the year 2004, Qasimi became a symbol for women empowerment in the United Arab Emirates. She went on to become the first women minister of State for Tolerance between the years 2016–2017 (Milken Institute, 2024). Besides her various accolades, throughout her governmental reign, along with her political decisions, it was her clothing choices which created an impact. Qasimi's clothing choices reflect pragmatism and institutional customs. Following the Arab customs, Qasimi has been seen wearing 'abaya' in most of her public gatherings. Similarly, she has been seen occasionally wearing 'hijab', 'headscarf' in international gatherings. Her ability to adorn both the traditional and western attire fulfils her dual commitment towards cultural values of UAE along with global diplomatic regulations. Her projection of feminine robustness gets highlighted in her attire, challenging the stereotypes of women in leadership in the Middle East. To cite an instance, the characteristic of international diplomacy gets reflected during the Dubai Expo, 2020, where Qasimi participated at the event donning an outfit with dual characteristics- western style suits with the authentic abayas highlighting the feature of international diplomacy. Qasimi's example reflects how her clothing goes beyond the characteristics of domination. Her clothing reflects cultural identity and influence. Her strategic clothing choices of donning ana 'abaya' aims at strengthening representation and identity. Similarly, provided the fact that the scrutiny over a women's clothing choices are more, Qasimi donning a traditional attire reckons with her position conveying a message that her sartorial preference is not a limitation to her power.

4.4 *Cristina Fernandez De Kirchner*

Cristina Fernandez de Kirchner is an Argentina lawyer and former president of the country from December 2007 to December 2015. She even served as the prime minister of Argentina between the years 2019 to 2022. Throughout her tenure, she made significant achievements and went on to be termed as the woman who created history. She was the second woman to become the president of Argentina, after Isabel Martinez de Peron. She is even the first woman to be directly elected, having the opportunity of being re-elected (Jones, 2025). Besides being convicted for corruption charges in the year 2022, Kirchner administrative decision making remains worth mentioning. As a president, she introduced a new tax system, which was protested by farmers, considering that it would reduce their profits. Additionally, she approached various social programs and in the year 2010, she signed the legislation, making Argentina the first country approving for same-sex marriage (BBC, 2010).

Kirchner has always expressed meaning through her attire. Authority along with cultural categorisation, has been reflected through her clothing. Kirchner even preferred wearing clothing having symbolic and regional significance. Her nationalistic image and pride towards the country is even reflected in gatherings where she is seen wearing the Argentina flag colours. The pinned flag in her attire, added to her role as the representative of the country. Her tailored suits and dresses were taken as a comprehensive blend of tradition and femininity. Kirchen even went on to be compared with Margaret Thatcher in terms of highlighting the communicative power of clothing. Her Chanel design suit acts as the synonym for power. Kirchen too aligns to clothing in alliance with gender norms. Her choice of attire is different during public gatherings, making it more approachable. Her choice of bold colours during public speeches has also been considered as a tool of political statement. Black too was used as a symbol of collective mourning, which she adorned in the year 2010, during the death of her husband, Nestor Kirchner (Friedman, 2014). Therefore, it has been an accepted fact that Kirchen's clothing played a major role in the arena of public communication (Ibid). In aligning with the research questions mentioned above, Kirchner's example clearly highlights the emulative power of clothing. Her clothing choice was primarily based on the audiences she encountered allowing them to resonate with her. Lastly, her strategic clothing choices allowed her to create a sense of collective identity.

The study has initially highlighted analysing concepts, the characteristics of which remain untapped. In all the above cases, besides the gender of the personalities, what remains similar are their conscious decisions towards their clothing choices in creating an impact. At this point, however, it becomes important to revisit the objective questions which were mentioned at the beginning of the chapter. Relying on the theory of Foucault for this study itself answers the need to view power beyond the characteristic of authority and domination, a requirement in order to address the dynamics of power. According to Foucault, the aspect of power is to establish structures which aim towards how we behave and present ourselves. In alliance with Foucault's analysis, dressing in a certain manner is considered as a response to the indirect systems of power (Geczy & Karaminas, 2024).

The choice surrounding dressing in a certain manner also includes an acceptance towards it. Again, a continuation to the ideology of Foucault, just as power, clothing too acts as a symbol of armour and resistance, while here the aspect of resistance is more complex, utilizing or undermining the visual cues, which connects both to contextual clues and the dressing norms. Coming to the second objective question, feminist theorists in their analysis of politics have considered a discussion surrounding women's clothing or dress not only detrimental but sexist in nature. For female leaders, the idea of them not being the natural holders of their positions creates a sense of doubt surrounding their presence. There have been instances where the attire of women leaders has made them being judged and scrutinized (Conway, 2016). Women leaders are often labelled as invaders who occupy the positions which inherently belong to men, in this case, it being politics (Puwar, 2004). One of the reasons behind the diversity in the clothing choices of women leaders owes to the cultural significance of the region they belong to. The attire of leaders therefore plays an important role in constructing one's identity and position a leader's institution towards economic, social and political contexts. Clothing not only locates but defines the changing characteristics of individual and social power across history (Conway, 2004). What remains worth noticing is the fact that in the similarity in the attire of all the three above-mentioned leaders have been the cultural characteristic, along with the individual personality, for instance, each of the leaders exercised authority through their attire. While Sirleaf and Gandhi's attire stressed on nationalism and their dismissal towards Westernization, Qasimi strengthened diplomatic relations by blending modest clothing with western, while Kirchner's attire was based in alignment with the audience she encountered. 'Clothing' in all of these aspects played a role in helping the leaders in retaining their power in their respective fields. Coming to the third objective question, as emphasised previously, concepts like 'gender', 'power' and 'politics' are very dynamic in their origin. However, it cannot be denied that as readers, we are often inclined towards having an expected understanding of the concept. The association of these concepts, with a term as ubiquitous as 'clothing', not only appears to be indeterminate to a few, but the explorative nature of such an alliance seems to be a successful possibility for many. Gender is a complex term. It is a discursive creation of representative interplay within the cultural and social activities (Xue, 2008). In the arena of politics, the association of all these three terms are collectively called 'political dress'. The impact thereby created by the association tends to be more nuanced and multidisciplinary in perspective.

5 Conclusion

The chapter throughout reflected on the need and possibility behind viewing power from the lens of the clothing of women political leaders. This section however will highlight the challenges and the possibility for further research related to such an idea. One of the prime reasons behind the difficulty in aligning 'clothing' in the arena of 'politics' is its informal nature. Clothing and fashion are often considered to be synonyms of each other. However, it becomes important to note here that each of the terms has its own unique characteristics. While 'fashion' may be the idea, 'clothing' becomes a representative of it. The second challenge which this study might encounter is the lack of data to quantify the theory. Taking in the perspective of women leaders would have made the study more authentic and credible in nature. The third challenge thereby lies in the lack of published works highlighting the significance between the political power of clothing. Moreover, the existing articles deal with comprehensive theories, with the mention of 'clothing' only as a characteristic.

Besides the challenges, the study would further highlight the possibility for further research. Taking the current situation into consideration, where world leaders are considering 'soft tools' as a medium of political administration, the diversity behind the clothing choices of political leaders in the geopolitical arena, requires attention. Moreover, the association between clothing and culture remains unexplored in the aspects of international relation, political and sociological history. In many areas, while the term 'power dressing' has been grabbing the attention of readers, its association surrounding the impact it creates in the arena of politics in terms of decision making, remains unnoticed. The role of the audience too becomes an important parameter here. Whether the clothing choices of political leaders are determined by the audience they are going to be encountered with, will be a remarkable discovery. This could also answer the question behind leaders having the desire of 'dressing down' and 'dressing up'. Therefore, including all the potentialities which this study possesses, one of the primary features lies in the need to study the above circumstances from a regional perspective, thereby creating room for comparative analysis in future.

References

Arvanitidou, Z., & Gasouka, M. (2011). Fashion, gender and social identity. *First Fashion Colloquia*. https://www.fibre2fashion.com/industry-article/6322/fashion-gender-and-social-identity

Balakrishnan, S. (2015). Antonio Gramsci and the concept of hegemony. *Shanlax International Journal of Arts, Science & Humanities*, *2*(4). https://www.shanlaxjournals.in/pdf/ASH/V2N4/Ash_V2_N4_001.pdf

BCC. (2010). Argentina legalises gay marriage: Your comments, NA, Other

Bera, T., & Saha, M. (2024). Evolution and significance of the saree as an expression of women's empowerment and nationalism in modern India. *International Journal of Research Publication and Reviews*, *5*(5), 5960–5965.

Bohan, J. S. (1993). Regarding gender: Essentialism, constructionism, and feminist psychology. *Psychology of Women Quarterly, 17*(1), 5–21.https://psycnet.apa.org/doi/10.1111/j.1471-6402.1993.tb00673.x

Bow tie and pinstripe, to Nehru coat and ikat prints: Your guide to Union budget fashion history from East India Company to Modi Government. (2022). *Economic Times*. https://economictimes.indiatimes.com/magazines/panache/bow-tie-pinstripe-to-nehru-coat-and-ikat-prints-your-guide-to-union-budget-fashion-history-from-east-india-company-to-modi-govt/articleshow/89262161.cms

Chafetz, J. S., & Dworkin, A. G. (1986). *Female revolt: Women's movements in world and historical perspective*. Rowman and Allanheld.

Clarke, V., & Braun, V. (2009). Gender. In D. Fox, I. Prilleltensky, & S. Austin (Eds.), *2008) Critical psychology: An introduction (second edition*. SAGE Publications.

Conway, D. (2016). Margaret thatcher, dress and the politics of fashion. In A. Behnke (Ed.), *The*. Being Fab in a Dangerous World. Routledge.

Conway, H. (2004). Clothing and power. In V. Steele (Ed.), The Encyclopedia of Clothing and Fashion (Vol. 1, pp. 317–320). Charles Scribner's Sons.

Entwistle, J. (2000). *The fashioned body: Fashion, dress, and modern social theory*. Polity Press.

Friedman, V. (2014, March 21). Latin lessons in dressing. *Financial Times*. https://www.ft.com/content/10369810-aeaf-11e3-aaa6-00144feab7de

Foucault, M. (1982). The subject and power. *Critical Inquiry, 8*(4), 777–795. https://www2.kobe-u.ac.jp/~alexroni/IPD2018%20readings/IPD1%202018%20No.8/Foucault%20Subject%20and%20Power.pdf

Foucault, M. (1998). *The history of sexuality: The will to knowledge*. Penguin.

Guzzini, S. (2017). Max Weber's Power. In R. Lebow (Ed.), *Max weber and international relations*. Cambridge Press.

Hauer, T. (2017). Power and politics. *Philosophy Studies, 7*(6), 292–297. https://pdfs.semanticscholar.org/597d/b2b61a4f4b26e4ba4ffc9f0bab512a828886.pdf

Haugaard, M. (2009). Introduction: Why power is the central concept of social sciences. *Handbook of Power.* 1–24. https://opus.lib.uts.edu.au/bitstream/10453/11724/1/2007005283.pdf

Hobbes, T. (1968). *Leviathan*. Penguin.

Hussain, A., & Saloi, P. (2024). Foucault's power/knowledge and its contemporary relevance. *Librar Progress International, 44*(1s). https://bpasjournals.com/libraryscience/index.php/journal/article/view/1085/658

Jones, M. P. (2025). Cristina Fernandez de Kirchner. *Britannica*. https://www.britannica.com/biography/Cristina-Fernandez-de-Kirchner

Jyoti, D. (2018). Saree as a weapon: The sartorial tastes of Indira Gandhi and Rattanbai Jinnah, *Hindustan Times*, NA, Other

Kalita, M. (2020). Wittgenstein's concept of language games and family resemblance. *Journal of Critical Reviews, 7*(4). https://www.jcreview.com/admin/Uploads/Files/61c7df47afd278.40197716.pdf

Karaminas, V., & Geczy, A. (2024). Power + Fashion. *Foucault Studies*. (36). https://muse.jhu.edu/pub/56/article/940819/pdf

Kumari, S. (2023). Indira Gandhi as Durga in Indian Politics. *International Journal of Enhanced Research in Educational Development, 11*(1). https://erpublications.com/uploaded_files/download/sunita-kumari_xnZkp.pdf

Maxwell, J. A. (2013). *Qualitative research design: An interactive approach* (3rd ed.). Sage.

Mikell, G. (2009). A woman you can trust: Ellen Johnson - Sirleaf and political leadership in Sub-Saharan Africa. *Georgetown Journal of International Affairs, 10*(1). https://www.jstor.org/stable/43134186

Milken Institute. (2024). Her Excellency Sheikha Lubna bint Khalid Al Qasimi.

Morgan, A. (2024, July 10). Angela Rayner's Green suit: why is it so difficult for women in power to dress correctly? *The Conversation*. https://theconversation.com/angela-rayners-green-suit-why-is-it-so-difficult-for-women-in-power-to-dress-correctly-234315

Murphy, E., & Mercille, J. (2019). (Re)Making labour markets and economic crises: The case of Ireland. *The Economic and Labour Relations Review, 30*(1), 22–38.

Patel, M., & Leslie, C. (2023). Power dressing and its importance in modern democracy. *Undergraduate Research Journal for Human Sciences, 16*(1). https://newprairiepress.org/cgi/viewcontent.cgi?params=/context/urjhs/article/1111/&path_info=Power_Dressing_in_Modern_Democracy___URJHS_Submission_Final.pdf

Pillai, S. (2017). *Michel Foucault*. IGNOU

Puwar, N. (2004). 'Space Invaders: Race', Gender and Bodies out of Place, Oxford and New York, Berg.

Rogers, L., & Murphy, E. (2014). Informal strategies of power in the local planning system. *Planning Theory, 13*(3), 244–268. https://doi.org/10.1177/1473095213492512

Rowchowdhury, A. (2021). An Indian dress code: How India debated what to wear and then decided not to enforce a style, *The Indian Express*, NA. https://indianexpress.com/article/research/an-indian-dress-code-how-india-debated-what-to-wear-and-then-decided-not-to-enforce-a-style-7234295/lite/?utm_source=chatgpt.com

Sinha, M. (2020). 'What is politics?', *Introducing Political Theory.* IGNOU.

Sarvesh & Tarushikha. (2022). *Michel foucault: Power and knowledge.* IGNOU.

Tijana, T. (2014). Clothes and Costumes as Forms of Non-Verbal Communication. *University of Ljubljana,* http://www.tekstilec.si/wp-content/uploads/2014/12/321-333.pdf

Tripathi, S. (2024, January 19). Indira Gandhi, A style icon as India's First Female Prime Minister. *India Times.* https://www.indiatimes.com/lifestyle/style/indira-gandhi-indias-first-female-pms-fashion-style-625606.html

United Nations. (2024). World economic situation and prospects 2024. United Nations. https://www.un.org/development/desa/dpad/wp-content/uploads/sites/45/WESP_2024_Web.pdf

Weber, M. (1946). "Politics as Vocation", In *From Max Weber: Essays in Sociology* edited and translated by H.H. Gerth and C. Wright Mills New Yor: Oxford University Press

West, C., & Zimmerman, D. (1987). Doing gender. *Gender and Society, 1*(2), 125–151. https://www.gla.ac.uk/0t4/crcees/files/summerschool/readings/WestZimmerman_1987_ngGender.pdf

Wickramasinghe, N. (2003). *Dressing the colonized body: Politics, clothing and identity in Sri Lanka.* Orient Blackswan.

Wrigley, R. (2002). *The politics of appearances: representations of dress in revolutionary France.* Oxford.

Xue, C. (2008). Critically evaluating the understanding of gender as a discourse. *International Education Studies, 1*(1). https://files.eric.ed.gov/fulltext/EJ1058023.pdf

Jacqueline Elisha Gomes is a PhD research Scholar, currently doing her research from JAIN (Deemed-to-be University) Bengaluru, with a keen interest in gender studies. Her research explores the intersections of culture, society, and gender, aiming to contribute to a deeper understanding of gender dynamics in contemporary political discourse. She aims to engage in critical discussions and scholarly analysis to drive meaningful conversations in the respective field.

Dr. Rubina Pradhan is an Assistant Professor at the Centre for Research in Social Sciences and Education (CeRSSE), JAIN (Deemed-to-be University), Bengaluru. She holds a Ph.D. from the Centre for International Politics, Organisation and Disarmament at Jawaharlal Nehru University (JNU), New Delhi. Her doctoral research focused on the theory of partnerships among international organisations in conflict resolution, with Libya as a test case. She has contributed to both academic and policy-oriented research, with prior engagements including her role as an Associate Researcher with WriteIgnite and experience as a freelance academic writer. Her research interests span international organisations, human rights, humanitarian intervention, climate change, and public policy. She has published extensively in peer-reviewed journals and edited volumes. Her recent contributions include Evaluating Public Policy Approaches to Women's Empowerment During the COVID-19 Pandemic: A Perspective from the Global South (Springer, 2023) and The Role of Green Budget in Promoting Environmental Sustainability in India (IGI Global, 2025), both Scopus-indexed book chapters. She is also the co-editor of the forthcoming volume Post-Pandemic World Order: Issues and Challenges, to be published by Routledge. In addition to her academic work, she is frequently invited as a resource person to deliver expert lectures and participate in academic forums.

Chapter 3
Women's Mobility, Leadership, and Inclusion in Bangladesh: A Call for Structural Reforms

Neeru Sidana, Firdous Ahmad Malik, Alaya Chhabra, and Divleen Kaur

Abstract Bangladesh has recorded significant improvements in terms of education, employment, and entrepreneurship among women after independence in 1971, but there are ingrained gender gaps in the country. Arising sectors like Ready-made garments(RMG) industry have opened up several opportunities for women, however, they are hindered by barriers such as the cultural norms of the country, lack of access to higher education by women, work place discrimination and wage disparity especially in male oriented fields in the country. Such sociocultural norms and social expectations limit the movement of women in their families, powers to make decisions as well as opportunities to advance in careers particularly in leadership roles. Although the government of the Bangladesh has enacted policies and initiatives to address such issues like domestic violence and digital literacy in women, various obstacles still exist. In doing this we get a deeper insight into how socio-cultural norms, structural barriers, and economic policies influence career progression in women in Bangladesh mostly in STEM, business, and entrepreneurship. It examines problem in labor markets and identifies the requirements of reforms for gender equality and leadership applicability. To understand socio-economic status of women in Bangladesh, recognize the necessity of targeted reforms, increased representation, financial inclusion, to ensure sustainability of women's economic and social performances as the country's contribution is recognised and valued and inform policymakers, communities, and industries to create a more fair and inclusive future for all people.

Keywords Women's empowerment · Gender equality · Socio-economic barriers · Workforce participation · Education · Leadership · Policy reforms · Financial inclusion · Cultural norms · Entrepreneurship

N. Sidana (✉) · A. Chhabra · D. Kaur
Amity School of Economics, Amity University Noida, Noida, India
e-mail: nsidana@amity.edu

F. A. Malik
Department of Management, University of People California, Pasadena, CA, US

H. Adam and F. A. Malik (eds.), *The Political Economy of Gender*,
https://doi.org/10.1007/978-981-92-2785-3_3

1 Introduction

The country of Bangladesh further develops as a fast-growing economy in the world market. With the support of the international economic direction of the International Monetary Fund and World Bank, the Bangladesh commenced its export-led industrial changes with the support of economic instructions in the early 1980s. The Bangladesh economy has been growing at an average rate of more than 6% a year in the last decade (Raihan & Khan, 2020). The small and medium-sized enterprises (SMEs) have become central forces in the promotion of economic growth over the past few years in the country. Practices of sustainable entrepreneurship in SMEs in Bangladesh are limited due to the fact that the traditional cultural practices of the country define the approaches to business (Meng et al., 2021). Group harmony and consensus-building are running as the core cultural values of the society. The developing country of Bangladesh, therefore, has to look at the education enrolment and student success rates, apart from the employment statistics of Bangladesh including the 56.7 million workers and 4.7% unemployment rates, and 49% workers in the industrial sector. The rural areas of Bangladesh experienced significant advancements in female economic activities and gender-sensitive human development during the last few decades because of both non-governmental organizations' development projects and supportive social policies from successive governments. The ready-made garments (RMG) sector, led by export production, became the major driver of female economic power growth in Bangladesh. 4 million operate in the ready-made garment industry across Bangladesh and women constitute between 50 and 60% of these workers. Surprisingly, Women remain underrepresented in leadership roles including general managers, line managers, quality managers, production and Quality production managers, heads of merchandisers, and other positions in the Ready-Made-Garment organizations that manufacture garments for western customers (Macchiavello et al., 2014). The presence of women on the board or in other leading positions improves performance and employees' engagement at work and their enthusiasm to excel at the workplace as they set role models for themselves, which also motivates them to work harder to set and achieve their goals. (Islam & Jantan, 2017) This has increased the participation of women in the industrial workforce and has marked a significant change in Bangladeshi society. (Akhter et al., 2017). In traditional society, men are responsible for providing all financial support to women, and any economic role of women is considered secondary. (Ward et al., 2004).

Against this backdrop, the paper examines the process of structural transformation in Bangladesh, focusing on how it affects inequality and the prospects for inclusive growth, particularly in relation to women's mobility, leadership opportunities, and broader inclusion in socio-economic development. Our findings aim to deepen the current understanding of how structural and cultural barriers continue to affect women's everyday experiences in both informal and formal sectors in Bangladeshi society. These challenges often intersect with each other and constrain women's agency, leadership opportunities, and mobility. Through this study we aim to provide insights that can help in developing structural reforms that help promote a more inclusive and equitable society for women in Bangladesh.

2 Review of Literature

Bangladesh, over the past few years, has seen a notable amount of economic growth and social development, even though the country has faced frequent amounts of natural disasters, it has seen significant poverty reduction and economic growth since it became independent in 1971. This growth has been driven by the country's RMG sector, microfinance initiative, and remittances. Despite the social development the government has over the past few years, their traditional socio-cultural structures remain to have a great amount of influence in shaping the norms around aspects such as family, employment, and gender roles (Emon & Khan, 2023).

Since 1990, the position of women in Bangladesh has changed greatly this can be seen in their increased participation in the labor market along with their improved literacy rates and enhanced political representation within the country. The industry that has contributed the most towards women's economic participation in Bangladesh is the readymade garment sector, but the sector also faces a lot of challenges for women regarding overworking conditions, assignments, and lack of career mobility (Jahan, 2024a). Women to this day experience long working hours, receive limited childcare support, and are provided inadequate healthcare services, which can cause excessive stress and anxiety to the women (Akhter et al., 2017). Female entrepreneurs also face challenges in establishing and sustaining their entrepreneurial ventures, this can be due to socio-economic, psychological, human, or organizational factors (Islam et al., 2025). While the micro-credit programs that have contributed to Bangladesh's economic growth have also facilitated female entrepreneurship, there still are structural inequalities and cultural barriers that remain a challenge for women when starting their ventures (Haque et al., 2023). As pointed out by Roy and Haider (2024), education also has played an important role in women's empowerment; this can be seen in how there is an increase in university enrollment amongst women in Bangladesh, while this is a net positive for the country there are still existing gender disparities in educational institutions especially in regards to higher education, especially in a field such as stem and business. This disparity shows how factors such as social and cultural Expectations can limit women's career choices. This is also pointed out in Haque et al. (2023) who point out how women's participation in industries such as it is seen to be rising, but issues of unequal pay, limited career advancement, and limited access to financial capital continue to be the challenge within the industry.

These problems show that even though Bangladesh has advanced as a country, there are still patriarchal values that shape the social norms and gender routes within the country, which can be seen in how women in the country experience lower wages, work-related harassment, and limited opportunities for professional growth, especially in male-dominated sectors (Jahan, 2024a). Women's participation in local government is also very limited with women only holding 25% of the seats in local government (Kaiser & Nabila, 2024). While in the labor market, women are mostly given lower-scale and lower-paying jobs, there has been an overall improvement in women's education, workforce participation, and decision-making autonomy in the household of Bangladesh. This has also caused a drop in the fertility rate in Bangladesh by a significant amount, as people with greater autonomy tend to have fewer children (Chowdhury et al., 2023). Some women challenge these cultural and social norms out of economic necessity; they often face social stigma and workplace discrimination. However, in some cases, despite these norms, women still can gain financial decision-making powers within their household, which shows there is a complex interplay between tradition and empowerment (Ahmed & Sen, 2018).

Even though there has been significant improvement in women's education for first participation and entrepreneurship, existing research does not show how the deeply entrenched patriarchal norms, gendered economic policies, and societal expectations limit women's career advancement and pressure opportunities in fields such as STEM and business in Bangladesh. Also, there is limited understanding of how workplace discrimination, social stigma, as well as family roles, affect women's decision-making powers and their professional lives. Through this we aim to highlight the need for structural reforms and further research in order to address these barriers that hinder women's participation and leadership in Bangladesh.

3 Current Status of Women in Bangladesh

Women's empowerment in Bangladesh shows key progress and continuing challenges. There have been improvements in recent decades, especially in areas like education and work. Government programs and NGO efforts have been important in making these changes. For instance, Union Digital Centers (UDCs) aim to close the digital gap that has often separated men and women in Bangladesh, allowing rural women to access information, technology, skill training, and business options (Akter & Husain, 2021). This access has helped with their financial independence and has also raised their social status. Initiatives supporting girls' education, such as stipends and focused programs, have led to more girls enrolling in primary and secondary schools, sometimes matching the number of boys in certain areas. This educational growth is seen as a significant achievement for Bangladesh, especially considering its past. These advancements have also played a role in changing societal views, with a growing acknowledgment of the importance of girls' education (Blunch & Das, 2015).

However, despite these positive developments, significant gender disparities remain. While female enrollment in primary and secondary education has improved drastically, the graduation rate for women in tertiary education, especially in STEM fields, lags (Ahmed et al., 2023). Patriarchal views, safety concerns, and gender-based violence continue to restrict women's agency and opportunities in both educational and professional settings (Ahmed & Hyndman-Rizk, 2020). Issues such as limited access to resources, discriminatory practices, and socio-cultural barriers still hinder full empowerment (Islam, 2016). The digital divide is still there, greatly affecting women's ownership of information and communication technology for their development (Akter & Husain, 2021). Despite an increased number of women in the work force, particularly in the ready-made garments (RMG) and agriculture sectors, this has most often not led to empowerment. Due to economic binding, many women do work that is often marked by poor pay, poor working conditions and chances of promotion (Islam, 2016). Following traditional gender roles and values still governs women's life in their houses and workplaces; thus, limiting women's decision-making powers and rejecting literal elimination of the countryside (Hossain & Tisdell, 2005).

Women's advancement in terms of political and business representation has improved greatly; however, their participation in higher education, especially in science and technology, is still low (Alam, 2009). Likewise, the other contributing factor of the education system itself is inequality because of resource allocation. Even considering education, women still suffer from the gender wage gap, where their earning lags behind that of men, especially in lower-skilled positions (Hossain & Tisdell, 2005). While some research maintains that women's increasing commercialization and participation in the political process are positive indicators of progress, cultural and socio-economic barriers remain to full equality. Although initiatives like the #missingdaughter program and the National Girls Programming Contest (NGPC) have encouraged girls to take part in ICT and programming (Jamal et al., 2020), more visible female role models and more support towards these programs are needed to address the socio-economic barriers and further enhance women's empowerment in these fields. While the progress made in women's empowerment in Bangladesh is undeniable, it is equally clear that varied efforts are necessary to address the remaining challenges and achieve true gender equality across all aspects of society in Bangladesh.

4 Methodology

To conduct this study various literatures have been studied regarding the concept and theoretical background of socio-economic status of women in Bangladesh, their structural barriers, and influence of economic policies on career progression of women in Bangladesh.

5 Findings

Cultural norms and traditional gender roles are still entrenched, thereby restricting women's participation in the public life and making them stand out in the decision making (Ahmed, 2024). MoWCA (Ministry of Women and Children Affairs) has a plan and tactics to work with and it manages to sign the marriage of the offspring by

2041 and under Homeland Action Plan to prevent the aggression against women and children (2019–2030). Bangladesh as a whole has faced various Public and Traditional Guidelines which have limited the progress of the common women in the form of monetary involvement to the attainment of the education and even overall happiness. Businesses are better off investing in collectivism than economic development because the traditional cultural values compel enterprises to be towards an approach of avoiding risks. Socially organizing as hierarchy by SMES puts barriers on two main elements that can never be overcome because of absolute obstacle they form: open dialogue and individual dependent advances (Emon & Khan, 2023). Rural Bangladeshi women encounter substantial obstacles in financing and opportunity access due to the traditional male-dominated social norms of their country that start shaping their development from childhood onwards. Men receive better distribution of resources than women because they receive more food and better attention while being given more opportunities in society (Sultana et al., 2018). After marriage rural women lose connections to their birth families while undergoing the control of their in-laws or husbands leading to common household violence and economic dependency along with social discrimination. The existing power dynamics because of these factors restrict women from effectively utilizing technology according to Sultana et al. (2018).

The public sphere remains limited for poor Muslim women to conduct economic activities because religious barriers of purdah practices hinder their access throughout Dhaka. Society maintains a strong segregation of spaces between men and women that prevents women from freely exploring public areas. Women face major life restrictions because of how purdah norms present themselves both through dress codes and through underlying social expectations. Girls and boys encounter restrictions regarding contact with each other as well as freedom of movement through the mahram and na-mahram principles. Economic needs force women to break norms which results in severe social discrimination along with harassment (Lata et al., 2021). The challenges affect women through the religious beliefs and economic influences as well as societal power dynamics of Bangladeshi society (Akhter & Sumi, 2014). The traditional practices represented by burqa-wearing in household settings and other components of women's wellness show direct associations in rural Bangladesh. Strong traditional family values discourage women from pursuing outside work which includes both agricultural and non-agricultural job sectors. Women experience increased risk of being overweight when household members maintain conservative views because such environments limit their movements along with providing limited access to nutritious food sources. Traditional values continue to shape women's opportunities for employment alongside their health status despite overall social changes throughout Bangladesh (Ahmed & Sen, 2018). Multiple cultural practices create significant barriers that prevent girls from receiving education until the finishing of their schooling (Sarkar et al., 2014).

6 Discussions

Women in the People's Republic of Bangladesh face many health and nutrition obstacles that significantly affect their happiness and their tribes. The high incidence of anaemia, particularly among pregnant and wet females, as well as the unacceptably high rates of unacceptably high dietary consumption and restricted intake of micronutrients (Ferdous et al., 2012). In addition, many females suffer from undernutrition, about one-third of whom are classified as sluggish (BMI 18.5 kg/m2), which may result in poor fitness outcomes for the mother and the child (Ferdous et al., 2012). Access to healthcare is inequitable, with lower antenatal care (ANC) service utilization rates among women in these areas (36% compared to 58.7% for other urban residents). Additionally, the quality of nutrition services in public primary healthcare facilities is suboptimal, resulting in lower client satisfaction than that experienced at private and NGO facilities (Islam Anne et al., 2022). Poverty significantly exacerbates these issues, with women in poorer households experiencing disproportionately higher rates of growth stunting in their children due to limited access to nutritious food and healthcare. Furthermore, the complex governance structure of the health system and inadequate funding contribute to these ongoing problems, impacting continuity of care and access to essential resources, including micronutrient supplements and educational materials (Hasan et al., 2023).Bangladesh women encounter severe abuse challenges mainly through congenial Companion brutality (IPV) because of multiple factors including extreme poverty and patriarchal traditions alongside systematic discrimination as well as illiteracy together with early marriage and unequal control interaction (Ahmed, 2005). Major findings of violence exposure in rural Bangladesh indicate that 50.8% of women endure bodily mistreatment by their husbands and 66.8% face verbal mistreatment (Bhuiya et al., 2003).

The current mistreatment exists from a deeply-rooted societal power mismatch and sociocultural customs which inflict severe physical and mental harm to females whose economic vulnerability and worry about social stigma makes their situation worse. The emergence of resistance against brutality occurs because Bangladesh has strong patriarchal customs which support patriarchal cultural norms. There exists a current wave of aggression stemming from within-family violence and dowry abuse including acid incidents and community actions (Hossain, 2016). Physical injuries and mental health problems including depression as well as anxiety and post-traumatic stress disorder are among the serious effects. Female exposure to violence during pregnancy deviates the health of newborns by creating nutritional deficits which cause stunted growth. Women put up with abuse because of their cultural situation which includes difficulties finding other support systems and worries about social repercussions as well as protection of their children (Bhuiya et al., 2003). The connection of economic and social conditions produces persistent violence which severely affects women's physical health as well as their mental condition. Women's autonomy leads to a decrease in violent incidents against women in Bangladesh. Women who experience few opportunities alongside patriarchal standards tend to face increased risks of being abused. (Koenig et al., 2003).

Early marriage is also a big issue that is highly associated with higher vulnerability to all forms of violence, such as domestic violence and sexual assault. The fact that the reference of increase of dowry practices is made implies a possible connection to violence against women. The Dowry disputes and the push to meet demands of Dowries are known to turn violent almost to death for Women in Bangladesh and many other South Asian places (Bates et al., 2004). Bangladesh, emphasizing that families often view daughters as financial burdens. Marrying them off at a young age allows parents to transfer this burden to the daughter's husband and his family, particularly in poverty-stricken areas where financial constraints are significant. Additionally, early marriage can reduce the size of the dowry that families must pay, as marrying off younger daughters is perceived to mitigate the higher dowry demands associated with older brides (Chowdhury, 2004). Family perspectives align with financial benefit when they choose early marriage since increasing dowry costs with age makes them prefer younger marriages to save expenses. Female children create financial burdens because of existing gender discrimination and therefore families choose early marriages to solve their economic problems (Kabir et al., 2019). Society continues to expose women to ongoing peril through early daughter marriages because they believe this method safeguards her safety despite potential victimization and exploitation. Because of this system parents continue following patriarchal traditions which in turn increases child marriage occurrences in the country (Chowdhury, 2010).

There is significant gender segregation in job allocation and the concentration of women in lower-skilled, lower-paying roles. However, it goes beyond simply noting the imbalance to explore the underlying mechanisms – managerial practices and broader patriarchal norms – that sustain this hierarchy and limit women's agency (Mawa, 2016). Women in Bangladesh have limited access to education and professional occupations; this suggests that this lack of access fundamentally limits their ability to progress within any hierarchical structure, whether in the political or economic sphere. This restricted access to professional and higher-level positions is a significant barrier to women's advancement and equitable representation across all sectors (Halder, 2004). The steep gender imbalance in workplace facilities of the RMG sector, compounded by the exclusion of women from leadership and skilled occupations despite their overwhelming dominance in workforce numbers, is a result of longstanding gender prejudice, social mores, and workplace discrimination. These plain and ubiquitous factors generate a hostile workplace climate and systematically stunt women's careers, reinforcement of which pushes their roles to lower-subordinate positions. (Jahan, 2024a). While women workers are concentrated in lower-skilled given that they are not allowed in higher-paid work areas, men's excessive representation in positions of supervision and management contributes mainly to the gender wage gap highlighted in the paper, exhibiting a clear lack of gender representation in the industry's hierarchy. (Hossain, 2012).

The absence of visible female success in these areas discourages young women from pursuing subjects such as sciences, technology, medicine, etc. This lack of representation reinforces societal stereotypes that these fields are not suitable for women, thus perpetuating the cycle of underrepresentation (Roy & Haider, 2024).

This absence of female role models discourages aspiring women in several ways. Seeing few women in leadership or successful positions can lead to a feeling of isolation and a lack of belief in one's potential to succeed. Without visible examples of women achieving their goals in their respective fields, young women may be less likely to pursue those careers in the first place. Even if they do enter the field, the lack of role models means a lack of mentorship, guidance, and networking opportunities that can be crucial for career advancement. There is a considerable gap regarding women in leadership positions, which prevents aspiring women in several ways. With so few women in senior or top-brass positions, feelings of alienation and a low belief in their potential for attaining such heights are prevalent. With very little evidence of women's prominence in their respective fields, young women tend not to pursue those careers in the first place. At times, even when they succeed, the lack of role models creates a vacuum where mentorship, advice, and networking opportunities, important factors in career advancement, are lacking (Islam & Jantan, 2017). The women lack mentors or examples of how to successfully balance these competing demands, leaving them feeling isolated and unsupported in their struggles. The limited resources and lack of empathy from supervisors and healthcare providers further compound the negative impact of this isolation and lack of appropriate role models (Akhter et al., 2017).

7 Conclusion

The research shows that Bangladesh experienced major gains in women's workforce participation, yet social and structural limitations prevent women from advancing further in Bangladeshi society. The challenges not only compromise the well-being of women but also restrict Bangladesh's broader social and economic development. In order to increase women's mobility, participation, and leadership roles and inclusion in Bangladesh society, there needs to be a more actionable framework. There should be more focus on enhancing education systems. As more women are gaining access to education, their enrollment in higher education, especially in STEM fields, remains disproportionately low, which is why it is important to create more scholarship schemes and networking platforms that can help promote more female role models in government, science, and entrepreneurship, which can encourage more women to pursue non-traditional career paths. Educational reforms should also prioritize skill-based learning with a special focus on rural women. Also there should be better enforcement of laws set to protect women from violence and discrimination, as there is still in consistent there should be better judicial accountability better legal literacy and better support services like legal aid, counselling centres, and survival shelters, which should be more accessible to women in rural and semi-urban areas. There should also be economics inclusion strategies which can help address financial access and workplace participation with a special focus on Women entrepreneurs in target support, such as access to credit without rigid Collateral conditions along training in business management and integration into values change.

In order to achieve a more inclusive Bangladesh for women, there need to be a change in social norms, which requires sustained community based efforts which involve men religious leaders, media influence and the public the scores should promote gender equitable values normalise shared domestic responsibilities; representation of women in policymaking and governance is a must to make sure that policies are inclusive and equitable.

8 Policies Recommendations

WHO (2022) indicates that sexual abuse affects 1 out of every 3 women at some point during their lives. On July 17 1995 the specialized Prevention of Women and Children Repression law officially came into effect while gaining its status as legislation. Under this legislation the government addresses both female and child mistreatment. By definition in this Act woman signifies any aged individual and child represents a person whose age falls below sixteen (Amended) (Khan & Karim, 2017). The term 'Repression comprises every physical or mental assault made against women or children. The legislation entered Bangladesh as a promising response to women and children suffering from violence. Bangladesh established new legislation and amended multiple existing laws to stop woman and female child abuse cases. Bangladesh has established the Dowry Prevention Act combined with legislation for preventing minor girl marriage together with the Women and Children Repression Prevention Act, 2000 among others. Thus, the government created Women Abuse Prevention Cell and rehabilitation centers that provide legal support services and counseling to stop women and children abuse. Numerous administrative orders have been issued to prevent woman and female child abuse in Bangladesh (Khan & Karim, 2017) while the Act establishes precise definitions of criminal activity. This legislation gives the panel exclusive authority to decide the case according to its According to (Khan & Karim, 2017), Sect. 26 of this Act declares that the tribunal is known as the "Prevention of Women and Children Repression Tribunal" and that its judges must be qualified as either District Judges or Sessions Judges. conducted a case study that illustrates the current situation and measures the extent to which the Prevention of Women and Children Repression Act has been put into practice. Case (1) - In the case of Abdul Kalam Azad alias Ripon v. According to court record of the required case the appellant received a death sentence because she tortured and killed her wife Mahmuda Sultan Mammi at the command of dowry. The trial court established through diary readings that the victim suffered torture because she failed to fulfil the dowry demands making the charges against the defendant solid according to the principle set by the court. The Act should undergo modifications to establish its success by including all criminal acts against women within its scope. The investigation process of offenses should maintain both proper and just procedures to prevent possibility of false charges from being filed. The current laws in Bangladesh lack a complete definition for gender-based violence. In 1993 the United Nations General Assembly incorporated the Elimination of Violence Against Women into its system. The definition of women's violence appears as 'any gender-related violence which generates physical damage or sexual mistreatment or psychological distress against women'. The Domestic Violence Prevention and Protection Act of 2010 supports a complete strategy for eliminating domestic violence across Bangladesh. The article begins by discussing domestic violence regulations that exist under international jurisdictions. This article examines the domestic violence laws in Bangladesh with emphasis on the Domestic Violence Prevention and Protection Act of 2010. This text provides specific suggestions to control domestic abuse in Bangladesh while advancing women's rights. The Constitution guarantees a society that is both secular and socialist along with freedom from exploitation because it will establish rules of law and basic human rights for all citizens. This text both protects people from discrimination founded on sexual identity and it establishes women's legal rights which match those of males for all public and state operations. The current 2010 Act and 2013 Rules of India protect women and children against religious domestic violence and mandate service organizations to offer besieged women and children assistance. The existing laws contain elements of gender-based violence legislation without purely focusing on gender inequality. The Act demonstrates its gender-specific focus through provision of shared residence arrangements and victim counseling services and child custody jurisdiction because initial assessment of women-specific needs remains vital for gender equality fulfilment (OECDDAC, 2016, p. 18). She can file a writ petition at the court to claim custody rights through rights infringement. It becomes complicated to use the concept of child welfare custody for mothers in certain situations. She must seek family court approval to gain custody of the children while seeking a court-ordered violence protection through Sect. 17 of the DVPPA. Well Intended disciplinary measures under the WCOPA fail to reflect the purpose of domestic violence resolution. The 2010 Domestic Violence Act together with the 2013 Rules secures protection for women and children who suffer abuse regardless of their religious backgrounds while mandating the responsible service organizations to offer needed assistance to disabled women and children. These legislations partially carry the characteristics of a legislation addressing gender-based violence but does not exclusively challenge gender inequality. The Act shows its dedication to gender-specific needs through provisions like 'shared residence' agreements and victim counseling services and child custody arrangements. Women-specific needs represent the initial step to obtain gender equality. (OECD, 2016). (OECD, 2016). The rights allow her to petition for custody through a writ demonstrating infringement (Jahan, 2024b). The doctrine of welfare as custody of the child to the mother may become complicated in certain complex situations. She should file her custody application to Family court while calling in court orders from Sect. 17 of the DVPPA for violence cases. Family violence settlement requires a different approach than the harsh punishment provided by the WCOPA because child marriages under special circumstances remain legal. The highest number of child marriages occurs in South Asia according to UNICEF statistics from 2020 (Unicef, 2020). Without providing proper education and health care along with development to minor brides after marriage they become more susceptible to violent situations. Approaches for preventing domestic violence situations remain absent from Bangladesh's domestic violence law which mainly responds to already occurred violence cases. Data indicates that financial deprivation has a direct connection with violent outcomes (UN Women, 2021).

References

Ahmed, N., Chowdhury, A. M., Urmi, T., & Jamal, L. (2023). Impact of socio-economic factors on female students' enrollments in science, technology, engineering and mathematics and workplace challenges in Bangladesh. *American Behavioral Scientist, 67*(9), 1104–1121.

Ahmed, R. (2024). The breaking barriers: Women empowerment transforming societies in modern times building a better future. *RADINKA Journal of Science and Systematic Literature Review, 2*(3), 451–461.

Ahmed, R., & Hyndman-Rizk, N. (2020). The higher education paradox: Towards improving women's empowerment, agency development, and labor force participation in Bangladesh. *Gender and Education, 32*(4), 447–465.

Ahmed, S. M. (2005). Intimate partner violence against women: Experiences from a woman-focused development programme in Matlab, Bangladesh. *Journal of Health, Population, and Nutrition,* 95–101.

Ahmed, T., & Sen, B. (2018). Conservative outlook, gender norms, and female wellbeing: Evidence from rural Bangladesh. *World Development, 111*, 41–58.

Akhter, R., & Sumi, F. R. (2014). Socio-cultural factors influencing entrepreneurial activities: A study on Bangladesh. *IOSR Journal of Business and Management, 16*(9), 1–10.

Akhter, S., Rutherford, S., Akhter Kumkum, F., Bromwich, D., Anwar, I., Rahman, A., & Chu, C. (2017). Work, gender roles, and health: neglected mental health issues among female workers in the ready-made garment industry in Bangladesh. *International Journal of Women's Health,* 571–579.

Akter, M., & Husain, T. (2021). The impact of Union Digital Centre on women empowerment: An assessment on rural areas of Bangladesh. *Dynamics of Public Administration, 38*(2), 188–197.

Alam, G. M. (2009). The role of science and technology education at network age population for sustainable development of Bangladesh through human resource advancement. *Scientific Research and Essays, 4*(11), 1260–1270.

Bates, L. M., Schuler, S. R., Islam, F., & Islam, M. K. (2004). Socioeconomic factors and processes associated with domestic violence in rural Bangladesh. *International Family Planning Perspectives*, 190–199.

Bhuiya, A., Sharmin, T., & Hanifi, S. M. A. (2003). Nature of domestic violence against women in a rural area of Bangladesh: Implication for preventive interventions. *Journal of Health, Population, and Nutrition,* 48–54.

Blunch, N. H., & Das, M. B. (2015). Changing norms about gender inequality in education: Evidence from Bangladesh. *Demographic Research, 32*, 183–218.

Chowdhury, F. D. (2004). The socio-cultural context of child marriage in a Bangladeshi village. *International Journal of Social Welfare, 13*(3), 244–253.

Chowdhury, F. D. (2010). Dowry, women, and law in Bangladesh. *International Journal of Law, Policy and the Family, 24*(2), 198–221.

Chowdhury, S., Rahman, M. M., & Haque, M. A. (2023). Role of women's empowerment in determining fertility and reproductive health in Bangladesh: A systematic literature review. *AJOG Global Reports, 3*(3), Article 100239.

Emon, M. H., & Khan, T. (2023). The impact of cultural norms on sustainable entrepreneurship practices in SMEs of Bangladesh. *Indonesian Journal of Innovation and Applied Sciences (IJIAS), 3*(3), 201–209.

Ferdous, J., Ahmed, A., Dasgupta, S. K., Jahan, M., Huda, F. A., Ronsmans, C., & Chowdhury, M. E. (2012). Occurrence and determinants of postpartum maternal morbidities and disabilities among women in Matlab, Bangladesh. *Journal of Health, Population, and Nutrition, 30*(2), 143.

Halder, N. (2004). Female representation in parliament: A case study from Bangladesh. *New Zealand Journal of Asian Studies, 6*, 27–63.

Haque, A., Haque, W., Ahmed, E., Islam, M. Z., & Islam, M. K. (2023). Empowering women through IT: The role of the IT sector in Bangladesh. *Saudi Journal of Economics and Finance, 7*(10), 459–465.

Hasan, S., Akter, T., Jahan, M., & Dewan, A. (2023). Proximity to healthcare centres and service use: The case of community clinics in Bangladesh. *Economics of Transition and Institutional Change, 31*(3), 819–849.

Hossain, A. (2016). The impact of domestic violence on women: A case study of rural Bangladesh. *Social Criminology, 4*(1), 135–142.

Hossain, M. A., & Tisdell, C. A. (2005). Closing the gender gap in Bangladesh: Inequality in education, employment, and earnings. *International Journal of Social Economics, 32*(5), 439–453.

Hossain, N. (2012). *Women's empowerment revisited: From individual to collective power among the export sector workers of Bangladesh.* IDS Working Papers, 2012(389), 1–40. https://mowca.portal.gov.bd/site/page/81115efe-f3cd-438a-b977-4884b088bc45/National-Action-Plan-for-the-National-Women-Development-Policy-2011

https://mowca.portal.gov.bd/site/page/81115efe-f3cd-438a-b977-4884b088bc45/National-Action-Plan-for-the-National-Women-Development-Policy-2011-

https://mowca.portal.gov.bd/sites/default/files/files/mowca.portal.gov.bd/law/a56e138b_0992_490b_8a23_aaed0c1fbeea/act2010.pdf

https://www.who.int/news-room/fact-sheets/detail/violence-against-children WHO (2022)

Islam Anne, F., Akter, S. M., Sheikh, S. P., Ireen, S., Escobar-DeMarco, J., Kappos, K., & Rasheed, S. (2022). Quality of nutrition services in primary health care facilities of Dhaka city: State of nutrition mainstreaming in urban Bangladesh. *PLoS ONE, 17*(12), Article e0278621.

Islam, M. A., & Jantan, A. H. (2017). The glass ceiling: Career barriers for female employees in the ready-made garments (RMG) industry of Bangladesh. *Academy of Strategic Management Journal, 16*(3), 1–11.

Islam, M. S., Azizzadeh, F., Islam, M. S., Adrita, U. W., Mazumder, A. H., & Akhter, R. (2025). Phenomenological insights into socio-psychological and network dynamics of women entrepreneurs. *Journal of Trade Science.*

Islam, S. (2016). Feminization of employment and gender inequality of Bangladesh labor market: The case of garment industries. *Developing Country Studies, 6*(2), 157–168.

Jahan, N. (2024). Inequality and discrimination against women in the workplace: Problems and prospects in the RMG (Ready-Made Garments) industry in Bangladesh (Master's thesis, Oslo Metropolitan University).

Jahan, S. (2024b). Is domestic violence (Prevention and Protection) Act 2010 successful in eliminating gender-based violence in Bangladesh? *Barishal University Journal of Social Sciences, 1719*(398694), 133.

Jamal, L., Hasan, M., & Sultana, M. (2020). Breaking the barriers: Empowering girls in information and communication technology education. *DEStech Transactions on Social Science, Education and Human Science (Issue ICEdDE).* DEStech Publications. https://doi.org/10.12783/dtssehs/icedde2019/33686

Kabir, M. R., Ghosh, S., & Shawly, A. (2019). Causes of early marriage and its effect on the reproductive health of young mothers in Bangladesh. *American Journal of Applied Sciences, 16*(9), 289–297.

Kaiser, Z. A., & Nabila, M. C. (2024). Assessing gender discrimination and inequality in local government in Bangladesh. *The Palgrave handbook of global social problems* (pp. 1–12). Springer International Publishing.

Khan, M. E. P., & Karim, M. A. (2017). The prevention of women & children repression act 2000: A study of implementation process from 2003 to 2013. *IOSR Journal of Humanities and Social Science, 2*(7), 34–42.

Koenig, M. A., Ahmed, S., Hossain, M. B., & Mozumder, A. K. A. (2003). Women's status and domestic violence in rural Bangladesh: Individual-and community-level effects. *Demography, 40*(2), 269–288.

Lata, L. N., Walters, P., & Roitman, S. (2021). The politics of gendered space: Social norms and purdah affecting female informal work in Dhaka, Bangladesh. *Gender, Work & Organization, 28*(1), 318–336.

Macchiavello, R., Menzel, A., & Woodruff, C. (2014). Managerial capital and productivity: Evidence from a training program in the Bangladeshi garment sector. *IGC Growth Week Presentation*, 25.

Mawa, B. (2016). *All Stitched up? Labour process regimes and patriarchal relations amongst female garment workers in Bangladesh* (Doctoral dissertation, University of Leeds).

Meng, L., Qamruzzaman, M., & Adow, A. H. E. (2021). Technological adaption and open innovation in SMEs: An strategic assessment for women-owned SMEs sustainability in Bangladesh. *Sustainability, 13*(5), 2942.

OECD, D. (2016). *Handbook on the OECD-DAC gender equality policy marker.*

Raihan, S., & Khan, S. S. (2020). *Structural transformation, inequality dynamics, and inclusive growth in Bangladesh (No. 2020/44).* WIDER Working Paper.

Roy, B. K., & Haider, T. (2024). Women in teaching: A Study on selected public universities of Bangladesh. *Law and Society Students' Journal, 2*(1), 19–19.

Sarkar, R. K., Reza, M. M., & Hossain, M. E. (2014). Socio cultural barriers of girls' educational attainment experiences from rural Bangladesh. *Cultural Anthropology, 349*, 358.

Sultana, S., Guimbretière, F., Sengers, P., & Dell, N. (2018, April). *Design within a patriarchal society: Opportunities and challenges in designing for rural women in bangladesh.* In Proceedings of the 2018 CHI conference on human factors in computing systems (pp. 1–13).

UN Women. (2021). Gender-responsive law-making. UN Women. Retrieved 02/05/2025, from https://www.unwomen.org/sites/default/files/2021-11/Handbook-on-gender-responsive-law-making-en.pdfRetrieved

UNICEF. (2020). *Ending child marriage: A profile of progress in Bangladesh.* United Nations Children's Fund.

Ward, K., Rahman, F., Saiful Islam, A. K. M., Akhter, R., & Kamal, N. (2004). The effects of global economic restructuring on urban women's work and income-generating strategies in Dhaka. *Bangladesh. Critical Sociology, 30*(1), 63–102.

Dr. Neeru Sidana is an accomplished academician with over 15 years of teaching and research experience. She holds a Ph.D., MBA, M.Ed., and M.A. in Economics, reflecting her strong academic foundation. Currently serving at the Amity School of Economics, Amity University Noida, she has previously worked with institutions affiliated to Kurukshetra University and as an Associate Professor at Lovely Professional University, Punjab. Passionate about teaching, training, and research, she has actively participated in over 50 seminars, workshops, FDPs, MDPs, and conferences, presenting papers at reputed national and international platforms. Her dynamic and extroverted personality makes her a distinguished educator.

Dr. Firdous Ahmad Malik, Assistant Professor of Economics at the University of People, is pursuing Post-Doctoral Research at Amity University Dubai. He holds a Ph.D. and MPhil in Economics from Babasaheb Bhimrao Ambedkar University, Lucknow, and a Master's from the University of Kashmir. His research focuses on microfinance, financial inclusion, and financial literacy, with publications in Scopus-indexed journals (Springer, Elsevier, Taylor & Francis) and six authored books, including Financial Inclusion Schemes in India (Springer). Actively engaged with the Young Scholars Initiative (YSI), he contributes globally as a presenter, session chair, and reviewer, earning awards for research and academic excellence.

Alaya Chhabra is a research Student at Amity University, Noida, with a strong inclination towards academic research and policy studies. Her research interests lie in development studies and women empowerment, where she seeks to explore how inclusive growth and gender equality can foster sustainable socio-economic progress. She is passionate about examining contemporary development challenges, analyzing policy frameworks, and contributing innovative solutions to bridge gaps in equality and opportunity. She aspires to create a meaningful impact through her research, focusing on empowering women and promoting inclusive development on a larger scale.

Divleen Kaur is a research Student at Amity University, Noida. With a strong academic foundation in economics, she has cultivated a keen interest in research, particularly in areas of Sustainable Development Goals (SDGs), women empowerment, and financial inclusion. Her work reflects a commitment to understanding how inclusive economic policies can drive social transformation and sustainable growth. As an emerging researcher, she aspires to contribute valuable insights that bridge theory with practice. Beyond academics, she is passionate about fostering innovation, equality, and development to create meaningful change in society.

Chapter 4
Two Decades of Gender Responsive Budgeting in India: A Stocktaking

Masroor Ahmad and Anam Ul Haq Ganie

Abstract Gender inequality continues to exist across the globe, though its form and intensity differ depending on a nation's stage of political and economic progress. In advanced economies, women have made significant gains in education, healthcare, and legal safeguards against domestic violence, yet their roles in economic activity and political decision-making remain limited. Bridging these gaps can stimulate economic development by boosting labor efficiency, fostering healthier generations, and ensuring more transparent governance. The global resolve to achieve this is embodied in Goal 5 of the Sustainable Development Goals (SDGs), which emphasizes gender equality and women's empowerment. One key strategy adopted worldwide to pursue this objective is Gender Responsive Budgeting (GRB). This chapter reviews the journey of GRB in India, beginning with its inclusion in the Union Budget of 2005–06 and following its progress through to the 2025–26 fiscal year. The scope of the study is to examine trends in gender budget allocations as a share of GDP and total expenditure, analyse budgetary allocations across key ministries and departments, and evaluate major gender-focused schemes in the Union Budget 2025–26. Relying solely on secondary data from official Gender Budget Statements, the analysis is based on percentage trends and graphical presentations. The findings reveal that, despite two decades of implementation, GRB allocations remain limited at around 5% of total expenditure and only 1% of GDP. Methodological inconsistencies, particularly in classifying schemes under Part A or Part B, diminish effectiveness. Moreover, the absence of an intersectional perspective excludes critical issues related to caste and religion. The study recommends enhancing targeted allocations, increasing ministerial participation, and revisiting the predominance of Part B schemes to ensure GRB better addresses the needs of vulnerable women and promotes substantive gender equality.

M. Ahmad (✉)
Department of Economics, Central University of Kashmir, Ganderbal, India
e-mail: masroor.econ@gmail.com

A. U. H. Ganie
School of Business, Woxsen University, Hyderabad, India

H. Adam and F. A. Malik (eds.), *The Political Economy of Gender*,
https://doi.org/10.1007/978-981-92-2785-3_4

Keywords Gender budgeting · India · Fund allocation · Gender equality · Sustainable development goals · Vulnerable women · Fiscal policy · Women empowerment · Intersectionality · Public expenditure

1 Introduction

The persistent gender inequalities that shape social and economic realities across the world have profound implications for economic growth and development (Das et al., 2017; Elborgh-Woytek et al., 2013; Ostry et al., 2018; Sahay & Čihák, 2018). This study is guided by a central research question: To what extent has Gender Responsive Budgeting (GRB) in India, from its inception in 2005–06 to the projected budget of 2025–26, influenced budgetary priorities in relation to GDP, total government expenditure, and the promotion of gender equity through key ministries and schemes? Addressing this question is crucial for understanding whether GRB in India has moved beyond symbolic commitments to deliver tangible and transformative outcomes for women's empowerment and inclusive growth.

The adoption of the Beijing Declaration by 189 United Nations member states and subsequent efforts to integrate gender concerns into policy interventions reflect the global acknowledgment of the link between gender equality and sustainable development. Governments worldwide have employed various policy tools to address these inequalities, with gender budgeting emerging as a significant fiscal instrument. Gender budgeting, as a macroeconomic and public financial management strategy, integrates gender considerations into the budgeting process by employing targeted procedures and analytical tools, with the objective of enhancing gender-responsive policymaking (Downes et al., 2017).

It does not imply a separate budget for women or confine itself to financing gender-specific initiatives. Instead, it is a comprehensive budgetary exercise that evaluates fiscal policies and budget decisions for their impact on gender equality and uses this analysis to inform inclusive policy design and implementation.

GRB must therefore be understood not only as a technical exercise but also as a moral and social imperative to advance fairness and justice. Eleanor Roosevelt's words—"Justice cannot be for one side alone, but must be for both"—underscore that without regular and rigorous impact assessments, GRB risks degenerating into a symbolic gesture. Efforts to achieve gender equality at the global level are anchored in key international milestones, with the "Convention on the Elimination of All Forms of Discrimination against Women" (CEDAW) of 1979 serving as a foundational framework. Over the years, this commitment has been reinforced through successive global development agendas, beginning with the MDGs and later expanded under the SDGs. Within this framework, SDG Goal 5 explicitly underscores that promoting gender equality and empowering women and girls is not only a matter of rights but also an essential prerequisite for inclusive growth and sustainable development.

From an economic perspective, GRB recognises that fiscal policies significantly influence macroeconomic outcomes, growth trajectories, and the distribution of income. In developing economies, well-structured fiscal frameworks are critical for sustaining growth and ensuring equity. Expenditure and taxation policies directly shape human capital development, investment decisions, and household welfare. However, technical challenges in measuring gender-differentiated outcomes and the historically limited political representation of women often result in the neglect of their developmental needs in public budgeting. Feminist economists such as Diane Elson have criticised traditional macroeconomic frameworks and institutions like the IMF and World Bank for promoting austerity measures that disproportionately affect women (Elson,). Budget cuts in health, education, and welfare expand the unpaid care burden on women, particularly those from low-income households. Gender budgeting thus emerged as a corrective to the gender-blind nature of so-called 'neutral' budgeting, advocating the mainstreaming of gender perspectives across the entire budget cycle.

Although its implementation varies across countries,[1] GRB has been recognised globally by institutions such as the IMF, UN Women, OECD, PEFA, and the G20 as a fiscal tool for advancing women-centric development (IMF, 2016; Nolte et al., 2021; OECD, 2019; PEFA, 2019; UN Women, 2018). In India, entrenched gender inequalities manifest from conception, as reflected in son preference, declining child sex ratios, and the rise in sex-selective abortions. These disparities extend into post-birth realities, with widespread issues including child abuse, sexual harassment, trafficking, and domestic violence. Socio-economic indicators further highlight the disadvantaged position of women, with the Periodic Labour Force Survey (PLFS) 2021–22 showing that only 32.8% of women aged 15–29 participated in the labour force compared to 77.2% of men (Government of India, 2023). This underutilisation of women's potential constrains economic growth, a reality compounded by India's low rank—127th out of 146 countries—on the Global Gender Gap Index 2023, and by women's continued underrepresentation in decision-making structures (Khullar, 2023).

In response, India has sought to integrate gender considerations into policy frameworks through women-specific initiatives in successive Five-Year Plans. Inspired by the global momentum for gender budgeting after the Beijing Declaration, India adopted GRB within its budgetary process. The introduction of a distinct Gender Budget Statement (Statement 19) in the Union Budget of 2005–06 signified the formal institutionalization of this approach. This practice has been sustained, with the Union Budget 2023–24 reiterating the government's commitment to gender equality.

Ultimately, GRB rests on the recognition that budgets are not gender-neutral; they reflect societal priorities and power structures (Akanji, 2022). When budgets fail to address the distinct needs and contributions of women—both in the formal economy and in unpaid care roles—they perpetuate structural inequalities. By examining GRB trends in India over two decades, and analysing allocations in key ministries and departments with a focus on the Union Budget 2025–26, this study seeks to assess whether India's budgetary practices align with the goal of achieving gender equity. In doing so, it not only contributes to the literature on fiscal policy and gender equality but also provides evidence relevant to policymakers, development practitioners, and advocates committed to advancing the transformative potential of gender-responsive public financial management.

2 Literature Review

2.1 Evolution of Women's Empowerment in Indian Planning

In India, the formal adoption of Gender Budgeting came more than fifty years after independence. Nevertheless, women had been part of the national planning discourse since its inception. Yet, their integration into the planning framework did not evolve in tandem with the broader shifts in India's development strategy—from the post-independence "mixed economy" model to the present market-oriented approach (Mitra, 2019). This gap is particularly evident when examining the long interval of nearly three decades between two significant documents—*"Women's Role in a Planned Economy" (WRPE)* and the *"Committee on the Status of Women in India" (CSWI)*. Both documents emphasized the necessity of women's empowerment, but the CSWI report (1974), released during the Fifth Five-Year Plan (1974–79), represented a turning point. Unlike the WRPE, which was more general in orientation, the CSWI provided robust statistical evidence to highlight the structural disadvantages faced by women across social and economic indicators. This evidence-based approach not only drew attention to the inadequacies of existing planning practices but also underscored the need for a comprehensive and gender-inclusive framework. As a result, planning discourse began to shift from perceiving women merely as passive recipients of welfare to recognizing them as active contributors to national development.

The Sixth Five-Year Plan (1980–85) responded by including, for the first time, a separate chapter dedicated to women's concerns. It emphasized that women's backwardness stemmed primarily from a lack of income-generating opportunities. To address these concerns, the plan placed strong emphasis on widening women's livelihood opportunities, ensuring better access to productive assets such as credit, land, and skills, and introducing legal measures to safeguard their rights within both the household and the labor market. Beyond programmatic priorities, this period also represented a turning point in institutional arrangements for women's development. A dedicated Department of Women and Child Development was created within the Ministry of Human Resource Development (MHRD), signalling a clear recognition of women's issues as a distinct policy domain rather than a peripheral welfare concern. This was further reinforced by the establishment of a national committee on women chaired by the Prime Minister, which provided political legitimacy and visibility to gender concerns at the highest level of governance.

The Seventh Five-Year Plan (1985–90) advanced the momentum of earlier initiatives by placing renewed emphasis on strengthening women's participation in the economy, with particular attention to rural wage employment and self-employment opportunities. A major contribution to this discourse came from the Shramshakti Report of the National Commission for Self-Employed Women and Women in the Informal Sector, which underscored the urgent need for ensuring job security, establishing minimum wage guarantees, and expanding avenues for skill development tailored to women in precarious work settings. Responding to these recommendations, the Government of India introduced the Support to Training and Employment Programme for Women (STEP) in 1986–87, designed to facilitate women's engagement in sustainable income-generating activities.

Equally significant was the launch of the National Perspective Plan for Women (1988–2000), a pioneering policy document that set out 360 comprehensive recommendations aimed at reshaping women's roles in both the economic and political spheres. Among its most transformative proposals were provisions for land distribution in women's favor and reservation of seats for women in local governance institutions—initiatives that not only addressed structural gender inequalities but also laid the foundation for subsequent policy reforms in India's democratic and developmental landscape.

The Eighth Five-Year Plan (1992–97) signalled a decisive shift by positioning *women's empowerment* as a central strategy of national planning rather than a peripheral welfare issue. It stressed that women must act as active contributors to development, not merely recipients of state benefits. Framed against the backdrop of the 1991 economic crisis and the onset of liberalisation and fiscal reforms, the plan sought to safeguard women from being sidelined in the new policy environment by embedding gender perspectives into development programmes. A significant institutional advance of this era was the 73rd and 74th Constitutional Amendments (1993), which guaranteed one-third reservation for women in local governance bodies, thereby securing their voice in grassroots decision-making and strengthening their political representation.

The Ninth Five-Year Plan (1997–2002) advanced the empowerment-oriented framework by emphasizing the creation of an enabling environment for women's socio-economic participation. Central to this strategy was the promotion of self-help groups (SHGs) and women's collectives, which provided a platform for solidarity, mutual support, and grassroots mobilization. The plan also prioritized improved access to credit and financial services, recognizing economic independence as a cornerstone of empowerment. This strategy found concrete expression in schemes such as *Swa-shakti* (1998) and *Swayam Siddha* (2001). At the same time, policymakers faced the challenge of reconciling progressive gender-focused planning with the principle of fiscal conservatism that characterized the post-1991 policy environment. To address this, the plan introduced the Women's Component Plan (WCP), under which all relevant ministries—including Health, Education, Labour and Employment, Rural Development, and Family Welfare—were required to earmark at least 30% of their plan budgets for women-specific programmes. This innovative mechanism ensured that women's programmes continued to receive funding without necessitating additional allocations that might strain fiscal policy.

The Tenth Five-Year Plan (2002–07) built upon the WCP framework and adopted a more comprehensive strategy for women's empowerment. The plan emphasized that the measurement of development should extend beyond GDP growth to include distributive justice, with a particular focus on gender equity. Special attention was directed towards women-headed households, who were disproportionately vulnerable to multiple forms of deprivation in both rural and urban contexts. The plan also called for the development of gender-sensitive indicators to assess human development and monitor progress over time. However, the WCP was increasingly criticized for its narrow scope, since it applied only to the Plan component of the budget and overlooked non-Plan expenditures (Das & Mishra, 2006; Mishra & Sinha, 2012).

To address these limitations, the Government of India established an expert group in 2003 under the Ministry of Finance to review the classification of public expenditure. The group recommended restructuring budget presentation to highlight the gender-sensitivity of allocations across ministries. In its 2004 report, it further proposed institutional mechanisms to integrate GRB into the national budgetary framework. These recommendations laid the groundwork for the formal adoption of GRB in India, setting the stage for a more holistic and transparent approach to gender-equitable public spending.

2.2 Gender Budgeting in India

As discussed earlier, the WCP introduced during the Ninth Five-Year Plan faced criticism for being confined to plan expenditures alone, which limited the resources available for women-oriented programmes. This shortcoming created the need to move towards a macro-level framework of gender budgeting that encompassed the entire budget. The Union Budget speech of 2000–01 also acknowledged this, noting that, *"There is an urgent need for improving the access of women to national resources and for ensuring their rightful place in the mainstream of economic development."* Recognising the need for a stronger institutional framework, the "Ministry of Women and Child Development" (MWCD) launched the National Policy for the Empowerment of Women in 2001, which stressed the importance of embedding gender considerations into all aspects of policy and planning. A central feature of the policy was the push to align the national budgeting process with gender priorities, ensuring that public spending translated into concrete outcomes for women.

Building on this mandate, the Ministry of Finance in 2003 set up an Expert Group to review the system of classifying government transactions, with the broader objective of making public expenditure more transparent, accountable, and gender-responsive. Within this initiative, a dedicated Gender Budgeting Subgroup was established to develop an institutional framework for gender-responsive budgeting (GRB). The subgroup also developed matrices to track allocations from a gender lens (Kumar & Vinodini, 2005). Its report, submitted in 2004, recommended the creation of formal institutional mechanisms for gender budgeting, thereby laying the foundation for its operationalization in India.

Following these recommendations, the MWCD adopted *"Budgeting for Gender Equity"* as its official mission statement in the Union Budget of 2004–05, signalling a decisive policy shift from intent to implementation. In the same year, the Ministry of Finance issued directives to all central ministries and departments to establish Gender Budgeting Cells (GBCs). These GBCs were envisioned as nodal institutional mechanisms tasked with integrating gender perspectives into every stage of the budgeting cycle—planning, formulation, and monitoring. By institutionalizing this framework, the government sought to move beyond ad hoc initiatives and ensure that gender-responsive budgeting became a systematic and cross-sectoral practice, reinforcing accountability in public expenditure toward women's empowerment. To aid implementation, a set of strategic guidelines and activities was circulated among ministries. This culminated in a major milestone in the Union Budget of 2005–06, which for the first time included a separate Gender Budget Statement. The finance minister observed, *"Although this is another first in budget-making in India, it is only a beginning and, in the course of time, all departments will be required to present gender budgets as well as make benefit incidence analyses"* (Budget Speech, Union Budget 2005–06).

At this point, India can draw valuable lessons from other countries that have advanced Gender Responsive Budgeting (GRB) practices. For example, Austria mandates every ministry to report on gender equality outcomes, thereby embedding accountability in governance. South Africa's GRB framework integrates gender concerns across planning, budgeting, monitoring, and evaluation—making gender equality an end-to-end process. Mexico improves transparency and trust by involving civil society in the monitoring of GRB implementation. These examples highlight how institutional accountability, multi-level coordination, and civic engagement can enhance the effectiveness of GRB.

Since then, as mandated by budget call circulars from the Ministry of Finance, the government has been regularly publishing the "Gender Budget Statements" along with the Union Budget. This statement indicates the extent to which ministries and departments allocate and utilize funds for women to achieve gender equality objectives, serving as a key mechanism for institutionalizing Gender Budgeting. The GBS was structured into three distinct sections: Part A consisted of *women-specific schemes* in which the entire allocation was dedicated to women and girls; Part B covered *pro-women schemes* where at least 30% of the provisions were directed toward women; and Part C included *residual schemes* in which less than 30% of the allocation benefitted women. This classification provided a systematic framework to track, monitor, and expand gender-sensitive allocations across ministries.

In March 2007, the Ministry of Finance released a charter specifying the structure and responsibilities of Gender Budgeting Cells (GBCs). The charter required each GBC to select between three and six of the ministry's largest programmes, based on budget allocations, to analyze the gender-related issues addressed by these initiatives.[2]

In parallel, India must embrace modern technological tools to make GRB more impactful and inclusive. Leveraging fintech solutions can enable real-time tracking of fund disbursements, ensure targeted delivery of subsidies, and remove access barriers to credit and financial services for women. Digital innovation, if integrated within the budgeting framework, can enhance transparency and efficiency. To support this,

India should invest in capacity-building of policymakers, develop standardised GRB frameworks across states, and allocate dedicated resources for gender-disaggregated data collection and monitoring. Such efforts would transform GRB from a procedural activity to a performance-driven mechanism of inclusive governance.

The Ministry of Finance played a pivotal role in laying the institutional foundation for GB, while the MWCD was designated as the nodal authority responsible for its operationalization in India. The successful adoption of GB at the central level also acted as a catalyst for state-level initiatives, encouraging subnational governments to embed gender perspectives into their fiscal frameworks. Odisha emerged as the first state to formally introduce Gender Budgeting in 2004–05, setting an important precedent. This momentum gradually spread across the country, with Dadra and Nagar Haveli becoming the first Union Territory to implement GB in 2011–12, thereby broadening the scope of gender-responsive fiscal practices beyond the central government. Overall, 16 states and two union territories have employed various mechanisms to implement Gender Budgeting.[3]

2.3 *Objectives of the Study*

In light of a comprehensive review of Gender Budgeting (GB) in India over the period 2005–06 to 2025–26, the present study is guided by the following key objectives:

- To examine the trends in GB in India from 2005–06 to 2025–26 as a share of GDP and total expenditure.
- To analyse the budgetary allocations of key ministries and departments under GB.
- To evaluate major gender-focused schemes and departmental priorities in the Union Budget 2025–26.

3 Methodology

This study employs a descriptive and analytical research design to trace the evolution and assess the present status of GB in India from 2005–06 to 2025–26. The analysis relies exclusively on secondary data drawn from official budgetary sources, including the Union Budget documents, Gender Budget Statements published by the Ministry of Finance, and annual reports of ministries and departments implementing gender-focused programmes. Additional inputs are taken from reports issued by the MWCD, NITI Aayog, and other relevant government agencies. To address the first objective, the proportion of Gender Budgeting in relation to both Gross Domestic Product (GDP) and total Union Government expenditure is calculated for each year within the study period. These ratios, expressed in percentage terms, facilitate year-on-year comparisons and help in identifying trends and shifts over time. For the second objective, the study compiles budgetary allocations of major ministries and departments under Gender Budgeting and presents them as percentages of the overall

Gender Budget. Special attention is given to ministries with significant gender-related outlays, such as the MWCD, Ministry of Rural Development (MRD), Ministry/ Department of Health and Family Welfare (MHFW), and Ministry of Education (MOE). For the third objective, major gender-focused schemes in the Union Budget 2025–26 is assessed using budget allocation figures and percentage distribution. The emphasis remains on the numerical trends rather than qualitative policy interpretation. The findings are presented through statistical tables and graphical representations, such as bar charts and line graphs, to illustrate the magnitude, distribution, and growth trends of Gender Budgeting across the study period.

4 Analysis

The size of allocations in the gender budget statement has increased almost nine times (from Rs 24,032.00 crore in 2005–06 to Rs 449,028.68 crore in 2025–26) since its inception in 2005–06. However, relative to the size of total budget allocations or the GDP of India, these allocations seem insufficient for elevating the performance of women on various indicators. Figure 1 shows that allocations under the gender budget, with some intermittent decrease and increase, range from 2.74% to 8.86% of the total union budget. Looking at the actual expenditure (for which data has been published since 2017–18), the highest figure that has been touched so far is 8.86% during 2025–26, following the COVID-19 pandemic. A significant shift occurs post 2021–22, when the gender budget begins to rise sharply, climbing from 5.52% in 2022–23 to 8.56% in 2023–24 (AE), and then to a record high of 8.86% in 2025–26 (BE). This significant rise can be viewed as a policy response to the increased socio-economic vulnerabilities experienced by women during and in the aftermath of the COVID-19 pandemic, which underscored the need for more robust gender-focused interventions.

For the first time, India's Gender Budget crossed the 1% of GDP mark in 2023–24, reaching a record 1.30%**,** marking a significant policy shift (Fig. 2). Between 2005–06 and 2022–23, it remained below 1%, reflecting limited fiscal commitment to gender equity. This sharp rise post-COVID indicates renewed focus, but sustained and institutionalized investment is essential to address structural gender disparities.

Looking at the allocations in disaggregate form (Part A, Part B and Part C), the allocations under Part B schemes (with at least 30% provisions for women) have always dominated the composition, Fig. 3. On average, Part B allocations constitute 72%, while Part A (100% women-specific) allocations constitute just 27% of total gender budget allocations. The share of Part A allocations was 33% in 2005–06, touched a minimum of 15% in 2020–21 and reached a maximum of 46% during 2021–22. Since then, it has started declining again, and as per budget estimates for 2025–26, it is 24%. The emergence of Part C allocations (below 30% for women) in recent years, beginning with 6% in 2021–22 and stabilising at 4% thereafter, suggests increasing efforts to recognise partially gender-responsive schemes. Overall, the data

Fig. 1 Gender budget as a percentage of total expenditure (*Note* All figures are Budget Estimates, except figures marked with * which are Actuals, and ^ which are Revised Estimates *Source* Government of India, Ministry of Finance. [2005–2025]. *Gender Budget Statements [2005–06 to 2025–26]*. New Delhi: Government of India. Retrieved from https://www.indiabudget.gov.in)

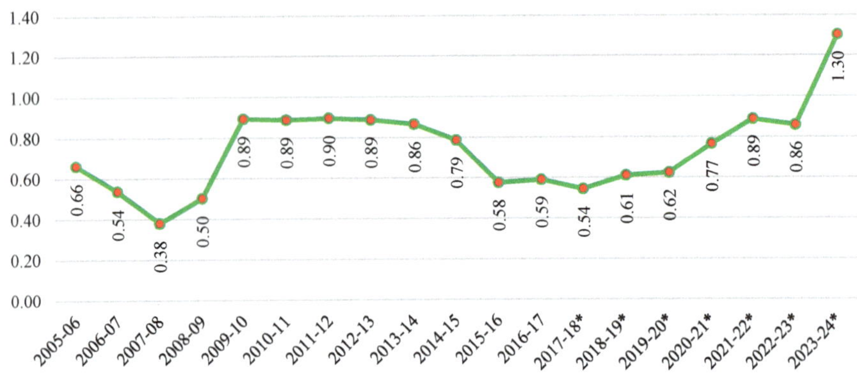

Fig. 2 Gender Budget as a percentage of GDP (2005–06 to 2023–24) (*Note* All figures are Budget Estimates, except figures marked with * which are Actual Estimates *Source* Government of India, Ministry of Finance. [2005–2025]. *Gender Budget Statements [2005–06 to 2025–26]*. New Delhi: Government of India. Retrieved from https://www.indiabudget.gov.in)

points to a persistent under-prioritisation of fully women-targeted programs within the Gender Budget, despite recent improvements.

To assess the seriousness of government towards making necessary expenditures under the gender budget, we have examined the difference between budget estimates and actual expenditures. From the available figures, it is clear that for the last six years, during three financial years, Actual expenditure has been lower than what was promised during budget speeches. Although this happened with overall expenditure, the extent of the decrease was more acute for gender budget allocations, as is evident in Fig. 4. As data is not available for the remaining years, we tried to assess the same using the difference between RE and BE and reached the same conclusion

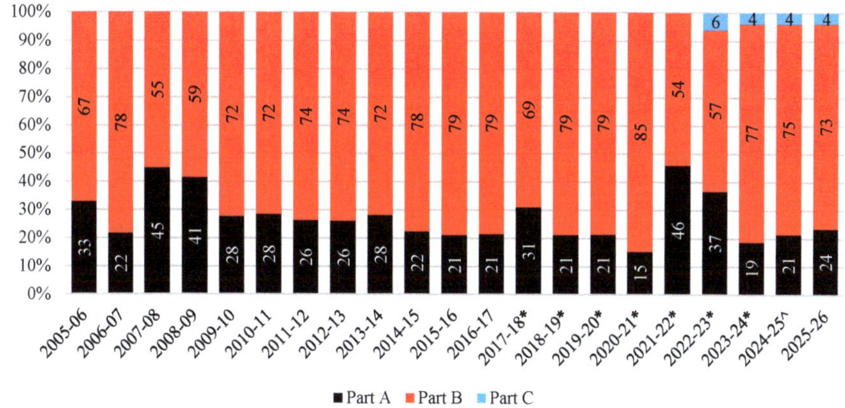

Fig. 3 Allocations to Part A, Part B and Part C as a proportion of gender budget (*Note* All figures are Budget Estimates, except figures marked with * which are Actuals, and ^which are Revised Estimates *Source* Government of India, Ministry of Finance. [2005–2025]. *Gender Budget Statements [2005–06 to 2025–26]*. New Delhi: Government of India. Retrieved from https://www.indiabudget.gov.in)

that if, for some reason, BE is not met, the axe falls more heavily on women-related expenditures.

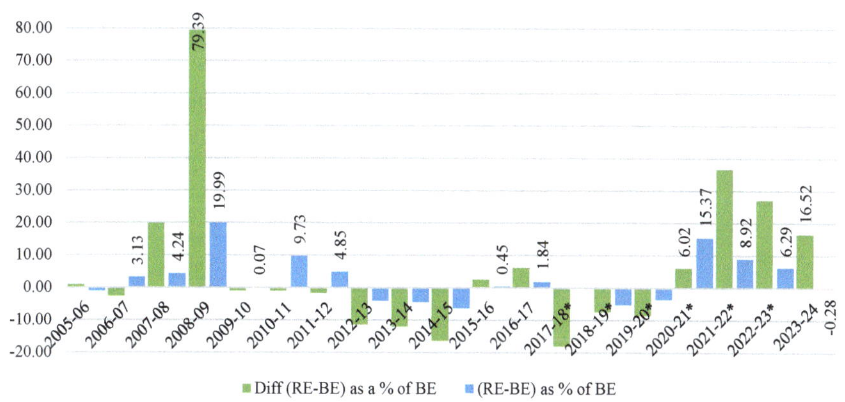

Fig. 4 Total expenditure & gender budget difference as a percentage of budget expenditure (*Note* All figures are Budget Estimates, except figures marked with * which are Actual Estimates, BE & RE represents budget & revised estimates *Source* Government of India, Ministry of Finance. [2005–2025]. *Gender Budget Statements [2005–06 to 2025–26]*. New Delhi: Government of India. Retrieved from https://www.indiabudget.gov.in)

4.1 Ministries: Participation in Gender Budgeting

The increased focus of union government towards Gender Budgeting is also reflected by the increasing number of ministries reporting in GBS. Having started with six different ministries in 2005–06 out of fifty, the number of reporting ministries increased to 27 during 2014–15, and in the latest budget, 39 different ministries of 55 reflected their allocations either under Part A or /and Part B or /and Part C. If the number of departments under any ministry is considered separately, then the number of ministries/departments has actually increased to 49.

Although the total number of ministries reporting under the gender budget has increased over the period of time, Fig. 5 reveals that the difference between the number of ministries/departments that are reporting under Part A, Part B and Part C is continuously increasing with a relatively more number of ministries reporting under part B. Looking at the number of ministries/departments that report under Part B only, this number has increased to 37, implying that these ministries, although women-related, have not planned/implemented any women-specific (100%) scheme. More importantly, during 2017–18, in comparison to the 2023–24 budget, nine ministries/departments have not shown their allocations under GBS, reflecting their lackadaisical approach towards gender budgeting. Part A reporting ministries remain limited, at 17 in 2025–26, indicating that few ministries implement 100% women-centric schemes. Notably, Part C ministries jumped sharply from 1 in 2024–25 to 22 in 2025–26, suggesting a growing number of departments are now implementing schemes with less than 30% gender focus. This sharp rise in Part C may reflect a broadening of gender tagging but also raises concerns about dilution of targeted efforts.

A deeper insight into data reveals that allocations under GBs have been dominated by Few ministries. The data for the last three years reveals that just six departments,

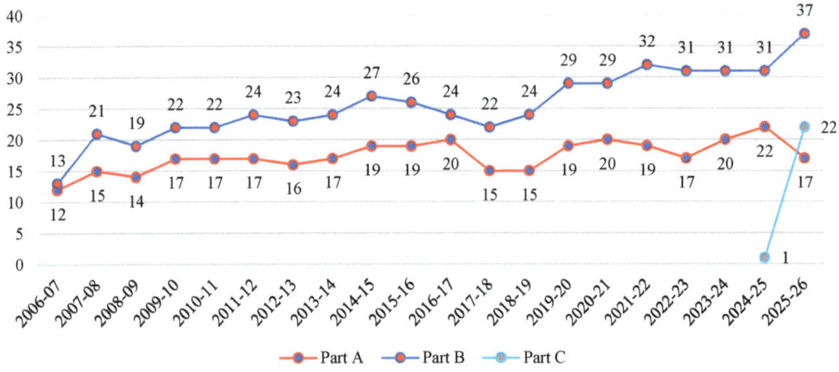

Fig. 5 Ministries/Departments reported in Part A Part B and Part C (*Source* Government of India, Ministry of Finance. [2005–2025]. *Gender Budget Statements [2005–06 to 2025–26]*. New Delhi: Government of India. Retrieved from https://www.indiabudget.gov.in)

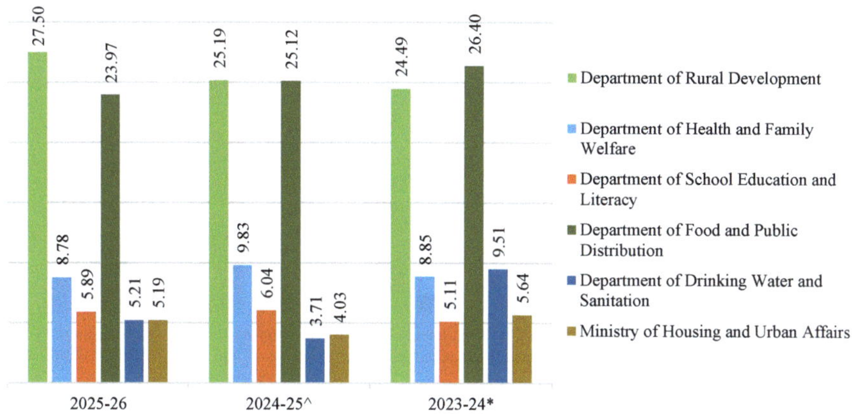

Fig. 6 Top six ministries/departments as a percentage of gender budget (*Note* All figures are Budget Estimates, except figures marked with * which are Actuals, and ^which are Revised Estimates *Source* Government of India, Ministry of Finance. [2005–2025]. *Gender Budget Statements [2005–06 to 2025–26]*. New Delhi: Government of India. Retrieved from https://www.indiabudget.gov.in)

on average, have been contributing more than 76% of total allocations Fig. 6. The actual expenditures, in fact, touched 80% during 2023–24. Figure 7 reveals that in 2025–26, the Department of Rural Development accounted for the largest share of the Gender Budget (27%) with 65.76% of its departmental budget directed towards gender schemes. The "Department of Food and Public Distribution" followed closely, contributing 24% of GB and allocating 50.92% of its own budget to gender. Although the MWCD allocated the highest proportion of its budget to gender (81.79%), its contribution to the total Gender Budget remained low at 5%. The Departments of Health and Education contributed 9% and 6% of GB respectively. The figure highlights the concentration of gender allocations in a few departments, underscoring the need for broader gender mainstreaming across ministries.

4.2 Schemes: Allocation Patterns in Gender Budgeting

Another limitation of Gender budgeting in India so far has been that only a few schemes constitute more than 50% of total allocations under GBs. During the last 6 FYs, the top five schemes, on average, have contributed 51% of total allocations under Part A, Part B and Part C, Fig. 8. Looking at the latest budget 23–24 top five schemes ("Rural Housing-Pradhan Mantri Awaas Yojana, Pradhan Mantri Awas Yojana-Urban, MGNREGS, Pradhan Mantri Garib kalyan Anna Yojana and Jal Jeevan Mission") constitute 54% of total allocations and these schemes are actually belonged to just four ministries, Fig. 9. The situation seems even more grim if one looks at the Part A schemes wherein just two schemes ("Rural Housing Pradhan Mantri Awas Yojna and Pradhan Mantri Awas Yojna -Urban") constitute about 71%

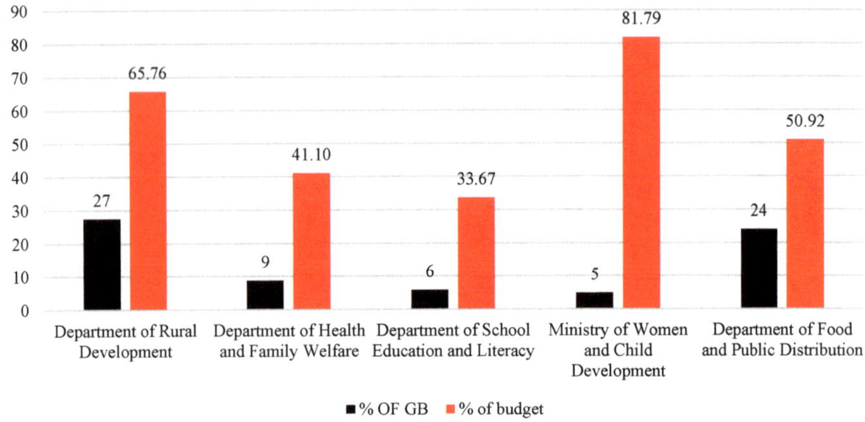

Fig. 7 Expenditure allocation of Top 5 ministries/departments (2025–26) (*Source* Government of India, Ministry of Finance. [2005–2025]. *Gender Budget Statements [2005–06 to 2025–26]*. New Delhi: Government of India. Retrieved from https://www.indiabudget.gov.in)

of total allocations under Part A, and both the schemes are related to housing for poor the benefits under which may not necessarily be counted as exclusively for women Fig. 10.

This brings to the fore a lack of seriousness on the part of different ministries regarding gender commitments, at least in quantitative terms. A mere reflection of a ministry under Part A or Part B or Part C of GBS will not suffice unless there are diverse schemes/programmes backed by sufficient funds.

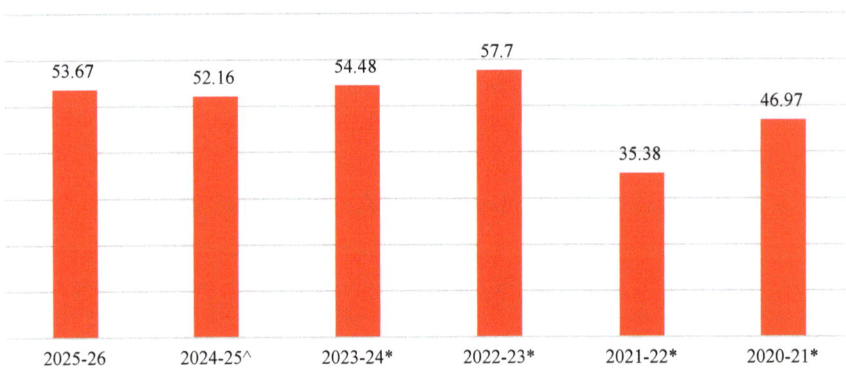

Fig. 8 Contribution of top five schemes in GB (*Note* All figures are Budget Estimates, except figures marked with * which are Actuals, and ^ which are Revised Estimates *Source* Government of India, Ministry of Finance. [2005–2025]. *Gender Budget Statements [2005–06 to 2025–26]*. New Delhi: Government of India. Retrieved from https://www.indiabudget.gov.in)

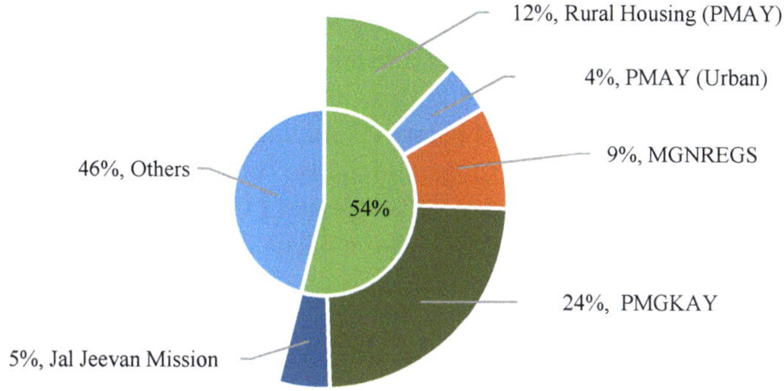

Fig. 9 Top five schemes as a % of GB allocation (2025–26) (*Source* Government of India, Ministry of Finance. [2005–2025]. *Gender Budget Statements [2005–06 to 2025–26]*. New Delhi: Government of India. Retrieved from https://www.indiabudget.gov.in)

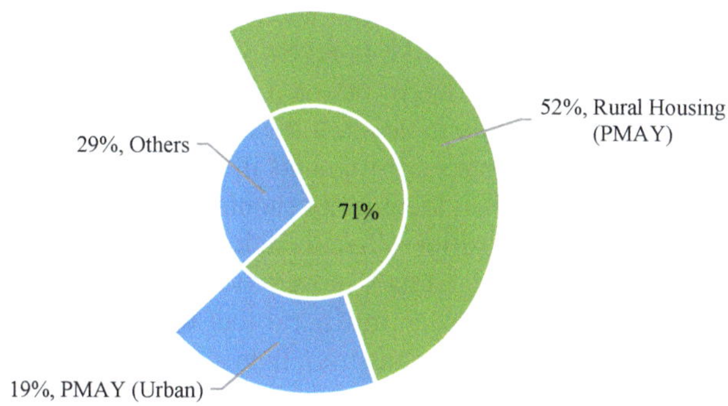

Fig. 10 Major two schemes in Part A (2025–26) (*Source* Government of India, Ministry of Finance. [2005–2025]. *Gender Budget Statements [2005–06 to 2025–26]*. New Delhi: Government of India. Retrieved from https://www.indiabudget.gov.in)

5 Conclusion and Policy Suggestions:

The recognition of the differentiated impact of budget led to the popularisation of gender budgeting as a fiscal innovation to address gender inequality. India, in an attempt to integrate gender budgeting with its budgetary process, published the first GBS in the Union Budget 2005–06. Since then, this statement has emerged as an important institutionalized tool that reflects India's sincerity in translating gender commitments to budgetary allocations with the ultimate aim of achieving gender equality goals. One of the biggest achievements so far has been the mainstreaming of the gender lens in fiscal discourse. The increasing quantum under gender budget statements, increasing number of ministries/departments reporting in GBs and appearance of new schemes in GBs over the period of time certainly reflect the government's commitment towards narrowing the gender gaps. However, the facts—a) that GB allocations as a percentage of total budgetary allocations hovered around 5 per cent since its inception and b) GB reached a historic high of 1.30% of GDP in 2023–24, crossing the 1% threshold for the first time. However, between 2005–06 and 2022–23, GB allocations remained below 1%, highlighting the persisting challenge of inadequate fiscal prioritization for gender equity. The methodological inaccuracies regarding the inclusion or exclusion of a scheme in GB and then its classification under Part A or Part B or Part C are also evident from the various iterations of GBs so far. For example, the Emergency Response Support Scheme (ERSS) of the Department of Police (Ministry of Home Affairs) is not exclusively a women-specific scheme but has been reported under Part A. In addition to the methodological and classification issues, Gender budgeting in India so far has not adopted the intersectionality approach, thereby ignoring the caste/religion-based discrimination faced by women. Further, instead of treating all women equally, there is a need to shift towards targeted GB so that programmes and policies could be framed for more vulnerable women. The government also needs to focus on increasing the number of ministries/departments that frame policies and programmes for the betterment of women and report the same under GBs. In recent iterations of GBs, the number of ministries/departments reporting ranges between 35–40 and the allocations Under Part B have been continuously dominating, a trend that needs to be reverted if the government is really serious about improvements in women's development indices. While allocating funds for gender, the priority should be for schemes that will help to change the existing gender positions. To conclude, integrating Gender Budgeting with the Budgetary process is a landmark move towards mainstreaming the idea of gender in the fiscal domain. However, this fiscal tool needs to evolve in line with changing demands and recommendations from field experts.

5.1 Limitations

This study relies solely on secondary data from official Gender Budget Statements, focusing only on percentage trends and graphical analysis. It does not include qualitative assessments or field-level evaluations of scheme outcomes. The findings may be influenced by inconsistencies in official reporting and classification of schemes. State-level gender budgeting has not been examined. Intersectional factors such as caste, religion, or region are not considered. These limitations suggest that the results provide only a broad fiscal overview rather than a comprehensive impact analysis.

Notes

1. So far, worldwide adoption experiences of Gender budgeting are different and to a stronger or lesser degree-about 80 countries have adopted it in one or other form (Cuberes et al., 2017).
2. CHARTER OF GENDER BUDGET CELLS, Department of Expenditure, Ministry of Finance 8th March 2007.

3. MWCD: Annual Report (2015–2016).

References:

Akanji, B. (2022). Rationale and entry points for gender-responsive budgeting in developing countries. *Gender-Responsive Budgeting in Practice: Lessons from Nigeria and Selected Developing Countries*, 35.

Cuberes, D., Newiak, M., & Teignier, M. (2017). Gender inequality and macroeconomic performance. *Women, work, and economic growth: Leveling the playing field*, 31–48.

Das, S., Jain-Chandra, S., Kochhar, K., Kumar, N., Kalpana, K., Jain-Chandra, S., & Newiak, M. (2017). Tackling gender inequality in Asia: India. *Women, Work, and Economic Growth: Leveling the Playing Field*, 117–26.

Das, S., & Mishra, Y. (2006). Gender budgeting statement: Misleading and patriarchal assumptions. *Economic and Political Weekly*, 3285–3288.

Downes, R., Von Trapp, L., & Nicol, S. (2017). Gender budgeting in OECD countries. *OECD Journal on Budgeting, 16*(3), 71–107.

Elborgh-Woytek, M. K., Newiak, M. M., Kochhar, M. K., Fabrizio, M. S., Kpodar, M. K., Wingender, M. P., Clements, B., & Schwartz, M. G. (2013). *Women, work, and the economy: Macroeconomic gains from gender equity*. International Monetary Fund.

Elson, D. (1992). Male bias in structural adjustment. *Women and adjustment policies in the third world* (pp. 46–68). Palgrave Macmillan UK.

Elson, D. (1995). Gender awareness in modeling structural adjustment. *World Development, 23*(11), 1851–1868.

Government of India, Ministry of Finance. (2005–2025). *Gender budget statements (2005–06 to 2025–26)*. Government of India. https://www.indiabudget.gov.in

Government of India. (2023). Ministry of statistics and programme implementation, Periodic Labour Force Survey (PLFS) Annual report (July 2021–June 2022). https://www.mospi.gov.in/sites/default/files/press_release/Press_note_AR_PLFS_2021_22_24022023.pdf

IMF. (2016). *Gender budgeting: Fiscal context and current outcomes*. IMF.

Kumar, N. G., & Vinodini, J. M. J. (2005). *Gender budgeting In India: A Strategy to achieve gender equality*.

Khullar, A. (2023, May). *Gender-responsive budgeting in India: A stocktaking. ORF Issue Brief No. 638*. Observer Research Foundation.

Mishra, Y., & Sinha, N. (2012). Gender responsive budgeting in India: What has gone wrong?. *Economic and Political Weekly*, 50–57.

Mitra, S. (2019). Planning and budgeting for women's empowerment in India: A historical process. *ANTYAJAA: Indian Journal of Women and Social Change, 4*(1), 51–69.

Nolte, I. M., Polzer, T., & Seiwald, J. (2021). Gender budgeting in emerging economies–a systematic literature review and research agenda. *Journal of Accounting in Emerging Economies, 11*(5), 799–820.

OECD. (2019). Designing and implementing gender budgeting. A path to action. *OECD, Paris*.

Ostry, M. J. D., Alvarez, J., Espinoza, M. R. A., & Papageorgiou, M. C. (2018). *Economic gains from gender inclusion: New mechanisms, new evidence*. International Monetary Fund.

PEFA. (2019). *Supplementary framework for assessing gender responsive budgeting*. PEFA Secretariat.

Sahay, M. R., & Cihak, M. M. (2018). *Women in finance: A case for closing gaps*. International Monetary Fund.

UN Women. (2018). Sustainable development goal indicator 5c1. https://gender-financing.unwomen.org/en/highlights/sustainable-development-goal-indicator-5c1

Dr. Masroor Ahmad is an Associate Professor in the Department of Economics, Central University of Kashmir. He specialises in Econometrics, gender economics, and public finance. He has published widely in reputed national and international journals and has over one decade of teaching and research experience. His recent work focuses on gender budgeting, inclusive growth, and fiscal policy.

Dr. Anam Ul Haq Ganie is an Assistant Professor of Economics at Woxsen University, Hyderabad, India. His research interests lie in energy economics, gender economics, and sustainable development. He has published in Scopus and ABDC indexed journals, presented at national conferences, and qualified UGC-NET in Economics. His recent research examines the nexus of financial development, energy consumption, and economic growth, with a strong focus on gender-responsive fiscal policies.

Part II
Cultural and Institutional Patriarchy

Chapter 5
Resisting Cultural Gender Domination in Africa: Insights from Drama and Legal Discourse

Stanley Timeyin Ohenhen, Princewill Chukwuma Abakporo, and Mary-Ann O. Ajayi

Abstract Most traditional societies in Africa have long been patriarchally organised, keeping women in secondary positions in social, economic, as well as political life. This study looks at the denial of such cultural domination through a study of dramatic portrayal as well as legal discourses that aim to knock down deep-rooted gender hierarchies. Focusing on a selected play by Ahmed Yerima, in conjunction with relevant African legal instruments ensuring gender equality, the research utilises a qualitative, text-based approach. Drawing on Socialist Feminism and Feminist Legal Theory, the study explores how dramas contain stories that act as sites of patriarchal resistance. Yerima's drama accounts for women characters exercising agency, challenging social oppression, and remaking themselves within the contexts of male-constrained worlds. Such dramatic constructs are consistent with recent legal efforts to intervene in gender discrimination, illustrating the way drama serves as both a reflection of and impetus to social change. The discussion draws attention to the intersection of drama and law as a critical location for contesting gender oppression and making the case for justice. By merging literary and juridical discourses, it emphasises the transformative potential of cultural and institutional coordination towards achieving gender equality. Lastly, the paper makes a contribution to intellectual debate in gender, power, and representation, calling for a new African society where women's agency is both recognised and institutionalised.

Keywords Feminine gender · Masculine gender · Feminist legal theory · Socialist feminism theory · Patriarchy · Cultural domination · Ahmed Yerima's Drama · Gender equality

S. T. Ohenhen (✉) · P. C. Abakporo
Theatre & Media Arts Programme, Bowen University, Iwo, Nigeria
e-mail: stanley.ohenhen@bowen.edu.ng

P. C. Abakporo
e-mail: princewill.abakporo@bowen.edu.ng

M.-A. O. Ajayi
College of Law, Bowen University, Iwo, Nigeria
e-mail: marryann.ajayi@bowen.edu.ng

H. Adam and F. A. Malik (eds.), *The Political Economy of Gender*,
https://doi.org/10.1007/978-981-92-2785-3_5

1 Introduction

The African cultural context, imbued with tradition and continuity, has long been shaped by profoundly entrenched patriarchal structures that determine gender roles and social hierarchies. Within this framework, women have commonly been relegated to subordinate roles, their agency curtailed by cultural norms that justify male dominance. Despite worldwide and regional progress toward gender equality activism, African societies continue to grapple with deeply ingrained traditions that resist transformation. The battle for gender equality, hence, goes beyond legal provisions and requires cultural and ideological change. While most African countries have passed legislations aimed at securing women's rights, statutory provisions are often sabotaged by cultural perceptions that consolidate gender differences. In this case, drama emerges as a suitable medium for challenging and questioning such norms. Playwrights from Africa have traditionally engaged with issues of power, identity, and transformation, and theatre has been a place of resistance against oppression (Ebewo, 2017). Drama not only mirrors social formations but also offers counter visions of reality, making it a desirable medium for criticising gender oppression and advocating for equity.

The continuous cultural subordination of women by African cultures despite the existence of legal means such as the Maputo Protocol aimed at gender equality constitutes the core of this study. Legal steps always fail to operate in actual life due to patriarchal values embedded in such societies where women are excluded. The gap between legal protection and day-to-day life necessitates intervention by cultural measures that facilitate internalisation of gender justice. Thus, this research explores the way drama can function as a counter-hegemonic force to resist patriarchal hegemony, with focus on one of Ahmed Yerima's plays. His play provides significant critical analysis of the way gender inequalities are reproduced culturally and how theater can turn such discourses around (Osofisan, 2001).

It is the objective of this study to explore the intersection of drama and law in gender equality debates, particularly how plays can be utilised to reinforce or undermine existing ideologies. Through an exploration of Yerima's plays, the study endeavours to demonstrate how theatre not only mirrors societal opinion but also acts as a catalyst for social change. Besides analysing Yerima's work, the research situates his plays within broader African gender politics. The research also addresses the interaction between legal rights for women and cultural resistance to gender equality (Osofisan, 2018). The research adopts a historical and contemporary stance in learning how patriarchal norms have evolved and continue to determine gender relations. By integrating legal discourse and dramatic literature, this book provides a multidisciplinary analysis of the persistent oppression of women.

The significance of this research is that it contributes to the African gender justice literature. It stresses the potential of drama to serve as a catalyst for change in bridging the gap between the law and society's acceptance of gender equality. Laws provide norms for correcting disparities, but public acceptance determines how effective they can be, an aspect that can be promoted through drama (Owomoyela, 2016; Yerima,

2015a, 2015b). Through theatre, audiences are prompted to challenge prevailing gender ideologies and to imagine more balanced social arrangements. Ultimately, the research argues that gender equality in Africa can only be achieved through the combined forces of legal activism and cultural change. Drama, with its power to provoke reflection and conversation, becomes an important tool in such efforts. By exploring the nexus of law and theatre, the research contributes to broad discussion on dismantling patriarchal structures and achieving sustainable gender justice in Africa.

2 Literature Review

The issue of gender dominance in Africa has been widely studied in the culture and law fields. Scholars continue to show how patriarchal structures—entrenched by cultural norms and legal frameworks—perpetuate the subordination of women. Cultural practices such as early marriage, female genital mutilation (FGM), and discriminatory inheritance laws persist, supporting gender subjugation (Ahimbisibwe, 2023; Ayoade, 2023; Bazaanah & Ngcobo, 2024). Ayoade (2023) contends that such customs, although harmful, are usually framed as "traditional" or "natural," therefore difficult to reverse (Chitando et al., 2024; Olusegun & Oyelade, 2022).

Feminist legal theory has played an important role in contesting patriarchal dominance and insisting on gender equality in Africa. It relies on critical legal studies, interrogating the impartiality of law by arguing that law systems have always been prone to advancing men's interests to the detriment of women's marginalisation (MacKinnon, 1989). Despite the existence of international and regional instruments such as CEDAW and the Maputo Protocol, implementation remains uneven due to entrenched socio-cultural resistance (Diala, 2018; Graness & Kopf, 2024; Masuku et al., 2023). Feminist legal activism in both South Africa and Rwanda has led to reforms such as gender quotas and constitutional protection (Burnet, 2011). Nonetheless, legal pluralism—where statutory law coexists with customary law—is still impacting the enforcement of women's rights (Otieno, 2020; Musingafi & Hungwe, 2023).

Feminist legal activists assert that equality cannot be confined to formal legal change but must include transformative justice strategies that dismantle structural patriarchy (Cornwall & Molyneux, 2006). Judicial decisions on discriminatory inheritance and spousal violence mark advances, while gender-sensitive policy in employment and property rights mark shifting norms (Amnesty International, 2021). Nevertheless, weak mechanisms of enforcement and deeply rooted cultural beliefs weaken their effectiveness. Thus, feminist legal activism remains an ongoing pursuit of structural transformation (Aikman, 2019; Dube et al., 2024a, 2024b).

Ngcobo (2021) notes that patriarchal culture is often internalised by women themselves, which reinforces cultural domination—a concept aligned with Gramsci's cultural hegemony (Chitando et al., 2024). Womanhood is frequently defined in terms of domesticity and submission, reinforcing limited societal roles (Bolt, 2021; Okongwu, 2024). The majority of African legal systems are shaped by colonial and indigenous patriarchal models, especially in marriage, inheritance, and property law (Barber, 2022; Sadouk & Bennouar, 2021). Adjei (2022) highlights that although there are legal reforms, enforcement is weak, in nations like Nigeria and Kenya where customary law prevails in regulating family life (Bazaanah & Ngcobo, 2024). Crenshaw's (1991) intersectional approach is still relevant, illustrating how African women face interlocking forms of oppression on the basis of gender, race, and class and thus require cross-cutting reforms (Oguamanam & Obah, 2024; Ojilere et al., 2019).

Drama has been employed as a potent weapon for social critique and transformation. In Nigerian perspective, Ahmed Yerima employed drama to counter and expose cultural and legal control of women. His dramas such as *Abobaku* (2015), *Jakadiya* (2017), and *Pegunrun* (2020) depict women as heroines, strong, and superior to men. This contrasts with more traditional portrayals in works like Ola Rotimi's *Our Husband Has Gone Mad Again*, Soyinka's *The Lion and the Jewel*, and J.P. Clark's *Song of a Goat,* where women are portrayed as passive or subservient. Yerima's dramaturgy aligns with Gramsci's notion of cultural hegemony; his characters challenge patriarchal assumptions and encourage ideological shifts (Aborisade, 2022). Adewale (2023) argues that Yerima's drama is in line with feminist legal theory to seek structural transformation both in law and in culture. By means of narrative, Yerima relocates women as agents of change, challenging dominant discourses validating their subordination (Ojaide & Ashuntantang, 2020; Pucherová, 2022).

Omotayo (2023) points out that the law must be supported by cultural transformation, and drama has a fundamental part to play in that. Kennedy (2023) thinks that it is time for legal scholars, activists, and cultural practitioners to collaborate in bringing patriarchy to an end. The intertwinement of legal discourse and cultural text in Yerima's dramas shows how drama not only reflects but also rebuilds social values (George-Ufot & Halkias, 2021; Ipadeola, 2022). This study situates Yerima's play as a prototype of how theatre challenges cultural norms and promotes gender justice. His female protagonists tend to occupy leadership roles, outshining men despite systemic inequalities (Asak, 2023; Ezeifeka, 2021; Oladosu et al., 2024). This representation is congruent with socialist feminist principles and challenges entrenched patriarchal norms (Anasiudu, 2022; Ogunyemi, 2024; Okongwu, 2024).

Gender injustice also appears in everyday life. The male children are privileged in the majority of African societies, while the girls continue to be under-valued. Ohenhen and Yerima (2022), citing Osezua and Agholor, observe that female children are derogatively termed "half current" in some Nigerian cultures. In development, women are forced to stick to gender roles, especially marriage, where they are objectified (Isanga, 2023; Omotayo, 2023). These patriarchal customs trace their historical origins from precolonial institutions, such as the Benin Kingdom, where women were held in concubine relations to reinforce political power (Ayoade, 2023; Dube, Musili & Owusu-Ansah, 2024a, 2024b). Widowhood is another area where cultural imperialism still holds sway. Widowed women undergo humiliating rituals, such as seclusion, compulsory public mourning, or drinking water employed to wash the corpse—a situation Ajima (2019) recorded. These ceremonies cement the idea that the identity of a woman is with her husband. With the illegality of most of these customs, their persistence prove the failure of legislation law where there is no shift in culture (Agbalajobi, 2021; Mugano & Dorasamy, 2023). Drama then becomes a critical space for challenging harmful traditions and social re-orientation.

3 Theoretical Frameworks

This study employs Socialist Feminism and Feminist Legal Theory to critically analyse the socio-legal structures perpetuating gender inequality. Socialist Feminism, articulated by Hartmann (1979) and Eisenstein (1979), assigns gender oppression to patriarchal and capitalist systems, illustrating how material realities build gender hierarchies. Concurrently, Feminist Legal Theory, spoken by MacKinnon (1989) and Crenshaw (1991), investigates the law's perpetuation of gender injustices while looking for avenues of reform. Together, these models elucidate how legal and cultural systems intersect in maintaining or subverting patriarchal norms. By means of the example of Ahmed Yerima's plays, the research examines the usage of drama as a site of resistance to legal and cultural domination of women and envisioning alternative gender relations (Makaudze, 2020a, 2020b). An interdisciplinary approach presents a nuanced understanding of how theatre and law intersect in efforts to attain gender justice in Africa.

4 Methodology

This research adopts a qualitative approach to examine the convergence of African cultural domination of the feminine gender through drama and legal implications. The study utilises a textual analysis of a selected play by Ahmed Yerima, examining themes of gender oppression, cultural practices, and women's resistance. Yerima's plays, particularly selecting Pegurun (2020) as a case study, is a key text used in this analysis that provides insight on how drama is used to satirise patriarchal norms among African societies. Data analysis within this study is largely based on thematic analysis, with key themes regarding gender oppression and resistance used within the play and dominant and operationalised legal guidelines. The play is analysed to understand how Yerima articulates the suffering of African women under patriarchal cultures and how such cultural discourses reinforce, or counteract the dominant legal orders. Textual and legal evidence are interpreted through the lens of the Socialist Feminist, and the Feminine Legal theoretical frameworks.

5 Analysis and Discussions

5.1 *Negating the Feminine Subjugation in Ahmed Yerima's Plays*

Ahmed Yerima's Pegunrun is a bold exploration of gender, power, history, and an established resistance to patriarchy's erasure of women's agency in society. Through dramatic confrontation, the play interrogates women's ongoing battle to be heard in a system that relegates them to the periphery of historical significance. In Pegunrun, Yerima looks at gender, power, and tradition through Oba Karounwi, who will not carry on a tradition a century in the making sealed under Oba Omole's rule with a woman.

Karounwi, a proud man and king, feels that it is below him to abide by a tradition that, in his view, robs him of his masculinity and kingly honor. As Adeoti, in the words of Yerima (2020), frames it, Karounwi was faced with "a patriarchal war to battle a humbling custom that will compel him 'lower' his royal self by dressing like a woman during the celebration like every other common commoner." His defiance is in patriarchal haughtiness and disrespect towards the legacy of a heroine who once saved the community. The Karounwi vs Pegunrun conflict reflects the larger ideological conflict between those who dismiss women's achievements as myths and those who try to discover their place in history.

Karounwi, patriarchy's voice, categorically rejects the legacy of the historical woman at the story's center. His cynicism reduces her narrative to an "old grandmother's tale confined in the fractured rotten teeth of age," and offers women's past roles as fanciful or extravagant. He diminishes her so-called return, inquiring if she has divine right:

"Is yesterday a hundred years? Has she the master key to the paradise that Olodumare will allow her 'come and go at will?'" (Yerima, 2020).

His revulsion evokes a profound unwillingness to accept women as active agents of the past. His final refusal—"I shall not tie a wrapper…or plait my hair just because a woman said so" (Yerima, 2020)—reaffirms his claim that the influence of a woman holds no authority over men.

In contrast, Pegunrun is a symbol of defiance against such historical neglect. Her indignation with Karounwi for demeaning her sacrifices is visceral:

"A fool! Hear his words that set my tempestuous soul ablaze like a fire-blazing volcano. I foam" (Yerima, 2020).

Her anger is not merely personal; it is centuries of angry frustration on the part of women whose work is lost or mutilated to further patriarchal ends. Pegunrun's anger takes the form of a last act of defiance—she kills the king who derided her sacrifice. She defends her act as revenge against an apparatus that consistently belittles women's struggles:

"Was it all? Was my blood a myth? Did my action mean nothing? His words reduced my sacrifice to nothingness, so I took him" (Yerima, 2020).

Her words express the painful reality of the women whose sacrifices, efforts, and contribution are ignored. She does not think her action as a murder but a show of power to make sure that her history is not forgotten without being held accountable. Even confronted by Adelu, the king's son, who is outraged at her conduct, Pegunrun holds her ground. She criticises the manipulation of women's voices, observing that even after a century, women are still accessories to men's ambitions:

"After a hundred years, men still use women. You have perfected the way of making our words sound like chippings of foolish birds…" (Yerima, 2020).

This is a line that carries on outside the play to the lived reality of most societies where women's voices are muffled as unimportant and not authoritative. She speaks in a dirge and an announcement tone—that history will continue repeating itself unless women take radical steps towards regaining their agency.

Yerima's Pegunrun interrogates the structures underpinning gender injustice. The play demonstrates how women's narratives are actively removed by patriarchal actors who desire to maintain male domination in history. Karounwi and Pegunrun represent opposing ideological forces—one sustaining the prevailing order and the other, which demands historical justice. Pegunrun's act of resistance, though radical, compels the audience to think about uncomfortable questions: to what extent is violence justifiable in the fight for gender justice? To what extent is erasure in history the cause of ongoing oppression of women? What happens to those who have been silenced for centuries who finally get their voice?

In placing drama as a site for investigating such questions, Yerima is asserting the role of theatre in shaping public awareness. Pegunrun is an intervention in culture that breaks the dominant ideologies and offering competing representations of gender relationships. It speaks to feminist critiques of traditional history as demonstrating how the patriarchal establishment controls whose stories are told and whose are forgotten. In this meeting, the play forces audiences to engage with history—not as an objective report but as a battlefield where power determines whose voices endure and whose do not.

Yerima satirises these entrenched patriarchal inclinations through the characterisation of Karounwi. The king demeans the work of an historic female character, violating the communal covenant with impunity. But for this erasure, there are terrible repercussions—Karounwi forfeits his life at the hands of Pegunrun, a woman who will not be erased. Through death even, the authority of womanhood reigns supreme, reaffirming the play's attack on gender-based oppression. The narrative follows Socialist Feminist Theory, which resists all forms of oppression, particularly oppressive in character and marginalising to women. In Pegunrun, resistance to patriarchal rule is not metaphorical in character—it has real and fatal consequences, emphasising the call for justice, equity, and gender affirmation. Yerima's message is clear: societies that dismiss women's contribution and decision-making do so at their own peril.

The play belongs to the Socialist Feminist genre, which examines the intersection of gender and class oppression in patriarchal societies. Pegunrun personifies this tension, resisting patriarchal control and the socio-economic institutions that perpetuate it. Her actions oppose patriarchal dominance and the socio-economic institutions perpetuating it. The play highlights how institutionalised gender oppression cannot be separated from general class exploitation, a crucial observation in Socialist Feminist theory. Yerima's critique is also not only of the traditional gender roles but of the wider socio-economic systems that maintain inequality. The themes of the play intersect with broader feminist concerns around representation in history, legal status, and cultural erasure. Pegunrun's character forces audiences to question how history is constructed and whose voices are validated.

By weaving history and drama together, Yerima critiques the continued marginalisation of women's voices and the patriarchal mechanisms that attempt to erase their contributions. Through Pegunrun's rage and Karounwi's resistance, the play exposes the tensions between those who seek to rewrite history in their favour and those who refuse to be forgotten. Yerima applies theatre skillfully not just as entertainment but as a tool of engagement concerning history and ideology, pushing society to value the underappreciated work of women towards its history, present, and future. Pegunrun is ultimately a political and cultural observation concerning the status of women in African society. It challenges traditional gender roles and the wider socio-economic structures perpetuating inequality, adding power to Socialist Feminist calls for cultural and legislative change in an effort to advance women's rights.

5.2 *Legal and Cultural Perspectives to Patriarchy and Women's*

5.2.1 Subjugation in Africa

Marriage is seen as a sign of respectability in African patriarchal societies, and spinsterhood, divorce, and single motherhood are stigmatised. Having only female children is also a social failure. Although most women aspire to economic independence, deeply rooted patriarchal values continue to keep them under male authority—by husbands, brothers, extended family, or even fellow workers. African patriarchy is marked by men dominating households and inheritance structures, which define masculinity and femininity in a way that supports the subordination of women.

Williams (2019) observes that "female subordination in Africa assumes complex forms rooted in patriarchal culture and tradition," and cultural beliefs tend to overpower the gains of education and media campaigns. Patriarchy is strongly rooted in Nigerian society, reproducing male dominance in social, cultural, and political life (Aina, 1998). Women are systemically barred from political offices, sexually objectified, and subjected to rights denial. Literature and societal culture continue to relegate women to secondary roles. Makama (2013) conceptualises women as being accorded second-class citizen treatment, where stereotypes like the notion that a woman's place is in the kitchen are reinforced.

Despite the UN's Sustainable Development Goal 5 of gender equality, progress remains limited due to entrenched patriarchy. Constitutional legal frameworks like

Nigeria's Constitution (Sections 17 and 42) prohibit discrimination, yet enforcement is weak. Similarly, the Convention on the Elimination of All Forms of Discrimination Against Women (CEDAW), which Nigeria ratified in 1985, advocates for the elimination of gender-based discrimination but is faced with opposition from culture. Discriminatory laws like the Nigerian Labour Act and Police Act still circumscribe women's rights to work and reproductive choice. Africa has made international legal commitments to gender equality under conventions like CEDAW and regional instruments like the Maputo Protocol (2003), which addresses reproductive rights, property rights, and harmful practices like female genital mutilation. Unlike CEDAW, the Maputo Protocol specifically addresses cultural barriers, and therefore it is contextually relevant. However, in the majority of African countries, customary law co-exists with statutory law and is usually supreme, especially in areas of marriage, inheritance, and land ownership (Diala, 2018).

South Africa and Rwanda provide examples of constitutional reform success stories in the area of law. The South African Constitution prohibits gender discrimination, and Rwanda, in the wake of genocide, established gender quotas, with women now holding over 60% of parliamentary seats (Burnet, 2011). However, issues of enforcement, corruption, and inaccessibility of justice in rural regions persist across the continent. Socio-economic barriers also erode legal safeguards. The majority of women, especially in rural areas, have restricted access to education and economic opportunities and therefore find it difficult to claim their rights (UN Women, 2020). Early marriage and teenage pregnancy account for school dropouts among girls, further deepening gender inequality (Aikman, 2019). In countries like Kenya, despite having ratified CEDAW and the Maputo Protocol, customary practices such as polygamy and wife inheritance continue to be prevalent, derailing efforts at reforms (Otieno, 2020).

Gender-based violence remains prevalent. While most African nations have domestic violence and sexual harassment laws—like Kenya's Sexual Offences Act (2006)—enforcement is typically weak, and cultural stigma discourages survivors from seeking justice (Amnesty International, 2021). The notion that GBV is a domestic matter also renders legal intervention complex. At the end of it all, legal mechanisms are insufficient. Advancement of gender equity in Africa involves a multi-pronged approach to address cultural, political, and economic challenges. Feminist legal activism has been central to conscientisation and challenging stereotypes (Banda, 2005; Tamale, 2020). The movements have made an impact, especially among the youth and urban dwellers. Cultural change is, nevertheless, incremental and must be accompanied by sustained education, activism, and rigorous enforcement of gender-responsive law. As Oyěwùmí (1997) and Mikell (1997) argue, durable gender equality in Africa must be founded not only on legal victory but on overall cultural transformation.

6 Key Findings

A dramatic analysis of Ahmed Yerima's Pegunrun portrays a compelling feminist narrative that combats patriarchal domination. Pegunrun, the protagonist, resists historical erasure and masculine hegemony, exerting agency in a world that marginalises women. She wages rebellion against Oba Karounwi, who disqualifies a woman-initiated covenant as "myth," to illustrate the way drama can expose institutional undervaluing of women's labour. Pegunrun's radical action of killing the king is a reclaiming of power and a challenging of oppressive cultural norms. This aligns with Socialist Feminism, which resists the structural roots of gender inequality, highlighting drama's potential to resist male-dominated historical narratives and provoke thought on gender justice (Yerima, 2020).

The play complements legal tools like the Maputo Protocol and CEDAW, which advocate for gender equality but find resistance where there are cultures in African societies. Pegunrun's argument of women's agency is complementary to the legal drive to dismantle discriminatory practices, particularly on succession and leadership. The criticism of patriarchy in the play reflects the legal fight for the transformation of customary ways, and the way legal storytelling is energised and the gap between formal law and social popularity is overcome (Diala, 2018). Yerima's narrative shows drama's double ability as both a mirror of civil values and a force of change. Karounwi's rejection of tradition led by a woman reflects entrenched patriarchal beliefs, while Pegunrun's resistance urges a redefinition of gender roles. Supported by Socialist Feminism, the play illustrates how cultural production can shift societal attitudes and support legal reforms in fostering gender equity (Aborisade, 2022).

The study creates a synergy between drama and law in the context of gender oppression. While legal instruments and tools are empowering in structure and design, drama like *Pegunrun* resonates emotionally and intellectually and societal cultural compliance to gender justice. Feminist Legal Theory bears testimony to this synergy, with evidence that legal change internalised societal cultural change (Omotayo, 2023). Despite gains in reforms, cultural opposition like patriarchal customary laws in Nigeria, and most other countries in Africa, continues to undermine societal statutory protections (Bazaanah & Ngcobo, 2024). In all, *Pegunrun* is a counter-hegemonic tool, using drama literature to invert gender norms and supplement legal advocacy. Through the intersection of art and law, the work highlights the imperative of cultural interventions in bridging the gap between legal obligations and lived experience, offering a model for advancing gender equality across Africa.

7 Conclusion

The present paper examines the centuries-old negative portrayal of women in Africa, driven by patriarchal writers, playwrights, and juridical institutions. But feminist academic scholars and playwrights of both sexes have resisted these conventions through studies and artistic portrayal. Feminist Legal Theory (FLT), particularly its socialist feminist branch, has been instrumental in resisting these repressive portrayals by advocating women's economic, social, and political empowerment. The study indicates how Ahmed Yerima's plays turn gender subordination in the standard way upside down, adopting socialist feminist ideologies seeking justice and equality for women, the laboring class, and marginalised groups (Napikoski, 2021). Yerima's positive portrayal of female characters purposefully confronts patriarchal control, affirming FLT's objective of systemic change. On that note, this research spotlights the progressive work of feminist literature and drama in reshaping gender narratives in Africa.

8 Recommendations

The study shows that drama, like *Pegunrun*, challenges patriarchal norms by showing women's agency and evoking critical thinking. Governments and NGOs need to include theatre in gender equality campaigns by using plays like Yerima's to stimulate debate in rural and urban spaces. These interventions are in line with SDG 5 by promoting cultural change as well as legal reforms. Cultural resistance would undermine law such as the Maputo Protocol and CEDAW, demanding improved enforcement by means of judicial training and surveillance. Compliance can be achieved through regional institutions like the African Union. Collaboration between interdisciplinary associations of legal and cultural institutions is necessary.

Institutions and universities could hold festivals that integrate performances like *Pegunrun* with gender law discourse, connecting legal obligations and popular compliance. On the other hand, Feminist Legal Theory points out the affective appeal of drama in promoting gender justice. Education systems can include gender justice in curricula, using drama and literature to tackle patriarchal narratives. Ministry of Education levels can include works by Yerima to support SDG 4 in raising critical consciousness from early on. Grass roots movements, rooted in Socialist Feminism, can change cultural patterns through participatory drama workshops (Bazaanah & Ngcobo, 2024). Community leaders and men must be involved as allies.

Financing needs to be invested more on how African theatre bolsters legal systems, with research on replicable models. Traditional laws always collide with statutory practices, and policy discussions have to bring them in conformity. Task forces that include traditional leaders and activists can recommend reforms, while media campaigns—under the guise of drama—can raise popular support (SDG 16). Broadcasting performances like *Pegunrun* on radio/TV can amplify gender justice tales, advancing SDG 5 via cultural outreach.

9 Recommendation for Further Studies

Future research should explore how contemporary African artists and feminist theatre makers reclaim existing theatre forms—oral storytelling, masquerade, and ritual theatre—to resist patriarchy. Unlike Western-influenced drama, these traditional arts rooted in cultural memory and people's participation offer organic sources of gender subversion. These works would highlight decolonial feminist resistance without eschewing cultural heritage, linking scholarly theory and street-level activism to gender justice in Africa.

References

Aborisade, R. A. (2022). Women and violent crimes in Nigeria: A theoretical, historical and contemporary overview. *Gender and Behaviour, 20*(2), 19423–19432.

Adewale, O. (2023). Counter-Hegemony through Drama: Ahmed Yerima's critique of african patriarchy. *African Theatre Review, 21*(1), 72–89.

Adjei, A. (2022). Legal reform and gender equality in Sub-Saharan Africa: The limits of formal laws. *Gender & Society, 36*(2), 145–167.

Agbalajobi, D. T. (2021). *Promoting gender equality in political participation: New perspectives on Nigeria.* Rowman & Littlefield.

Ahimbisibwe, J. (2023). *Determinants of domestic violence reporting culture among rural women in Kabale Municipality-Uganda* (Doctoral dissertation, Makerere University).

Aikman, S. (2019). *Education and gender equality in Africa.* _Oxford Review of Education_.

Aina, I. O. (1998). Women, culture and society. In A. Sesay and A. Odebiyi (Eds.), *Nigerian women in society and development* (p. 15). Ibadan, Dokun Publishing House.

Ajima, M. (2019). A feminist reading of three plays on negative widowhood practices in Nigeria: Asen's *The Woman in Black*, Mbachaga's *Widows Might* and Okoh's *Our Wife Forever*in. *The Oye Journal of Arts, 1,1 & 2*, 1-17.

Amnesty International. (2021). _Report on Gender-Based Violence in Africa_. Available at: (www.amnesty.org).

Anasiudu, O. (2022). Transcending Hegemonic Phallic-Culture and Imaginaries: Afropolitan feminism and relocation as an Emancipatory Metaphor. *Journal of Language and Literature, 22*(2), 293–305.

Asak, M. O. (2023). Understanding critical and cultural theories: An African perspective. *Media and Communication Theory in Africa* (pp. 71–104). Springer International Publishing.

Asiedu, A. (2019). Gender equality and African Customary Law: The challenge of bridging the gap. *African Studies Review, 62*(1), 45–66.

Ayoade, B. (2022). African feminist movements: Cultural and legal strategies for gender equality. *Women's Studies International Forum, 91*, Article 102474.

Ayoade, M. A. (2023). Spatiotemporal patterns of female genital mutilation in Nigeria: Evidence from the 2008, 2013 and 2018 NDHS. *The Social Science Journal*, 1–20.

Baltzer, N. (2021). On the Woman Question: A Defense of Alexandra Kollontai against Liberal Critics.

Banda, F. (2005). Women, law and human rights in Africa. *Hart Publishing*. https://doi.org/10.5040/9781472563480

Barber, K. (2022). *Routledge handbook of African popular culture* (p. 1). G. A. Musila (Ed.). Routledge.

Bazaanah, P., & Ngcobo, P. (2024). Shadow of justice: Review on women's struggle against gender-based violence in Ghana and South Africa. *SN Social Sciences, 4*(7), 126.
Bolt, M. (2021). Homeownership, legal administration, and the uncertainties of inheritance in South Africa's townships: Apartheid's legal shadows. *African Affairs, 120*(479), 219–241.
Burnet, J. E. (2011). Women have found respect: Gender quotas, symbolic representation, and female empowerment in Rwanda. Politics & Gender.
CEDAW. (1979). Convention on the Elimination of All Forms of Discrimination against Women (CEDAW).
CEDAW. (1979). Convention on the elimination of all forms of discrimination against Women.
Chamallas, M. (2020). *Feminist Jurisprudence: Cases and Materials.* Academic Publishing.
Chitando, A., Kamaara, E., & Chitando, E. (Eds.). (2024). *Routledge handbook of contemporary African Women.* Taylor & Francis.
Cornwall, A., & Molyneux, M. (2006). The politics of rights: Dilemmas for feminist praxis. *Third World Quarterly, 27*(7), 1175–1191.
Crenshaw, K. (1991). Mapping the margins: Intersectionality, identity politics, and violence against Women of Color. *Stanford Law Review, 43*(6), 1241–1299.
Diala, A. C. (2018). The shadow of legal pluralism in marriage law reform in Nigeria. *Journal of Legal Pluralism and Unofficial Law.*
Dube, M. W., Musili, T. K., & Owusu-Ansah, S. (Eds.). (2024a). *African women legends and the spirituality of resistance.* Routledge.
Dube, M. W., Musili, T. K., & Owusu-Ansah, S. (Eds.). (2024b). *Gender and African indigenous religions.* Routledge.
Dube, M. W. (2024). *Gender, African philosophies, and concepts.* T. K. Musili, & S. Owusu- Ansah (Eds.), Oxfordshire: Taylor & Francis Group.
Ebewo, P. (2017). African theatre and gender: An exploratory study. *Journal of African Studies, 32*(2), 203–218.
Eisenstein, Z. R. (1979). *Capitalist patriarchy and the case for socialist feminism.* Monthly Review Press.
Ezeifeka, C. R. (2021). Chinweizu and woman's place: A response to anatomy of female power. *African and Asian Studies, 20*(1–2), 179–199.
George-Ufot, D. & Halkias, D. (2021). Challenges of Women micro-entrepreneurs in the Niger delta region of Nigeria for business survival: A narrative inquiry. *ISM Journal of International Business, 4*(1).
Gramsci, A. (1971). *Selections from the Prison Notebooks.* Edited and translated by Q. Hoare and G. Nowell-Smith. International Publishers.
Graness, A., & Kopf, M. (2024). Changing the frame: New epistemic frameworks and social transformation in African feminist theory. *The Monist, 107*(3), 279–293.
Hartmann, H. (1979). The unhappy marriage of Marxism and feminism: Towards a more progressive union. *Capital & Class, 3*(2), 1–33.
Ipadeola, A. P. (2022). *Feminist African philosophy: Women and the politics of difference.* Routledge.
Isanga, J. M. (2023). The intolerably slow implementation of African Women's rights and its impact on African Economic Development. *Mich. St. Int'l l. Rev., 31*, 191.
Kennedy, S. E. A. (2023). *Women's agency in the Nigerian art world: modernist legacies and contemporary moves across African art networks* (Doctoral dissertation, University of Birmingham).
MacKinnon, C. (1989). *Toward a feminist theory of the state.* Harvard University Press.
Makama, G. A. (2013). *Patriarchy and gender inequality in Nigeria: The way forward. European Scientific Journal, 9*(17), 115–144. https://doi.org/10.19044/esj.2013.v9n17p%25p
Makaudze, G. (2020a). Drama as a tool for gender equality in African Societies. *African Cultural Studies Review, 27*(1), 33–50.
Makaudze, G. (2020). *Theatre, law, and gender in Africa: A critical discourse on Ahmed Yerima's Plays.* African Humanities Press.

Masuku, M. M., Mthembu, Z., & Mlambo, V. H. (2023). Gendered effects of land access and ownership on food security in rural settings in South Africa. *Frontiers in Sustainable Food Systems, 7*, 1158946.
Mikell, G. (Ed.). (1997). *African feminism: The politics of survival in Sub-Saharan Africa.* University of Pennsylvania Press.
Mitchell, J. (1966). *Woman's Estate.* Pantheon Books.
Mugano, G., & Dorasamy, N. (Eds.). (2023). *SMEs and economic development in Africa.* Taylor & Francis Group.
Musingafi, M. C. C., & Hungwe, C. (Eds.). (2023). *Women empowerment and the Feminist Agenda in Africa.* IGI Global.
Napikoski, L. (2021). Socialist feminism: Definition and comparism, https://www.thoughtco.com/socialist-feminism-womens-history-definition-3528988
Ngcobo, M. (2021). The cultural subjugation of Women in Southern Africa: Rethinking patriarchy and tradition. *Journal of African Cultural Studies, 33*(3), 201–218.
Oghoadena, C. O & Agholor, N. A. (2019). Patriarchy, cultural prejudices and spousal violence in the ancient city of Benin of Southern Nigeria. *Journal of International Women Studies, Article 26*, 20, 7, 409–422
Oguamanam, G. O., & Obah, A. I. (2024). The cultural factors affecting women's rights to property inheritance: A study of the Njikoka local government area of Anambra State. *Journal of Interdisciplinary Research in Education, Social Sciences and Arts (JIRESSA), 1*(2).
Ogunyemi, O. (2021). Law and culture in Africa: Challenging the Patriarchal Systems through Feminist Drama. *African Journal of Law and Society, 9*(3), 118–134.
Ogunyemi, C. B. (2024). The epistemic codification of satiric indictment and the decrying gender Grotesque in Winnie Madikizela-Mandela's 491 days and the Zimbabwean Maverick Movie, Neria. *Imbizo, 15*(1), 14-pages.
Ohenhen, S & Yerima B. (2022). Culture and modernity: A case for social media advocacy against sexual violence in Afica. In E. Dandaura & A. Yahuza (Eds.), *Culture and sexual violence in Nigeria.* Abuja:NICO Publications. 229–245
Ojaide, T., & Ashuntantang, J. (Eds.). (2020). *Routledge handbook of minority discourses in African literature.* Routledge.
Ojilere, A., Onuoha, R., & Igwe, T. (2019). New Directions for Securing African Women's right to property under customary law: The Case of Nigeria. *Asian Women, 35*(1), 95–119.
Okongwu, O. C. (2024). The need for a national legislation for the protection of women from workplace discrimination in Nigeria: Lessons from the existing UK legal framework. *International Journal of Discrimination and the Law*, 13582291251322180.
Okonkwo, N. (2021). Traditional practices and the gender question in Africa: A socio-legal inquiry. *African Studies Quarterly, 22*(2), 56–72.
Oladosu, A. A., Ojebode, A., & Afolayan, A. (Eds.). (2024). *The human and humanities in the age of globalization.* Cambridge Scholars Publishing.
Olusegun, O. O., & Oyelade, O. S. (2022). Access to justice for Nigerian women: A veritable tool to achieving sustainable development. *International Journal of Discrimination and the Law, 22*(1), 4–29.
Omotayo, I. (2023). *Gender and customary law: Examining Women's Rights in Africa.* Legal Studies Press.
Osofisan, F. (2018). Theatre as resistance: Gender dynamics in contemporary African Plays. *Theatre Research International, 43*(3), 229–243.
Osofisan, F. (2001). *Literature and the pressures of freedom: Essays, speeches and songs by Femi Osofisan.* Opon Ifa readers
Otieno, T. (2020). Customary Law and gender equality in Kenya: A critical analysis. Kenya law Review.
Owomoyela, O. (2016). *Theatre and social change in Africa.* Ibadan University Press.
Oyěwùmí, O. (1997). *The invention of women: Making an African sense of Western gender discourses.* University of Minnesota Press.

Maputo Protocol. (2003). _Protocol to the African charter on Human and Peoples' Rights on the Rights of Women in Africa.
Pucherová, D. (2022). *Feminism and modernity in anglophone African women's writing: A 21st-century global context*. Routledge.
Sadouk, H., & Bennouar, L. (2021). *Patriarchy, gender discrimination and resistance in Buchi Emecheta's second class citizen (1974) and Kehinde (1994)* (Doctoral dissertation, Université Mouloud Mammeri Tizi Ouzou).
Tamale, S. (2020). *Decolonization and Afro-feminism.* Daraja Press.
Williams, Catherine, (2019), Patriarchy and the representation of Women in Africa and Asia, https://www.iias.asia/the-newslette/article/patriarchy-and-representation-womens-africa-and-asia
UN Women. (2020). *Women's Rights in review: 25 Years After Beijing.* United Nations Entity for Gender Equality and the Empowerment of Women. https://www.unwomen.org/sites/default/files/Headquarters/Attachments/Sections/Library/Publications/2020/Gender-equality-Womens-rights-in-review-en.pdfUN Women+1UN Women+1
Yerima, A. (2015a). *Culture.* Ebony Books & Creation.
Yerima, A. (2015b). *Abobaku.* Kraft Books Limited.
Yerima, A. (2017). *Jakadiya.* Kraft Books Limited.
Yerima, A. (2020). *Pegunrun,* Rochester: Alpha Crownes Publishing Limited.

Stanley Timeyin Ohenhen is a Professor of Theatre Management, Arts Administration, Advocacy, and Entrepreneurship. He earned a B.A. in Theatre Arts from the University of Benin and M.A. and Ph.D. degrees from the University of Ibadan, Nigeria. His research spans performing arts management, indigenous epistemologies of the Global South, eco-criticism, and theatre's role in resisting colonial and neo-colonial structures. A former Provost, and Head of Theatre Arts Programme at Bowen University, Iwo, Nigeria, he serves on its Senate. He is also an editor and peer reviewer for international journals on theatre, culture, decolonisation, and sustainable development.

Princewill Chukwuma Abakporo (Ph.D.,) teaches Theatre Arts at Bowen University, Iwo, Osun State, Nigeria. He is a member of the Guild of Nigerian Dance Practitioners, the Society of Nigerian Theatre Artists, and a research associate with Theatre Emissary International. He also serves as artistic director of African Pot Theatre (Owerri) and director of research and strategic collaborations for Bowen's Theatre Arts Program. His work applies autochthonous epistemologies and indigenous performative arts to explore decoloniality, environmental sustainability, and African aesthetics. His productions include Oyi Dance, This is Nigeria, and Ara Wa Ninu Jigi, reflecting his cultural and political engagement.

Mary-Ann Onoshioke Ajayi is the Head of Law Programme at Bowen University, Nigeria. She holds two doctoral degrees one from the Faculty of Law and another from the African Law Unit, Institute of African Studies, both at the University of Ibadan, showcasing her commitment to advancing legal education and research. She began her academic career in 2008 at Lead City University, where she served as Sub-Dean for five years. Her scholarly interests include Gender Justice, Comparative African Customary Law, and Human Rights. Professor Ajayi has published over 60 peer-reviewed articles in leading national and international journals.

Chapter 6
Bhutan and the Female Agency: Intersection of Social Norms, Religion and Gender in Bhutanese Literature

Vanya Srivastava

Abstract The youngest democratic and modernized nation of Bhutan is known for its unique approaches for consummate development, environmental conservation and female representation. The country was in isolation till the greater half of the twentieth century and with its end, it emerged as a "Shangri-la" (heaven) on earth. Popular for its breathtaking beauty and gender inclusive romantic culture, there are traces of masked projection of gender performativity and liminality in the traditional matriarchal society of Bhutan. The overwhelming influence of Buddhism and modernization is said to be shifting the existence and identity of Bhutanese women into the growing 'culture of silence'. Thus, the present paper is an attempt to examine the interplay of gender agency and the grand narratives of gender neutrality in the kingdom of Bhutan. The paper posits that there is a disjunction between the said egalitarian principles and the lived experiences of women in the country. It will analyze the works of Kunzang Choden and Karma Ura using theoretical considerations of Buddhist Feminism and Marxist Feminism to establish that the intersection of religion and socio-political transformation has weakened the gender agency where Bhutanese women are grappling to bring coherence to their existence and identity. The paper aims to contribute to the contemporary discourses on gender studies within the SAARC vicinity by focusing on the significant concerns coming from the underrepresented and poorly studied cultures and nations of South Asia.

Keywords Bhutan · Gender agency · Buddhism · Modernization · Buddhist feminism · Marxist feminism · SAARC literature · Gender studies · Kunzang Choden · Karma Ura

V. Srivastava (✉)
Department of Languages (English), FOHSS Integral University, Lucknow, India
e-mail: vanya.srivastava29@gmail.com

H. Adam and F. A. Malik (eds.), *The Political Economy of Gender*,
https://doi.org/10.1007/978-981-92-2785-3_6

1 Introduction

The kingdom of Bhutan is a "small sparsely populated kingdom at the eastern end of the Himalayas, often described as one of the most isolated countries on earth" (Ahmad, 236). Popularly known as Druk-yul, the Land of the Thunder Dragon, its national identity is intimately tied to its religious identity as the last bastion of Tibetan Buddhism. Bhutan was never colonized and remained in isolation till the greater half of the twentieth century. Despite being geo-politically alienated, this Himalayan kingdom grappled with issues of cultural negotiations and monastic dogmatism that led to the institutionalized subordination of gender system in an otherwise matriarchal society of Bhutan.

The first breach in the country took place in seventeenth century with the arrival of Tibetan Buddhist lamas. Tibet was seized by the Mongolians leading to the religious annihilation, known as the "Dark Age" of Buddhism. Bhutan then was economically independent, culturally rich but politically fragmented. Thus, it emerged as the fertile ground for the relocation and restoration of Buddhism. This was at the cost of indigenous Bon tradition. Bon was fundamentally a matrifocal religion with animistic and shamanistic elements. The female deities were highly revered and considered the guardian deity of the land and the resources consumed by the Bhutanese. Conversely, Bon stood in sharp contrast to the core teachings and principles of Buddhism.

To establish the strong base and influence of Buddhism, monastic institutions associated Bon with everything evil and delusional, that needed absolute purification. The very first step towards purification started with the identification of Bon female deities as 'primordial chaos', who were required to be subdued using the masculine powers of lamas, thus necessitating the legitimization of androcentric reforming of Bhutanese society. Subsequently, the monastic institutions regressively misinformed Bon worldviews and further circumscribed female sexuality, This initiated gender exclusivity in the socio-cultural and political set-up of Bhutan.

In addition to the monasticization, the end of isolation and simultaneous introduction of modernization further pushed Bhutanese women in the anonymity of existence. In the "new emerging realities" (Choden 3), the rise of consumerist culture, profit-making and westernization, Bhutanese women who were already struggling with monastic domination to bring coherence to their existence, were conditioned to a "vacant" state of "incomprehension and confusion" (Choden 145). Modernization was though cautiously implemented, it tussled Bhutan between the sustenance of tradition and aspiration for development. In this tussle, Bhutanese women were subjected to new forms of vulnerabilities and social pressures. They suffered economic disempowerment, workplace discrimination, and new forms of sexism. Thus, the advent of modernizing mission further intensified persistent socio-cultural patters of "gender-specific frustration" (Gilbert and Gubar) against the acclaimed gender neutrality of Bhutan.

2 Objectives of the Study

The research problem in the present paper lies in the disconnection between Bhutan's projected ideal of gender neutrality and lived experiences of its women. The influence of Buddhism and modernization resulted in the implicit gendered hierarchies which perpetually shifted its women to the 'culture of silence'. This has left Bhutanese women helplessly navigating their position between religious identity and embracement of changing socio-political dynamics in their country which is popular for its unique socio-cultural policies of valuing happiness of its people over the metrics of development.

The paper examines how the works of Choden and Ura portray female agency in Bhutanese society? It also explores in what ways Buddhism and modernization influence gender question in Bhutanese literature? It will analyze how literary narratives challenges or reinforce the country's claim of gender neutrality?

The objective of the study is to understand the intersection of social norms, religion and gender in Bhutanese literature. It aims to assess the impact of Buddhism and modernization on the female agency as represented in *The Circle of Karma* (2005) and *The Hero with a Thousand Eyes* (1995). It attempts to situate the female question of Bhutan within the broader framework of contemporary gender studies.

The present study thus contributes to the contemporary feminist discourses, particularly, South Asian gender studies by exploring emerging yet significant theoretical concern of Buddhist Feminism. It also uniquely employs Marxist feminist critique to understand the evolving socio-cultural setup of Bhutan which further contributes to the important concerns of gender inclusivity and identity in the context of underrepresented cultures and traditions.

3 Literature Review

Recent scholarship has seen Bhutan as a place of "no reading culture" (Namgay Zam) because of which its literature has not received substantial academic attention. Majorly, the country was either romanticized as "a modern 'Shangri-la' or as a genocidal state" (Phuntsho 166). Thus, the seriousness of its socio-cultural transformation suffered far sprung representation. Additionally, gender studies in the South Asian literary context, have gradually evolved significantly but in the context of Bhutan it is still marred by inaccurate projections and external prejudices. There are dynamic works by the Bhutanese writers who have challenged the monolithic representation of the country. Writers like Karma Ura in *The History of Bhutan* (2013) has lucidly captured the rise and development of Bhutan from an isolated kingdom to the youngest modernized nation, covering every dimension of Bhutanese life but has not specified the effects of nation's transition on its women. Dorji Penjore, an eminent writer of Bhutan, has written many articles on the country and even runs a prominent website, *A Bowl of Suja*, to disseminate research materials focused on

Bhutanese studies but research gap in the feminist discourses in Bhutan have not been comprehensively covered by him. There are also foreign writers who have written extensively on Bhutan such as Linda Leaming, Madeline Drexler, Jamie Zeppa but these writers have overtly romanticized exotic customs and breathtaking beauty of the country and even criticized its attempt at consummate development rather than reflecting on its realities and important developments. So far, the most significant contribution to the Bhutanese feminist concerns is dealt by Kunzang Choden, the first Bhutanese woman to write a novel in English. But her works have largely been analyzed to understand the socio-political transition of Bhutan with a generalized approach towards the condition of Bhutanese women.

Overall, there is a lack of nuanced understanding of gender dynamics in the literature of Bhutan. The present study thus becomes significant in its approach in expanding the cliched interpretations of female agency by presenting it as the active site of social negotiations and transformation. It also explores the important issues of feminism in Buddhism thereby adding to the multifaceted experiences of women across the world and contributing to the global gendered-cultural context.

4 Methodology

The study employs a qualitative approach combining textual and contextual cultural analysis to understand female agency in Bhutan. Through a close textual reading of *The Circle of Karma* and *The Hero with a Thousand Eyes* the study will focus on representations of female characters, portrayal of their experiences, implicit gender discourses to understand functioning of gender agency in the country. The contextual cultural analysis will be situated within Bhutan's historical, religious and cultural contexts to examine gender practices, dynamics and evolution enabling the interpretations of selected works with the broader cultural narratives about gender neutrality, modernization and Buddhist traditions.

4.1 Theoretical Framework

The concerns of Buddhist feminism present a dynamic convergence of feminist issues with pacific traditions of Buddhism. Buddhist feminism as a branch of theoretical study emerged in twentieth century emphasizing on the tension between the egalitarian impulse and ethos of Buddhism, and the subsequent androcentric organization of monastic institutions and practices. The Buddhist feminists trace this institutionalized subordination of female gender back to Gautam Buddha when he denied request of his foster mother, Mahaprajapati Gotami, for ordination from himself. Later, on the insistence of his disciple Ananda, Mahaprajapati Gotami's wish was granted but

Buddha imposed a concept of Bhikkuni, a fully ordained Buddhist nun, on Mahapajapati Gotami and subsequently on those women who wished to be ordained in future. This came to be known as eight Garudhammas-the heavy rules:

1. A nun who has been ordained even for a hundred years must greet respectfully…do proper homage to a monk ordained but that day.
2. A nun must not spend the rains in a residence where there are no monks.
3. After the rains a nun must 'invite' before both orders in respect of three matters, namely what was seen, what was heard, what was suspected.
4. A nun, offending against an important rule, must undergo manatta discipline for half a month before both orders.
5. When, as a probationer, she has trained in the six rules for two years, she should seek higher ordination from both orders.
6. A monk must not be abused or reviled in any way by a nun.
7. From today, admonition of monks by nuns is forbidden. (Mohr and Tsedroen)

These rules evidentially subordinate nuns to monks. Contrastively, Buddhism focuses on the supremacy of mind for attaining nirvana-emancipation and enlightenment, and directs path for such liberation for all class, color, creed and gender. Hence, attacking this all-embracing philosophy, Buddhist feminist question, 'does mind have a gender?'.

The primary concern of Buddhist feminism is to debunk the systematic othering of female gender propagated by the three influential sects-Hinayana, Mahayana and Vajrayana. The latter two have profound influence in establishing and popularizing the strong base of Buddhism. The Mahayana sect cultivates the idea of universal empathy by renouncing delusional inclination towards desires and materialism. Additionally, it considers female sexuality as the focal point of all kinds of desires and attachments, reducing these categories to more sexual than spiritual. This restrictive conditioning of female sexuality is essential to eliminate and control such evil aversions. This belief could be called an extension of the seventh garudhamma where female sexuality is directly associated with the abuse and defiling of masculine monastic customs.

Likewise, the Vajrayana tradition reduces female sexuality to a mere passive requisite for its rituals. This tradition fundamentally follows occult procedures to reach powerful stage of enlightenment, which majorly involve acts of sexual consummation. Moreover, a meticulous system is followed for the selection of women who are to be chaste, virtuous, and young. These women are classified as Dakinis, the spiritually potent women chosen by Buddha for the pure sustenance of Buddhism. But they ultimately end up helping tantric masters for the rituals and later managing their household and offsprings. Thus, while Vajrayana Buddhism claims to historically celebrate divine forms of femineity, it has perpetuated embedded forms of misogyny by restricting women's spiritual potential within the domestic boundaries.

The systematic liminality of female sexuality propagated by Buddhism is evidentially manifested in the socio-cultural set up of Bhutan. The women are denied monastic education as it might corrupt pious monk tradition. Moreover, under the pretext of romantic culture, extra marital affairs, unmarried pregnant teenagers are destigmatized to brazenly support the claim of sexual freedom. But in practice, these women have to undergo demeaning rituals to apparently cleanse themselves to live in society. Whereas, there are no such prescriptions for men.

The effective disparity between symbolic representation of Buddhist principles concerning gender neutrality and its lived reality in Bhutan further extends to economic structures and class relations with the advent of modernization. The country's transition from absolute to constitutional monarchy reflects how economic transformations have intersected with class structures, religious traditions affecting gender relations. This paradigmatic shift in the socio-cultural setup of Bhutan has further revealed the 'myth of emancipation' of Bhutanese women. The present study has analyzed this "sexual imbalance of power" (Firestone 9) using Marxist Feminist lens, particularly using Shulamith Firestone's *The Dialectic of Sex: The Case for Feminist Revolution* (1970).

The Marxist Feminism is an offshoot of Social Feminism which builds upon Marxist theory of class division to highlight the unacknowledged exploitative subordination and conditioning of women in the social hierarchy through family structures. The Marxist feminists basing their premises on Friedrich Engels' *The Origin of the Family, Private Property and the State* (1884) believes:

> The first division of labor is that between man and woman for the propagation of children...The first class opposition that appears in history coincides with the development of the antagonism between man and woman in monogamous marriage, and the first class oppression coincides with that of the female sex by the male. (66)

The aforementioned concern considers set up of 'marriage' and 'family' as the primary sites of domestic and sexual labor of women, which propagates into larger gendered specific subjection and suppression where biological conditioning of female sex is used for socio-cultural and financial suppression. In such setup the female sexuality is reduced to a private property owned by men for free reproductive and domestic labor.

In the context of Bhutan, the Marxist feminist analysis has busted the hyped culture of "cloying romanticism" (Firestone 27) revealing the exhaustion, financial dependency and unrelenting demands of domestic duties beneath the celebratory image of independent Bhutanese women. Particularly significant is that how the introduction of modernization and subsequent market system has created new forms of gender oppression along with the existing traditional patriarchal structures. The contemporary literature of Bhutan effectively navigates the strong claim of gender inclusivity and material reality to explore the status of women in cultural preservation and economic development. The present study will evaluate this "strategic essentialism" (Spivak) to understand the dynamics and interplay of Buddhism and Marxism in defining the traditional identity and modern existence of Bhutanese women.

5 Buddhist Feminism in Choden

Kunzang Choden's *The Circle of Karma* (2005) is the first novel written in English by a Bhutanese woman. The novel was significant in many aspects, firstly it deconstructed the representation of Bhutan as the *Shangri-la* by bringing to forefront real challenges of the youngest democratic-modernized nation. Secondly, it was the precursor to the feminist question in the literature of Bhutan. The novel features the story of Tsomo-her quest for spiritual knowledge and emancipation through monasticism in the rapidly changing and modernizing Bhutan. Tsomo's journey manifests androcentric interjection of emancipatory Buddhist principles amidst the creeping urbanization and new forms of sexism.

Her journey raises serious concerns on the role and position of apparently free women in Buddhist Bhutan. She oscillates between attachment and rejection, emancipation and circumscription, highlighting gendered performativity and interpolation of Buddhist ethos and customs. The very title of the novel hints towards limiting outturn of monastic customs. It signifies the 'law of moral' causation-what goes around comes around. As per Buddhism, human actions are directly proportional to eternal emancipation, good actions are followed by good life and easy emancipation, bad actions have retributions. Moreover, the effect of law continues to next birth. If a person constantly suffers it means the karmas of previous life have extended to the current life. Thus, the novel traces the karmas of a Buddhist woman to question its transcendental determination of gender agency and functionality.

Tsomo, wanted to study religion but was bluntly denied by her monk father. He establishes that being born a woman in the current life is an indication of bad karmas of previous life. Since, Tsomo is still bound to her karmic retributions, she cannot pursue religion, at least, in this life. Hence, she was advised "to learn other things" that will "make her a good woman and a wife" (Choden 15). This gender determinism of karma propagated by the monks effectively dismantles female participation and acceptance in the monastic communities, and adversely in society.

The social implications of manipulative dependent origination (*pratityasamutpada*) of karmic nemesis are further evident through the sufferings of Tsomo's friends, Chimme. Her friend had an affair with a monk. Chimme got pregnant and her monk lover refused the public acceptance of their relationship because he was a ordained monk-thus supposed to be celibate. In gender-inclusive Bhutan, pregnancy out of marriage is considered impure unless the child has "a willing father" (Choden 36), thus Chimme had to undergo a purification ceremony, tshangma. Moreover, she was socially condemned for causing a celibate monk lose his virginity. This religious despotism was well countered by Chimme when she retaliates:

> Well, I did not pull him into my bed. He came begging and sweet-talking night after night and then conveniently disappeared... (Choden 44)

Thus, the religious restrictions for Tsomo's education and limiting her existence to 'woman and wife' highlights androcentric circumscription of women identity. Even Chimme's trial signifies androcentric imposition of "habitual, obsessive and mimetic" (Bell 19) projection and othering of women in monastic communities where men can freely manipulate and even negate customs but women are made the ultimate scapegoat.

The systematic normativity of distorted female participation and acceptance in Buddhism and, at large, apparent matrilineal culture of Bhutan also evident in Tsomo's marriages. Her first marriage was with a married man and father, Wangchen. She only had a random fling with him which resulted into pregnancy after which Wangchen decided to leave his wife and child for her. But Tsomo's happiness was short lived. She delivered a still born child resulting into a mysterious disease which left her disfigured. Out of his growing impatience with the sorrow and disfigurement of Tsomo, Wangchen developed an illicit affair with her younger sister, Kesang. The final blow to Tsomo's married life was when she found out that her younger sister was pregnant with her husband's child.

Tsomo was ultimately left "-barren desolate and infertile" (94). She begged and revolted against Kesang to leave her husband but without any success. Her relatives though sympathetic, urged Tsomo to accept Kesang as the younger wife because Kesanga's is more useful to Wangchen as a woman and mother than Tsomo. Tsomo was engulfed by "overwhelming sense of defeat" (94). She considered Wangchen's betrayal as her 'karmic retribution'. She made Wangchen leave his first wife and child for her, and now, her child dead, she lost him to another woman. The restrictive karmic conditioning and understanding did not let her see that her suffering is the consequence of rash acceptance of a wrong man who is now playing with the life of her sister. She never for once questioned Wangchen, but either cursed her sister or blamed herself. Finally, she decided to run away, only to return after proving Wangchen and Kesang her usability and desirability as a 'woman'.

Tsomo's marriage with Wangchen highlights the inseparability of 'personal' and 'public' in the socio-religious functioning of Bhutan. The graving mistreatment and subordination of women has religious sanction in gender-liberated Bhutan. The country boasts destigmatization of unmarried pregnant women, extra marital affairs, polygamy as the markers of gender and sexual freedom under its pennant of romantic culture. The sufferings of Chimme, Tsomo and even Wangchen's first wife establishes the manipulation of religion promoting gender objectification which is resulting in a disordered society in the name of gender emancipation.

This objectification corresponds to the identification of women as a lowly, corrupt beings who should be set on the path of dharma but only by superior men. Tsomo's second marriage further highlights this controlled derivation of Buddhist ethos. After leaving her home, Tsomo landed among men of religion but she was only objectified as a woman. She met Lhatu, who was a monk under the patronage of Lama Rinpoche. From their first meeting, Lhatu's behavior made it clear that Tsomo was just an option to support his financial and physical needs. But Tsomo saw Lhatu as her 'karmic remuneration' for all her struggles and miseries. She was tired of being rejected and needed companionship. Her friend, Ani Decho warned her of dependency on men by making her realize the emancipation in her isolation:

> …would you have come here if you were well and happily married off with your children clinging to you? Think of all the choices that a solitary and unattached pilgrim has, choose wisely. It is not easy for women whatever choices we make. (189)

Ani Decho's words stands for the institutional de-valorisation of female question in Buddhism which Tsomo has been suffering by the men of religion in religion. She warms Tsomo of the limited choices women have, even less the opportunity to break away from circumscribed existence, but Tsomo failed to understand. She finally realized her liminality as a woman when Sherab, Lhatu's friend, exposed Lhatu's lies and affair to her. But again, she blamed her karmas instead of her wrong choices and decisions. She was so much enraged by the loss of her worth as a woman that she decided to chop off the nose of Lhatus's mistress. She was calmed by Sherab who gave her the most reasonable advice that, "women have to learn to think things differently" (269).

Sherab's advice to Tsomo forms the core of Buddhist Feminism-the reorganization and revaluation of the androcentrism of the Buddhist doctrines. Throughout her life Tsomo desired to study religion, but had to be dependent on monks. After breaking away from her family she had the opportunity of studying religion but she was dependent on men than monastic sisterhood. For all her sufferings, she held her karmas and women around her accountable. She failed to understand that it was the centrality of "men and sex" (Choden ix) in her life that have always deviated her from her path and true liberation. Finally, when she decided to break all her attachments and pursue strict path of religion, she was found by her family. The children and grandchildren of Wangchen and Kesang came "calling sister, aunty, granny, expecting nothing in return, but giving her the best of what they had" (298). Once again, Tsomo was caught by the 'circle' of family and belonging, and her desire "to do something remarkable in life, to prove her worth to those she thought had caused her to leave" (298) faded away as she felt among her family her 'circle of karma' is complete.

Tsomo's karmic journey and mis-understanding of emancipation presents an unflinching examination of femininity as a site of monastic manipulation and social control. This manipulation also reveals disparity between the country's official narrative of gender inclusivity and women lived experiences. The country uses sexual liberty as a marker of female emancipation where in reality it justifies monastic reduction of femineity as the most potent means of delusion from spiritual emancipation. This justification further transfers to their systematic subordination in societal participation and representation.

Tsomo presents the cause of Bhutanese women who have been made to internalize this sexual objectification and social exclusion as inherent part of their identity and existence. They have been made to understand karma as deterministic force informed by gender. Thereby, they tend to relate the purpose and meaning of karmas in domestic and reproductive spheres. In Bhutanese society, the underpinning of this restrictive karmic interpretation culminates into libertine relations and marriages under pretext of gender inclusivity where women are free to assert their sexuality. Thus, it can be argued that the celebratory romantic concept of gender neutrality of Bhutan majorly glories destigmatization of female sexuality and underscores their economic participation, religious equality and social representation. Tsomo, Chimme, Kesang represents this lopsided freedom of Bhutanese women where their subordination and reinforcement of societal expectations is manipulated as karmic destiny.

5.1 Marxist Feminism in Ura

Karma Ura's *The Hero with a Thousand Eyes: A Historical Novel* (1995) subtly presents the oppressive socio-cultural mechanism of Bhutan. The novel traces the historical transition of Bhutan from a medieval kingdom to modernizing nation. Ura claims his novel an attempt to rewind the history of Bhutan with "an abiding nostalgia for an era from which even shadows are fading" (Ura). It is a semi-autobiographical narrative from the 'eyes' of a fictional courtier, Shingkhar Lam, working in the court of the Second King of Bhutan, Jigme Wangchuk. The novel basically is a celebratory narrative-dedicated to the Royal Institution of Bhutanese Monarchy. The protagonist Shingkhar becomes the mouthpiece of Ura, a courtier himself, glorifying the nation, its tradition, attempts at consummate development, emphasizing on the role of Bhutanese monarchy in all these. However, beneath this grand narrative, there are traces of reductive participation and acknowledgement of women in the transforming society of Bhutan.

The novel provides a nuanced insight into the culmination of monastic structural inequalities into the social stratification Bhutan. The analysis of the novel expands the gender question to examine the impact of intersection of modernization with the traditional structures of the country. The novel though focuses on glorification of modernization and Bhutanese monarchy, the signs of emerging "sexual class system" (Firestone 29) are deeply manifested. In the novel, the protagonist's transition from rural to urban Bhutan is paralleled with the transition of the country. Ura in his work attempted to promote the unique cultural heritage and socio-economic policy of Gross National Happiness but it challenges Bhutan's self-image as the bastion of social harmony and egalitarian nation.

Shingkhar is shown as the victim of his uncle's "highly discourteous behavior for the court" (Ura 15). His uncle was a courtier who abandoned his services without proper protocol. To compensate, Shingkhar was sent to the court to replace his uncle. Shingkhar never wanted to join the court, he desired to be a monk. Thus, this transition was a huge blow to him and his family. The news of Shingkhar's appointment spread in his neighborhood following which the young girls of his village came to console and declare their longing for him through their "haunting dance" (Ura 17). This dance has an "evocative declaration of love and constancy" (Ura 18) which is the first instance in the novel of the "sex class system" (Firestone 146) where under the pretext of sexual liberty women become the 'givers' of emotions, sexuality and desires and men become the 'passive receivers'. Such evocations in the name of liberty and freedom are natural extensions for the objectification of femineity.

Another incident of this "corrupted romantic love" (Firestone 146) was evident when Shingkhar during his journey to court mentions about the vibrant customs and traditions of rural Bhutan which he regretted to leave behind. He describes about a group of youngsters he saw on the way. The boys of the group were slipping tadpoles inside the kira-national dress of women in Bhutan, and in "mock surprise and fear, the girls screamed a bit and began to unbutton their upper part of the dress, as they dislodge the tadpoles" (20). Such valorization of free display of female sexuality under the pretext of gender inclusivity is the "concentration of sexuality" (Firestone 147) which reduces them to a mere "sexually charged objects" (Firestone 147). Such objectification prepares women from their childhood to use their body 'freely' for male pleasure.

The reinforcement of gender materialization was further reflected in Shingkhar's description of one of the highly revered festivals of Bhutan, the "Fair of Wandicholing" (Ura 55). It commemorates the building of first dzong which is "the biggest spectacle in Bhutan" (Ura 51). One of the main highlights of the fair is archery match, the national sport of Bhutan. The match is accompanied by evocative songs and dance where the woman dancers "heckled and harassed the other team by occasionally levelling personal criticism in the form of songs" (Ura 55). One such refrain even point towards "royal seduction":

You will not propel your arrow on to the target,
If you must shoot, you could launch it below my navel! (Ura 56).

Such songs point towards "sexual dualism" (Firestone 7) by pushing women into the category of "otherness" (Firestone 7) and not acknowledging them beyond bodily and sexual pleasure. This distortion of the "myth of emancipation" (Firestone 25) is further manifested in the institution of marriage of the country.

Ura's description of Shingkhar's marriages was an attempt to glorify the unrestrained carefree life but they eventually come out as a tool to naturalize women's systematic subordination. The basis of marriages in Bhutan is the custom of 'night-hunting'. Under this custom, a boy sneak into the house of a girl at night and if he remains in the morning until the family finds that means he is ready to commit, or else it is considered just a fling. Such practices are kept alive in Bhutan to prevent its 'culture of romance' from being monotonous and dull. Likewise, Shingkhar's marriages also set the examples of "biological determinism" (Firestone) of Bhutan's free women.

Shingkhar's first marriage was with a woman named Pendon Wangmo. Their romance initially started with the exchange of betel nuts which was a sign of "romantic lavishness" (Ura 79) in the country. Pendon was already married and Shingkhar was not aware of this. When he came to know about it, he decided to continue this relationship in secret as he didn't want to lose his much-valued bachelorhood. Thus, he called his relation a "safe clandestine affair" which is a normal practice in Bhutan.

Eventually, Shingkhar's safe affair became public and Pedon's husband finds about them. Moreover, Pendon was also pregnant with Shingkhar's child. In Bhutan, to preserve the sanctity of apparent gender liberalization, the women under such circumstances are kept "blamelessly out" (Ura 79) and men are supposed to pay "restitution for marital dissolution" (Ura 93). Thus, all at once Shingkhar's life took unwanted turn, he lost his bachelorhood as he had to marry Pendon. He paid a hefty restitution amount to Pedon's husband to avoid any social scandal. Tired of his miseries, Shingkhar sent his pregnant wife to his village and stayed back at court.

After moving over his first wife, Shingkhar's began a new search for love which ended Pema. She was the desired diversion Shingkhar wanted and their affair took no time in escalating. After a few meetings one day Pema removed Shingkhar's "bedding from the dzong (palace) and took it to her place" (Ura163). But just like his first love, Shingkhar's second romantic encounter also proved disastrous. Pema was also married and again Shingkhar paid the restitution money to her husband and was bound to marry her. In order to clear his way for the second marriage, his first wife was married off to his brother. Eventually, Shingkhar was bored of his second marriage also and left her at his village home and moved to court.

After moving over his two affairs and consequent wives, Shingkhar finally found his 'true love' in the third woman of his life, Lakhi, who worked for the elder sister of the Queen of Bhutan. Shingkhar claims to feel genuine pangs of love for the first time. He desperately wanted to settle down with Lakhi and faced no objections from his ex-wives. Since there are no legal and simultaneous moral code of conduct for marriages and divorces in Bhutan, even if the wives wanted to object, they had no means. Ultimately, Shingkhar settled with his third wife who he claimed to love truly but had a child from her younger sister.

Shingkhar's subsequent marriages are effectively used to emphasize the context of gender neutrality and female emancipation in Bhutan. His wives are shown to be infidel, avaricious, who are being looked after by Shingkhar even after their betrayal. Shingkhar, on the other hand is shown as the ultimate victim of femme fatal, and largely representing men as the sufferer of the unrestrained romantic culture of Bhutan. He is shown to be bearing the financial, social and traditional responsibilities of the love affairs, where his lovers are left 'blamelessly out' with no onus and nemesis. Questionably, the condition of Shingkhar's wives highlight "biological conditioning" (Firestone 10) of women, where the matriarchal Bhutan privilege the female rights and desires but are at the continual mercy of patriarchal conventions. His wives, under the pretext of 'blameless' emancipatory culture, were kept out of the decisions and settlement of their affairs, it was settled among men and they 'had' to oblige.

The exclusionary liberation and neutrality of female gender reinforces "archetypal male and female roles" (Firestone 15) that completely neglect the women's voice, rights and choice over their lives. This celebrated culture of gender inclusivity becomes a "cultural tool to reinforce class system" (Firestone 147) where female body is used for the voyeuristic pleasure of men. The moment this pleasure turns into any kind of restriction on men, like marriage and child, the sexual freedom of women is confiscated under the pretext of keeping them 'blamelessly out' from any stigmatization. Shingkhar's wives were similarly eliminated when they became a liability for his freedom. He conveniently sent them back to his village and nowhere their choice and decisions are given voice or importance. Shingkhar knew about the marriage of his first wife yet continued his 'safe affair' and with the second wife he had a consenting affair. Yet, as soon as the affairs became public scandal, it was the women who were circumscribed in marriage and family while Shingkhar's freedom remained unaffected.

In the gender liberated Bhutan, the set-up of marriage and family appears to be a punitive institution, depriving women of their sexual, economic and social freedom to create a way for men for exercising his tyranny over women and children. This institution presents "amazing set of contradictions" (Firestone 28) where on one hand female sexuality is celebrated and the other if their sexuality becomes burden on men in the form of children and marriage, they are literally pronounced "civilly dead" (Firestone 17) with men regaining the control. Shingkhar's marriages display the reality of illusive freedom of Bhutanese women. His continued exploitation of women, even of his genuine love Lhaki, where he had a child with his younger sister, establishes the interplay of freedom of sexuality and its repression in the culture of romance of Bhutan.

The simple story which claims to highlight the significant socio- political transformation of Bhutan raises pertinent questions on the gender-neutral sex-class system of the country. Where the life of apparently free Bhutanese women who married Shingkhar became "inferior and parasitical" (Firestone 138), Shingkhar was thriving without any restraint, or remorse. This concern becomes critical as Ura' represented Bhutan as the center of most unique approach to modernization. The country aims to achieve Gross National Happiness with egalitarian happy existence and representation of its citizens. But the female characters represent the continuum of gender hierarchy and fractured identity amidst the new realities of Bhutan.

6 Findings and Discussion

The analysis of Choden and Ura's work reveal that the female agency in Bhutan suffers extensive intersection of religious manipulation and implicit modern constraints, contradicting nation's grand narrative of female emancipation and gender neutrality. The works analyzed expose the intricate ways of religious subjection and incoherent modern existence leading to displaced female identity and representation. The present study counters that Bhutanese female agency is tussling between personal autonomy and complex socio-cultural landscape.

The findings from this research demonstrate circumscriptive influence of Buddhism and modernization on the female agency in Bhutan. As global influences permeates Bhutan, its women are facing identity crisis and new forms of subjugations-existing monastic constraints while adapting to modern configurations. The study also contributes to broader scholarly discussions about gendered modernization and Buddhist feminism as poorly studied tools of female subjugations, especially in the context of overlooked SAARC nations.

7 Conclusion and Recommendations

The study concludes that the female agency in Bhutan operates at the complex interplay of Buddhist traditions, modernization process and emerging female consciousness. Primarily, the pervasive dominance of Buddhism is pivotal in offering constraints and misplaced opportunities for the female agency. While preaching the ethos of compassion and spiritual potential, monastic institutions reinforce gendered hierarchies through manipulation of the concept of karma. It is used to justify androcentric validation of female inferior status.

Similarly, modernization in Bhutan further extends paradoxical emancipation of female agency and gender inclusivity. Despite its progressive and celebrative veneer, modern Bhutan fails to address let alone understand fundamental gender inequalities. Beneath the celebratory narratives of modernization there are strong traces of how this significant transition of Bhutan is reproducing more disparaging socio-cultural and political hierarchies in the gender system rather than dismantling them.

Based on the above findings and discussions, future research can explore various dimensions of feminism in Bhutan, which is otherwise known as a gender-neutral country. The romantic portrayal of the country as 'Shangril-la' can be further examined to analyze its unique policies of Gross National Happiness and its influence on Bhutanese gender system. and brings to light one of the most overlooked issues of the social silencing and cultural castration of women. The study can also be used to address important questions of gender inclusivity and identity in the underrepresented nation of Bhutan to widen the contemporary feminist discourses, particularly in the SAARC vicinity. These recommendations aim to advance understanding of female agency to support Bhutanese women's complex navigation of tradition and modernity while addressing gender disparities.

References

Brown, J. S. (2001). *Dakini's warm breath: The feminine principle in Tibetan Buddhism*. Shambhala.
Choden, K. (2005). *The circle of Karma*. Penguin Books India.
Choden, K. (2009). *Tales in colors and other stories*. Zubaan.
Engels, F. (2010). *The origin of the family, private property, and the state. In Gender violence: Interdisciplinary perspectives* (2nd ed., pp. 12–32). New York University Press.
Firestone, S. (2015). *The dialectic of sex*. Verso Books.
Gilbert, S. M., & Gubar, S. (2020). *The madwoman in the attic: The woman writer and the nineteenth-century literary imagination*. Yale University Press.
Gross, R. (1993). *Buddhism after patriarchy: A feminist history*. State University of New York Press.
Hooks, B. (1984). *Feminist theory: From margin to center*. South End Press.
Tomalin, E. (2006). The Thai Bhikkhuni movement and women's empowerment. *Gender and Development*, *14*(3), 385–397. http://www.jstor.org/stable/20461161
Ura, K. (1995). *The hero with a thousand eyes*. CBS, Thimpu.

Chapter 7
Unwritten Codes: The Individual Struggle with Gender Norms and Postcolonial Identities

Sakshi Shukla

Abstract This chapter explores how women IT professionals negotiate and navigate gendered expectations at workplace and socio-cultural norms. By bringing in a postcolonial feminist framework at the center of the study, chapter examines the under explored but pervasive "unwritten rules" that govern women's career advancement, professional image, and identity formation. For this 43 semi-structured interviews with women from different regional and caste backgrounds analyzed, highlighting the manner in which nationalist imaginaries, corporate cultures, and digital surveillance reinforce traditional expectations of femininity in the workplace. The respondents described their coping mechanisms for navigating expectations of emotional work, care work, and leadership—often struggling to perform these expectations despite institutional barriers and unwritten prejudices. Further, the study explores the internal strategies used by women—self-monitoring, strategic ambition, and solidarity through support groups—to navigate these constraints. By centering these everyday negotiations, the chapter contributes to debates on gendered labor, postcolonial identity, and the imperative for reform in India's rapidly growing IT industry.

Keywords Gender norms · Postcolonial identities · Femininity · Masculinity · I.T. Professionals · Nationalist ideologies · Gendered spaces · Identity negotiation · Professional challenges and mobility

1 Introduction

In India's evolving socio-economic context, personal identity is rarely separate from nation's social expectations and cultural identity—particularly when it comes to gender. From an early age, women learn to navigate a space created by deeply rooted societal norms. These unwritten rules (or codes), often shaped by nationalist idea of

S. Shukla (✉)
M S Ramaiah University of Applied Sciences, Bengaluru, India
e-mail: sakshishukla.ss@msruas.ac.in

H. Adam and F. A. Malik (eds.), *The Political Economy of Gender*,
https://doi.org/10.1007/978-981-92-2785-3_7

ideal women carrying the traditional values, extend beyond the boundary of home. This naturalization subtly start influencing how women participate in public life, including how they shape careers, manage professional relationships, and pursue leadership roles (Menon, 2012; Uberoi, 2006). The IT sector in India is often celebrated as a space of opportunity, especially for women seeking financial independence and professional advancement (Fuller & Narasimhan, 2008). Yet beneath this image of progress, many continue to face long-standing challenges. Gender bias in hiring, limited access to mentorship, and the persistent expectation that women must embody both technical competence and emotional care continue to shape their professional journeys (Kelkar & Nathan, 2002). The structural inequalities of the past haven't disappeared—they've taken new forms within corporate frameworks. For many women, success in IT requires constant negotiation: balancing ambition with social expectations, confidence with humility, and growth with familial duty. Even in workplaces that promote gender inclusion, informal expectations persist. Women who express dissent or speak assertively risk being labeled "too aggressive," while those who remain quiet may be seen as lacking initiative. Leadership spaces still often reflect masculine norms, requiring women to work harder to be heard, seen, and promoted (Patel, 2014). At the same time, many still face the underlying belief that a woman's career must never eclipse her family responsibilities—a belief that often transforms the idea of "work-life balance" into a personal burden, especially for mid-career women (Radhakrishnan, 2011).

This chapter focuses on those invisible scripts—the unwritten workplace norms and social expectations that influence how women in India's IT sector experience success, credibility, and belonging (Mohanty, 2003). While these rules are not formally written into company policies, they operate powerfully through peer behavior, performance reviews, and leadership expectations. Women are expected to deliver results and uphold professionalism while also conforming to gendered ideals around caregiving and emotional labor—usually without institutional safeguards to support them. This chapter provides an intersectional perspective on how these professionals comprehend, adjust to, and defy gendered expectations based on in-depth interviews with women of various castes, classes, and regions. The narratives shared in this chapter reflect the quiet tension that women professionals continually navigate—the desire to belong, layered with silent refusals and small acts of adjustment. These are not always visible forms of resistance, but subtle ways of negotiating space, legitimacy, and credibility in an environment shaped by inherited codes (Bhattacharya et al., 2016). It shows how gendered labor manifests itself at various scales—individual, familial, institutional, and cultural—their experiences challenge oversimplified conceptions of empowerment.

Bringing in postcolonial and feminist theoretical work at the center of discussion especially that of Mohanty (2003), Connell (2005), and Menon (2012), this study frameworks offer a prism through which we can view the continued existence of gendered labor, even in fields that are characterized as "inclusive" or "modern" and space where gender is performed, controlled, and contested. The voices here do not fit easily within narratives of inclusion promised by modern institutions. Instead, they expose how gendered labor remains coded into daily life—even in so-called progressive industries. This chapter seeks to put lived experiences front and center by drawing attention to these subtle forces, going beyond institutional analysis. Rather than limiting analysis to formal policies or institutional discourse, this chapter turns to lived experience as evidence of how power functions through routine, through expectation, and through norms that are rarely named aloud but deeply felt.

2 Gendered Workspaces and Unwritten Codes in India's I.T. Sector

Postcolonial feminist, labor studies, and digital economy scholarship have rigorously examined India's information technology industry workplace gendered dynamics. Scholars have examined the means in which implicit workplace norms, hierarchical workplace cultures, and patriarchal codes, hidden behind supposedly inclusive policies, shape women's participation in male-dominated fields (Ghosh, 2022; Patel, 2014). The impact of informal practices, digital surveillance, and intersecting social identities that covertly perpetuate gendered exclusions are among the major gaps in these analyses, despite the fact that they detected obstacles to career advancement. This section critically reviews the primary literature to identify these gaps and suggest spaces for further inquiry.

2.1 Gendered Expectations and Unwritten Workplace Codes

India's IT industry is still influenced by enduring gendered expectations that are frequently ignored in business discourse, even in spite of official pledges to diversity. Cultural views of femininity and masculinity still shape professional interactions, influencing who is regarded as a "natural" leader, whose opinions are taken seriously, and who advances through the ranks (Athanasopoulou et al., 2018; Holmes, 2008; Radhakrishnan, 2011). Organizations may place a strong emphasis on "gender-neutrality," but this frequently conceals more subtle forms of behavioral control. Although they are never specifically required, collaboration, emotional control, and self-control are still expected of women professionals and serve as unofficial prerequisites for legitimacy (Ok & Eniola, 2024).

These unwritten codes are rarely codified in policy, yet they exert pressure through informal feedback, peer perception, and the unspoken criteria embedded within performance evaluations and promotion decisions (Budhwar et al., 2013; Fleming, 2009). The expectation to maintain "workplace harmony" often falls squarely on women, who are required to manage interpersonal dynamics while demonstrating technical acumen. This expectation positions them in a double bind—where assertiveness risks backlash, and compliance risks invisibility (Shukla, 2023; Shukla & Chaudhuri, 2023). Women who adopt direct leadership styles or resist inequitable treatment are often labeled "difficult," quietly excluded from key decisions, or perceived as uncooperative (Wijayanti et al., 2022).

It is still necessary to investigate how women internalize, negotiate, or challenge these behavioral expectations in their day-to-day work, even though research has shown how gender manifests in organizational settings. The persistence of "invisible codes" calls for more investigation, particularly in India's tech sector, which is frequently portrayed as modern and meritocratic. Understanding how women professionals interpret, react to, or defy these expectations provides a window into the cultural framework that underlies official workplace structures. In this study, gender is not only performed but also strategically reimagined in these micro-navigations, which are sites of tension and meaning-making.

2.2 Digital Surveillance and Gendered Workplace Scrutiny

New forms of visibility—and therefore, new forms of gendered scrutiny—have been brought about by the digitization of work. The lines between official evaluation and informal judgment have become blurred as corporate monitoring tools, video-based communication, and remote work have become commonplace. In addition to simplifying workflow, these digital infrastructures also introduce covert behavioral surveillance mechanisms that disproportionately affect female professionals (Masoodi et al., 2021). In order to maintain an image of "professionalism" that is subtly gendered, participants talked about the constant need to adjust how they appeared on screen, including their voice tone, facial expressions, email phrasing, and responsiveness. As Vitak and Zimmer (2023) note, this is not simply about visibility, but about the kind of emotional legibility expected of women in professional roles. Women spoke of self-monitoring in ways that felt both exhausting and necessary—strategically adjusting their digital presence to avoid being seen as either "too assertive" or "too passive" (Shukla, 2023).

These dynamics are not neutral. Digital scrutiny often reinforces normative ideas of the "ideal woman employee"—responsive, composed, communicative, and emotionally attuned—without ever naming these criteria in formal performance rubrics. As a result, women are left to navigate a terrain where success depends not only on technical competence, but on their ability to manage how they are perceived through screens, emails, and message trails. The pressure to be legible, likable, and emotionally intelligent is rarely imposed on their male peers in the same way.

While corporate surveillance tools have received growing academic attention, few studies have examined how women specifically interpret and adapt to these technologies in their professional routines (Mosseri et al., 2023). The current work foregrounds these lived experiences, treating them not as peripheral, but as central to understanding the evolving forms of gendered labor in India's I.T. sector.

2.3 Intersectional Barriers: Caste, Class, and Regional Disparities

Much of the scholarship on gender in India's corporate sector continues to center urban, upper-caste, English-speaking women, often treating their experiences as representative of all professional women. This framing risks obscuring the distinct and layered barriers faced by women from marginalized caste, regional, and class locations (Rani et al., 2022; Shenoy-Packer, 2014; Shukla, 2022). Several participants from non-metropolitan areas shared that even after gaining access to corporate spaces, they remained under scrutiny—judged not only by their gender, but also by language fluency, accent, attire, and cultural performance. These women described moments of exclusion that were not overt, but woven into the texture of workplace interactions: being overlooked in meetings, talked over by colleagues, or subtly marked as "less polished." As Belliappa (2009) argues, professional legitimacy in Indian tech spaces is often silently tied to markers of caste-class privilege, which continue to shape perceptions of who belongs and who leads.

Despite the fact that gender inclusion has gained popularity in corporate India, caste hierarchies and regional disparities are frequently overlooked in the pursuit of this goal. Even with official pledges to promote diversity, women from privileged social backgrounds continue to hold a disproportionate number of leadership positions. Researchers have noted that caste-based exclusions still exist in prestigious fields like information technology (IT), which restricts access to networks, informal sponsorship, and mentorship—all of which are essential for career advancement (Banerjee et al., 2024; Jameel, 2024). However, very few business initiatives specifically address these disparities; instead, they concentrate on general "women in leadership" initiatives that ignore the intersectional realities that exist in the real world.

Gender bias is not something that women from marginalized communities face alone; rather, it is a combination of exclusions that work together. Departing from universal narratives of empowerment and focusing on the complex, situation-specific negotiations that influence women's careers in India's IT industry is necessary to comprehend these dynamics.

2.4 Gaps in the Literature & Contribution of this Study

While gender and labor in India's I.T. sector have been widely studied, less attention has been given to the informal norms that quietly shape women's career paths. Much of the literature focuses on structural issues—like pay gaps and lack of leadership—but rarely engages with the everyday expectations that influence how women behave at work. Though agency and resistance are emerging areas of interest, few studies explore how women actively navigate and challenge these unwritten rules in their professional lives. This study makes three key contributions to existing literature:

- **Unwritten Codes and Gendered Expectations**: By foregrounding the lived experiences of women professionals, this study provides an in-depth analysis of unwritten codes—the implicit gendered expectations that shape professional credibility, leadership potential, and workplace interactions. These findings extend existing research by illustrating how these codes enforce dual behavioral expectations, requiring women to balance professional assertiveness with domestic expectations. Unlike previous studies that focus on formal policies, this research highlights how gendered negotiations manifest in daily experiences, influencing career mobility and personal identity.
- **Gendered Self-Monitoring and Professional Navigation**: The study examines the ways women professionals engage in self-monitoring and behavioral adaptation to navigate workplace hierarchies. Women adjust their communication styles, assess their professional personas, and employ strategies of self-regulation to balance conflicting expectations. While some scholars have discussed workplace bias, fewer studies explore the emotional and psychological toll of constantly modifying one's behavior to fit both professional and domestic spheres.
- **Intersectional Barriers and Workplace Inequities**: By incorporating caste, class, and regional identity, this study expands the discourse on intersectionality in corporate environments. Unlike studies that primarily focus on urban, upper-caste women's experiences, this research acknowledges the layered exclusions that shape workplace outcomes. Women from marginalized communities face compounded discrimination, not only based on gender but also on socioeconomic and regional hierarchies. This study highlights the need for more inclusive frameworks that consider these overlapping barriers in career advancement.

By addressing these gaps, this research contributes to ongoing discussions on gender, labor, and corporate culture in postcolonial India. It emphasizes the necessity for institutional reforms, workplace policy changes, and broader societal shifts that recognize and challenge gendered workplace norms.

3 Research Methodology

Participants were initially identified through professional networks, LinkedIn outreach, and referrals, with the pool expanding via peer recommendations. This approach enabled access to women in leadership and technical roles, often underrepresented in corporate gender diversity discourse. The study purposefully included participants across varied career stages, technical and non-technical roles, and socioeconomic locations, allowing for a layered, intersectional reading of their professional trajectories. Semi-structured interviews facilitated a dialogic space for participants to narrate detailed personal experiences, while enabling the researcher to follow emergent thematic threads. The interview guide explored critical terrains such as workplace culture and unwritten norms, career progression and institutional barriers, surveillance practices, negotiation strategies, and the entanglement of caste, class, and regional histories in shaping access.

To further deepen the understanding of lived realities, in-depth interviews—conducted in-person and virtually—spanned 60 to 90 minutes. Conversations were audio-recorded with consent, transcribed, and anonymized to protect participant identities. Employing a thematic analysis approach (Clarke & Braun, 2017), we traced recurring patterns, silences, and dissonances within these narratives (see Table 1). Rather than applying fixed theoretical models, themes emerged inductively through participants' accounts, ensuring findings remained grounded in their voices.

Key threads that surfaced included: behavioral expectations within professional spaces, pressures of self-regulation, invisibilized bias in leadership evaluation, subtle resistance tactics, and the complex layering of caste, class, and linguistic capital in navigating mobility. Given the personal and, at times, sensitive content around discrimination and gendered inequities, ethical considerations were central. Participants were fully briefed, provided with consent forms, and reminded of their right to withdraw at any point. All data was pseudonymized.

Table 1 Mapping literature review across Key Themes developed based on my data analysis

Theme	Core idea	Key authors & studies
Gendered workspaces in IT	Gender biases in leadership, workplace culture, and career growth.	Athanasopoulou et al. (2018), Butler (1999), Budhwar et al. (2013)
Intersectionality: Caste, class & gender	The interplay of caste, class, and gender in shaping professional experiences.	Banerjee et al. (2024), Chander (2019), Crenshaw (2013)
Postcolonial identities & Work culture	Colonial legacies influencing gender roles in workspaces.	Chatterjee (1993), Radhakrishnan (2011), Mohanty (2003)
Unwritten codes & Workplace norms	Informal expectations, implicit biases, and workplace behaviors.	Holmes (2008), Mosseri et al. (2023), Patel (2014)
Digital economy & Gendered surveillance	Tech-driven inclusion/exclusion and monitoring practices.	Masoodi et al. (2021), Rani et al. (2022), Vitak and Zimmer (2023)
Leadership & power dynamics	Gendered challenges in leadership, authority, and decision-making.	Ok and Eniola (2024), Wijayanti et al. (2022), Fuller and Narasimhan (2008)
The 'good girl' ideology & Work-Life balance	Societal norms and expectations impacting career decisions.	Uberoi (2006), Menon (2012), Shenoy-Packer (2014)
The future of gender equity in IT	Progressive policies, movements, and inclusivity measures.	Ghosh (2022), Kelkar and Nathan (2002), Shukla and Chaudhuri (2023)

Although the study adopted an intersectional feminist lens, caste was not explicitly addressed in the interviews to ensure participant comfort and voluntary disclosure. This omission is acknowledged as both a limitation and a reflection of caste's unspoken presence in professional conversations. The qualitative approach—melding semi-structured interviews, thematic interpretation, and an intersectional lens—offers a textured account of how women in India's I.T. sector negotiate gendered expectations, navigate surveillance regimes, and reimagine leadership pathways. The following table provides a structured summary of key themes identified in my data analysis, mentioning relevant studies that support each theme:-

4 Gender and the Postcolonial Individual

In postcolonial India, gender identity continues to be shaped by history, culture, and societal norms. The ideology of nationalist defining 'ideal women' formed during and after colonialism period played a crucial role in reconstructing gender roles and identities. The idea often reinforces patriarchal norms while projecting the illusionary image of progression (Shukla, 2023). Consequently for women, this created a dual expectation: first, to embody tradition through familial duty and modesty, and second, to also symbolizing the modern, progressive face of the nation in public and professional space.

This struggle is not an aspect of past but it extends into the present and dwell into regular life. Certainly, in contemporary time women are encouraged to study and succeed, but with an instruction that they should not disturb societal and familial norms. The origins of this conflict lie in nationalist portrayals of women as carriers of cultural virtue—images that celebrated their strength but simultaneously confined their autonomy. As Radhakrishnan (2011) argues, identity remains closely tethered to collective acceptance, and women's choices are often viewed not as personal, but communal. These layered expectations become even more visible in professional settings. Anita, a systems software engineer from Bihar, speaks to the recurring questions she faces:

> Why focus on your career when family should come first? she recalls being asked. People see professional success as a disruption to a woman's traditional role, even when she's excelling at her job.

Similarly, Meera, a senior analyst, moved from Orissa shares how assumptions about family support shape perceptions of working women:

> If I work late, colleagues assume I must have a very supportive family—as if my success needs to be justified by others' approval.

These experiences are a microcosm of a broader, structural dynamic: women's ambition is still perceived as unnatural. Rather, it's almost always challenged, mediated or subtly rejected. But there are subtler systemic filters in addition to the visible barriers. Women are judged not by professional performance alone but also by how well they juggle domestic imperatives — something almost never required of men. Therefore, their accomplishments in the workplace are hailed; as long as they fall within socially-accepted norms. Priya, a marketing executive from Bihar, explains the discomfort this creates:

> Even in companies that promote gender equality, there's an unspoken rule—you can be ambitious, but not 'too ambitious.'

These emotions perpetuate an enduring prejudice which links leadership with men, making higher-rank women seem out of place instead of as peers. The back-and-forth contest between personal strive and set expectations unfolds as a never ending struggle. Self-advocating women experience some sort of friction—overt, covert, or somewhere in between. This friction, over time, shapes their future outlooks and confines their aspirations within a stifling box. This relentless pursuit of set societal role expectations in career pathways results with numerous women stuck in the middle, attempting to satisfy two contradictions. Adapt, and so many attempt to break through. In this case, relentless effort stands testament to defiant resolve—not seeking attention, but quietly, and almost entirely, behind closed doors. The boundaries of which change the focus of what is deemed 'normal.' Providing context specific telling tales of restraint, where the removal of these boundaries poses more than obstacles.

Where identity and professionalism intertwine, restricting the boundaries set on careers, re-draws these boundaries defining which and how society approach women. Structures within society need to move with evolving organizational settings. In more practical terms, these changes look at responsive shifts towards institutional structures themselves, while actively paying heed towards the constraints set on these boundaries.

The next section explores how these negotiations unfold in real settings, drawing attention to both institutional reactions and the strategies women use to challenge constraints.

4.1 *The Postcolonial Ideologies in the Professional Space*

India's expanding I.T. sector carries a layered contradiction. On one side, it appears to offer professional spaces for women, but on the other, it quietly absorbs long-standing gender codes that shape everyday workplace dynamics. While more women are part of the workforce now, leadership and core technical roles remain male-dominated, keeping the link between authority and masculinity intact. This leaves women in a difficult space—where proving their capability must go hand in hand with meeting social expectations about how women should behave. These contradictions often appear in daily interactions. Siya, a 27-year-old infrastructure engineer at a German-based I.T. company and originally from Rajasthan, shares:

> We're told not to be too opinionated because it disrupts harmony. If we speak up, we're labeled domineering; if we stay silent, we're considered incompetent.

Such experiences reflect how women must constantly adjust. They are asked to participate, but only within quiet boundaries. Over time, this pressure affects how they see themselves and shapes how they express their thoughts at work.

These challenges aren't just social—they are built into how organizations function. Leadership roles are usually shaped around traits like ambition, decisiveness, and assertiveness. But when women show these qualities, they are often questioned or seen as too aggressive. If they stay within traditional expectations, they risk being seen as too passive. This creates an ongoing conflict between career growth and the need to fit social norms.

The idea of meritocracy adds to this tension. Though companies speak of rewarding talent, many women's successes are viewed as the result of quotas, mentorship, or luck—not their own efforts. This weakens their credibility, making it seem like they don't fully belong in high-level positions. Added to this is the expectation that women must balance both work and family without letting either suffer. Some hesitate to take on larger roles for fear that personal responsibilities will be seen as a liability. These pressures are often not talked about openly, but they affect how women make decisions about their careers.

Still, many women continue to move forward—sometimes quietly, often without support—pushing boundaries and reshaping the system in small but meaningful ways. Yet this push often comes at a cost. Until both workplace culture and social thinking change, the fight for gender equity will continue to be slow, demanding, and deeply personal.

4.2 Postcolonial Ideologies in the Private Space

In postcolonial India, the private sphere is where gender identities are constructed, reproduced and contested. Even though women have more opportunities for professional employment now, traditional values still hold sway in their own homes. Postcolonial femininity which draws on nationalist ideologies is about selflessness, nurturing and caring—values that have been central to a woman's identity in India. Women who want to pursue a career are caught between deeply rooted social norms and their own goals. Women are expected to put their family's needs before their own and be the moral and emotional pillars of the household. For professional women it means an infinite double burden—managing career requirements while adapting to traditional gender roles at home. Swati, a computer programmer working for a German IT company from New Delhi explains:

> I am expected to be a good wife, mother, and daughter-in-law while maintaining my job. Every decision I make revolves around these roles. Anything less is seen as failure.

Her personal experience shows that professional success doesn't take away household duties but adds to them. This pressure is further reinforced by the social construct of the "balance woman" which presents success as conditional on being able to excel in both the home and professional space. But the idea goes beyond what is expected of it; it creates a mandate that expects women to balance the two spaces and act according to cultural norms. Any failure to meet this standard is criticized, making the private space more of a conduit for work related stress than a haven.

The distinction between private and public expectations is particularly distressing for working women. While ambition, assertiveness and autonomy are valued in the workplace, they are seen as emotional labor, self-sacrifice and submission at home. It's emotionally and physically draining to switch between these two roles and leaves little space for oneself. Rina, a local of Madhya Pradesh and data consultant with one of the US's top information technology firms, says:

> At work, I have to be confident and decisive. But when I come home, I must switch roles—be softer, more accommodating, and put family first. It's like living two different lives.

Nationalist ideologies introduce another layer of complexity in the sense that they portray women as guardians of national culture. Their value is often gauged on their ability to maintain familial as well as social harmony, thereby supporting that personal wants should always take a backseat. The ideology encourages an internalized sense of guilt, given that most working women cannot come to terms with the fact that progress of their profession may be at the cost of family duties. The pressure to conform to the norms is not only externally applied; it tends to become deeply internalized to the extent that women internalize that they are personally responsible for conforming to such practices. The burden is especially seen when it comes to professional decisions. Women constantly filter professional prospects against probable impacts on the family setup—something not really done against men. Meena, a young woman from Uttar Pradesh who is a team leader with a multinational information technology firm, shares:

> I turned down a promotion because it would require more travel. My husband was supportive, but I knew that my in-laws and neighbors would see it differently. A 'good woman' doesn't prioritize work over family.

Swati, Rina and Meena's stories show how these social norms are present in our daily lives. Their stories not only show the struggles of women but also the determination to overcome them. Women are pushing boundaries despite these constraints, quietly but successfully challenging the gender norms. The relationship between domestic space and gender is tied to the larger social structures. As the character of professional spaces change, the gap between job goals and home duties grows; the need for change in both is more evident. The blurring of work and domestic life for women in postcolonial India shows the complexity of gender and power. Till the attitudes in the society change and institutional support is in place, women will continue to bear the burden of multiple identities—often at great personal cost.

5 The Unwritten Codes: Discussion and Results

The postcolonial dilemmas for women in India is a constant navigation and negotiation between the identities that lead to professional progress and those expected at home (Shukla & Chaudhuri, 2023). Such continues shift demands complex and tiresome balance, which usually ends up in the loss of individual identity as suggested by participants of this study. As per societal norms, women are expected to be nurturing, selfless, and submissive at home, while traits stereotypically associated with men, such as independence, assertiveness, and authority, are valued and rewarded in professional settings. The lived experiences of women in both personal and professional contexts are shaped by these implicit norms, which have their roots in cultural and societal expectations. The duality of domesticity and career emphasize how colonial and patriarchal ideologies continue to dictate gender roles. Such norms, argues gender theorist Judith Butler (1999), are not inherent; rather, they are constantly evaluated by social norms and behavior.

In professional settings, women often encounter resistance when they display leadership traits. While assertiveness and confidence are admired in men, women who exhibit the same qualities are frequently labeled as aggressive or difficult. As a result, many feel compelled to temper their ambitions to align with expectations of acceptable femininity. At home, the pressures are different but equally restrictive—women are expected to prioritize caregiving and household duties, reinforcing the belief that career success should never come at the expense of family responsibilities (Chaudhuri et al., 2024; Shukla, 2023).

These challenges are not same for all women. Factors such as caste, class, and region shape each woman's experience of balancing work and home. Middle-class professionals in urban settings may struggle with the demands of a hyper-competitive corporate culture, while women from marginalized backgrounds often face compounded biases. Regional differences also play a role, with patriarchal norms in northern India often being more rigid than those in the south. The lived experiences of working women reveal how these invisible rules operate in everyday life. Arpita, a systems analyst, working in an Indian multinational IT company, and native of Chandigarh shares her frustration:

> At work, I am called unapproachable because I behave differently than my male colleagues. At home, I am criticized for being too focused on my career. It feels like society wants women to follow a manual that doesn't exist.

Her words reflect the double standard women face—expected to be competent professionals while also conforming to domestic expectations. Jyothi, an entrepreneur, moved from Kerala, recalls the assumptions people make about her career choices:

> I have had clients ask if my husband supports my business decisions, as if I need his approval. No one asks men these questions.

In many of the conversations I had, women described how they still felt the need to explain or justify decisions in ways their male colleagues didn't. That pressure doesn't come from one place—it comes from years of being told, in subtle ways that they have to prove their worth twice over. Over time, this seeps in, creating quiet doubts and moments of self-questioning. Several women spoke of second-guessing themselves, checking their tone, their words, and their presence— adapting constantly to fit into different versions of themselves depending on the space.

While these informal codes, prefer to say unwritten codes of conduct remain resilient, women are however, increasingly rewriting the script. Their growing capacity to redefine gender roles is a slow but tangible shift. But the persistence of these issues is what drives the urgent need for institutional and cultural transformation—transformation that would allow women to thrive at work and in life without having to sacrifice their sense of self.

6 Conclusion

The participants of this study described their experiences of work in professional settings under the relentless pressures that are invisible. Their accounts reveal how the negotiation of gender is more than organizational policy; it is the articulation of expectations within the mundane interactions. These expectations, whether implicit or explicit, greatly affect the way women talk, desire leadership positions, and interact with colleagues and individuals outside the workplace. Whereas previous research has explored structural barriers, the focus here is on the lived experience of living with double expectations. Examples like Arpita's bring alive why doing gender in workplaces is not a theoretical concept; it has real-life implications in terms of who gets promoted, heard, and identified as being right to lead. Such expectations are not evenly distributed across the population. The women in this study spoke of carrying pressures that weren't always visible, yet constantly shaped how they moved through professional life. Their caste, class background, and where they came from often became part of how they were perceived, judged, or dismissed. These weren't isolated experiences—they were part of a deeper institutional silence around who is expected to belong, and who must work harder to prove that they do.

But these women weren't just adjusting to fit in. Many participants reported the small ways women in industry trying to push back—sometimes by setting boundaries, sometimes by refusing to perform stereotypical expected roles, and often by supporting each other through informal networks. These acts of refusal, though quiet, are significant. They carry emotional weight, and often come at a cost. Institutions, however, rarely acknowledge this cost. The burden of navigating contradictions is left to the women themselves, expected to carry it with composure. Their stories point to something larger: the idea that women can succeed only if they play by rules that were never made with them in mind. Even in spaces that claim to value merit or diversity, the expectation is still clear—don't disrupt, don't push too far. Change is welcome, but only if it's polite, contained, acceptable. These unspoken limits reflect a deeper discomfort with challenging the norms that have long gone unexamined. They are rooted not only in workplace culture, but in social history, caste memory, and postcolonial frameworks of order.

Leadership programs and policy reforms are not enough if the deeper cultural discomfort with women's ambition and anger remains untouched. What's needed is a shift in how we listen to women—especially those who have been historically silenced. This chapter doesn't offer a roadmap, but it does insist on the importance of asking different questions: What do we mean by inclusion? Who is asked to be silent? And what happens when women refuse?

Rather than expecting women to adjust to outdated ideals, we might begin to imagine spaces where care, vulnerability, and refusal are not weaknesses—but forms of leadership. The women in this study aren't simply adapting to systems. They are reshaping them, sometimes in ways that are barely visible, but deeply felt. In doing so, they offer glimpses of a future that is more just, more honest, and grounded in the realities they live every day.

References

Athanasopoulou, A., Moss-Cowan, A., Smets, M., & Morris, T. (2018). Claiming the corner office: Female CEO careers and implications for leadership development. *Human Resource Management, 57*(2), 617–639.

Banerjee, D., Memon, N. Z., & Sharma, A. (2024). Casteism and career change in India: A gender-based explanation of retention. *Australian Journal of Career Development, 33*(1), 105–115.

Belliappa, J. (2009). *Relational identities: Middle class Indian women negotiate the consequences of globalization and late modernity (Doctoral dissertation).* University of York.

Bhattacharya, K., Ghosh, A., Monsivais, D., Dunbar, R. I., & Kaski, K. (2016). Sex differences in social focus across the life cycle in humans. *Royal Society Open Science, 3*(4), 160097.

Budhwar, P. S., Saini, D. S., & Bhatnagar, J. (2013). Women in management in the new economic environment: The case of India. In *Women in Asian management* (pp. 41–55). Routledge.

Butler, J. (1999). *Gender trouble: Tenth anniversary Edition* (2nd ed.). Routledge. https://doi.org/10.4324/9780203902752

Chander, R. K. (2019). *Combating social exclusion: Inter-sectionalities of caste, gender, class and regions.* Studera Press.

Chatterjee, P. (1993). *The nation and its fragments: Colonial and postcolonial histories.* Princeton University Press.

Chaudhuri, M., Karmakar, S., & Shukla, S. (2024). Intersectionalities and im/mobilities in family and marriage: A comparative study of Germany and India. *Humanities & Social Sciences Communications, 11*, 539. https://doi.org/10.1057/s41599-024-03075-5

Clarke, V., & Braun, V. (2017). Thematic analysis. *The Journal of Positive Psychology, 12*(3), 297–298.

Connell, R. (2005). Advancing gender reform in large-scale organisations: A new approach for practitioners and researchers. *Policy and society, 24*(4), 5–24.

Crenshaw, K. W. (2013). Mapping the margins: Intersectionality, identity politics, and violence against women of color. In *The public nature of private violence* (pp. 93–118). Routledge.

Fleming, P. (2009). *Authenticity and the cultural politics of work: New forms of informal control.* OUP Oxford.

Fuller, C. J., & Narasimhan, H. (2008). From landlords to software engineers: Migration and urbanization among Tamil Brahmans. *Comparative Studies in Society and History, 50*(1), 170–196.

Ghosh, S. (2022). Gender and financial inclusion: Does technology make a difference? *Gender, Technology and Development, 26*(2), 195–213. https://doi.org/10.1080/09718524.2022.2073323

Holmes, J. (2008). *Gendered talk at work: Constructing gender identity through workplace discourse.* John Wiley & Sons.

Jameel, A. (2024). *Intersectionality in the workplace in India: Navigating the impact of race, ethnicity and socio-economic status on women's experiences (Doctoral dissertation).* Glocal University.

Kelkar, G., & Nathan, D. (2002). Gender relations and technological change in Asia. *Current Sociology, 50*(3), 427–441.

Masoodi, M. J., Abdelaal, N., Tran, S., Stevens, Y., Andrey, S., & Bardeesy, K. (2021). *Workplace surveillance and remote work.* Cybersecure policy exchange, Ryerson University.

Menon, N. (2012). *Seeing like a feminist.* Penguin UK.

Mohanty, C. T. (2003). *Feminism without Borders: Decolonizing theory, Practicing Solidarity.* Duke University Press. https://doi.org/10.2307/j.ctv11smp7t

Mosseri, S., Vromen, A., Cooper, R., & Hill, E. (2023). Between frustration and invigoration: Women talking about digital Technology at Work. *Work, Employment and Society, 37*(6), 1681–1698.

Ok, E., & Eniola, J. (2024). The power dynamics of male and female leadership: A comparative study.

Patel, R. (2014). Today's 'good girl': The women behind India's BPO industry. In *Women, gender and everyday social transformation in India* (Vol. 1, p. 21).

Radhakrishnan, S. (2011). *Appropriately Indian: Gender and culture in a new transnational class.* Duke University Press.

Rani, U., Castel-Branco, R., Satija, S., & Nayar, M. (2022). Women, work, and the digital economy. *Gender and Development, 30*(3), 421–435.

Shenoy-Packer, S. (2014). *India's working women and career discourses: Society, socialization, and agency.* Lexington Books.

Shukla, S. (2022). Sarita Devi: A Mother's fight against her community to support her Daughter's education. In *Women community leaders and their impact as global Changemakers* (pp. 199–204). IGI Global.

Shukla, S. (2023). *Postcolonial intersections in digital India: Navigating gendered spaces in information and communication technology (Doctoral dissertation).* Indian Institute of Technology Jodhpur, Department of Humanities and Social Sciences.

Shukla, S., & Chaudhuri, M. (2023). Intersectional Im/Mobilities: Gender, family and information technology professionals in digital India. *Applied Mobilities, 8*(1), 47–64.

Uberoi, P. (2006). Freedom and destiny: Gender, family, and popular culture in India (no title).

Vitak, J., & Zimmer, M. (2023). Surveillance and the future of work: Exploring employees' attitudes toward monitoring in a post-COVID workplace. *Journal of Computer-Mediated Communication, 28*(4), zmad007.

Wijayanti, F. I., Djatmika, D., Sumarlam, S., & Sawardi, F. X. (2022). Portraying leader characters through speech acts and politeness strategies in job interview: A gender perspective. *International Journal of Society, Culture & Language, 10*(1), 41–57.

Sakshi Shukla is an Assistant Professor in the Department of Sociology, School of Social Sciences, at M.S. Ramaiah University of Applied Sciences, India. She holds a Ph.D. in Gender Studies from the Indian Institute of Technology Jodhpur. Her research lies at the intersection of gender, mobility, and postcolonial studies, with a particular focus on the Indian IT industry. A trained anthropologist and qualitative researcher, Dr. Shukla has received international recognition, including the MAXQDA Research for Change and a Global Research Scholarship in South Korea. She is a full member of the Sigma Xi Scientific Research Honor Society and currently serves as an Associate Editor with the Springer Nature HSS Editorial Community.

Chapter 8
From Home to Workplace: Gender Equality and Domestic Labor Division in Malaysian Dual-Career Couples

Daisy Mui Hung Kee, Jamin Kun Peng Xia, and Louis Yong Yu Lee

Abstract This study explores gender equality and the domestic labor division among dual-career families in Malaysia, with a specific focus on how demographic variables and satisfaction with labor division influence marital outcomes. Data were collected from 1120 urban dual-earner couples with young children. Our findings identify persistent gender disparities in household responsibilities. Although parenting and personal time are more evenly split across ethnicities, women still shoulder most housework, whereas men dominate paid labor contributions. Men report higher satisfaction with both labor divisions and exhibit greater marital investment than women. Moreover, socio-demographics, age, educational attainment, and race, significantly predict satisfaction levels, underscoring the influence of cultural and structural elements in shaping perceptions of household equity. Notably, satisfaction with the domestic labor division emerged as a significant predictor of marriage satisfaction, reinforcing the relevance of equitable labor sharing in nurturing relationship quality. As the first empirical study of its kind in Malaysia, this research highlights the challenges and progress in gender role transformation within dual-career households. Findings offer practical implications for policymakers, employers, and families, especially in shaping inclusive work-life policies and promoting gender-balanced domestic responsibilities. The study contributes to ongoing discussions on gender equality, supports the aspirations of Malaysia's Shared Prosperity Vision 2030, and the United Nations Sustainable Development Goals.

Keywords Gender equality · Domestic labor division · Marital satisfaction · Dual-career couples · Relationship investment · Malaysia · Household responsibilities · Work-life balance · Demographic factors · Sustainable development

---

D. M. H. Kee (✉) · J. K. P. Xia · L. Y. Y. Lee
Universiti Sains Malaysia, Penang, Malaysia
e-mail: daisy@usm.my

H. Adam and F. A. Malik (eds.), *The Political Economy of Gender*,
https://doi.org/10.1007/978-981-92-2785-3_8

1 Introduction

The emergence of dual-career couples, where both husbands and wives engage in professional careers, has been one of the prominent social developments since the 1980s, constituting a break from traditional gender roles towards more egalitarian relations within the family. Despite observable progress in developed areas, the persistence of gendered activities among families indicates the need for deeper exploration, particularly among regions where traditional norms are binding (Deb et al., 2024; Lee et al., 2020). Malaysian societal norms have traditionally positioned women in subservient roles, entrenching gender inequality concerns (Saigaran & Bada, 2023; Thimm, 2025). Deeply rooted in conservative gender norms founded on religion and modesty, male attitudes assume domestic responsibilities, such as housework and parenting, to be primarily the women's role (Chelliah et al., 2023). Amidst these societal intricacies, limited research has looked into crucial predictors of marital satisfaction among Malaysian dual-career couples, such as satisfaction with the domestic labor division (SwDL), satisfaction with the paid labor division (SwPL), and the impact of marital investment (MI) on overall well-being (Gorchoff et al., 2008; Hortaçsu, 2007; Kubricht et al., 2017).

Dual-career couples have undergone a significant transformation, particularly magnified by the global COVID-19 pandemic. Kee et al. (2021) described the pandemic as a double-edged sword. This crisis has exacerbated gender and economic inequalities, compelling working parents to reconcile domestic and paid labor within the confines of their homes. Malaysian couples navigating the challenges of this unprecedented global crisis have grappled with relationships in working, learning, teaching, partnering, and parenting. About 80,000 divorce cases were filed in Malaysian courts during the period from March 2020 to August 2021, revealing the strain experienced by couples during the pandemic. Issues su Datuk Seri Ismail Sabri Yaakob, Former Prime Minister of Malaysia, in September 2021, highlighted a significant economic shift, with around 580,000 households transitioning from the middle 40% (M40) to the bottom 40% (B40) category. This economic transition has placed an increased burden on married couples.

The unequal division of domestic labor is a well-documented feature of gender inequality, particularly in Western countries. Studying the division of labor in households has become increasingly relevant as female participation rates in paid labor have risen and employment systems have evolved. Our research represents the first study examining gender equality among Malaysian dual-career couples, making a unique and significant contribution to the understanding of domestic labor in this context. We focus on satisfaction levels, demographic influences, and the relationship between household labor division and marital satisfaction. Our study's findings contribute to the broader discourse on gender equality by highlighting the persistent challenges and potential areas for policy intervention to promote a more balanced division of labor. Our research aligns with global efforts to address gender inequality and supports Malaysia's Shared Prosperity Vision 2030 and the United Nations' Sustainable Development Goals. Our research questions are as follows:

1. What is the current status of dual-career couples in Malaysia concerning the division of household labor?
2. Do SwDL, SwPL, and the investment in the relationship differ by gender?
3. Do demographic determinants, such as age group, race, education level, and annual income, impact SwDL, SwPL, and investment in the relationship?
4. What is the relationship between SwDL and marital satisfaction?

Our study is a pioneering effort to provide evidence of the gender division of labor within Malaysian families, specifically focusing on dual-earner couples with children. Gender equality is a fundamental aspect of diversity and equity. Our paper significantly contributes to the understanding of gender diversity and equity in both domestic and professional settings. Also, our study highlights how an equitable division of labor can promote a sense of inclusion and belonging within the family unit. This concept parallels the principles of diversity, equity, inclusion, and belonging (DEIB) in the workplace. While our study is not directly focused on organizational settings, the findings gained from understanding gender equality and satisfaction in dual-career couples can inform organizational policies related to work-life balance, parental leave, and support systems for dual-career households. Our findings can indirectly contribute to organizational excellence by promoting employee well-being and retention. When organizations understand the context of dual-career couples and implement supportive policies, they can create a more inclusive and productive work environment. Our research thus serves as a critical bridge between gender equality and organizational DEIB efforts, offering a better understanding of both family and workplace contexts.

2 Literature Review

We conceptualize the division of labor into domestic labor and paid labor. Domestic labor involves unpaid work that is performed to look after members of the family and the home (Coltrane, 2000; Deshpande & Kabeer, 2024). Domestic labor encompasses cleaning, cooking, childcare, grocery shopping, laundry, and other duties necessary for a household to be maintained day by day (Humphries, 2024). We define paid labor as work performed in exchange for monetary compensation, which contributes to the economic support of the household. In this study, we classify the division of labor into four main activities: *parenting*, *housework*, *personal time*, and *paid work*, parenting and housework fall under domestic labor, which includes unpaid work undertaken to maintain the household and the family (Coltrane, 2000; Deshpande & Kabeer, 2024); paid work falls under paid labor, encompasses work for pay, whereas personal time is considered as leisure time, which involves activities that one engages in for relaxing and personal enjoyment.

2.1 Satisfaction with Domestic Labor Division, Paid Labor Division, and Marital Investment

The shift away from traditional gender roles has been observed gradually in more and more societies, with couples adopting more egalitarian patterns of household labor (e.g., Bianchi & Milkie, 2010; Murray & Durrheim, 2024; Nasurdin & Ahmad, 2013; Perry-Jenkins & Gerstel, 2020). The greater entry of women into the workforce has been a main driver of this transformation. Despite progress, challenges to achieving a more equal division of domestic labor persist. Societal expectations (Birkett & Forbes, 2019; Deb et al., 2024; Ueno, 2021), cultural norms (Deb et al., 2024; Lusiba et al., 2017; Mussida & Patimo, 2021; Tjorring, 2016), and ingrained stereotypes (Christopher, 2024; Couprie et al., 2020; Thebaud et al., 2021) continue to influence perceptions and behaviors, leading to imbalances in the division of household tasks. Under such conditions, the concept of work-life balance has been a salient theme (Mathur et al., 2024; Selim & Kee, 2023), calling for the sharing of household responsibilities for ensuring personal well-being and the health of marital relationships (Arunima & Nangia, 2022; Panzhi et al., 2022).

The transformation from a family based on traditional gender roles to a dual-career family requires a reduction in women's involvement in domestic labor as they seek additional paid employment and therefore reshaping spouses' MI (Davis & Greenstein, 2004; Shockley et al., 2025). This transition may result in a complex situation. To some degree, wives who are disproportionately burdened with domestic labor find it challenging to commit to the labor force like their husbands. Contrarily, husbands need to take a greater proportion of active participation in domestic tasks that might result in decreased SwDL and SwPL.

Age is also widely regarded as an important determinant in family and marriage research (Chung & Kim, 2013; Sorokowski et al., 2017). Younger generations are more liberal in their perceptions of gender roles, and they tend to desire egalitarian marital relationships. However, attitudes among older generations might be different, though, since they might still adhere to more traditional expectations. Other demographic factors also play significant roles. Different racial or ethnic groups may have distinct cultural perspectives on gender roles, family relationships, and the division of labor. Cultural norms can influence spouses' expectations and satisfaction levels regarding domestic and paid labor responsibilities (Riggs & Bartholomaeus, 2020; Yu et al., 2012). In addition to that, race-related cultural values can impact beliefs and perceptions about the importance of investing time, energy, and resources in a marital relationship (Juhari et al., 2019).

Besides, higher levels of education have often been found to be associated with more modern and egalitarian values and with the increased acknowledgment of the importance and worthiness of investing in a relationship. Individuals with higher education might put a higher importance on equality in domestic and paid labor, and this will also impact their levels of satisfaction as well as on negotiation of tasks within the relationship. They may seek out relationship education resources and employ tactics to enhance their MI (Tokal et al., 2023). Furthermore, annual income can exert itself on satisfaction with the labor division (Thebaud, 2010). Financial stability may provide individuals with more options in terms of working arrangements, household support, and outsourcing tasks, influencing their degree of satisfaction. As such, it is critical to determine if any variation by gender and the remaining demographic variables, including age, race, education level, and annual income, exists in how dual-career couples' SwDL and SwPL influence their MI. Given this, we hypothesized:

H1 Gender differences exist in SwDL, SwPL, and MI among Malaysian dual-career couples.

H2 Malaysian dual-career couples' SwDL, SwPL, and MI vary based on their age, race, education level, and annual income.

2.2 *Satisfaction of Domestic Labor Division and Marital Satisfaction*

The division of domestic labor is the distribution of tasks and responsibilities related to household chores, caregiving, and family management between spouses in a relationship (Tartakovsky, 2023). Marital satisfaction is a broader measure of the overall happiness, contentment, and fulfillment individuals derive from their marriage (Li et al., 2022). According to Equity Theory (Adams, 1965), SwDL is closely tied to perceptions of fairness, and when individuals perceive an imbalance, it can affect overall marital satisfaction. Another related, well-established theory is Role Theory, originally formed by Talcott Parsons (Turner, 2001), which emphasizes the significance of defined roles within relationships. Based on this theory, SwDL will be influenced by how well individuals' roles align with their expectations, impacting their overall marital satisfaction.

The predicted effect of SwDL on marital satisfaction has been proven in various societies outside Malaysia. A satisfied division will sweeten the marital satisfaction of dual-career couples, especially when male spouses assume more domestic responsibility (Arunima & Nangia, 2022; Durtschi et al., 2017; Kang, 2015; Qian & Sayer, 2016; Schieman et al., 2018). Notably, the household labor division and the subjective assessment of it differ according to social context. While social contexts may influence the subjective assessment of domestic labor, evidence suggests a positive association between SwDL and marital satisfaction. Thus, we posed:

H3 SwDL will predict higher marital satisfaction among dual-career couples in Malaysia.

3 Methodology

Employing a quantitative approach, our study investigates gender disparities in the division of labor among dual-earner couples with children. We employed purposive sampling, specifically targeting those residing in Malaysian urban areas who have at least one child below 18 years old. Both spouses must meet the following criteria: (1) being parents with at least one child below 18 years old, (2) being married, and (3) both being engaged in paid employment. In addition, participation in the survey required mutual agreement from both the husband and wife within each couple. Participants had to be currently working in key urban cities in Malaysia, which provided a focused examination of dual-career couples in urban settings. Urban cities were chosen due to their economic activities and significant representation of dual-earner families. This study involved 1120 participants with an equal gender distribution (50% male, 50% female), as both spouses needed to consent to participate. The largest age group involved was 51 years and above (29%), followed closely by 41–50 years (28%), indicating a mature participant base. In terms of ethnicity, Malay respondents formed the majority (45%), followed by Chinese (41%) and Indian (11%). Educational backgrounds varied, with 40% holding a bachelor's degree, while high school (28%) and diploma (18%) holders also formed significant portions, reflecting Malaysia's growing emphasis on higher education. 60% of urban participants earned RM50,000 or less annually, and another 28% earned between RM50,001 and RM100,000, suggesting that a large portion of dual-earner couples in urban Malaysia face economic challenges.

3.1 Measures

Division of labor was measured in four key activities, namely, parenting, housework, personal time (or leisure), and paid work, to capture perceptions of responsibility allocation within the household and understand the division of tasks between spouses in dual-career relationships. Participants were asked to assess "who does more of each of the following activities?" and indicate the relative division of labor between themselves and their spouse. They could choose one from three options: (1) equally divided between husband and wife, (2) the male spouse does much more than the female spouse, and (3) the female spouse does much more than the male spouse.

We assessed all measures using a five-point Likert scale ranging from 1 (strongly disagree) to 5 (strongly agree). *SwDL* was measured using a 3-item scale. Sample items include "I am satisfied with the family labor division between my spouse and me." The scale has a Cronbach's alpha of 0.92. *SwPL* was evaluated through a 3-item scale developed specifically for this study. A sample item is "I am satisfied with the paid labor division between my spouse and me." The scale showed acceptable internal consistency, with a Cronbach's alpha of 0.93.

Investment in the relationship was assessed using five items adapted from Coy (2013), with minor modifications to replace the term "partner" with "spouse". Sample items include "Compared to other people I know, I have invested a great deal in my relationship with my spouse." The Cronbach's alpha reported by Coy was 0.71.

Marital satisfaction was assessed using a 5-item scale, incorporating established measures. Four items were adapted from the Investment Model Scale (Rusbult et al., 1998). A sample item is "Our relationship makes me very happy." Another item,

"My relationship is close to ideal," was adapted from the Satisfaction with Married Life Scale by Johnson et al. (2006). The Cronbach's alpha reported in this study was 0.95.

4 Results

Initially, we investigated the distribution of responsibilities within the household and how tasks are allocated between spouses in dual-career relationships. We employed Cross-Tabulation Analysis and visualized the findings into a Stacked Percentage Column Chart (see Fig. 1) to explore how domestic tasks, personal time, and paid work are divided between spouses across different ethnic groups.

Parenting. Most couples reported equal parenting responsibilities, especially among Malay (73.72%), Indian (62.71%), and Chinese (62.20%) couples. However, Chinese (36.26%) and Indian (34.75%) couples showed higher rates of female spouses taking on more parenting duties. Male-dominated parenting was rare (3.39%).

Housework. An unequal distribution was evident, with only 44.55% reporting an equal share. Chinese couples (57.14%) showed the highest rate of female spouses

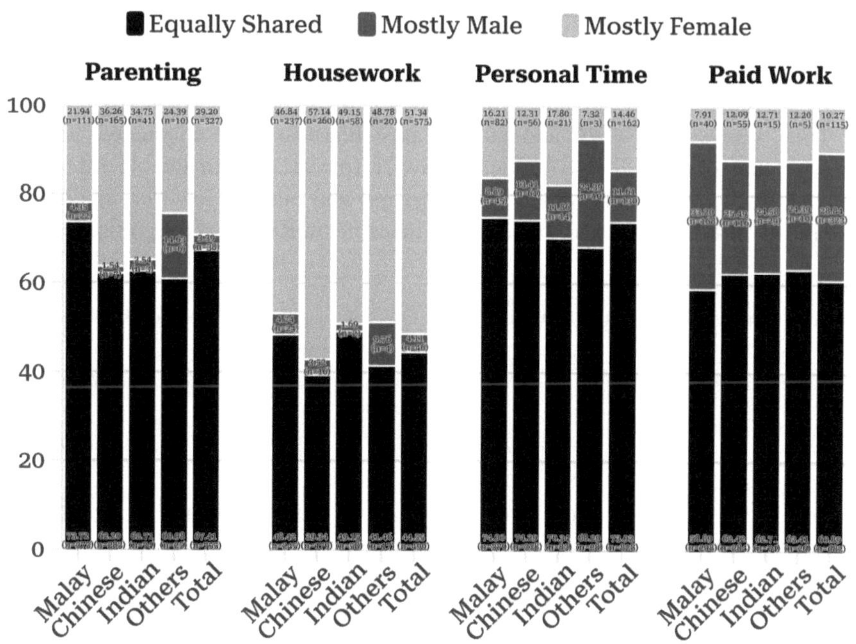

Fig. 1 Stacked Percentage Column Chart: Division of Domestic Labor, Paid Labor, and Personal Time by Ethnicity (N = 1120). *Source* Created by the authors

doing most housework. Overall, 51.34% of all female spouses assumed a greater share of housework, highlighting a persistent gender imbalance.

Personal Time. The division was mostly equal (68.29–74.90%) across all ethnicities. However, male spouses often had more personal time, particularly among other ethnicities (24.39%). Female spouses having more personal time was less common.

Paid Work. A majority (58.89–62.71%) reported equal involvement in paid work. However, male spouses often did more paid work, especially among Malay and Chinese couples (25.49–33.20%). Female spouses took on more paid work in fewer cases, with Chinese couples reporting the highest (12.09%).

To summarize, the current status of dual-career couples in Malaysia regarding the division of household labor reflects a mixed scenario. While parenting and personal time are moving toward gender equality, housework remains largely the responsibility of female spouses, and male spouses dominate in paid work. Ethnic differences are notable. Chinese couples show higher female involvement in domestic tasks, while Malay couples show more male participation in paid labor.

Next, independent samples t-tests were conducted to test Hypothesis 1. Table 1 revealed significant gender differences across all three variables. Men reported higher SwDL ($M = 4.07$) compared to women ($M = 3.88$, $p < 0.001$), likely reflecting traditional norms where men contribute less to household chores. Similarly, men expressed greater SwPL ($M = 4.03$ vs. 3.88, $p < 0.01$), suggesting they perceive the current arrangement as more equitable or favorable. In addition, men reported a higher level of relationship investment ($M = 3.94$) than women ($M = 3.75$, $p < 0.001$), indicating that they may feel more committed or benefit more from existing relationships. These findings support Hypothesis 1 and confirm that significant gender differences exist in satisfaction and investment levels within dual-career marriages.

Then, one-way ANOVA and Tukey's post hoc test were conducted. Table 2 revealed that age significantly influenced SwDL ($p = .021$), with notable differences between the youngest age group (19–20 years) and others. However, age had no significant effect on SwPL or relationship investment. Race was a significant factor

Table 1 Gender Differences in Satisfaction with Division of Labor and Relationship Investment ($N = 1120$)

Variable	Gender	M	SD	Mean Difference	t-value	df	p-value
SwDL	Male	4.07	0.79	0.19	3.731	1090.38	.000***
	Female	3.88	0.93				
SwPL	Male	4.03	0.8	0.15	2.872	1093.39	.004**
	Female	3.88	0.93				
Investment in a relationship	Male	3.94	0.77	0.19	3.962	1109.13	.000***
	Female	3.75	0.84				

Notes $^{*}p < .05$, $^{**}p < .01$, $^{***}p < .001$
Source Created by the authors

across all three variables ($p < .01$), with Malay participants reporting higher satisfaction levels than other racial groups, highlighting cultural influences. Education level also had a significant impact ($p < .05$), suggesting that individuals with higher education perceived household roles and relationships differently than those with only a high school education. In contrast, annual income did not significantly affect any of the satisfaction measures ($p > .05$), indicating its limited role as a differentiator in this context. These findings support Hypothesis 2, emphasizing the role of these socio-demographic factors in influencing perceptions of domestic responsibilities and relational investment.

Finally, we tested Hypothesis 3. Table 3 shows the correlations and Cronbach's Alpha for the variables. Based on Table 4, the regression analysis shows that SwDL is a significant predictor of marital satisfaction ($\beta = .723$, $p < .001$), providing evidence supporting Hypothesis 3. This finding indicates that higher satisfaction with how domestic labor is divided is associated with higher overall marital satisfaction among dual-career couples in Malaysia.

Table 2 One-way ANOVA and Tukey's Post Hoc Tests for Differences in Satisfaction and Relationship Investment by Demographic Variables

Demographic Variable	SwDL F (Sig)	SwPL F (Sig)	Investment in Relationship F (Sig)
Age group	2.664 (.021*)	1.937 (.086)	1.137 (.339)
Race	9.163 (.000***)	7.122 (.000***)	4.167 (.006**)
Education level	3.584 (.003**)	3.601 (.003**)	2.341 (.040*)
Annual income	0.624 (.646)	0.492 (.741)	0.308 (.873)

Notes Values in the table represent means unless otherwise indicated. Detailed statistics for each subgroup have been omitted in keeping with the principle of brevity. The comprehensive results are available on request. *p <.05, **p <.01, ***p <.001
Source Created by the authors

Table 3 Means, SD, Cronbach's Alpha, and Correlation Coefficients

Variable	M	SD	1	2	3	4
SwDL	3.97	0.87	**0.919**			
SwPL	3.95	0.87	.807***	**0.926**		
Investment in a relationship	3.84	0.81	.539***	.546***	**0.899**	
Marital satisfaction	4.14	0.82	.723***	.700***	.642***	**0.946**

Notes Cronbach's alpha was reported on the diagonal (in bold). *p <.05, **p <.01, ***p <.001
Source Created by the authors

Table 4 Linear Regression Predicting Marital Satisfaction

Variables	Marital Satisfaction
SwDL	.723***
R^2	0.523
F value	1226.266
Durbin-Watson statistic	2.014

Notes *p <.05, **p <.01, ***p <.001
Source Created by the authors

5 Discussion

The division of labor among dual-career couples reflects societal norms, cultural expectations, and marital relationships. In Malaysia, as in many societies, traditional gender roles historically assign domestic responsibilities predominantly to women (e.g., Boo, 2020; Chelliah et al., 2023; Mumtaz, 2022; Sunaryo et al., 2019). However, with the rise of dual-career households, these traditional divisions are changing, though not uniformly across all tasks. Our findings show a more equitable distribution of parenting tasks compared to housework among different racial groups, in which husbands are generally more willing to engage in childcare, especially in enjoyable activities, than in housework. The observed trend towards more equitable distribution of parenting responsibilities suggests a gradual shift towards shared caregiving responsibilities, possibly fueled by shifting social norms towards gender equality in childcare. Disparities persist in the division of housework, however, reflecting entrenched gender stereotypes and traditional expectations of women's roles in domestic chores. This imbalance continues to place an uneven load on women, which can impact their career advancement and perpetuate gender gaps in the labor market. Women's disproportionate share of household chores affects their SwDL and, subsequently, their overall marital satisfaction. Higher satisfaction levels reported by men may stem from societal expectations that legitimate men's lower contribution to housework, and women's lower satisfaction levels are likely caused by the strain of combining work life with a greater share of domestic duties.

The gender disparities in relationship investment can be attributed to varying views of commitment and contribution to the relationship. Men's higher self-reported MI may relate to societal norms placing men as providers rather than caregivers, influencing their perspective on MI. Conversely, women would possibly put more weight on emotional support, mutual chores, and equal partnership in their investment in the relationship (Gorchoff et al., 2008). These gender-based differences in satisfaction and relationship investment have significant implications, potentially resulting in strained relationships, less emotional intimacy, and conflicts among dual-career couples.

Besides, age, race, and education level play a part in the development of perceptions and behaviors in relation to the division of labor among dual-career couples. Our study shows that younger couples are likely to hold more egalitarian views on gender roles and household responsibilities because of changing societal beliefs that promote gender equality. On the other hand, older couples might expect more traditional gender roles and, therefore, may expect women to do a larger share of household tasks. Our study indicates that education level has a strong impact on SwDL and relationship investment. Our findings also report that racial identity emerged as a significant determinant factor, with Malay respondents reporting much higher satisfaction levels compared to other races. More educated couples tend to be more likely to adopt equitable labor distribution, viewing household tasks as joint responsibilities and not gender-specific duties. Respondents with higher levels of education report different satisfaction levels compared to those with only high school education, suggesting that higher educational attainment is associated with more egalitarian views and expectations regarding the sharing of household tasks and investment in relationships, aligning with previous studies (e.g., Narender, 2024). These findings reveal the importance of educational attainment in shaping attitudes towards gender roles and household responsibilities.

Our study also found a positive relationship between SwDL and overall marital satisfaction. When couples perceive the division of household tasks as fair and balanced, it contributes positively to their marital satisfaction. Our findings highlight the importance of equitable domestic labor distribution in promoting overall marital satisfaction among dual-career couples in Malaysia. Addressing imbalances in household responsibilities supports gender equality and also contributes to stronger, more fulfilling marital relationships.

5.1 *Theoretical Implications*

Our study is a pioneering effort to provide evidence of the gender division of labor within Malaysian families, specifically focusing on dual-earner couples with children. By exploring the division of domestic labor and its impact on marital satisfaction among Malaysian dual-career couples, our research significantly contributes to the theoretical understanding of gender diversity and equity in both domestic and professional settings. This study enhances the body of knowledge on how demographic factors such as age, race, and education level might influence household labor division and marital satisfaction. The insights into gender differences in satisfaction levels with domestic and paid labor, as well as relationship investment, add depth to existing theories on gender roles, labor division, and marital relationships.

5.2 *Practical Implications*

Our findings can inform organizational policies related to work-life balance, parental leave, and support systems for dual-career households. By understanding the needs of dual-career couples, organizations can implement supportive policies that promote employee well-being and retention, creating a more inclusive and productive work environment. For example, targeted educational programs can address traditional gender roles and work-family policies like flexible working or parental leave that enable work-life balance. In addition, attempts at resisting stereotypes and promoting co-responsibility at home must be structured in a way that targets multicultural populations, bearing demographic realities in mind to reinforce gender equality. Our research serves as a critical bridge of rigor between gender equality and organizational DEIB efforts, offering insights from family and workplace settings to contribute to crafting a more balanced and inclusive society. This approach fills the gap between gender equality in the household and within the workplace by determining how more equitable practices in one setting can have a positive influence on the other.

5.3 Limitations and Future Research Directions

There are some limitations in our study. First, social desirability bias could have occurred due to the use of self-reporting data, affecting the validity of the responses. Future research should attempt to incorporate objective measures or social desirability questionnaires to counter such biases. In addition, the cross-sectional design of our research limits the ability to determine the dynamics of perceptions. Longitudinal designs are recommended to track the dynamics of relationships and household responsibilities over time. Finally, future research could try to clarify the influence of cultural context and societal norms in determining gender equality within households. Investigating the intersectionality of gender, culture, and domestic labor division will further shed light on gender equality in cultural contexts and inform strategies for promoting inclusive practices in both the home and workplace.

6 Conclusion

Our study represents the first study to introduce new knowledge about dual-career couples in Malaysia. Our findings have provided clear evidence of the gender inequalities that dominate Malaysian society. Specifically, our findings highlight significant challenges for dual-career couples with children in managing professional careers and household responsibilities. We reveal the burden placed on women within these relationships, with unequal division of domestic labor leading to decreased levels of satisfaction. These disparities show the prevalence of gender inequality in Malaysia, even among dual-career families. Our findings offer a baseline framework for future studies seeking to address gender equality, marital relationships, and the intersection of work and family interface for dual-career couples in Malaysia.

References

Adams, J. S. (1965). Inequity in social exchange. In L. Berkowitz (Ed.), *Advances in experimental social psychology* (Vol. 2, pp. 267–299). Academic.

Arunima, & Nangia, R. (2022). Gender stereotyping and work-life balance: A study of dual-career couples. *Pacific Business Review International, 14*(10), 79–87.

Bianchi, S. M., & Milkie, M. A. (2010). Work and family research in the first decade of the 21st century. *Journal of Marriage and Family, 72*(3), 705–725.

Birkett, H., & Forbes, S. (2019). Where's dad? Exploring the low take-up of inclusive parenting policies in the UK. *Policy Studies, 40*(2), 205–224.

Boo, H. S. (2020). Familial influences on the division of household labour in Malaysian families. *Malaysian Journal of Society and Space, 16*(3), 1–13.

Chelliah, H. D., Boo, H. S., & Karupiah, P. (2023). Gender, ethnicity, and unpaid domestic work before and during the COVID-19 pandemic in Malaysia. *Pertanika Journal of Social Sciences & Humanities, 31*(3), 975–993.

Christopher, E. (2024). 'It's a Man's job: Doing gender and male gatekeeping in the division of household labor. *Journal of Family Issues, 45*(11), 2851–2874.

Chung, K., & Kim, H. (2013). Family change in Korea through the examination of family relationship satisfaction: Between 1991 and 2008. *Korea Journal of Population Studies, 36*(1), 175–202.

Coltrane, S. (2000). Research on household labor: Modeling and measuring the social embeddedness of routine family work. *Journal of Marriage and Family, 62*(4), 1208–1233.

Couprie, H., Cudeville, E., & Sofer, C. (2020). Efficiency versus gender roles and stereotypes: An experiment in domestic production. *Experimental Economics, 23*(1), 181–211.

Coy, A. (2013). *The contribution of partner investments to romantic relationship commitment (master's thesis, Virginia Commonwealth University).* VCU Scholars Compass.

Davis, S. N., & Greenstein, T. N. (2004). Cross-national variations in the division of household labor. *Journal of Marriage and Family, 66*(5), 1260–1271.

Deb, A., Kusimova, T., & Hominis, O. (2024). Perpetuation of gender inequalities in households: From culture to cognition. *Journal of Cognition and Culture, 24*(3–4), 373–409.

Deshpande, A., & Kabeer, N. (2024). Norms that matter: Exploring the distribution of women's work between income generation, expenditure-saving, and unpaid domestic responsibilities in India. *World Development, 174*, 106435.

Durtschi, J. A., Soloski, K. L., & Kimmes, J. (2017). The dyadic effects of supportive co-parenting and parental stress on relationship quality across the transition to parenthood. *Journal of Marital and Family Therapy, 43*(2), 308–321.

Gorchoff, S. M., John, O. P., & Helson, R. (2008). Contextualizing change in marital satisfaction during middle age: An 18-year longitudinal study. *Psychological Science, 19*(11), 1194–1200.

Hortaçsu, N. (2007). Family-versus couple-initiated marriages in Turkey: Similarities and differences over the family life cycle. *Asian Journal of Social Psychology, 10*(2), 103–116.

Humphries, J. (2024). Careworn: The economic history of caring labor. *The Journal of Economic History, 84*, 319–351.

Johnson, H. A., Zabriskie, R. B., & Hill, B. (2006). The contribution of couple leisure involvement, leisure time, and leisure satisfaction to marital satisfaction. *Marriage & Family Review, 40*(1), 69–91.

Juhari, R., Yaacob, S. N., Arif, N. A. M., & Sabri, M. F. (2019). Marital commitment as a function of marital satisfaction, marital investment, and marital alternatives among working women in Malaysia. *Pertanika Journal of Social Science and Humanities, 27*, 61–76.

Kang, Y. (2015). Effects of the division of housework, perceived marital fairness, and communication on marital satisfaction in elderly households: The moderating effect of communication. *The Korean Journal of Community Living Science, 26*(2), 361–374.

Kee, D. M. H., Al-anesi, M., Chandran, S., Elanggovan, H., Nagendran, B., & Mariappan, S. (2021). COVID-19 as a double-edged sword: The perfect opportunity for GrabFood to optimize its performance. *Journal of the Community Development in Asia, 4*(1), 53–65.

Kubricht, B., Miller, R., Yang, K., Harper, J., & Sandberg, J. (2017). Division of household labor and marital satisfaction in China: Urban and rural comparisons. *Journal of Comparative Family Studies, 48*(2), 261–274.

Lee, I. C., Hu, F., & Li, W. Q. (2020). Cultural factors facilitating or inhibiting the support for traditional household gender roles. *Journal of Cross-Cultural Psychology, 51*(5), 333–352.

Li, F. Z., Chen, C., Wang, J. R., Peng, H. Y., Wu, L., Ren, L., Song, L., Jin, Y. C., & Yang, Q. (2022). A cross-temporal meta-analysis on marital satisfaction of Chinese couples. *Frontiers in Psychology, 13*, 903276.

Lusiba, G. S., Kibwika, P., & Kyazze, F. B. (2017). Intra-household gender division of labour and decision-making on rice postharvest handling practices: A case of eastern Uganda. *Cogent Social Sciences, 3*, 1296323.

Mathur, G., Gulati, C., Sankpal, S., & Kee, D. M. H. (2024). Work-life balance and withdrawal behaviors among knowledge workforce: High performance work system comes into play for managing boundaries. *Global Business and Organizational Excellence*, 1–17. https://doi.org/10.1002/joe.22257

Mumtaz, R. (2022). Does gender differences matter? Investigating the prejudiced practices and gender-role conflict among female professionals working in male-dominated professions. *International Journal of Business and Society, 23*(2), 1297–1315.

Murray, A. J., & Durrheim, K. (2024). Studying intersectionality using ideological dilemmas: The case of paid domestic labour. *British Journal of Social Psychology, 63*, 1743–1756.

Mussida, C., & Patimo, R. (2021). Women's family care responsibilities, employment, and health: A tale of two countries. *Journal of Family and Economic Issues, 42*(3), 489–507.

Narender, S. G. V. (2024). *The role of gender and age in shaping attitudes towards childcare and financial roles in American families*. South Dakota State University.

Nasurdin, A. M., & Ahmad, N. H. (2013). Comparing work-family conflict and facilitation among male and female entrepreneurs in Malaysia. *International Journal of Business and Society, 14*(1), 149–162.

Panzhi, Lee, U. S., & Jo, D. H. (2022). A study on the effect of work-life balance conflict of working mothers on parental role satisfaction: The mediation effect of mother's child-rearing stress and parenting guilt. *Global Business Administration Review, 19*(3), 142–164.

Perry-Jenkins, M., & Gerstel, N. (2020). Work and family in the second decade of the 21st century. *Journal of Marriage and Family, 82*(1), 420–453.

Qian, Y., & Sayer, L. C. (2016). Division of labor, gender ideology, and marital satisfaction in East Asia. *Journal of Marriage and Family, 78*(2), 383–400.

Riggs, D. W., & Bartholomaeus, C. (2020). 'That's my job': Accounting for division of labour amongst heterosexual first-time parents. *Community, Work & Family, 23*(1), 107–122.

Rusbult, C. E., Martz, J. M., & Agnew, C. R. (1998). The investment model scale: Measuring commitment level, satisfaction level, quality of alternatives, and investment size. *Personal Relationships, 5*(4), 357–391.

Saigaran, N. G., & Bada, A. B. (2023). Perceptions of Malaysian Indian women on domestic violence in Malaysia: A peek into the Indian households. *Kajian Malaysia, 41*(2), 173–194.

Schieman, S., Ruppanner, L., & Milkie, M. A. (2018). Who helps with homework? Parenting inequality and relationship quality among employed mothers and fathers. *Journal of Family and Economic Issues, 39*(1), 49–65.

Selim, I., & Kee, D. M. H. (2023). Using job demands-resources theory to predict work-life balance among academicians in private universities in Egypt during the COVID-19 pandemic. *Information, 14*(1), 12. https://doi.org/10.3390/info14010012

Shockley, K. M., Shen, W., & Dodd, H. (2025). Dual-earner couples. *Annual Review of Organizational Psychology and Organizational Behavior, 12*, 369–394.

Sorokowski, P., Randall, A. K., Groyecka, A., Frackowiak, T., Cantarero, K., Hilpert, P., Ahmadi, K., Alghraibeh, A. M., Aryeetey, R., Bertoni, A., Bettache, K., Blazejewska, M., Bodenmann, G., Bortolini, T. S., Bosc, C., Butovskaya, M., Castro, F. N., Cetinkaya, H., Cunha, D., et al. (2017). Marital satisfaction, sex, age, marriage duration, religion, number of children, economic status, education, and collectivistic values: Data from 33 countries. *Frontiers in Psychology, 8*, article 1199.
Sunaryo, S., Sukoco, B. M., Ratmawati, D., & Ekowati, D. (2019). The glass ceiling: Investigating the dynamics surrounding the election of a female regent. *International Journal of Business and Society, 20*(2), 463–481.
Tartakovsky, E. (2023). A dyadic study of the spouses' assessment of the division of domestic labour and marital satisfaction. *Journal of Family Studies, 29*(5), 2356–2371.
Thebaud, S. (2010). Masculinity, bargaining, and breadwinning understanding men's housework in the cultural context of paid work. *Gender & Society, 24*(3), 330–354.
Thebaud, S., Kornrich, S., & Ruppanner, L. (2021). Good housekeeping, great expectations: Gender and housework norms. *Sociological Methods & Research, 50*(3), 1186–1214.
Thimm, V. (2025). Reconfiguring gender, kinship, and spirituality: Space—and place-making in Muslim Malaysia. *Journal of the Royal Anthropological Institute, 31*, 82–99.
Tjorring, L. (2016). We forgot half of the population! The significance of gender in Danish energy renovation projects. *Energy Research & Social Science, 22*, 115–124.
Tokal, P., Sart, G., Danilina, M., & Ta'Amnha, M. A. (2023). The impact of education level and economic freedom on gender inequality: Panel evidence from emerging markets. *Frontiers in Psychology, 14*, 1202014.
Turner, R. H. (2001). Role theory. In J. H. Turner (Ed.), *Handbook of sociological theory* (pp. 233–254). Springer US.
Ueno, K. (2021). Gender-stratified labor market, heterosexual marriage expectation, and LGBQ young adults' career plans in contemporary Japan. *Socius: Sociological Research for a Dynamic World, 7*, 23780231211052807.
Yu, W.-h., Su, K.-h., & Chiu, C.-T. (2012). Sibship characteristics and transition to first marriage in Taiwan: Explaining gender asymmetries. *Population Research and Policy Review, 31*(4), 609–636.

Daisy Mui Hung Kee is an Associate Professor at the School of Management, Universiti Sains Malaysia (USM). She is also an External Professor at Qingdao Hengxing University of Science and Technology, China, and an International Adjunct Faculty at IMS Ghaziabad, India. She holds a Ph.D. in Business and Management from the University of South Australia and an MBA from USM. With over 80 Web of Science-indexed publications, her research focuses on HRM, OB, Work Values, Leadership, and Entrepreneurship. She is Country Director for AIBPM (Indonesia) and STAR Scholars Network (USA), and serves as an Entrepreneurship Fellow at USM (2024–2025).

Jamin Kun Peng Xia is a research assistant at the School of Management, Universiti Sains Malaysia. His research interests include organisational behaviour, human resource management, strategic management, and innovation. Mr. Jamin has made notable contributions to academia, including a recent publication in the high-impact journal *Energy Policy*. He is also an active member of the Association of International Business & Professional Management (AIBPM).

Louis Yong Yu Lee is a research scholar at the School of Management, Universiti Sains Malaysia. Alongside his academic pursuits, he is actively involved in research activities as a research assistant. His areas of academic interest span corporate social responsibility, financial analysis, organisational behaviour, human resource management, and corporate governance. He has recently co-authored a paper published in Corporate Social Responsibility and Environment Management, a reputable international journal. In addition to his research work, Mr. Louis is affiliated with the Association of International Business & Professional Management (AIBPM).

Chapter 9
Breaching Institutional Patriarchy in Banking: Case Study of the Mann Deshi Bank

Sumedh Dalwai, Sameena Dalwai, and Rajdeep Pakanati

Abstract Financial inclusion of women, especially of poor women, remains a challenge across the globe. When a poor rural woman seeks a loan from a mainstream bank, she is told that she will not be able to pay back the loan or the instalments, that she does not possess the knowhow for starting or running a business. The refusal of the bank not only breaks the spirit of an individual woman but also makes it difficult for India to reach its goals of achieving financial inclusion and thus deepening democracy. The mainstream banks personify the hegemonic features of society such as urban, male, upper class, upper caste. Their denial of loan to those from the lower strata and women embody institutional patriarchy. Our research question for this chapter is: can microfinance lead to financial inclusion? What kind of alternate financial models can make this happen? Can financial inclusion of women can result in larger social political entitlements and enhancement of citizenship? We consider the case study of the Mann Deshi Bank based in Satara district in Maharashtra. The research is based on mixed methodology, which entails analysis of data provided by the bank as well as interviews with stake holders and bank officers. This chapter contends that the work of Mann Deshi Bank can serve as a new benchmark in the microfinance industry in India as it addresses the cash flow needs of marginalized clients, as it works with innovative models based on client demands. We argue that microfinance can, if undertaken with innovation and care, can lead to financial inclusion and that in turn could enhance other entitlements for women.

All the authors of this chapter—a lawyer, an economist and a political scientist—are connected to the bank in different capacities. We thank the Mann Deshi family for sharing their data and providing insights.

S. Dalwai
University of St Andrews, St Andrews, UK
e-mail: sd293@st-andrews.ac.uk

S. Dalwai
Jindal Global Law School, OP Jindal Global University, Sonipat, Haryana, India
e-mail: sdalwai@jgu.edu.in

R. Pakanati (✉)
Jindal School of International Affairs, OP Jindal Global University, Sonipat, Haryana, India
e-mail: rpakanati@jgu.edu.in

H. Adam and F. A. Malik (eds.), *The Political Economy of Gender*,
https://doi.org/10.1007/978-981-92-2785-3_9

Keywords Banking · Financial inclusion · Microfinance · India · Global south · Intersectionality · Political economy · Gender · Rural · Empowerment

1 Introduction[1]

> Vaishali Anile Pise got married at age 17. Soon after, her husband was driven out of his family business due to family feud. This left them in a dire situation with no source of income. With no formal education or skills under her belt, Vaishnavi was forced to work as an agricultural wage laborer and fended for herself. But with the birth of her first son, Vaishali wanted to find another source of income. She decided to start her own vada pav (street food consisting of bread and vegetable gravy) stall. With the little money she was able to save, she set up her stall beside an auto stand. With her newborn baby on her hip, she would sell Vada Pav earning profit of just ₹ 40 per day. Eager to expand her business, she decided to move her stall outside of her relative's hotel. She was able to borrow the hotel's equipment at night, only after they had used it, to make her Vada Pav. Only selling her vada pav at night, Vaishali knew she could earn more if she had her own equipment.

Vaishali Pise is one of the clients of Mann Deshi Bank, village Mhaswad in Satara district in Maharashtra. Her story captures the lives of many women in rural communities: underage marriage, domestic labor and violence, lack of financial autonomy and access to formal economy leading to precarity of everyday life. In myriad ways, intersectionality of patriarchy, caste and class encircle poor lower caste women blocking their full human potential and aspirations to live with dignity as the citizens of India.

Vaishali is also an example of a person who is excluded from the formal banking system. Businesses operated by women in rural areas generally commence with limited capital borrowed from friends and family and have a substantially smaller financial footprint. This also leads to lower asset accumulation and reduced cash flows. Consequently, the formal banking sector perceives lending small loans and providing savings accounts as cost-inefficient to service. Moreover, the nature of women-led businesses often entail cash flow cycles and financial needs that diverge from the mainstream banking products. For example, their operations may align with local or weekly markets, necessitating short-term liquidity during the day and cash reconciliation by day's end.

1.1 Economics to Politics: A Continuum

In India, adult franchise became universal upon independence empowering women at one go. Despite this, their representation in elected bodies remained poor. One step to address this, was carried out through the 73rd Amendment to the Indian Constitution,

[1] An earlier version of this paper is available as a preprint at https://ore.exeter.ac.uk/articles/thesis/Three_essays_in_development_economics/29764832?file=56793983. The current manuscript is the revised and original version.

enacted in 1992, which extended elected representation at the grassroots level of village, block and district. The provision of reservation of at least one-third of the elected seats for women at this level saw increased number of women contesting elections (Bhavnani, 2009). Despite women getting elected at the local level their role was sometimes marginalized due to the dominance of their husbands. This led to a phenomenon of *sarpanch pati* (elected village head's husband) exercising real power (Ghosh & Mahajan, 2019; Turnbull, 2022).

To contextualize such proxy participation, we need to understand that in a patriarchal context, men exercise power as they hold the strings of the purse. This extends from a dominant control of income earned by women to assets like land and houses which are usually registered in the name of the men only. Hence economic autonomy of women is crucial for them to participate in the economic and political life in a society.

In this chapter, we look at the work of Mann Deshi Bank to see how they have carved out a niche pathway undergirded by the women-centric principles to provide financial inclusion and a sense of entitlement. We argue that economic autonomy and financial inclusion of women to be pivotal to their political participation and widening meaningful democracy on the ground in the developing world. We study the Mann Deshi Bank as a model that endeavors to assist women attain their economic goals and thereby finding pathways into other social and political entitlements.

The research questions we raise here are:

1. Can self—help groups and microfinance lead to financial inclusion?
2. What kind of alternate financial models can make this happen?
3. Can financial inclusion of women lead to enhanced socio-political entitlements?

In the next section, we lay present the methodology. We then engage with the relevant literature pertaining to financial inclusion, microfinance and gender to provide context for the chapter. We then elaborate on the discussion of financial inclusion, microfinance and undertake a case study of the Mann Deshi Bank.

2 Methodology

The paper adopts a mixed methodology approach. A quantitative approach deals with how women clients of the Bank see an increase in their incomes. This analysis is based on details of 4914 Joint liability group borrowers. The forms stored in the main bank office in Mhaswad were accessed and studied for several months of 2019. Descriptive statistics are used to tease out the sustainable model of microfinance. Qualitative approach is built on a post Covid context and teases out the dynamics of the functioning of this microfinance institution. This includes case studies of select borrowers and interviews with bank officials.

3 Literature Review

This paper is at the intersection of the functioning of the formal banking sector, financial inclusion goals and operation of microfinance institutions.

Financial inclusion is beset with gender gaps around the world, especially in developing countries, legal and systemic barriers (Aterido et al., 2013; Demirgüç-Kunt et al., 2015; World Bank, 2022) and lowering these barriers will benefit the economy (Khera, 2018). In such circumstances, Microfinance can offer solutions to women and communities trying to overcome poverty. Pioneering studies of the Grameen Bank model in Bangladesh (Khandker, 2005) and studies which use randomized evaluation that microfinance generally has positive effects on female entrepreneurship (Banerjee et al., 2015).

A big portion of the literature sheds light on the mechanisms of microfinance which are successful in generating higher repayment rates. Ghatak and Guinnane (1999) points out four potential problems which would affect loan repayment negatively when comparing formal banking institutions and microfinance institutions. They are *adverse selection, moral hazard, enforcement and auditing problems.*

To mitigate the effects of these problems microfinance institutions have developed loan products which are offered based on joint liability of borrowers, since the clients do not have collateral and cannot access the formal banking system. This is called the joint liability model. There are two major types of joint liability models in India. Self-Help Groups (SHGs) which consist normally of 10–20 people and Joint Liability Groups (JLGs) with about 5 people in one group. This design mitigates the three major problems identified above.

Group lending (Ghatak, 1999; Stiglitz, 1990; Varian, 1990) is considered to provide a screening mechanism by taking advantage of information available among borrowers to mitigate the problems of adverse selection. Peer monitoring enables microfinance institutions to mitigate the issue of moral hazard (Stiglitz, 1990; Wenner, 1995) and default rates are reduced (Armendáriz de Aghion & Morduch, 2000; Ghatak & Guinnane, 1999). Wydick (1999) shows some contrary evidence that members' monitoring costs affect the repayment rate negatively. Enforcement of loans can be enhanced through group lending which can impose sanctions on group members who have defaulted irresponsibly (Besley & Coate, 1995; Montgomery, 1996). Some studies place emphasis on social ties (Paxton et al., 2000; Zeller, 1998) while some studies argue that peer monitoring and intra-group insurance drives the success of group lending whereas social sanctions just play a secondary and supporting role (Wydick, 1999).

As MFIs are consolidating their operations, the need to increase profits or efficient management of operations is becoming an imperative for them. A study by Kodongo and Kendi (2013) compares individual lending versus group lending suggests a possible way out—i.e. to establish a form of credit risk assessment of individual borrowers in a group and then target them for offering progressive individual loans.

More recent literature takes a comprehensive stock of the relationship between microfinance and gender along three axes—the potential of microfinance to empower women, negative gender discrimination in the microfinance sector and power relations within and beyond the household shaping the context and outcomes of microfinance initiatives (Chakraborty & Abraham, 2025; Garikipati et al., 2017). Financial inclusion of women can have far reaching effects on the communities. It helps strengthen women's economic agency and position (Datta & Sahu, 2023; Malik & Yadav, 2022), enabling them to resist and thus bring about a reduction in violence (Dulhunty, 2025).

While quantitative studies in microfinance underline economic rationale of market model, qualitative studies can update the assumptions to better frame the economic theory.

4 Financial Inclusion Trends

According to the World Bank, the total number of adults without a bank account over the age of 15 in India was 190 million which accounts for 14% population in 2017. A twofold growth of the banked population during the period of 2011 and 2017 was due to the strong push of biometric identification card by the government. The Pradhan Mantri Jan Dhan Yojana (PMJDY), launched in 2014, gave every household a bank account and basic insurance cover. This flagship scheme of the government attracted a mass of 15 million on the day it was launched.[2] Later, the license to payments banks and small finance banks and the launch of Micro Unit Development and Refinance Agency (MUDRA) in 2015 showed the determination of the government to promote financial inclusion to the poor. Since then. According to the government, over $380 billion collateral free loans have been disbursed, of whom 70% are women beneficiaries.[3] The account ownership for women experienced a rapid increase of from 2014, but still one-fifth of the women are un-banked. Based on the census in 2011, 46% of households in the rural areas and 32% of households in the urban areas do not have access to banking services.[4]

Microfinance financial intuitions (MFIs) in India reached out to 177.5 million households by 2023 through self-help groups (SHGs) who are linked to 14.42 million savings bank accounts, averaging a credit of ₹ 3,35,000 per SHG. India is also the country with the largest number of borrowers borrowing from MFIs. The loan portfolio stands around $46 billion as of 2024 (NABARD, 2024). There are 163 microfinance lenders as of Financial Year 2023–24, including banks, small finance banks (SFBs), non-banking financial companies (NBFCs), and non-banking financial companies—microfinance institutions (NBFCMFIs) in the microfinance sector (NABARD, 2024).

[2] https://economictimes.indiatimes.com/news/economy/policy/pm-jan-dhan-yojana-launched-1-5-crore-bankaccounts-opened-in-a-day/articleshow/41093413.cms

[3] www.mudra.org.in/

[4] We wait for updated data as the Census 2021 has been delayed and is expected to be completed by 2027.

Based on the data of 163 MFIs collected by NABARD in 2024, we find NBFC-MFIs and NBFCs took the lead in client outreach with amounts of 1,49,721 (₹ in crore) and 1,31, 165 (₹ in crore) which is 43.6% and 33.1% respectively (Fig. 1).

On the other hand, while NBFC-MFIs still account for the largest share of amount disbursed at 40%, Banks account for 35% of the amount disbursed, even though they are in a small number at 13 (Fig. 2).

The strong growth in microfinance can be attributed both to the demand of the market and to RBI's agenda of extending credit to the poor. For example, RBI requires all domestic banks with at least 20 branches to have at least 40% of loans lent to the priority sector, which MFIs are categorized as. Moreover, agriculture, micro

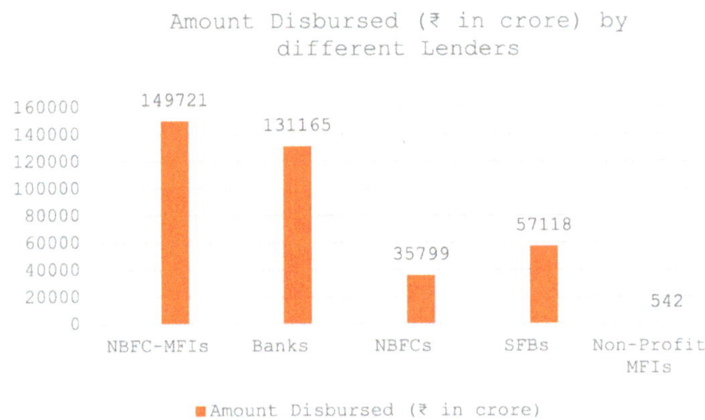

Fig. 1 Amount disbursed by different lenders. *Source* Status of microfinance in India 2023–24, p. 242. (NABARD, 2024)

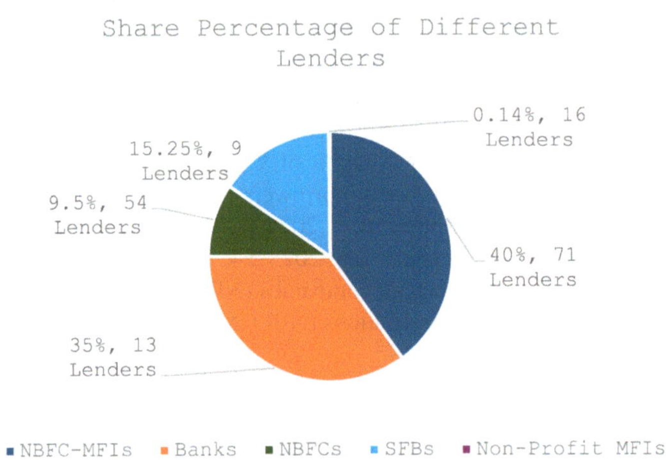

Fig. 2 Share percentage of different lenders. *Source* Status of microfinance in India 2023–24, p. 242. (NABARD, 2024)

enterprises and weaker sections should be allocated at least 18%, 7.5% and 12% of loans. However, the public sector banks tend to fall short of the target set by RBI.[5] In 2017, they fell short of 7.5% of the target. The current solution for the shortfall is to require the banks to contribute to the Rural Infrastructure Development Fund for further allocation.[6] To control the portfolio risk and encourage lending to the poor, banks are allowed to have unsecured loans of 10%.

5 Mann Deshi Bank

5.1 Choice of the Case Study

Amongst the wide variety of microfinance models and institutions why do we choose Mann Deshi Mahila Bank as the case study here? It is because it recognizes the interconnected nature of poverty and caste and strives to offer financial opportunities for lowest caste women. This comes from the background of activism that the Founder Chetna Sinha and her partner came from. As part of the Socialist Movement, they had led agitations for employment guarantee schemes for rural landless labor. In order to fight poverty and to create income generation activities poor women from these movements came together to first build a credit society and later, a bank. The products they offer, the policies they pass and the vision they hold show their understanding of the intersectionality of caste, class and gender.

The four steps that underlie Mann Deshi Bank's success are—Doorstep Banking, Joint Liability, customized financial products and providing Business Training and Support.[7]

As of Financial Year 2023–24, it provides financial services to over 120,000 clients. These services include loans, savings, pension, and insurance, and doorstep banking which are provided by field agents who travel to clients' doorsteps. Mann Deshi has eight branches covering 7 districts (Satara, Solapur, Sangli, Raigarh, Ratnagiri, Pune and Kolhapur) in Maharashtra with 10,000 transactions daily. There are in total around 100 employees including around 20, who work in the headquarter office. The bank was at the forefront in convincing RBI that higher priority lending requires higher upper limit for unsecured loans. When RBI came up with a circular in 2016 to allow any banks which have more than 90% priority lending to lift the original cap on unsecured loans of 10% to 35%,[8] Mann Deshi is the only bank in India to fulfil the criteria.

[5] https://m.rbi.org.in/Scripts/FAQView.aspx?Id=87

[6] https://www.thehindubusinessline.com/money-and-banking/banks-can-now-meet-their-msme-priority-sector-lending-target-better/article22682033.ece Accessed on July 14, 2023.

[7] https://manndeshibank.com

[8] https://www.rbi.org.in/Scripts/NotificationUser.aspx?Id=10361&Mode=0 Accessed on July 14, 2023.

Mann Deshi goals were distinct from other MFIs from its inception. While other MFIs started with lending where lack of access to capital was identified as a reason for low productivity and low income of the poor, Mann Deshi started with savings. Lack of saving opportunity for women was identified as the problem. Banks were not ready to accept these poor rural women's savings, as such small deposits were not seen viable by the banks. Women needed access to banking to save, because they understood the benefits of having the savings both as precautionary money and as an investment. But, not having control on their finances they were not able to save. Quite often the men in the family would force the women to spend the money. Hence, an external secured option to save was in demand. Mann Deshi started with an objective to offer that. While many MFI's relied on external support in terms of grant as a gift or as a loan, Mann Deshi raised capital for its operations from the savings of the rural poor women, whom they were committed to serve. It is not an investor driven institution, but a cooperative, which means every member's vote carries equal weight irrespective of the investment the member had in the organization.

Mann Deshi also approached financial inclusion from a women's development point of view. They aim was to have the women exercise greater control on her finances. This was to enable women to have more liberty. An opportunity to invest, own assets in their name, and have a fair share in ownership of family assets.

5.2 *Financial Products*

Mann Deshi's flagship product is the JLG loan. Primary Research was carried out in 2019, by digitizing 4914 first JLG loan application forms. It showed that between 2011 to 2015, a third of the borrowers are in their 30 s and the other one third of borrowers are in their 40 s. As shown in Fig. 3, more than half (54.35%) of the borrowers are self-employed as tailors, street vendors of fruits and vegetables, bakers, cobblers and so on. One out of three (34.35%) borrowers work as wage labour. Most of them are farm hands or builders. Only 6.88% of the borrowers are in salaried jobs whereas only 4.42% of women are only undertaking household duties. 75% of the borrowers have a family size between 3 to 5. 82% of co-applicants are husbands whereas 12% of co-applicants are sons. Out of five borrowers, two come from a household with monthly income ranging from ₹ 10,000 to ₹ 15,000, one comes from the income range from ₹ 5000 to ₹ 10, 000 and another from ₹ 15,000 to ₹ 20,000, respectively. Nearly 90% of borrowers contribute less than half to the family income.

Figures 4 and 5 summarize the distributions of occupation and caste category. The forward caste clients happen to be 20%, out of which 16% are Maratha, which is the most populated caste in the region. A large proportion i.e. 31% of borrowers are from schedule caste which were traditionally considered "untouchables". 10.48% are from Mahar and 10.07% are from Matang. Matang is a community which is considered to be on the lowest step of the caste ladder.As per the national definition of Other Backward Caste (OBC), 43% of the borrowers are in this category. Among 48 castes in OBC category, 7.59% are Ramoshi and 4.93% are Mali. Vadar, Dhangar, Lohar,

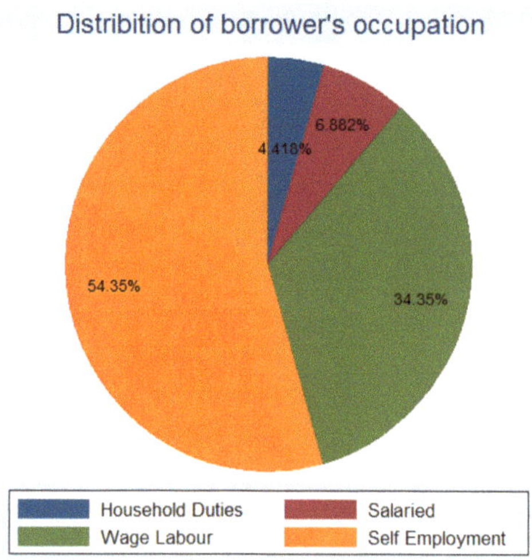

Fig. 3 Distribution of borrower's occupation. *Source* Data collected by Sumedh Dalwai in 2019

Nhavi and Wani are all small and marginalized communities that are represented here. 12.58% are Muslims, which is the largest religious minority in the region. This shows that the borrowers are well diversified in the caste and communities. Since literature shows that access to rural credit is skewed in favor of landed and upper caste borrowers, the borrower profile of Mann Deshi shows a distinctive pattern of credit distribution.

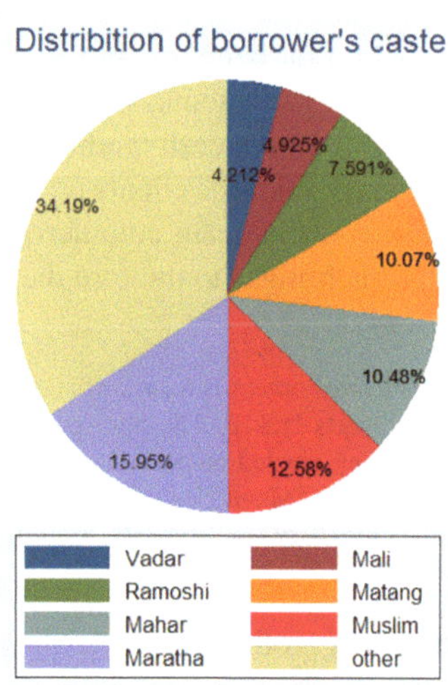

Fig. 4 Distribution of borrower's caste. *Source* Data collected by Sumedh Dalwai in 2019

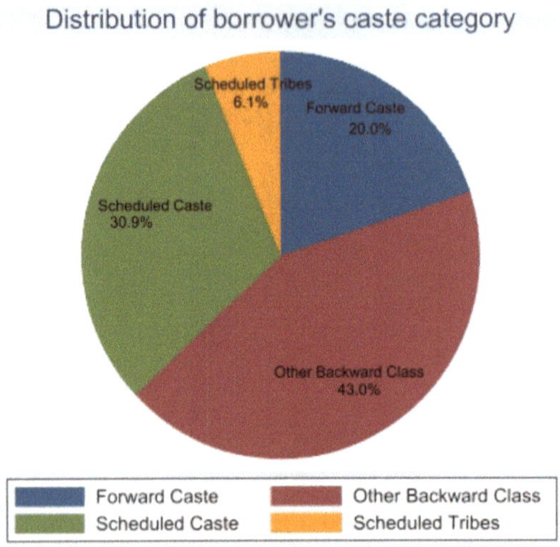

Fig. 5 Distribution of borrower's caste category. *Source* Data collected by Sumedh Dalwai in 2019

Mann Deshi Bank was a pioneer in developing a novel customized 'Weekly Market Loan' product. This product provides credit to small scale vendors who sell at weekly markets and have hitherto taken short-term loans from moneylenders or purchased stock from wholesalers on credit. These short-term loans or credit were accessed at a high interest rate. To address this need Mann Deshi Bank undertook a year-long survey in four markets in the region of the bank's operations, by building financial diaries of weekly vendors to understand their cash flows. The result was "a product custom-designed to suit the variable and daily income streams of low-income customers [which] could offer better client value and be serviced profitably by the bank (GIZ, 2014)". Kumar (2020) found that even though Mann Deshi Bank charges a flat interest rate of 15% on the cash credit product, which is higher than borrowers from other commercial banks, the clients prefer Mann Deshi Bank as they are not the focus of business for mainstream commercial banks and the service is not accessible. He posits that this brings "to the fore the issue of availability versus accessibility (Kumar, 2020, 143)."

> "The preference for Mann Deshi over others is a case of successful outreach efforts made by this bank which their counterparts lacked. The poor probably needed social inclusion to precede financial inclusion. They needed respect, recognition, timeliness and doorstep service more than interest rate benefits. Mann Deshi Bank probably succeeded in capturing the sense of these excluded segments of society with customized products and delivery mechanism. (Kumar, 2020, 143)"

These two kinds of unsecured loan products make up the primary portfolio of Mann Deshi Bank (Table 1).

They are now providing a new loan product, named *Unnati* (growth) specifically for the graduating borrowers of JLG, who are seasoned women entrepreneurs and keen to scale their businesses. The weekly market credit loan is a growing product and

Table 1 Weekly market cash credit loans vs joint liability group loans

Items	Weekly Market Cash Credit Loans	Joint Liability Group Loans
Instalment	Varies and flexible amount equal and fixed amount	Varies and flexible amount equal and fixed amount
Loan received	Depending on the withdrawal amount up to the limit	Fixed lump sum at the beginning
Amount to be borrowed	Decided by borrowers up to the limit	Options fixed by bank
Type of loans	Overdraft term loan	Term loan
Age	21–59	18–59
Group size	3	4 to 7
Credit limit	₹10,000 to ₹40,000	
Loan tenure	3 years	1 and 2 years
Interest rate	26%	
Repayment frequency	Weekly	Weekly/monthly
Repayment rate	95%	99%

Source Data collected by Sumedh Dalwai in 2019

reached more than 60,000 clients. In terms of loan performance, the Non-Performing Assets (NPA) rate remained stable with net ratio of two percent, which is far below the industry average of 10%.

When there was upheaval in the microfinance sector in 2010, the bank was affected for a few months and then retained its market share through its long-stand brand image and its close ties with local borrowers, as it had an embedded business model (Bhawe & Jha, 2025). Pre-COVID, the JLG loans with repayment rate of 99% outperformed other loan products. After reaching as low as 86% in COVID period it has been steadily improving and stands at around 94% now. The capital adequacy ratio, which measures a bank's credit risk exposure, remains in a range between 14% to 18% which is much higher than 9% which is required by RBI for commercial banks. The bank's net profit is 1% due to high operating cost, especially the door-step service which is 3%. Apart from the three unsecured loans, the bank offers secured loans for housing, agriculture allied, gold, vehicle and business loans.

5.3 *Bank plus: The Contribution of Mann Deshi Foundation*

Complementing the banking services is the Mann Deshi Foundation (MDF),[9] a non-profit program which provides a lot of non-financial support through a business school to help women gain financial knowledge to build up their business. The

[9] https://manndeshifoundation.org

program is called *Udyogini* and it's motto is 'never provide poor solutions to poor'. The 14-hour financial literacy course, offered by Mann Deshi *Udyogini*, is a key component to Mann Deshi Bank's successful operations. Completing the financial literacy course is the must-do requirement for each of Mann Deshi Bank's loan clients. "The courses offered by Mann Deshi Udyogini have three important components: training in technical skills; training to build financial literacy and marketing skills; and training for confidence building (Shukla, 2017)".

The non-financial services provided by the Foundation include skills development, mentoring and technical support to empower women entrepreneurs and their communities. These are week-long, fifteen day-long, and one-year Deshi MBA courses on financial and adult literacy and business development.

There are 13 business schools, along with 12 mobile business schools which have served 7,91,456 women so far. 80% of these women see an increase in their monthly average income by 56%, while 92% have started new business or expanded their business, and 70% of women have gone on to gain ownership of assets..[10]

Apart from the Business Schools, there are 13 Chambers of Commerce (CoC) which provide support for existing entrepreneurs on how to expand their businesses. They have served 2,24, 337 women. The support includes networking, mentorship and access to new market. This is a customized financial education for women entrepreneurs to establish a sound business.

6 Mann Deshi Social Impact

Recalling the story of Vaishali Pise at the beginning of this chapter, we can now contextualize her engagement with the bank. Vaishali approached the Mann Deshi Bank for a loan of ₹5000. She used this money to purchase her own cooking equipment. She was then able to make and sell *vada pav* all day, without the need to depend on anyone. Naturally, her income grew from ₹40 a day to ₹70. Encouraged by this, Vaishali enrolled in the Mann Deshi business School to learn how to run her business more effectively. She listened to Mann Deshi Radio for business tips. She learnt that by listening to her customers and understanding their needs would make her successful. When her customers enquired for mineral water, she decided to take another loan of ₹10,000 to purchase and sell mineral water. This loan allowed her to expand into a wider variety of other food items like tea, rice and dal, and baked goods. She built a shed to store and protect her raw materials. Since then, Vaishali is earning over ₹1500 a day and can save ₹5000 per month. She is the major bread winner in her family and manages to send her children to school. She hopes to run her own restaurant one day. Vaishali's inspiring story is what helped her become a recipient of the 2017 Successful Entrepreneurship Award from Mann Deshi.

---

[10] Mann Deshi Foundation, Annual Report 2023–2024. https://manndeshifoundation.org/annual-reports/MDF_AR_2023-24.pdf

The first thing that we see from the illustrative story is the obvious fact that these are entrepreneurial women who have overcome immense structural challenges thrown at them in life—from crushing poverty to cruel patriarchy from lack of capital to denial of family support. Women are not allowed to fail in patriarchy; if they fail in one venture, it becomes impossible for them to start another venture again. Hence, they work endlessly to ensure success. This is also a reason why their credit return is so high to their bank and why Mann Deshi has a low default rate.

A less known aspect of the work of Mann Deshi Bank is their work in moments of instability and crisis. When the Indian government demonetized currency notes of 500 and 2000 rupees in November 2016, the Bank stepped in to innovatively access small value coins and bundle them in pouch of 500 each which were exchanged in the weekly market in lieu of the 500-rupee currency notes. This suited need of the small borrowers and clients very well and earned goodwill in the community (Kumar, 2020).

Similarly, during the Covid pandemic the Mann Deshi Foundation led their community from the front by working with the government to enhance emergency medical facilities and organizing vaccination camps, specifically for women. They began a mask unit to create and distribute masks which makes aprons and PPE for those working in the healthcare sector.[11]

Usually banks sell a product, but Mann Deshi develops a product based on the clients' needs and capability.

6.1 Political Participation

The multiplier effect of the Mann Deshi Bank's work can be seen in how the clients now avail various government welfare schemes, which have hitherto remained difficult to access. Experienced and empowered clients of Mann Deshi Bank engage with mainstream banks to avail loans underwritten by the government. As members of the Bank, women gain identity and visibility. They participate in meetings and are even felicitated for being 'Best Borrowers'. Women become ambitious in other fields once they gain economic autonomy. As their self-esteem rises and practice of self-determination ensues, it follows in all aspects of their lives, including local politics.

Women's political participation has always been high in India. Contrary to popular belief, poor women participate in elections, stand in long queues and cast their vote. The system of 'secret ballot' protects them from the influences of husbands, family members and political parties that pay for votes. As interviews in *Why India Votes* (Banerjee, 2017) reveal, women may get sarees and money for votes, but they cast their vote based on their own independent criteria. In the 2024 Parliamentary elections, 65.78% of eligible female electors voted as compared to 65.55% of eligible

[11] Mann Deshi Foundation, Annual Report 2021–2022. https://manndeshifoundation.org/annual-reports/MDF_AR_2021-22.pdf

male electors. As the clients grow in stature and recognition, political opportunities come their way. Local leaders scout women with their own networks, identity and confidence. They get invited to participate in politics and become representatives of people.

In an interview with the founder and Chairman of the bank, Mrs. Chetna Sinha, she says,

> Poor women lack many different entitlements. Financial inclusion can be a pathway towards those entitlements: Saving account. Ownership of money. Ownership of assets. With financial inclusion, the woman's journey of entitlements begins. This journey then empowers her to face the domestic violence, societal abuse. It is a myth that poor women need awareness, they need to understand their own rights. The truth is that they are well aware, but they lack the tools to assume those rights. To turn awareness into action, anyone would need support, strategy, safety, money. Control over finances helps women shape their own destiny.

Today the Bank faces two major challenges. One is how to localize the JLG products by considering the local community's needs and culture. This is essential when microfinance wants to penetrate new areas. The other is how to provide the 'right' financial tools to those borrowers who have completed several loan cycles and are ready to scale their business or get into new business but still struggle to get into the formal banking system due to various reasons. This group of borrowers have different requirements of cash flows and loan amount. So new types of products should be explored to meet clients' needs.

7 Policy Recommendations

Reflecting from the experience of the Mann Deshi Bank, we make the following policy recommendations. These could be incorporated into the proposed National Strategy for Financial Inclusion for the period 2025–2030 of the Reserve Bank of India. Further, when we refer to the parameters of the Financial Inclusion Index prepared by the RBI, we see that access, which covers the supply side of financial inclusion through banking, digital reach, pension and insurance coverage has increased steadily. It has grown from 43.4 in 2017 to 64.2 in 2024 (Reserve Bank of India, 2024, p.105).

On the other hand, usage which reflects the demand side of financial inclusion which measures usage of financial infrastructure and quality of financial inclusion which captures the efforts of financial institutions to make citizens aware of appropriate financial services, has reached only half the population (Reserve Bank of India, 2021).

The shortcomings of usage and quality of financial products is a severe challenge, and we emphasize that banks and other financial institutions should, learning from the experience of Mann Deshi Bank, adopt the following:

(i) Design customized banking products, so that the contextual needs of households and borrowers are addressed as these vary by the profile of the population, region, climate, state and even sometimes within a district. A one-size fits all microfinance loan products cannot meet the credit requirements of the borrowers.

(ii) Provide comprehensive financial training, to borrowers based on their borrowing needs, so that their business proposals reach fruition.

(iii) Synchronize with other government welfare programs, like the Pradhan Mantri MUDRA Yojana which facilitates loans up to ₹ two million rupees for small and micro enterprises, so that the user base is widened.

(iv) Provide additional support to borrowers when faced with systemic effects like demonetization or the pandemic.

8 Conclusion

This paper considers financial inclusion of poor women through the lens of understanding everyday democratic process in India. Though the case study of a unique experiment of the Mann Deshi Bank, we surmise that economic policies can be successful if they are led by the recipients and participants; the Bank has great returns and very low defaults as it listens to women and caters new financial products. As women grow in financial planning and autonomy, they aim for other social and political achievements. They contest elections and run local governance. This way economic autonomy of women shows results of widening democracy.

Whereas the Grameen Bank of Bangladesh viewed women as the best medium for achieving development through microfinance, Mann Deshi Bank views microfinance as the best medium for achieving development of women.

References

Armendáriz de Aghion, B., & Morduch, J. (2000). Microfinance beyond group lending. *The Economics of Transition, 8*(2), 401–420.

Aterido, R., Beck, T., & Iacovone, L. (2013). Access to finance in sub-Saharan Africa: Is there a gender gap? *World Development, 47*, 102–120. https://doi.org/10.1016/j.worlddev.2013.02.013

Banerjee, A., Duflo, E., Glennerster, R., & Kinnan, C. (2015). The miracle of microfinance? Evidence from a randomized evaluation. *American Economic Journal: Applied Economics, 7*(1), 22–53. https://doi.org/10.1257/app.20130533

Banerjee, M. (2017). *Why India votes?* Routledge India.

Besley, T., & Coate, S. (1995). Group lending, repayment incentives and social collateral. *Journal of Development Economics, 46*(1), 1–18. https://doi.org/10.1016/0304-3878(94)00045-E

Bhavnani, R. R. (2009). Do electoral quotas work after they are withdrawn? Evidence from a natural experiment in India. *American Political Science Review, 103*(1), 23–35. https://doi.org/10.1017/S0003055409090029

Bhawe, N., & Jha, S. K. (2025). MFIs and financial inclusion: The role of business models. *The Journal of Development Studies, 61*(1), 133–151.

Chakraborty, R., & Abraham, R. (2025). Microfinance and Women's empowerment: A comparative study between two developing countries. *Business Strategy & Development, 8*(2), e70133.

Datta, S., & Sahu, T. N. (2023). *Financial inclusion and livelihood transformation.* Springer Books.

Demirgüç-Kunt, A., Klapper, L. F., Singer, D., & Van Oudheusden, P. (2015). *The global findex database 2014: Measuring financial inclusion around the world* (Policy Research Working Paper No. 7255), World Bank.

Dulhunty, A. (2025). A qualitative examination of microfinance and intimate partner violence in India: Understanding the role of male backlash and household bargaining models. *World Development, 186*, 106805.

Garikipati, S., Johnson, S., Guérin, I., & Szafarz, A. (2017). Microfinance and gender: Issues, challenges and the road ahead. *The Journal of Development Studies, 53*(5), 641–648. https://doi.org/10.1080/00220388.2016.1205736

Ghatak, M. (1999). Group lending, local information and peer selection. *Journal of Development Economics, 60*(1), 27–50. https://doi.org/10.1016/S0304-3878(99)00035-8

Ghatak, M., & Guinnane, T. W. (1999). The economics of lending with joint liability: Theory and practice. *Journal of Development Economics, 60*(1), 195–228. https://doi.org/10.1016/S0304-3878(99)00041-3

Ghosh, P., & Mahajan, C. (2019). Inequality, politics and exploitation in a Rajasthan Village. In *Development and deprivation in the Indian sub-continent* (pp. 411–419). Routledge.

GIZ. (2014). *Mann Deshi Bank's Cash Credit Product for Micro-Entrepreneurs A Case Study.* Published by Deutsche Gesellschaft für Internationale Zusammenarbeit (GIZ) GmbH GIZ NABARD Rural Financial Institutions Programme.

Khandker, S. R. (2005). Microfinance and poverty: Evidence using panel data from Bangladesh. *The World Bank Economic Review, 19*(2), 263–286. https://doi.org/10.1093/wber/lhi008

Khera, P. (2018). Closing gender gaps in India: Does increasing womens' access to finance help?. International Monetary Fund. 10.5089/9781484377468.001.

Kodongo, O., & Kendi, L. G. (2013). Individual lending versus group lending: An evaluation with Kenya's microfinance data. *Review of Development Finance, 3*(2), 99–108. https://doi.org/10.1016/j.rdf.2013.05.001

Kumar, A. (2020). Cooperative and social innovation in finance—A case study of Mann Deshi Mahila Sahkari Bank. In D. Rajasekhar, R. Manjula, & T. Paranjothi (Eds.), *Cooperatives and social innovation.* Springer. https://doi.org/10.1007/978-981-15-8880-8_10

Malik, F. A., & Yadav, D. K. (2022). *Financial inclusion schemes in India.* Springer.

Montgomery, R. (1996). Disciplining or protecting the poor? Avoiding the social costs of peer pressure in micro-credit schemes. *Journal of International Development, 8*(2), 289–305. https://doi.org/10.1002/(SICI)1099-1328(199603)8:2<289::AID-JID368>3.0.CO;2-2

NABARD. (2024). *Status of Microfinance in India 2023–24.* https://www.nabard.org/auth/writereaddata/tender/0808244223NABARD-SOMFI%20%20%20%20%20%20%20%202023 2024%20%20%20%20%20%2030072024.pdf

Paxton, J., Graham, D., & Thraen, C. (2000). Modeling group loan repayment behavior: New insights from Burkina Faso. *Economic Development and Cultural Change, 48*(3), 639–655. https://doi.org/10.1086/452613

Reserve Bank of India. (2021). *Financial Inclusion Index for India.* https://rbi.org.in/scripts/BS_ViewBulletin.aspx?Id=20502

Reserve Bank of India. (2024). *Annual Report 2023–24.* https://rbidocs.rbi.org.in/rdocs/AnnualReport/PDFs/0ANNUALREPORT202324_FULLDF549205FA214F62A2441C5320D64A29.PDF

Shukla, S. (2017). Mann Deshi Bank and Udyogini: Successfully collaborating to empower women. In *Overcoming challenges to gender equality in the workplace* (pp. 189–199). Routledge.

Stiglitz, J. E. (1990). Peer monitoring and credit markets. *The World Bank Economic Review, 4*(3), 351–366. https://doi.org/10.1093/wber/4.3.351

Turnbull, B. (2022). *Women who only serve chai: Gender quotas, reservations and proxies in India.* Routledge India.

Varian, H. R. (1990). Monitoring agents with other agents. *Journal of Institutional and Theoretical Economics (JITE)/Zeitschrift für die gesamte Staatswissenschaft*, 153–174.

Wenner, M. D. (1995). Group credit: A means to improve information transfer and loan repayment performance. *The Journal of Development Studies, 32*(2), 263–281.

World Bank. (2022). *Women, Business and the Law*. https://wbl.worldbank.org/

Wydick, B. (1999). The effect of microenterprise lending on child schooling in Guatemala. *Economic Development and Cultural Change, 47*(4), 853–869. https://doi.org/10.1086/452435

Zeller, M. (1998). Determinants of repayment performance in credit groups: The role of program design, intragroup risk pooling, and social cohesion. *Economic Development and Cultural Change, 46*(3), 599–620. https://doi.org/10.1086/452360

Sumedh Dalwai was an Associate Lecturer at the University of St Andrews. Ph.D. in Economics at the University of Exeter in December 2019, following a Master's degree in Financial Economics from the University of Exeter. Prior to that I earned a Master's degree in Economics from Gokhale Institute of Politics and Economics, India and a Bachelor's degree in Financial Accounting and Auditing from Mumbai University.

Sameena Dalwai is Professor at O. P. Jindal Global University, Sonipat, specializing in gender, sexuality, and law. Her research examines the intersections of law, globalization, caste, and sexuality in India. She is the author of Love Jihad: A Feminist Retelling (2026), Bans & Bar Girls: Performing Caste in Mumbai's Dance Bars (2019), and Babri Masjid: 25 Years On (2017).

Rajdeep Pakanati is a Professor at OP Jindal Global University, Sonipat, India. His research interests include International Relations, Comparative Politics, International Law and Global Governance. Rajdeep has been engaged with issues of transparency and accountability, and how they contribute to good governance. Rajdeep's present teaching includes courses on Comparative Politics, Indian Foreign Policy, India and China in International Relations, International Law, Research Methods, Accountability and Academic Writing.

Chapter 10
The Intersectional Politics of Gender: Pedagogy and Practice in Indian Universities

Nisha Nair and Samanvi Narang

Abstract The role of Higher Education Institutions (HEIs) as transformative agents of sustainability has gained increasing recognition in both policy and academic discourse. SDGs, particularly SDG 4 (Quality Education), emphasize the need for higher education to not only impart knowledge but also equip students with the skills, values and competencies necessary to lead sustainable transitions. The importance of higher education in achieving greater sensitivity towards the social, political and economic complexities that emerge from gender inequalities is uncontested. The chapter examines how academia is shaping the understanding of political economy of gender (PEG) by analysing the experiences of faculty, the curriculum and pedagogy of gender & women studies programmed offered in India HEIs. By collecting and analysing the classroom narratives from faculties of different HEIs, the chapter highlights the challenges in pedagogy and policy framework viz. classroom resistance at the intersection of class, caste, religion and sexuality, gender fatigue i.e., indifference towards issues of gender, ideological resistance, politicisation and tokenism. The scope of the chapter is limited to the narratives collected from faculty members teaching Gender focused courses on Indian HEI that engages with the concept of PEG. The objective of the chapter is to understand, deconstruct and reimagine the approach(es) being adopted by the faculties in the classroom to engage with the questions of power dynamics, social and cultural conditioning, distribution of resources that shape PEG. The outcome of this chapter is a deeper understanding of how pedagogy functions as both a site of resistance and possibilities, offering pathways to reimagine PEG in Indian HEI while presenting critical perspectives on the relevant policy framework.

Keywords Political economy · Gender · Sustainability · Intersectionality · Social capital · Cultural capital · Caste · Higher Education · HEIs · Pedagogy

N. Nair (✉) · S. Narang
O.P. Jindal Global University, Sonipat, India
e-mail: nnair@jgu.edu.in

S. Narang
e-mail: snarang@jgu.edu.in

H. Adam and F. A. Malik (eds.), *The Political Economy of Gender*,
https://doi.org/10.1007/978-981-92-2785-3_10

1 Introduction

Historically, the concept of political economy seemed indifferent to the way gender operated. Their presence or contribution didn't alter the assumptions of the political economy on how gendered division of labour operated, which was considered a given universal truth rather than a historically constructed structure (O'Connor, 2016). Over the years a nuanced and intersectional understanding of the political economy has emerged which moves beyond the binaries of cultural and economic system also referred to as the 'new political economy' (Anthias, 2013). This understanding of Political Economy of Gender (PEG) recognises the way gender, class, race, religion, and in the Indian context, caste operated in different ways to pave a complex intersectional framework. This framework is unique to its socio-cultural context. Hence, PEG establishes that economic forces are embedded in social, cultural, and political conditions which affect all genders (Anthias, 2013).

In the South-Asian context, women's participation in the workforce is highly determined by social and cultural realities. Women continue to shoulder lion's share of unpaid household work, and their jobs are considered supplemental income. In the context of PEG, two important aspects where HEIs can exercise significant influence besides working towards transferable skills are cultural capital, and social capital both individual (Pierre Bourdieu, 1986) and collective (Robert D. Putnam, 1994) which can be tremendously shaped by the HEIs over a period of time by engaging with the ideas of class/caste relations, and how these realities influence access to resources and opportunities to grow. In this background, the chapter answers how these courses engage with intersectionality embedded in the operation of PEG? What has been the experience of faculty members who are teaching these courses, in terms of pedagogy & practice? Most importantly, how are students responding to the course curriculum?

2 Literature Review

2.1 The Role of Higher Education Institutions in Shaping the Political Economy

HEIs are increasingly recognized as central players in shaping not only knowledge systems but also the political economy of nations. They function as ideological and cultural apparatuses, simultaneously reproducing dominant social hierarchies and opening spaces for contestation and transformation (Connell, 2022; Marginson, 2022). Within the Global South, and particularly in India, HEIs operate in a layered terrain shaped by postcolonial state-building projects, neoliberal reforms, and subaltern struggles for epistemic and material justice (Ahmed, 2012; Ghosh & Menon, 2018; Naidu, 2023). This complex environment makes the PEG central to understanding how higher education reflects, negotiates, and reshapes power relations.

2.2 HEIs as Ideological and Neoliberal Apparatuses

Drawing from Althusser's (1971) notion of ideological state apparatuses, universities normalize hierarchies of caste, gender and capital. In the Indian context, these must be understood through postcolonial lenses that foreground intersecting structures of caste, religion, and colonial legacies (Rege, 2003; Guru, 2011; Paik, 2025). Neoliberal reforms viz. metrics-driven funding, privatization, global rankings, have reshaped HEIs into what Gill (2009) terms the "neoliberal university," privileging employability over critical knowledge (Burton et al., 2015; Hall, 2020; Kadmos & Taylor, 2024; Musselin, 2021). These logics marginalize disciplines like gender studies, often considered "non-productive" or "non-essential" academic labor (Menon, 2020). Academic precarity, especially among women and marginalized faculty, compounds these inequities (Burton et al., 2015; Pereira et al., 2016).

2.3 Global Frameworks, National Policy Gaps and Gender

HEIs are expected to advance sustainability and equality agendas through the United Nations' SDGs, particularly SDG 4 (Quality Education) and SDG 5 (Gender Equality) (UNESCO, 2017; United Nations, 2023; UNESCO GEM, 2024). However, operationalizing these goals in Global South contexts faces persistent barriers (Mok & Neubauer, 2021; Leal Filho et al., 2019). In India, while female enrollment has improved significantly with a Gender Parity Index (GPI) above 1 since 2017–18 (AISHE, 2022; MOSPI, 2023), structural inequities remain. The National Education Policy (NEP) 2020 promotes interdisciplinarity, equity, and value-based education (Government of India, 2020), yet scholars critique its depoliticised approach that overlooks caste, sexuality, and exclusion (EPW, 2022; Kumar, 2020; Nair, 2020). Institutional requirements like the UGC's POSH Regulations (2015) and the Transgender Persons (Protection of Rights) Act (2019) show promise, but implementation remains fragmented (Rangarajan, 2025).

2.4 Feminist Pedagogy and Epistemic Justice

Feminist and decolonial scholars challenge the dominance of Eurocentric feminist theory in pedagogy, advocating for "epistemologies of the South" (Connell, 2022; Madhok, 2021; Santos, 2014). In India, Brahmanical epistemes continue to exclude Dalit and marginalized perspectives (Guru, 2002; Rege, 2013; Paik, 2025). Recent literature underscores the moral and pedagogical responsibility of faculty to move beyond tokenistic intersectionality toward historically conscious, relational, and epistemically just practices (Ahmed, 2012; Chakravarty, 2023; Nanda, 2016), even while confronting institutional "diversity fatigue" and representational burdens (Ahmed, 2012).

2.5 *Intersectionality and the Classroom*

Intersectionality first formulated by Crenshaw (1991) must be re-grounded in India to address caste's foundational oppression along with class, religion, region, and sexuality (Guru & Sarukkai, 2019; Paik, 2014; Rege, 1998). Contemporary research insists that intersectionality must be embedded in classroom praxis, not treated as a thematic add-on (Kamal, 2024). Faculty commonly confront student defensiveness, institutional invisibility, and emotional economies shaped by upper-caste fragility and administrative silences (Ahmed, 2012; Subramaniam, 2020), illustrating systemic barriers in HEIs for feminist pedagogy (Khanna & Mukherjee, 2024).

2.6 *Emerging Pedagogical Innovations*

Despite these challenges, educators are creatively reimagining the classroom. Dalit feminist pedagogies leverage oral narratives and testimonial forms to reclaim marginalized voices (Paik, 2022). Queer pedagogies disrupt binary norms of gender and sexuality (Campbell & Taylor, 2024; Shlasko, 2005), while vernacular rights cultures (Madhok, 2021) ground gender-justice pedagogy in lived, local experience rather than universalist frameworks. These approaches reconfigure classrooms into dialogic and affective political spaces (Ahmed, 2012; Deshpande, 2019; Hooks, 1994). However, scholars caution that without structural shifts such as inclusive staffing, co-created curricula, and pluralistic governance, these innovations remain precarious (Kapur, 2022).

Current literature consistently highlights three major issues: (1) Impact of neoliberal institutional structures on gender pedagogy, and academic autonomy is under explored; (2) There is a gap between intersectional theory and classroom praxis; and (3) insufficient institutional reform to address intersectional marginalization. Empirical research that systematically examines how Indian faculty navigate these issues in teaching is scant. Moreover, classroom narratives are seldom integrated into wider arguments about epistemic justice, neoliberalism, and the SDGs.

As we transition to the next section of this chapter, these theoretical and narrative insights inform our understanding of how classroom praxis intersect with broader institutional structures and disciplinary frameworks. Through fieldwork with faculty members across diverse HEIs, we aim to explore how these tensions between structure and agency, theory and experience, resistance and compliance, manifest within the everyday practices of teaching and doing gender in India.

In the context of lack of sustained analysis of how gender is negotiated and contested within the everyday pedagogical practices in the context of PEG, this chapter becomes important because it looks at courses that are being offered on PEG currently and presents narratives of pedagogy & practice mapping student response and resistance.

3 Objective of the Study

1. To understand and analyse the perspective of pedagogue and their pedagogy of PEG.
2. The way it is being shaped in the classroom; visible in the responses, resistance and change in the perspectives of students.

4 Research Methodology & Methods

This study employed a qualitative research design using in-depth, semi-structured interviews to explore lived experiences and perspectives of educators offering courses on Gender in State, private and central HEIs. Purposive sampling was used to identify 20 academicians between the ages of 28 to 42 teaching interdisciplinary courses focused on gender and intersectionalities to students of sociology, journalism, economics, literature, law and political sciences courses. The term gender explicitly appeared in their course titles. An indicative list of the stated course objectives offered by the faculty participants is given (Table 1):

Table 1 Course objectives of the gender related courses

S. No	Stated objectives of the courses offered by participants of the study
1	Developing a critical understanding of how gender is constructed, lived, and contested within the specific historical, social, and political realities of India
2	Examining gender through its intersection with caste, class, sexuality, and other social hierarchies. This also included nationality and religion
3	Interrogating all gender categories, not just women and norms of masculinity and femininity—both through institutional structures and everyday practices
4	Gendered inequalities in care. In both national and international contexts
5	Norms and habits which govern human behavior, access to resources and opportunities and the construction of social identity

Source Prepared by the authors to indicate the courses being offered by the HEIs that focused on gender and intersectionality

The interviews were conducted in-person and through a video-conferencing platform, audio-recorded with prior consent, and transcribed verbatim. Each interview lasted between 60–90 minutes. Authors mapped how gender as both a structural and relational category shapes classroom interactions, pedagogical approaches and educator subjectivities. Data were analyzed using Braun and Clarke's thematic analysis approach, a widely used and flexible method suitable for capturing patterns of meaning across qualitative datasets (Braun & Clarke, 2006). The analysis followed their six-phase process: (1) familiarization with the data, (2) generating initial codes, (3) searching for themes, (4) reviewing themes, (5) defining and naming themes, and (6) producing the report. A reflexive approach was maintained throughout with authors critically reflecting on their positionality and potential biases, particularly in relation to educational values and assumptions.

The interview questions were designed to probe the theoretical underpinnings, pedagogical strategies and in-class experiences of educators. Some of questions posed by the authors included:

1. How do you engage with and understand the concept of PEG? What has been your experience of teaching the course?
2. How do students respond to the course? What kind of challenges/resistance/transformations/changes, if any, have you experienced while teaching/offering the course?

The study identifies three broad thematic issues: (1) Conceptualisation of PEG (2) students' responses to gender-focused pedagogy, including instances of resistance and change; (3) pedagogical practices and faculty experience. These themes and their subthemes are explored not through a binary lens of compliance or resistance but as embedded within a broader continuum of discomfort and contestation that characterizes gender discourse in academic spaces. The analytical orientation is thus attentive to both the micro-politics of classroom interaction and the broader sociocultural matrices within which Indian HEIs are embedded.

5 Results and Discussion: Thematic Analysis

This section will present a comprehensive account of the experiences from faculty members from HEIs and emancipate the discussion on the role of pedagogy and pedagogue in shaping the different connotations of PEG. The interviews reveal that faculty are not only shaped by PEG but also actively respond to it through their teaching practices. Many described how caste, gender and class hierarchies are reproduced in the classroom, echoing Althusser's (1971) idea of education as an ideological state apparatus. At the same time, they highlighted the unequal burden placed on certain pedagogues, especially women and those from marginalized backgrounds, to address issues of diversity and justice. Pedagogy thus becomes a key site where structural pressures like casualisation, employability metrics, and "diversity fatigue" (Gill, 2009; Pereira et al., 2016) are directly experienced and negotiated.

Yet, the narratives also show how pedagogues witness the classroom as spaces of resistance. Faculty members who integrate oral histories, vernacular materials, or queer perspectives exemplify Santos' (2014, 2018) "epistemologies of the South," challenging dominant canons and opening new ways of teaching. Such practices embody Hooks' (1994) idea of the classroom as a space of "emancipatory possibility," even when student resistance limit their reach. By centering the role of pedagogy, these accounts show that HEIs and the classrooms witness faculty members as active agents who both navigate and reshape the structures of inequities.

The following themes emerged post transcription and immersive engagement with the data collected:

5.1 Conceptualisations of PEG

5.1.1 Nexus of Personal, Political, Public in Gendered Economy

During the interview, faculty members were asked to share their understanding of the PEG and how does their course intersect with it. Respondents looked at PEG from the private space (home), and the way it influences gender positioning in public space, to the extent of feminising certain sectors in terms of labour market, reinforcing gendered distribution of work and vice-versa.

One respondent traced the idea of PEG through everyday lived experience of individuals, including non-heterosexual people and their systematic exclusion.

They have to work with the systems that are set not accounting for them, captured in the narrative account:

> Just walking down, the street to buy vegetables ... is not very easy. I don't know how people will judge me. The shopkeeper will be very rude to me, and he'll say *Ki Madam aapko lena hai to lelo nahi to niklo yahan se (Madam, if want to buy then buy the vegetables or leave).* You don't know how they'll respond. Which is sometimes very unsettling for many of us.

Adding further,

> Public spaces are not very well designed for women, queers, non-gender affirming individuals. It's defined from the lens of heterosexual male gaze. What can we do as citizens and what can institutions do to ensure that anyone who's not male, who's not upper caste, not heterosexual, is treated equally as citizens, reclaiming the public spaces?

Bringing such nuanced perspective to classroom helps learners appreciate the subtilities in which gender operates and reinforces social hierarchies in spaces that should be accessible to all. Another faculty member offering a course on feminist economy located the meaning of PEG in societal norms and the way in the context of development, gender impacts households and society at large:

> I look at the PEG, the context in which it is situated, the society and its specific norms, whether it's about gender or caste or any of its historical context that has evolved...that is actually the PEG. Something that recognizes the intersections between these different

> positions and then speaks to the notions of divisions between resources, rights, opportunities to grow. How is it that gender shapes into something from the development of people in our household but also within the larger community and society?

In context of care work and economy, PEG was understood as restricting women to private spaces to do free labour:

> PEG as a mode of production, where women are at home, they are producing unpaid care work, which is then freeing up men to perform more highly valorized tasks. But why do women end up in these positions? So that's colonization, "housewifeization", kicking women out of more public occupations, pushing them into private occupations, re-enforcing violent ways of primitive accumulation."

The narrative amplifies the feminisation of certain types of work, which can also be traced back to academia itself. They are also indicative of how positionality bias should be brought in the classroom.

A senior faculty while conceptualising PEG mentioned,

> How politics and economics both inform gender. Or perhaps it could be also the other way around, how perhaps gender informs politics and economics. So, for example how gig economy is becoming feminised, particularly in the context of India, and how feminized understanding of job roles impact the structure of labour norms or the way government looks at it.

These narratives are indicative of how understanding of PEG is based on positionality of the faculty and their disciplinary expertise, which informs the epistemology of developing the social and cultural capital in the higher education sphere.

5.2 *Experience of Teaching the Course and Student Response*

5.2.1 Making the Course Relevant

The faculty members are keenly aware of the power dynamics embedded in the classroom between faculty and students. They are mindful of the unease the subjects may cause among learners, greater sensitivity is exercised while engaging with the subject. There is an attempt to establish a sense of safety within the classroom to encourage students to voice their thoughts even if it is unpopular. Students are encouraged to back their ideas by research.

> As professors, we have to ensure that this course makes sense to the students as well, and for that we have to keep revisiting the course. Making sure that it's up to date with the lived realities of the present day, the nuances, because today with digital worlds, social media, and all the discussions on range of topics, including Andrew Tate or the idea of misogyny, the idea of alimony. All of these discussions are rampant all across social media. Issues we thought that we were past. But then it is still being discussed. All of them are brought to the classroom.

The narratives indicate unconscious and conscious biases of student. While they are open to discussing and engaging with views on gender in its various intersectionalities, they are resistant to recognizing the way oppression operates, believing in narratives of reverse oppression and misandry.

Respondents highlighted that most students who take these courses unless offered as compulsory courses are female students. In one instance when the course was offered as an optional course, 30% male students enrolled, but the class size was relatively small and the male students assumed that since the course is also focussed on developmental economics and looks at gender in the context of economics, there would be more data analysis component.

> I've been teaching this course for almost three years, and I have had a quite range of students in my class from different courses. Many students are interested and have engaged with the nuances of the course. Students have a lot of strong opinions. So, I tell my students that you need to clear your mind of any prejudices, make sure that you're respectful to everybody. If you find anything too sensitive, you can always tell me that I'm feeling uncomfortable.

5.2.2 Challenges: Questioning Relevance of Learning About Gender

Faculty members also reported that while majority of students are appreciative of the course and learning, some students also question the relevance of learning about Gender related issues, highlighting gender fatigue:

> There are some students who ask why we are learning about these things? It's difficult to teach or convince students who are not very receptive. And that is the challenge. But then I've accepted that as a part of the teaching journey. You do your best, teaching them the nuances of concepts. They also influence each other, and they discuss and learn from each other.

In some instances, the male students felt attacked and questioned the neutrality of discussion, if men are held accountable for historical wrongs perpetrated on women and other genders. At the same time, female students, particularly felt validated that their concerns or experiences are being voiced and they can see the interconnectedness of their individual experiences, which is also shared experiences with larger social realities and how it affects their position in domestic and employment space:

> There is another segment of the class who, I think, because the patriarchal structure or the dominant structure suits them and challenging their own position to an uncomfortable spot at all times is unsettling for them. Also, because these are undergraduate students. So, there is resistance to saying why this is problematic? Why is this my fault? Why do I have to study this when it doesn't relate to me? So, the first barrier that we need to break in this class is that it's not about women. At times, there is some backlash from male students. Because they feel that they are being attacked by all of this...one has to be careful in making sure that all participants in the class are comfortable.

As extension on the discussion of gender fatigue takes us to the larger discussion on the idea of gender while addressing the connotations of PEG. It was found that male students were supportive of the idea of contributing to domestic work and paternity leave if it did not hamper their ability to gain employment and grow, the way women have been affected historically.

5.2.3 Resistance Around Intersections of Religion and Caste with Gender

Resistance was also experienced on the question of caste and religion. As the narrative indicates:

> Once we were discussing sexualities and a student said that my religion does not allow me to talk about such things, especially with women, so I'm not going to be in your class and they left.

Another instance when caste and gender was being discussed, a faculty reported,

> At times when we give examples from films on how caste complicates PEG and share experiences from daily life with students, they also question, why should I believe that? When I ask them if they have different utensils for domestic workers? And they respond, no, (and defend) but that's because my brother also has a different plate than I do because my brother breaks things. They could also break things. That's why these plates are different. So sometimes there is a challenge because we're trying to ask them to introspect in terms of how they've lived their life, how their homes could be a site of discrimination of any kind, maybe gendered, maybe based on caste.

The narrative demonstrates how unconscious bias is reinforced, visible in the rejection of suggestion that students' home could be a site of discrimination as it difficult for them to accept how caste operates in their immediate social setting. Considering most of them are from urban areas in which the subtilities of caste oppression makes them invisible and are often hidden behind the ideas of purity and pollution (hygiene) which they are unable to otherwise distinguish.

5.2.4 Ideological Resistance and Change in Perspective

Some faculty members shared stories of ideological resistance and change, where towards the end of the course the student was able to consider and appreciate the Dalit feminist perspective:

> By senior years students have already been instructed in certain ways of thinking. They have gone in their own directions, found their own spots within ideological spectrums. I do not demand from my students that there was one way in which they should critique. I introduced them to the 'capabilities approach', coming from the human development approach of Amartya Sen.
>
> During the course, students were required to develop essays through workshops & seminars. A student was looking at the NEP 2020 and since they were coming from the Marxist perspective of political economy, they were convinced that education is merely approved by the ruling class to subjugate the working class. It was clear that the student had not considered the idea of individual agency and the transformation that lies within the educational experience because of the dominance of Marxist structure in their thinking. So, in the student's interpretation of NEP, the policy reinforced solidarity with capitalist system of education that only reproduces inequality. I felt it was a bit mechanical as the student was not considering that education is not only instrumental and have a latent intrinsic value which sparks autonomous thinking. Therefore, it forces people to, despite their social locations, position, gender and other disadvantages, to question the system and aspire for upliftment.

> In the end the student added a Dalit feminist perspective to the existing Marxist approach in analysing NEP 2020.

5.2.5 Innovative Pedagogy

In terms of pedagogy some innovative pedagogical practices came to light during the interviews. In one of the courses;

> Instead of writing a reflective paper, students wrote a play to engage with certain concepts like desire, caste, queerness and show the intricacies of lived experiences. I was amazed by the nuances that they showed in the play and it was great to see that their classmates also came in considerable numbers despite the fact that it was staged after the class hours.

Another example was a project of gender performativity called "Gender in Action" where students were asked to observe the reaction of those around them; Peer-group, teachers, parents if they break the gender norms. For example, both male and female students applying nail polish or lip color. Students were asked to observe the responses or reactions and bring that understanding to their project while supplementing them with research.

5.2.6 Faculty's Experience

While discussing their own experiences as faculty and researchers working in the field of gender, the respondents shared that some of their colleagues do not consider gender to be an important area of engagement and often nudge them to engage with core-disciplinary areas in teaching & research. All respondents shared that they try to be assertive while navigating the dichotomies of equality that they profess in class and the wisdom they must exercise while dealing with normative challenges and complex biases of daily life.

Some of the key-take aways from the faculty interviews were the way these courses were encouraging students to think about their own lives and experiences from intersectional lens while being reflective of the biases and status-quos that they considered universal.

Even though faculty members approached these discussions from their epistemological and experiential standpoints to help students understand, question and reimagine gender norms in their personal and professional lives. These attempts garnered both acceptance and resistance from the students.

While there were stories of change in perspective and greater consideration, there were also experiences of continued discomfort, and absolute rejection evident in silent disengagement in some cases. Nonetheless, the participants emphasised upon the need to offer more of such courses in HEIs. Participants opined gender should be embedded in courses across disciplines. This should be further supplemented by specialised gender focussed programmes. For this a robust policy framework must be implemented across HEIs. The study also revealed that the faculty are not connecting their gender pedagogy to any of SDGs directly. It is to be noted that in some cases the

HEIs are trying to align with SDGs yet faculty has not considered it, though in the context of PEG they are already discussing intersectionalities and sectoral overlap and related impact which can be traced to SDGs.

One of the most persistent normative challenges in Indian HEIs is the entrenchment of patriarchal values, moral conservatism, and institutional silence to disrupt dominant social hierarchies. Discussions on gender, sexuality and autonomy continue to face ideological and cultural resistance, often framed as violations of Indian cultural values or as unnecessary politicization of the classroom (Subramaniam, 2020). Gender studies is frequently viewed as a subversive or non-essential academic field, leading to its symbolic inclusion without substantive institutional commitment. This is evident in the fact that only 64 HEIs out of a total of 70,018 HEIs in India are offering courses and programmes related to gender and women studies (PIB, 2025).

6 Policy Implications

6.1 Normative Constraints: Culture, Morality, Policy and Silence

This resistance is not only cultural but increasingly shaped by the regulatory and policy landscape, particularly in light of the NEP 2020. While the NEP articulates a vision of inclusion and equity, its practical implementation reveals significant normative tensions. The policy largely approaches gender through a technocratic and instrumentalist lens, framing inclusion in terms of access, enrolment, and skill development, while eschewing deeper engagement with structural inequalities related to caste, religion, and gendered forms of knowledge production.

Notably, the NEP fosters a tokenistic approach as it articulates a vague commitment to "gender-inclusivity" and "respect for diversity". Albeit, a vision document it lacks a clear outline for curricular mandates or institutional mechanisms to critically engage students with feminist theory, queer politics, or caste-gender intersectionality.

Furthermore, the regulatory shift towards centralized accreditation and homogenized curriculum under bodies such as the University Grants Commission (UGC), the National Assessment and Accreditation Council (NAAC) presents additional barriers. These mechanisms prioritize quantifiable metrics, employability outcomes, and institutional rankings, while sidelining critical pedagogy, deliberative learning, and reflective inquiry hallmarks of gender-conscious education. The increasing reliance on digital and online learning formats, promoted under the rubric of "flexibility" and "access," risks eroding the dialogic and experiential nature of gender pedagogy, which relies heavily on classroom conversations and the safe space model of teaching.

Additionally, gender sensitization workshops are frequently bureaucratized as checkbox activities, stripped of political content, and administered through HR cells rather than academic departments. As a result, gender is taught not as a lens of structural analysis, but as a matter of behavior, etiquette or sexual harassment compliance. This diminishes the transformative potential of gender pedagogy and recasts it within a disciplinary rather than emancipatory paradigm.

6.2 Structural Challenges: Institutional Hierarchies and Curricular Marginalisation

On a structural level, departments focused on gender studies are often underfunded, insufficiently staffed, or institutionally marginalized. They are perceived as lacking rigour compared to other disciplines, thereby diminishing their academic legitimacy. Gender-focused courses are typically offered as electives rather than core curriculum components, reinforcing the impression that gender is a niche concern rather than a central analytic lens through which broader societal processes must be understood (Patil, 2011). In the current study also, the faculty members shared similar experiences of marginalisation.

7 Conclusion and Recommendation

In conclusion, this chapter identifies classrooms as a complex and contested space that governs the notions of PEG. PEG based on the narratives is conceptualized in the 'personal' spaces which further shapes how gender operates in 'public' spaces. While the curricula of most gender-focused courses attempts to integrate contemporary connotations of gender, pedagogy is affected by conscious and unconscious biases. Faculty experiences reveal that narratives of resistance in the classroom discussion is a complex terrain for further scrutiny by their own gender identity (females) and that of students, where majority are females unless the course being offered is a compulsory credit course. Student responses are marked by ambivalence ranging from defensiveness, discomfort and resistance when confronted with privilege to transformative moments of critical engagement, recognition, and acceptance. Taken together, these findings underscore that pedagogy is not simply about transmitting content but about negotiating power, resistance, and possibility within the classroom.

Most faculty members teaching gender related courses are not consciously treating gender or related discussions as SDG, thus, adopting an SDG framework in the teaching gender would help in embedding it across disciplines with greater acceptance. This will also help in anchoring gender from the periphery to the center of the conversation, given HEIs are keen on incorporating SDGs in their institutional framework. This reimagining is not just about reforming content but reshaping the ethics, impact, and purpose of pedagogy itself in the formulation of the PEG.

Reimagining gender pedagogy requires recognizing and valuing the everyday pedagogical strategies that faculty already employ; practices that are grounded in thoughtfulness, critical reflexivity, and a commitment to gender-conscious higher education. Their narratives point to the need for institutional structures that are responsive to feminist ethics of teaching and allow space for dissent, vulnerability, and experimentation. Rather than isolating gender as a thematic optional course, the faculty envision it as central to broader questions of power, knowledge, and justice across disciplines. Their reflections call for a structural rethinking of how universities understand academic legitimacy and success, moving beyond output-based metrics towards cultivating classrooms that are sites of transformation.

While the courses foreground critical feminist thought, intersectionality, and engagement with Global South perspectives, faculty also spoke of challenges such as regulatory uncertainty, over-bureaucratization, limited curricular autonomy in some instances and the undervaluation of gender-conscious teaching practices. Moreover, policies that prioritize fragmented reforms without tackling entrenched structural inequalities risk reinforcing the very exclusions they claim to address, leaving the responsibility of change disproportionately on the classroom and the pedagogue. Despite these barriers, their pedagogical labor affirms a deep investment in creating intellectually and emotionally generative classroom spaces. The authors would like to call it the "pedagogy of hope".

References

Ahmed, S. (2012). *On being included: Racism and diversity in institutional life*. Duke University Press.

Althusser, L. (1971). Ideology and ideological state apparatuses. In *Lenin and philosophy and other essays* (pp. 127–186). Monthly Review Press.

Anthias, F. (2013). Intersectional what? Social divisions, intersectionality and levels of analysis. *Ethnicities, 13*(1), 3–19. https://doi.org/10.1177/1468796812463547

Azam, M., & Bhatt, V. (2015). Like father, like son? Intergenerational Educational Mobility in India. *Demography, 52*(6), 1929–1959. https://doi.org/10.1007/s13524-015-0428-8

Bourdieu, P. (1986). The forms of capital. In J. G. Richardson (Ed.), *Handbook of theory and research for the sociology of education* (pp. 241–258). Greenwood Press.

Bourdieu, P. (1996). *The state nobility: Elite schools in the field of power* (L. C. Clough, Trans.). Stanford University Press.

Braun, V., & Clarke, V. (2006). Using thematic analysis in psychology. *Qualitative Research in Psychology, 3*(2), 77–101.

Burton, L. J., Summers, J., Lawrence, J., Noble, K., & Gibbings, P. (2015). Digital literacy in higher education: The rhetoric and the reality. In M. K. Harmes, H. Huijser, & P. A. Danaher (Eds.), *Myths in education, learning and teaching* (pp. 151–165). Palgrave Macmillan. https://doi.org/10.1057/9781137476982_9

Campbell, C.P., Taylor, C.G. (2024). Queer-Expansive Education. In *The Palgrave Encyclopedia of Sexuality Education*. Palgrave Macmillan, Cham. https://doi.org/10.1007/978-3-030-95352-2_40-1

Connell, R. (2007). *Southern theory: The global dynamics of knowledge in social science*. Polity Press.

Connell, R. (2022). *The good university: What universities actually do and why it's time for radical change* (1st ed.). Bloomsbury Academic.
Collins, P. H. (2000). *Black feminist thought: Knowledge, consciousness, and the politics of empowerment* (2nd ed.). Routledge.
Crenshaw, K. (1989). Demarginalizing the intersection of race and sex: A Black feminist critique of antidiscrimination doctrine, feminist theory and antiracist politics. *University of Chicago Legal Forum, 1989*(1), 139–167. https://chicagounbound.uchicago.edu/uclf/vol1989/iss1/8/
Crenshaw, K. (1991). Mapping the margins: Intersectionality, identity politics, and violence against women of color. *Stanford Law Review, 43*(6), 1241–1299.
Delhi University. (2022). *Annual report 2021–22*. University of Delhi.
Freire, P. (1970). Pedagogy of the oppressed. Herder and Herder.
Gill, R. (2009). Breaking the silence: The hidden injuries of neo-liberal academia. In R. Flood & R. Gill (Eds.), Secrecy and silence in the research process: Feminist reflections (pp. 228–244). Routledge.
Gill, R., & Donaghue, N. (2016). Resilience, apps and reluctant individualism: Technologies of self in the neoliberal academy. *Women's Studies International Forum, 54*, 91–99.
Global Education Monitoring Report Team. (2024). Global education monitoring report 2024/5: Leadership in education—Lead for learning. UNESCO.
Guru, G. (2002). How egalitarian are the social sciences in India? *Economic and Political Weekly, 37*(50), 5003–5009.
Guru, G. (2011). The idea of India: Derivative, desi and beyond. *Economic and Political Weekly, 46*(1–2), 36–42.
Guru, G., & Sarukkai, S. (2019). Introduction. In *Experience, caste, and the everyday social* (pp. 1–16). Oxford University Press. https://doi.org/10.1093/oso/9780199496051.003.0001
Haraway, D. (1988). Situated knowledges: The science question in feminism and the privilege of partial perspective. *Feminist Studies, 14*(3), 575–599.
Hartigan-O'Connor, E. (2016). The personal is political economy. *Journal of the Early Republic, 36*(2), 335–341. https://doi.org/10.2307/jearlyrepublic.36.2.335
Hooks, b. (1994). *Teaching to transgress: Education as the practice of freedom*. Routledge.
Iversen, T., & Rosenbluth, F. (2006). The political economy of gender: Explaining cross-national variation in the gender division of labor and the gender voting gap. *American Journal of Political Science, 50*(1), 1–19. https://www.jstor.org/stable/3694253
Jacobs, S., & Klesse, C. (2014). Introduction: Special issue on gender, sexuality and political economy. *International Journal of Politics, Culture, and Society, 27*(2), 129–152. https://www.jstor.org/stable/24713309
Jansen, J. D. (2009). *Knowledge in the blood: Confronting race and the apartheid past*. Stanford University Press.
John, M. E. (2008). Feminism, Poverty and the emergent social order in the global south. *Feminist Studies, 34*(3), 572–578.
Kadmos, H., & Taylor, J. (2024). No time to read? How precarity is shaping learning and teaching in the humanities. *Arts and Humanities in Higher Education, 23*(1). https://doi.org/10.1177/14740222231190338
Kamal, U., & Roluahpuia. (2024). Educational inequality and household dynamics in India: Exploring the role of caste capital. *Journal of South Asian Development, 20*(1), 117–138.
Khanna, G., & Mukherjee, M. (2024). Intersectionality and women academics in Indian higher education. *Journal of Underrepresented & Minority Progress, 8*(SI(1)). https://www.ojed.org/jump/article/view/5918
Kumar, K. (2020). Public university in India: Crisis and response. *Social Scientist, 48*(5–6), 1–10.
Madhok, S. (2021). *Vernacular rights cultures: The politics of origins, human rights, and gendered struggles for justice*. Cambridge University Press.
Magazine, A. (2024, November 3). *'More than half of Indian women remain outside labour force due to care duties': International Labour Organization report. The*

Indian Express. https://indianexpress.com/article/business/indian-women-remain-outside-labour-force-international-labour-organization-report-9650392/
Marginson, S. (2022). Research on international and global higher education: Six different perspectives. *Oxford Review of Education, 48*(4), 421–438. https://doi.org/10.1080/03054985.2022.2087619
McHugh, M. C. (2020). Feminist qualitative research: Working toward transforming science and social justice. In P. Leavy (Ed.), *The Oxford handbook of qualitative research* (2nd ed., pp. 200–242). Oxford University Press. https://doi.org/10.1093/oxfordhb/9780190847388.013.16
Menon, N. (2020). Is gender studies obsolete? *EPW Engage, 55*(5), 9–13.
Ministry of Education, Department of Higher Education. (2024). All India Survey on Higher Education (AISHE) 2021–22: Final report. *Government of India*. https://aishe.gov.in/aishe-final-report/
Ministry of Labour and Employment, Government of India. (2025, January 31). *Labour market indicators show substantial improvement in last few years: Economic Survey 2024–25* [Press release]. https://labour.gov.in/sites/default/files/pib2097939.pdf
Ministry of Statistics and Programme Implementation. (2023, December 18). Year end review 2023: Ministry of Statistics and Programme Implementation. Press Information Bureau, Government of India. https://pib.gov.in/PressReleasePage.aspx?PRID=1986994
Musselin, C. (2021). University governance in meso and macro perspective. *Annual Review of Sociology, 47*, 305–345. https://hal.archives-ouvertes.fr/hal-03367341/document
Nagar, R. (2014). *Muddying the waters: Coauthoring feminisms across scholarship and activism.* University of Illinois Press.
Naidu, R. (2023). Postcolonial higher education and epistemic struggles in India. *Higher Education Quarterly, 77*(3), 534–552.
Nair, S. (2020). Feminism and the university: From invisible labor to epistemic justice. *EPW, 55*(50), 17–22.
Nanda, M. (2016). *Science in saffron: Skeptical essays on the history of science.* Three Essays Collective.
Narayan, U. (1997). *Dislocating cultures: Identities, traditions, and third world feminism.* Routledge.
Paik, S. (2014). *Dalit women's education in modern India: Double discrimination.* Routledge.
Paik, S. (2025). Dalit womanism-humanism: Against caste and gender hierarchies. In *The Routledge handbook of subalterns across history* (pp. 252–260). Routledge.
Patil, S. M. (2023). Raving with equality? On protean forms of caste and gender in the women's/gender studies departments in India. *CASTE: A Global Journal on Social Exclusion, 4*(2), 383–402. https://doi.org/10.26812/caste.v4i2.675
Pereira, D., Flores, M. A., & Niklasson, L. (2016). Assessment revisited: A review of research in Assessment & Evaluation in Higher Education. *Assessment & Evaluation in Higher Education, 41*(7), 1008–1032. https://doi.org/10.1080/02602938.2015.1055233
Press Information Bureau. (2024, November 18). *Enhanced female workforce participation in economic activity: Data shows improved employment indicators over last six years [Press release].* Ministry of Labour & Employment. https://www.pib.gov.in/PressReleasePage.aspx?PRID=2074399
Priya, L. (2020, July 25). How does the National Education Policy accelerate the privatisation of higher education? *Economic and Political Weekly, 55*(30). https://www.epw.in/engage/article/education-policy-2020-privatisationhigher-education
Putnam, R. D. (1994). Social capital and public affairs. *Bulletin of the American Academy of Arts and Sciences, 47*(8), 5–19. https://doi.org/10.2307/3824796
Rangarajan, R. (2025). Relational pedagogy for inclusion in (in)action: Exploring relational encounters in teaching and learning at a rural small school in India. *International Journal of Educational Research, 132*, Article 102620. https://doi.org/10.1016/j.ijer.2025.102620
Rege, S. (1998). Dalit women talk differently: A critique of 'difference' and towards a Dalit feminist standpoint position. *EPW, 33*(44), WS39–WS46.

Rege, S. (2003). *Sociology of gender: The challenge of feminist sociological knowledge.* SAGE.
Santos, B. de S. (2014). *Epistemologies of the South: Justice against epistemicide.* Routledge.
Shlasko, G. D. (2005). Queer (v.) pedagogy. *Equity & Excellence in Education, 38*(2), 123–134. https://doi.org/10.1080/10665680590935098
Spivak, G. C. (1988). Can the subaltern speak? In C. Nelson & L. Grossberg (Eds.), *Marxism and the interpretation of culture* (pp. 271–313). University of Illinois Press.
Subramaniam, M. (2020). *Holy science: The biopolitics of Hindu nationalism.* University of Washington Press.
UNESCO. (2017). Education for Sustainable Development Goals: Learning Objectives. UNESCO. https://doi.org/10.54675/CGBA9153
United Nations. (2023). The Sustainable Development Goals report 2023: Special edition—Towards a rescue plan for people and planet. United Nations. https://unstats.un.org/sdgs/report/2023/
UN Women. (2024, September 16). *UN report urges immediate global action to close critical gender gaps: Investing in women and girls and ending discrimination are key to fulfilling the promise of the 2030 Agenda for Sustainable Development.* https://www.unwomen.org/en/news-stories/press-release/2024/09/un-report-urges-immediate-global-action-to-close-critical-gender-gaps
Wagh, A. C., & Rayaprol, A. (2023). Marginality and Gender in Educational Institutions in Contemporary India. *Sociological Bulletin, 72*(4), 367–374. https://doi.org/10.1177/00380229231196444

Prof. (Dr.) Nisha Nair is currently a Professor at Jindal Global Law School (JGLS) and Vice Dean at the Office of Admissions and Outreach, O.P Jindal Global University. She is a Fellow at the International Institute for Higher Education Research and Capacity Building (IIHEd) at O.P. Jindal Global University (JGU). Her research work explores education policy, quality and strategies to enhance educational outcome in tertiary education. Prof. Nair has been a key contributor and co-author of the State Higher Education Plan for Haryana under Rashtriya Ucchatar Shiksha Abhiyan and has contributed to developing the implementation plan for NEP 2020, a project undertaken by IIHEd in collaboration with the Association of Indian Universities.

Prof. Samanvi Narang is associated with Jindal Global Law School as Assistant Professor and Assistant Dean, Office of Admissions and Outreach, O.P. Jindal Global University.

Part III
Resistance, Right-Wing Populism, and Gendered Narratives

Chapter 11
The Quiet Uprising: Gender, Power, and Women's Roles in Right-Wing Populist Regimes in the Global South

Jyot Shikhar Singh and Hebatallah Adam

Abstract This chapter explores the gendered dynamics of right-wing populism (RWP) in the Global South by examining women's political agency in Indonesia and the Philippines. Beyond the crude dichotomies of co-optation and resistance, it examines how women negotiate, navigate, and occasionally reinforce the moral and patriarchal ideologies that underpin populist governments. The chapter conceptualises populism as a performative political logic that creates meaning, stages moral legitimacy, and distributes affective authority, rather than as an ideology. It does this by drawing on Ernesto Laclau's discourse theory and Saba Mahmood's idea of strategic agency. Using a comparative perspective, it demonstrates how culturally rooted roles such as mother, caregiver, or moral guardian become means for women's political participation under RWP. Although Indonesia and the Philippines have different regime styles, both situations show how women use moral scripts and affective legitimacy to increase their political visibility. The tensions at the core of populist gender politics are exposed by the chapter's argument that these forms of agency are strategically equivocal rather than emancipatory.

Keywords Right-Wing Populism · Gender · Strategic Agency · Southeast Asia · Moral Legitimacy · Populist Discourse · Feminist Politics · Indonesia · Philippines · Political Performance

1 Introduction

The global political landscape has witnessed the ascendance of right-wing populist (RWP) regimes marked by hyper-nationalism, anti-elitism, and a strong moral rhetoric that often reasserts patriarchal norms (Grewal, 2022; Love, 2020; Sauer, 2024). Whether in established democracies or transitioning polities, these regimes frequently mobilise strongly gendered national imaginaries, evoking idealised

J. S. Singh (✉) · H. Adam
Jindal School of International Affairs (JSIA), Jindal Global University (JGU), O.P, Sonipat, India
e-mail: jssingh@jgu.edu.in

H. Adam and F. A. Malik (eds.), *The Political Economy of Gender*,
https://doi.org/10.1007/978-981-92-2785-3_11

conceptions of womanhood, family, and community as emblematic pillars of national authenticity (Dietze, 2022; Heinemann & Stern, 2022; Sauer, 2020). The ideological, communicative, and institutional aspects of populism have received a lot of scholarly attention (Ádám, 2020; Aslanidis, 2015; Canovan, 2002; Chernov, 2019; Devinney & Hartwell, 2020; Rašković et al., 2024; Sengul, 2019), but little is known about how it relates to gender, especially in the Global South. Two notable blind spots have resulted from this gap in the literature. On the one hand, even though leaders such as Eva Perón in Argentina, Pia Kjaersgaard in Denmark, and Marine Le Pen in France have been instrumental in the growth and mainstreaming of RWP movements, the majority of populism studies have focused on male leadership, frequently to the exclusion of female populist figures (Eksi & Wood, 2019; Löffler et al., 2020). The way that populist language defines female leadership has also been ignored in populism studies. On the other hand, dominant definitions of populism, especially those that focus on its procedural or institutional attributes, tend to ignore the substantive and symbolic gendered elements that emerge from within populist rhetoric. The manner in which gender operates both as a discursive tool and a political identity within populist formations remains under-theorised.

A counterintuitive yet crucial paradigm for comprehending the gendered aspects of right-wing populism will assist in breaking from such oversights. This chapter looks critically at how women interact with, oppose, and strategically align themselves with RWP discourse and institutions rather than viewing them as passive victims of regressive political agendas or as anomalies within a masculinist political order. It contends that while RWP governments support traditionalist, protectionist, and patriarchal ideals, they also frequently produce conflicts and discursive fissures that women strategically navigate. The inquiry that this chapter prompts is: How do RWP governments in the Global South enable the emergence of women as influential actors within their political and cultural spheres? Based on Ernesto Laclau's discourse theory of populism and the idea of strategic agency, this chapter asserts that women function within these regimes rather than in binary opposition to them, negotiating situated, frequently ambivalent issues that enable them to take on public roles, change the discourse, and amass political capital.

Indonesia and the Philippines are the two comparative case studies that are the focus of this chapter to examine this dynamic. These are two large democracies in Southeast Asia that have pluralistic elections and have seen a recent rise or consolidation of right-wing populist leadership (Hadiz, 2018; Webb & Curato, 2019). Due to Prabowo Subianto's political return and connections to Jokowi's administration, Indonesia is exhibiting populism that is both developmentalist and moralised by religion. The Philippines is a prime illustration of how violence, affect, and spectacle come together to form a gendered dictatorship under Rodrigo Duterte's hypermasculine populism. Despite these differences, both regimes are based on symbolic femininity, affective legitimacy, and moral narratives, which give women conditional possibilities to wield power through socially acceptable positions. The chapter unfolds in the following structure. Section 2 details the literature review, which incorporates the conceptual framework, the methodological approach, and the research objectives that guide this study. The examination of Indonesian populism is discussed in Sect. 3, which also looks at the gendered dynamics and tactics used by women to negotiate visibility and agency. The findings of the examination of Philippine populism are shown in Sect. 4, with particular focus on the dynastic, performative, and hypermasculine aspects that influence women's political positions. In tandem with the research question and thesis statement, Sect. 5 offers a comparative evaluation of the two case studies, emphasising their similarities, differences, and wider theoretical implications. Section 6 concludes the chapter by summarising the main inferences and providing suggestions for activism, policy, and research.

2 Theoretical and Literature Review: The Gendered Logic of Populism

Following Ernesto Laclau, populism is a political logic that articulates diverse social demands into a single collective identity known as "the people" (Laclau, as cited in da Silva & Vieira, 2019). It is not an ideology. This unity is created through chains of equivalence, by linking various concerns under a shared hostility towards an "other," usually a corrupt elite, the establishment, or the system. In this manner, populism is defined by the discursive process that creates "the people" as a political subject in opposition to power, not by its intellectual conten (Laclau, as cited in Katsambekis, 2020). For Laclau, populism is a hegemonic technique in which meaning is stabilised by elevating empty signifiers, such as "the people," "the nation," or "sovereignty," which momentarily bring disparate political sentiments together (Laclau, as cited in Katsambekis, 2020). RWP is a particular expression of this logic, even if Laclau's theory is ideologically agnostic. It centres the chain of equivalence on nationalism, moral traditionalism, and cultural nativism.

2.1 Gender and the Historical Construction of "the People"

Populism tends to function on ambiguity (Mény & Surel, 2002). It both excludes and incorporates, demonises and valorises. This dialectic is particularly pronounced in gendered narratives, where women are simultaneously recognised as cultural icons and excluded from formal power (Caravantes & Lombardo, 2022). This tension forms the discursive terrain on which women negotiate visibility and political capital. Historically, populism and female political participation have frequently arisen at the same time, as is shown in Latin America. Juan Domingo Perón in Argentina, Getúlio Vargas in Brazil, and Lázaro Cárdenas in Mexico mobilised women as vital supporters in their nation-building endeavours during the classical populist era of the 1920s to 1940s. Like the leaders themselves, women were portrayed as political outsiders since they were barred from the political mainstream. Women's suffrage evolved into a nationalist reform and populist gesture, reflecting the gendered construction of "the people" as a single, but divided, entity (Betz, 2013).

In Europe, the rise of globalisation, migration, and supranational integration made room for radical RWP to transition from fringe players to serious competitors. Meanwhile, new waves of women's activity, particularly third-wave feminists, addressed concerns such as gender-based violence, welfare reform, and reproductive rights. These issues collided with populist discourses of state abandonment and marginalisation (Gunnarsson Payne, 2023). An overlap resulted from this: populists used feminist agendas to further their own nativist and nationalist goals while also denouncing feminism. E.g., many populist RWP parties in Europe shifted from pure traditionalism to advocating women's rights but only in opposition to immigrants, particularly Muslim communities (de Lange & Mügge, 2015).

RWP tends to rely heavily on gendered moral narratives, often framing women as guardians of the community or reproducers of tradition. In Southeast Asia, these roles are saturated with religious and nationalist significance. E.g., the Indonesian concept of ibuism (motherism) has been reappropriated by political actors to moralise economic and political participation (Kabullah & Fajri, 2021). However, women themselves strategically adopt, contest, and reconfigure these gendered roles rather than having them imposed from above. For Butler (2013) and Yuval-Davis (2006), gender is a contested site of political performance and negotiation rather than a set category of oppression. Because of the performative aspect of populism, women might embrace populist positions without internalising their ideological tenets, a phenomenon known as affective performativity (Ostiguy & Moffitt, 2020). RWP's deliberate use of feminist rhetoric is among its most notable and little-studied characteristics.

2.2 *Contested Empowerment in Right-Wing Populist Regimes*

RWP reframes feminist issues into a paradoxical narrative that is both pro-women and anti-feminist. Feminism is portrayed as a destructive, modernist philosophy that has weakened the natural order of gender roles, motherhood, and families rather than as a historical force for freedom (Stopler, 2021). Thus, anti-feminism becomes not an accidental by-product but an essential ideological pillar of RWP. Women aligned with these movements often present themselves as guardians of traditional values, which may be described, borrowing from Zygmunt Bauman (Bauman as cited in Kociatkiewicz & Kostera, 2018), as a "retrotopian affect": the nostalgic invocation of the past as a utopian vision for the future. Drawing on Saba Mahmood's (Mahmood as cited in Christensen, 2009), strategic agency refers to the capacity of actors to navigate and inhabit structures of domination without necessarily resisting them in overt or liberal ways. Agency, in this sense, is not freedom from power but action through constraint.

Although RWP has made traditional family values a central theme, mainstream assessments of RWP ideology have rarely taken this into account. It has not been acknowledged enough that gender discourse itself might play a significant role in understanding the emotional appeal and cultural resonance of RWP. A conceptual tension is present here. On the one hand, populism is often characterised as an open-ended political logic that articulates diverse and unsatisfied demands into a unified collective identity. On the other hand, its gender politics tend to be rigid, essentialist, and exclusionary. This raises framing questions: Is there a unique gender dimension intrinsic to populist politics? Is the populist support base gendered in both makeup and affect? How do gender norms mix with the primacy of personalisation in contrast to the charismatic, masculinist leadership style common in populist politics?

Strategic agency becomes legible when viewed through the lens of intersectionality (Diggs, 2022). Marginalised women, lacking access to liberal scripts of resistance, often employ culturally resonant roles such as caregivers, educators, or moral reformers to obtain legitimacy inside populist regimes (Cohen, 2019). These performances connect with the populist invocation of "the people" as a moral collective, making exclusion politically costly. In Indonesia and the Philippines, as analysed in the upcoming sections, women have exploited nationalist, religious, and familial themes to enhance their political influence. However, visibility alone does not imply empowerment. As Nancy Fraser (2015) argues, visibility must be examined through the discourses that offer it legitimacy. Substantiating with Butler (2013), gender here is performative, i.e., iterated to obtain recognition. Women gain authority by reproducing hegemonic norms while subtly reshaping them, resulting in ambivalent empowerment, a central paradox explored in the case studies that follow.

3 Methodology

This study adopts a comparative, qualitative approach, using critical discourse analysis (CDA) to explore how RWP in Southeast Asia constructs and engages with gender. Examining how women's political positions are shaped, negotiated, and challenged in Indonesia and the Philippines, the focus is on the performative and moral aspects of RWP.

Influenced by both Laclau's populism as a political logic and Saba Mahmood's concept of strategic agency, the objective is to highlight how action occurs both inside and occasionally in response to established power structures. Following these frameworks will assist in studying the structure women tend to find themselves in the discursive framework of RWP regimes. The Philippines and Indonesia were selected as case studies for a purposeful reason. In the past 20 years, both sizable, multiethnic democracies in Southeast Asia have seen substantial political changes characterised by the emergence or strengthening of populist leadership. Their institutional arrangements, populist inclinations, and gendered repertoires, however, differ substantially. Indonesia offers a hybrid form of RWP that blends Islamic moral nationalism and technological developmentalism, while the Philippines, under Rodrigo Duterte, offers a hypermasculine, personalist variant that depends on emotive spectacle and coercive state authority.

To guarantee exposure to a wide, rigorously reviewed corpus of literature, the study is dependent on secondary sources. These include peer-reviewed journal articles in political science, gender studies, Southeast Asian studies, and discourse analysis, books and edited volumes on populism, nationalism, and feminist political theory. To showcase how gender is utilised to define "the people" and delineate the limits of the political community, these patterns are then interpreted through Laclau's concept of the populist "chain of equivalence." This makes it possible to explore not only the official, state-led narratives of moral guardianship, motherhood, and national virtue, but also the ways in which women craft alternative or subversive readings of these roles through affective politics, symbolic reinterpretation, and everyday acts that subtly challenge dominant scripts. This approach responds to a gap in existing research. The ideological, institutional, and communication facets of RWP have been extensively studied, but the role of women in these movements in the Global South has received far less attention. Specifically, the deficit lies in how women gain political prominence in environments where moral conservatism predominates or how populist governments use women's practical and symbolic responsibilities to support their own legitimacy.

This study addresses that gap with three main aims: first, to examine how RWP governments construct gendered forms of moral legitimacy; second, to explore the different ways women in Indonesia and the Philippines engage with and shape these political environments; and third, to consider what these dynamics reveal about rethinking empowerment, belonging, and agency outside of liberal feminist frameworks.

4 Findings: Women's Agency in Populist Regimes

4.1 Indonesia: Religion, Developmentalism, and Strategic Ibuism

Populism in Indonesia has attracted growing academic attention. Jakarta's example is unique, though, in that it includes several overlapping currents comprising Islamic populism, left-wing populism, and RWP, all of which are influenced by the nation's social and political environment (Hatherell & Welsh, 2019). This diversity has resulted in a hybridised populism that sits at the intersection of Islamic conservatism, nationalism, and democratic pluralism. A moralised state, decentralised government, and a changing capitalist economy are examples of this hybridity, which creates lopsided and frequently incongruous political participation landscapes (Hatherell & Welsh, 2019).

4.1.1 Inside Indonesia's Populist Turn: Leaders, Religion, and Competing Moral Visions

The emergence of RWP rhetoric in Indonesia must be situated within the broader post-Suharto political transformation, which witnessed a fragmentation of elite power, a resurgence of Islamic identity politics, and the decentralisation of state authority (Webber, 2006). Within this evolving landscape, President Jokowi is often portrayed as a technocratic reformer (Hatherell & Welsh, 2021). However, his alliances with figures such as Prabowo Subianto, a former general, known for his militarist and nationalist views, have significantly shaped the ideological contours of contemporary Indonesian populism. Mietzner (2014) characterises Jokowi as a polite populist, advocating a form of "light" populism distinct from more confrontational global variants (see also Aspinall & Mietzner, 2014, 2019).

In the 2014 general elections, Jokowi was described as a "pluralist-centrist" (Mietzner, 2014), representing what Mietzner (2020) later termed a technocratic and ideologically pluralist populism. Crucially, this form of populism was not rooted in systemic overhaul or anti-foreign antagonism, but rather in an inclusivist appeal that refrained from targeting enemies or engaging in divisive rhetoric. Nevertheless, there remains academic contestation on Jokowi's populist credentials. Hatherell and Welsh (2019) argue that Jokowi is best understood not as a populist at all, but as a pragmatic technocrat whose governance style lacks the polarising populist hallmark of constructing an enemy. Prabowo appeals to numerous marginalised groups, including women, with his pledge to restore national dignity through military might, economic protectionism, and moral rejuvenation (Muhtadi, 2025). Prabowo portrayed himself as Sukarno, who spoke for the people, but he also gave the impression that he was a king, complete with all the opulent possessions he owned. But he was unable to establish himself as a spokesperson for the general populace in the setting of populist politicians. Jokowi and Duterte, who are from and belong to the common people in the Philippines, stand in stark contrast to this.

Religious conservatism further deepens the moral underpinnings of Jakarta's populism. Islamic groups such as *Nahdlatul Ulama* and *Majelis Ulama Indonesia (MUI)* have been instrumental in crafting a public morality, particularly around gender roles (Malik, 2023). But these same institutions frequently serve as platforms for community-based leadership and women's advocacy, illustrating the contradictory spaces within which gendered agency can emerge. This interaction between religious nationalism and decentralised governance forms what Hadiz (2018) refers to as "authoritarian populism with Indonesian characteristics," where moral principles are central to the political imaginary yet remain subject to contestation and strategic interpretation. However, not all expressions of Islamic politics in Jakarta fit comfortably within RWP. Many actors, particularly those aligned with hardline movements such as the *Front Pembela Islam* (FPI), embody what might more accurately be termed "populist Islamists" rather than Islamist populists. The distinction is crucial. While populism is typically a thin-centred ideology open to articulation with other ideologies, Islam is a comprehensive ideological system. To subsume Islamist actors within a populist master frame risks overlooking the theological dimensions of their politics. FPI's controversial leader Rizieq Shihab, known by his followers as an *Imam Besar*, does not embody the populist principle of people's sovereignty. He claims his authority via a religious hierarchy in which virtue lies not in the will of the people but in the will of God. In this manner, democracy and pluralism are subordinated to divine law, and the notion of a unified, secular general will is absent. Rizieq provides an example of a leader who has historically mobilised not against elites per se, but against moral enemies, such as non-orthodox Muslims, religious minorities, communists, and ethnic Chinese communities, drawing from a long-standing tradition of exclusionary virtue politics. Therefore, while populist and Islamist discourses may converge tactically, their foundational logics and sources of authority often diverge in fundamental ways.

4.1.2 Strategic Ibuism and Developmental Citizenship in Populist Indonesia

The return of the state to protectionist economic policies, particularly under Jokowi's vision of "Golden Indonesia 2045" and earlier programs such as *Nawacita*, has led to a renewed interest in microfinance, infrastructure, and rural economies (Bräuchler, 2025). These economic efforts, sometimes presented in populist terms as a return to national sovereignty from global capitalism, have paved unexpected avenues for women to participate. But initiatives such as Program Keluarga Harapan (PKH), which offers conditional cash transfers, have disproportionately targeted women as the home administrators of the family (Maizunati & Sulistyaningrum, 2019). In addition to legitimising women's increased involvement in public administration and economic decision-making, this framework also serves to uphold traditional gender roles. On the other hand, state and religious institutions have aggressively promoted the growth of MSMEs. Women entrepreneurs in rural Java, Sulawesi, and parts of Sumatra are celebrated as promoting resilience on a local and national level. These women often practice a form of developmental citizenship by embodying the values of piety and patriotism (Marwah, 2019). They find legitimacy in adhering to religious and nationalist values, and they live inside the moral economy of RWP. However, this agency is highly situated and ambivalent.

Buehler notes that the decentralisation of governance has enabled local elites to impose gender-discriminatory bylaws (*perda syariah*) that restrict women's mobility and dress (Buehler et al., 2021). The same RWP decentralisation that creates room for female leadership in local economies also facilitates the formalisation of patriarchal norms. In this manner, women must continually negotiate this unstable landscape, using one set of populist discourses to counterbalance the limitations imposed by another. Ibuism is a key paradigm that permits women's participation in Indonesia's RWP environment. Despite its past use as a patriarchal control mechanism, ibuism's contemporary manifestation under populist governments paints a more nuanced picture. Ibuist principles are commonly invoked by female political actors to defend their positions of authority in civil society, education, and local government. This invocation is strategic rather than inherently submissive; women acquire credibility in a society that views caring and selflessness as symbols of national virtue by associating with these moral ideals. Religious organisations also reinforce this strategic ibuism. Female religious scholars (ulama perempuan), community organisers, and school administrators can participate in policy discussions under the aegis of moral reform through the women's wings of Nahdlatul Ulama and Muhammadiyah (Maftuhin, 2023). Instead of challenging the male-centric framework of formal politics, these platforms provide an alternate route to public exposure that quietly changes it from the inside out. The modalities of agency that function within normative power rather than against it are reflected in such behaviours, according to Mahmood (Mahmood as cited in Christensen, 2009).

Indonesian women's movements also show a range of reactions to RWP, from appropriation to opposition. Groups such as Aisyiyah and Fatayat NU have used their religious foundations to promote women's education, economic engagement, and gender-sensitive interpretations of Islamic law (Arnez, 2010). These organisations often use the ideological frames of RWP (religious virtue, anti-Westernism, and national pride) to obtain legitimacy and evade state repression, even when they do not directly challenge them. They can participate in the larger populist moral economy while keeping a critical distance thanks to this selective alignment. It also explains why some women's groups oppose liberal feminist agendas, which they perceive as elitist, foreign, or insufficiently moral. Thus, rather than a simple binary between feminist resistance and populist complicity, what emerges is a continuum of negotiated identifications, rooted in local, religious, and national idioms of legitimacy. The capacity to appropriate hegemonic discourse without completely internalising its ideological substance is a crucial aspect of strategic agency that is highlighted by such actions (Herschinger, 2012). In response to the opportunities and limitations of populist power, Indonesian women who are active in civil society or local administration frequently embody several subjectivities, including mother, entrepreneur, moral guide, and citizen. It would be an underestimation of the complexity of women's strategies to interpret their involvement in Indonesian populist politics as only co-optation. These women work amid a complex web of conflicting ideologies that provide both opportunities and solutions, such as religious nationalism, economic populism, and moral ibuism. Adaptive, performative, and discursively situated methods enable people to survive and occasionally flourish in morally restrictive regimes, rather than expressing their agency through overt resistance.

4.2 The Philippines: Hypermasculine Populism and Dynastic Legitimacy

In the study of gendered agency in RWP governments, the Philippines differs from but complements Jakarta. Rodrigo Duterte's administration (2016–2022) was defined by an extreme style of performative populism founded on hypermasculinity, moral spectacle, and harsh governance (Encinas-Franco, 2022). He articulated a populist style that valued vulgar speech, personalistic leadership, and the use of violence to maintain social order, which contained highly gendered features that reinforced patriarchal power. The term *Dutertismo*, now widely used to describe this political phenomenon, is generally attributed to columnist and sociologist Randy David (David as cited in Parcon, 2021), who identified the emotional and affective nature of Duterte's appeal even before his presidential victory. David compared Duterte's sudden rise to that of previous fascist strongmen such as Benito Mussolini and Adolf Hitler, pointing out that he failed to establish an ideological framework throughout his campaign (David as cited in Parcon, 2021). Instead, he used anecdotal storytelling and emotionally charged narratives of governmental failure to arouse the electorate's collective frustration. This narrative populism, based on grievance rather than policy, strengthened his populist legitimacy and established the moral and emotional context for gendered performances of power.

4.2.1 Masculinity, Misogyny, and Dynastic Legitimacy

Rodrigo Duterte's populism was inseparable from his hypermasculine persona. He positioned himself as the protector of the people, frequently citing his working-class roots and contempt for elite institutions while pursuing a punitive law-and-order politics (Curato, 2016a). His controversial war on drugs, which resulted in thousands of extrajudicial deaths, was foretold in moral terms of cleansing and justice, mirroring RWP narratives that portray violence as required for national salvation (Mendoza & Jaminola, 2020). Duterte's gendered populist power featured a lengthy history of misogynistic speech, which was frequently tinged with threats of sexual assault. E.g., while addressing state soldiers, Duterte once delivered a horrific order directed at female communist rebels: "*We will not murder you. We will simply shoot your vagina*," meaning that, without reproductive potential, women are deemed useless (Banquiles, 2025). On another occasion, he suggested that under martial law, soldiers would be permitted to rape up to three women without fear of prosecution (Banquiles, 2025). These utterances were not isolated outbursts, but rather part of a larger political style that normalised violence against women while using the language of humour and bravado.

What is even more alarming is that such words were made not only by a head of state, but also in front of an applauding audience. His populist performance was centred on a gendered moral economy in which the ideal "good citizen" was obedient, heteronormative, and loyal, characteristics usually associated with feminine roles such as mothers, wives, and moral guardians of the home (Kusaka, 2017; Tuğal, 2023). Curato (2016b) characterises Duterte's leadership as a form of penal populism, built on fear and anxiety, but also offering hope to the socially excluded. Excluded groups, such as those marginalised by an elitist democracy governed by oligarchic hegemony, discovered in Duterte a person who channelled their disillusionment. Curato claims that his ascent to power was the result of a protest vote against a disconnected political elite and a broader political culture that had failed to confront structural injustice. Duterte's frequent misogynistic remarks, which range from rape jokes to attacks on female critics, have been well documented (Kwon & Valdez, 2024). However, such speaking acts did not simply reflect personal prejudice; they were integral to his populist style, supporting patriarchal power, reifying gender hierarchies, and displaying dominance for public consumption.

One of the most prominent female figures during and after Duterte's presidency is his daughter, Sara Duterte-Carpio, who served as mayor of Davao City and is now vice president of the Philippines. Her dynastic status within the Duterte family, a significant source of symbolic capital in a political system that values familial loyalty and continuity, and her administrative background both contribute to her political legitimacy. Sara Duerte has carefully allied herself with her family's populist brand while also enhancing its perception by making emotional appeals to discipline, motherhood, and moral leadership (Arguelles, 2021). This type of dynastic legitimacy has strong gendered connotations. While adhering to a paradigm that normalises political authority as an extension of household obligation, it permits women to participate in high-level politics. Other female politicians' careers exhibit similar trends, such as Imee Marcos, whose public image as the daughter and devoted supporter of former dictator Ferdinand Marcos has played a significant role in reviving authoritarian nostalgia in populist rhetoric (Novio, 2022). These women are not outliers; rather, they are representative of a larger tactic wherein female political actors enter the field by assuming roles that are approved by the patriarchal-populist system.

4.2.2 Performing Power: Women, Morality, and Strategic Agency

Many women in Duterte's regime established political and social space outside the dynastic elites by exhibiting culturally acceptable types of femininity, which are rooted in civic duty, religiosity, and maternal sacrifice. These performances found a particularly fruitful root in local governance (Calva, n.d.). To assert their moral authority and public legitimacy, councilwomen and female mayors have often relied on stories of selfless devotion and communal care. These positions tend to be symbolic and give women considerable influence over decisions and prominence in their communities. The performative nature of this femininity echoes Butler's (Butler as cited in Mills, 2000) notion of gender as reiteration: by enacting socially expected roles, women become intelligible within the populist moral regime. Women can, however, redefine prevailing discourses from inside through such performances, which also have the potential to be disruptive.

Sandra and Jenkins (2022) argue that women can quietly change the norms of populist discourse from coercion to compassion and from violent sovereignty to maternal responsibility by emphasising care, moral reform, and community survival. Rodriguez (Rodriguez as cited in Parcon, 2021) provides theoretical support for this dynamic by arguing that deliberative democracy, as defined by Jurgen Habermas, informs Philippine politics and that rational communication is essential. At the same time, Rodriguez uses the hospitality concept of Jacques Derrida, which permits a more emotive, contingent, and disruptive form of political engagement. He uses both philosophical frameworks to analyse critical democratic moments, most notably the EDSA Revolution, suggesting that an uneasy tension between rational consensus and disruptive popular intervention shapes Philippine democracy. Within this paradigm, populism can be understood through what academics have called a democratic paradox (Papaioannou, Slewe, Pantazi, & van Prooijen, 2025): it frequently undermines liberal democratic principles while claiming to return authority to "the people." Because populist appeals question the elitist democratic structures that have historically marginalised familiar people, they are particularly compelling. Thus, women's involvement in this environment, even when framed within conservative moral standards, represents a multifaceted political action that balances tradition and change, obedience and disruption.

While elite and local female leaders have navigated Duterte's populism, feminist civil society actors have adopted a range of critical responses. To appeal to public sentiment, organisations such as Gabriela Women's Party, Lila Filipina, and Rise Up for Life and for Rights have openly criticised Duterte's misogyny, human rights abuses, and militarised government. They frequently phrase their criticisms in moralistic and religious terms (Navera, 2021). These organisations practice what Dean and Maiguashca (2020) call affective counter-politics, grounding their opposition in emotional registers like grief, compassion, and social solidarity instead of defining resistance in exclusively liberal-feminist terms. These groups confront populist masculinism on its moral level by mobilising the stories of faith-based community organisers, mothers of deceased victims, and survivors of gender-based violence. Their opposition is based on the moral languages and lived experiences of regular Filipinos rather than being oppositional in the abstract. However, to obtain funds, legitimacy, or operational space, several women's organisations have strategically realigned, momentarily aligning with populist moral norms. This ambivalence highlights how moral alignment and political critique conflict on the uneven terrain of agency. Therefore, it is not a question of whether these players are complicit or resist; rather, it is a question of how they manage power, legitimacy, and visibility in the paradoxical world of RWP.

Duterte's masculinist populism creates what Cornwall and Lindisfarne (2016) term an opportunity structure for hegemonic masculinity, but it also inadvertently reveals the cracks within that structure. Through moral code alignment, re-signification of familial legitimacy, and mobilisation of localised care work, these fractures enable women to exert power. Duterte depended on women to spread his populist brand, soften his image, and expand his moral authority, including his daughter, allies, and grassroots organisers (Laguilles-Timog, 2020). To preserve legitimacy, it must be viewed as a regime of performative excess that necessitates complementary performances, frequently femininely. The strategic usage of these roles allows women to acquire symbolic power and distributive and discursive power. The popular spectacle both empowers and limits their agency. The Philippine situation complicates linear conceptions of populist repression or female emancipation. It demonstrates that even in morally orthodox and masculinist regimes, women can rise to positions of political authority, acquire local legitimacy, and change the goals of governance. This does not imply that these regimes are emancipatory or feminist, but rather that it is possible to resolve the conflicts between patriarchal exclusion and populist inclusion strategically.

5 Comparative Analysis: Ambivalence and Gendered Belonging

At a structural level, both regimes rely on morally coded populist discourse to consolidate political legitimacy. This leads to the creation of gendered imaginaries of "the people" that emphasise conventional femininity, which is frequently represented by the mother, caretaker, or moral guardian (Löffler et al., 2020). Gender and the Nation (2004) by Nira Yuval-Davis was one of the first books to analyse the ways in which gender influences national affiliation thoroughly. In her subsequent work, The Politics of Belonging: Intersectional Contestations (2011), she makes a significant distinction between the politics of belonging, which deals with the active construction of boundaries around inclusion and exclusion, and belonging, which is defined as an emotional attachment and sense of "feeling at home" in daily life. The hegemonic reproduction of communal boundaries by dominant powers and their contestation and disruption by alternative actors and marginalised voices are both aspects of these politics, which are by their very nature contested.

5.1 Performing Belonging: Moral Legitimacy and Gendered Inclusion

When analysing gendered RWP rhetoric, where women are frequently included conditionally, this conceptual perspective is especially helpful. This gendered moralism turns into a contradictory source of political mobilisation in both Indonesia and the Philippines. Women's access to public life is mostly due to their alignment with culturally valued values rather than ideology. These attributes become a form of moral legitimacy, permitting women to claim visibility and authority within RWP regimes that are otherwise patriarchal and exclusionary (Spierings et al., 2015). A crucial concept for comprehending how women's participation is both facilitated and restricted is the politics of belonging. Ironically, women's admittance into public life is based on this gendered moralism. For women to participate in both Indonesia and the Philippines, moral legitimacy is a crucial currency. Their perceived alignment with cultural values, such as piety, sacrifice, and family loyalty, rather than their political ideology or activism, is what makes them understandable within the populist framework (Spierings et al., 2015).

This convergence draws attention to a fundamental contradiction in RWP: although it uses patriarchal and moralistic discourses to subjugate women symbolically, it is unable to completely exclude them without compromising its claim to speak for "the people." To maintain their hegemonic appeal, populist formations depend on internal heterogeneity, as Laclau (Laclau as cited in Thomassen, 2019) contends. Without directly challenging the regime's legitimacy, women can strategically fill the structural voids created by this ambiguity. To access these opportunities, women in Indonesia and the Philippines use emotive and moral performances, embodying positions of moral virtue, communal caring, and authenticity. The moral and symbolic borders of the community are framed by nationalist discourses, which mediate these performances. Umut Özkırımlı (Özkırımlı as cited in Güçler, 2020) observes that nationalism divides the world into binaries of "us" and "them," produces hierarchies among social actors, and naturalises these distinctions through institutions such as the family, school, media, religion, and law enforcement. Women's presence in such a system is contingent upon their ability to perpetuate prevailing ideals in both public and private domains.

The key to comprehending these interactions is the idea of strategic agency. Women from Indonesia and the Philippines frequently use culturally acceptable roles to advance politically, not in opposition to them. According to Nurmila (2020) and Rinaldo (2011), their behaviour demonstrates an embeddedness in moral discourses that influence what constitutes leadership, authority, and morality in populist regimes. Furthermore, populism in both regimes is founded on performance, with moral and emotive spectacles being used to establish political legitimacy. Under these circumstances, gendered performances become an essential part of the regime's representational apparatus, not just symbolic, but as systems that bestow moral clarity and cultural validity. The nationalisation of gender equality is a clear illustration of this, since gender rights are framed as a component of a dominant national culture that is thought to be threatened by the culturally "other." Similar processes can be seen worldwide, even though these tales are frequently linked to Nordic nations with robust formal pledges to gender equality. According to Andreassen (2014), Muslim women are either overtly or implicitly denied gender equality, which is increasingly being framed as a universal European norm. This allows RWP actors to advocate specific types of women's rights to further exclusionary nationalist objectives by redefining gender equality as a symbol of cultural limits and civilizational identity. As active co-producers of populism's emotive economy, women thus participate in this performative moral order in addition to serving as symbolic bearers of tradition or modernity.

5.2 *Ambivalence as Strategy: Rethinking Empowerment Beyond Liberal Scripts*

These commonalities cast doubt on the notion that women's autonomy cannot pass via RWP. Rather, populism is better understood as a gendered political construction characterised by performative demands, emotive appeals, and internal inconsistencies, all of which produce contextual chances for gendered negotiation, they contend.

Despite these commonalities, there are notable distinctions between Indonesian and Philippine women's political assertion in terms of style, organisation, and avenues. These differences show how the boundaries of strategic agency are shaped by regional political cultures, institutional setups, and populist practices.

First, the populist style of each regime varies considerably. Populism in Indonesia is typified by technocratic and developmentalist nationalism, especially under Subianto. It relies more on institutional mobilisation and is less individualistic. On the other hand, the Philippines under Duterte is a quintessential example of personalist governance, where legitimacy is fostered by emotional attachment to a single strongman character. Within each regime, gender mobilisation and contestation are shaped by these stylistic variances. Eleanore Kofman (Kofman as cited in Mense-Petermann, Welskopp, & Zaharieva, 2022) notes that RWP lack a unified or consistent stance on the family and its social relationships. While this suggests variability in how gender roles are articulated, Cas Mudde (Mudde & Kaltwasser, 2015) identifies a core gender ideology common to many RWP actors. He claims that this comprises three fundamental ideas: (1) linking women's politics with family politics; (2) defending natural differences between the sexes; and (3) advancing the notion that women must be protected because they are the only ones who are capable of bearing children, and their survival depends on them. The conceptual instability of gender within RWP ideology is highlighted by these differing scholarly interpretations: gender is fundamental but variously operationalised and theorised across settings. This variation has a significant impact on women's access to power. Through MSMEs, local government, and religious NGOs, decentralisation and economic protectionism have created opportunities for women in Indonesia. On the other hand, women's access to political power in the Philippines is more mediated via dynasties. Rather than through grassroots activism or economic leadership, individuals such as Sara Duterte and Imee Marcos acquire prominence and legitimacy through symbolic capital and familial allegiance.

Secondly, discursive sources of legitimacy differ. When Indonesian women establish their legitimacy in developmentalist and religious idioms, they often comply with the criteria of piety and output. However, when Filipino women organise against state violence, they typically utilise emotional registers like maternal compassion, sacrifice, or mourning (Pratt, 2009). Filipinas tend to practice emotive politics of kinship and caring in a hyper-mediated public sphere, while Indonesian women function under institutional logics of state-religious moralism. The forms of agency also differ. Without overt conflict, Indonesian women frequently carry out covert change from within hegemonic institutions, such as Islamic schools, village cooperatives, or cash transfer schemes. Rinaldo (Rinaldo as cited in Marwah, 2019) asserts that their agency is reformist rather than revolutionary and is predicated on discursive alignment with the moral economy. To resist the populist spectacle, Filipino women, on the other hand, use affective counter-politics, mobilising public mourning, survivor narratives, and maternal grief. This results in a sort of resistance that is more obvious but also more vulnerable.

The significance of contextual specificity is highlighted by these differences. Populism and women's agency are not uniform. Analysing these distinctions assists in avoiding oversimplification and instead draws attention to the situated, historically embedded practices of female political assertion under authoritarian populism. This comparative analysis tilts towards reevaluating the definition of empowerment in RWP environments. Too often, feminist study confuses empowerment with resistance to patriarchal authority, visibility, and voice. However, rather than rejecting prevalent beliefs, women's agency in Indonesia and the Philippines especially results from their compliance with them. This kind of agency, which operates within the affective and symbolic logics of populist speech while subtly undermining its constraints, is best described as ambivalent (Bargetz, 2023).

Ambivalence differs from passivity. It is a strategic position that allows women to occupy dominant roles without truly understanding their importance. It permits subversion, co-optation, and navigation without necessarily resulting in overt confrontation. These behaviours expose a non-liberal female politics predicated on survival, moral legitimacy, and context-specific kinds of power. These contradictory agencies also challenge the binary distinction between resistance and complicity. According to Grewal and Kaplan (Grewal and Kaplan as cited in Hundle et al., 2019), transnational feminisms must avoid using Western liberation scripts and instead concentrate on how women in the Global South negotiate community, morality, and modernity. Although they lack liberal empowerment, women in Indonesia and the Philippines have political clout. Though they also occupy public space, influence discourse, transfer resources, and shape government processes, they are nonetheless understandable within culturally accepted moral systems.

6 Conclusion and Recommendations: Rethinking Empowerment Beyond Liberal Scripts

The convergence of moral discourse, gendered affect, and strategic agency in RWP regimes challenges inherited binaries of victimhood and resistance. Women in Indonesia and the Philippines have neither been overt opponents of populist authority, nor have they been passive recipients of it. As active participants in negotiating the limits of political power and morality, they have instead become co-constructors of populist legitimacy. These discussions occur within the symbolic logic of the populist moral order, not in opposition to it. The fact that the same ideologies that are used to restrict women can also be instrumentalised as political ploys highlights a fundamental contradiction: populism both empowers and disciplines in the same gesture. This tension is not coincidental. Rather, it is a component of the structure of populist politics. RWP needs to stage a cohesive moral community to uphold its claim to represent "the people," and this cannot be accomplished without symbolically integrating women. However, this inclusion is always subject to conditions, negotiated through affective repertoires, and validated by cultural norms. It is impossible to reduce what women do with this equivocal visibility to co-optation. They create comprehensible spheres of influence inside populist moral economies through emotive counter-politics, re-signification of moral codes, or strategic compliance.

Comparatively, this chapter highlights the ways in which regime style (hypermasculine spectacle or technocratic) significantly influences the ways in which women express themselves. These distinctions serve as a warning against viewing women's populist behaviour as a single entity or presuming that symbolic authority equates to real change. Not that populism gives women more power, but rather that women intentionally use populist paradoxes to their advantage. Still, these insights remain insufficient if they are only read through the lens of populism's internal grammar. Future research will need to address the conditions of agency under illiberal regimes in a more rigorous manner, taking into consideration the limitations of liberal feminist presumptions and emphasising non-Western expressions of resistance, legitimacy, and empowerment. Understanding how RWP's gendered scripts are modified, disputed, or reinforced in various contexts is becoming more than just an academic exercise with the movement's continued global encroachment, particularly in areas of democratic backsliding. It is now a political necessity. The question, then, is no longer simply how women resist populism but how they shape it.

From this critical investigation, there are major implications that extend beyond theoretical debates. First, research on RWP must move beyond Western liberal feminist assumptions that situate empowerment solely with resistance. The necessity for frameworks that recognise the practice of negotiation, moral compliance, and strategic ambiguity is illustrated by the ambivalent forms of agency that are evident in Indonesia and the Philippines. To properly account for the affective and cultural registers through which women exercise agency under illiberal regimes, future inquiry should embrace intersectional and Global South-oriented methodologies. However, because class, caste, religion, and ethnicity do not always intersect in linear or equivalent ways, making it difficult to generalise across contexts, intersectionality in the Global South poses unique analytical issues. As a result, when applying intersectional frameworks to various populist contexts, researchers run the risk of either repeating essentialisms or failing to recognise the dynamic, situational nature of identity politics. Second, policy interventions must recognise that women's visibility in RWP regimes is often conditional, symbolic, and mediated through moral legitimacy. This necessitates supporting community-based networks and grassroots organisations that empower women to transform symbolic inclusion into institutional and tangible impact. Even though visible, with the absence of such reinforcement, women run the risk of being politically marginalised in such regimes.

Third, feminist advocacy should alter its strategies by engaging with the moralised repertoires that RWP regimes mobilise. Rather than discarding notions of care, sacrifice, and guardianship as inherently conservative, advocacy can strategically re-signify these idioms to challenge exclusionary populist narratives on their own terms. This re-signification emphasises how feminist actors can challenge illiberal regimes without eschewing culturally relevant moral vocabulary by reversing the very emotive tropes that uphold patriarchal populism into counter-hegemonic tools. Lastly, comparative research ought to go beyond Southeast Asia (as this study is situated in Southeast Asia as well) and explore the differences and similarities across the various areas where RWP thrives. Particularly crucial are longitudinal studies that closely monitor shifts in women's status over time so as to determine whether conditional inclusion leads to long-term empowerment or maintains patriarchal dominance. In addition to capturing the fluidity of women's political agency, this kind of diachronic investigation improves the epistemology of populism studies by avoiding static events in favour of a more comprehensive conception of the formation, contestation, and transformation of gendered power under illiberal regimes. The overarching focus is on how important it is to see women as key players in the performance, legitimacy, and contradictions of populism rather than as supporting/subservient characters. Attending to these dynamics is vital not only for academic understanding but also for the pursuit of a more inclusive political future.

References

Ádám, Z. (2020). Re-feudalizing democracy: An approach to authoritarian populism taken from institutional economics. *Journal of Institutional Economics, 16*(1), 105–118. https://doi.org/10.1017/S1744137419000304

Andreassen, R. (2014). Political Muslim women in the news media. In Negotiating identities in Scandinavia: Women, migration and the diaspora (pp. 61–90). New York and Oxford: Berghahn Books. https://www.torrossa.com/en/resources/an/5817304#page=71

Arguelles, C. V. (2021). The populist brand is crisis: Durable Dutertismo amidst mismanaged COVID-19 response. Southeast Asian Affairs, 257–274. https://www.jstor.org/stable/27075086

Arnez, M. (2010). Empowering women through Islam: Fatayat NU between tradition and change. *Journal of Islamic Studies, 21*(1), 59–88. https://doi.org/10.1093/jis/etp025

Aslanidis, P. (2015). Is populism an ideology? A refutation and a new perspective. Political Studies, 64(1_suppl), 88–104. https://doi.org/10.1111/1467-9248.12224

Aspinall, E., & Mietzner, M. (2014). Indonesian politics in 2014: Democracy's close call. *Bulletin of Indonesian Economic Studies, 50*(3), 347–369. https://doi.org/10.1080/00074918.2014.980375

Aspinall, E., & Mietzner, M. (2019). Southeast Asia's troubling elections: Nondemocratic pluralism in Indonesia. *Journal of Democracy, 30*(4), 104–118. https://doi.org/10.1353/jod.2019.0055

Banquiles, V. C. T. (2025). 'We will shoot you in the vagina': Phallocentric populism and women in time of Rodrigo Duterte. Revista de Estudiantes de Ciencia Política, 23–24, 19–48. https://revistas.udea.edu.co/index.php/recp/article/view/360126/20818072

Bargetz, B. (2023). Affect, populism, politics: Paradoxical promises of agency. In The complexity of populism (pp. 73–89). Routledge. https://www.taylorfrancis.com/chapters/edit/https://doi.org/10.4324/9781003302513-7

Betz, H. G. (2013). A distant mirror: Nineteenth-century populism, nativism, and contemporary right-wing radical politics. *Democracy and Security, 9*(3), 200–220. https://doi.org/10.1080/17419166.2013.792250

Bräuchler, B. (2025). Golden Indonesia 2045: Neoliberal development policies and environmental journalism. Journal of Current Southeast Asian Affairs, 0(0). https://doi.org/10.1177/18681034251345832

Buehler, M., Nataatmadja, R., & Anugrah, I. (2021). Limitations to subnational authoritarianism: Indonesian local government head elections in comparative perspective. *Regional & Federal Studies, 31*(3), 381–404. https://doi.org/10.1080/13597566.2021.1918388

Butler, J. (2013). Gender as performance. In J. Butler, A critical sense (pp. 109–125). Routledge. https://www.taylorfrancis.com/chapters/edit/https://doi.org/10.4324/9780203754238-7/gender-performance-judith-butler

Calva, J. C. (n.d.). Women's role in local governance and development in Mindanao, Philippines: Views and challenges. International Journal of Social and Management Studies, 7(2). https://doi.org/10.51386/25815946/ijsms-v7i2p113

Canovan, M. (2002). Taking politics to the people: Populism as the ideology of democracy. In Y. Mény & Y. Surel (Eds.), Democracies and the populist challenge (pp. 25–44). London: Palgrave Macmillan. https://doi.org/10.1057/9781403920072_2

Caravantes, P., & Lombardo, E. (2022). The symbolic representation of the 'People' and the 'Homeland' in Spanish left populism: An opportunity for feminist politics? *Journal of Contemporary European Studies, 31*(3), 902–915. https://doi.org/10.1080/14782804.2022.2090322

Chernov, G. (2019). European populism: A communicative aspect. Studies in Media and Communication, 7(1), 89–94. https://shorturl.at/QOkEU

Christensen, H. R. (2009). Pieties and gender. Leiden, The Netherlands: Brill. https://doi.org/10.1163/ej.9789004178267.i-236

Cohen, J. L. (2019). Populism and the politics of resentment. *Jus Cogens, 1*, 5–39. https://doi.org/10.1007/s42439-019-00009-7

Cornwall, A., & Lindisfarne, N. (2016). Dislocating masculinity: Gender, power and anthropology. In A. Cornwall & N. Lindisfarne (Eds.), Dislocating masculinity (pp. 27–61). Routledge. https://www.taylorfrancis.com/chapters/edit/https://doi.org/10.4324/9781315408309 9

Curato, N. (2016a). Flirting with authoritarian fantasies? Rodrigo Duterte and the new terms of Philippine populism. *Journal of Contemporary Asia, 47*(1), 142–153. https://doi.org/10.1080/00472336.2016.1239751

Curato, N. (2016b). Politics of anxiety, politics of hope: Penal populism and Duterte's rise to power. *Journal of Current Southeast Asian Affairs, 35*(3), 91–109. https://doi.org/10.1177/186810341603500305

da Silva, F. C., & Vieira, M. B. (2019). Populism as a logic of political action. *European Journal of Social Theory, 22*(4), 497–512. https://doi.org/10.1177/1368431018762540

de Lange, S. L., & Mügge, L. M. (2015). Gender and right-wing populism in the Low Countries: Ideological variations across parties and time. *Patterns of Prejudice, 49*(1–2), 61–80. https://doi.org/10.1080/0031322X.2015.1014199

Dean, J., & Maiguashca, B. (2020). Did somebody say populism? Towards a renewal and reorientation of populism studies. *Journal of Political Ideologies, 25*(1), 11–27. https://doi.org/10.1080/13569317.2020.1699712

Devinney, T. M., & Hartwell, C. A. (2020). Varieties of populism. *Global Strategy Journal, 10*(1), 32–66. https://doi.org/10.1002/gsj.1373

Dietze, G. (2022). Right-wing populism and gender. In M. Oswald (Ed.), The Palgrave handbook of populism (pp. xx–xx). Cham: Palgrave Macmillan. https://doi.org/10.1007/978-3-030-80803-7_16

Diggs, S. N. (2022). Chapter 8: Intersectionality of gender and race in governmental affairs. In S. N. Diggs (Ed.), Handbook on gender and public administration. Cheltenham, UK: Edward Elgar Publishing. https://doi.org/10.4337/9781789904734.00016

Eksi, B., & Wood, E. A. (2019). Right-wing populism as gendered performance: Janus-faced masculinity in the leadership of Vladimir Putin and Recep T. *Erdogan. Theory and Society, 48*, 733–751. https://doi.org/10.1007/s11186-019-09363-3

Eliyanah, E., Yannuar, N., Choiron, N. F., & Zahro, A. (2023). Islamising neo-ibuism: Representations of the ideal wife in marriage self-help books in Indonesia. *Indonesia and the Malay World, 51*(151), 330–347. https://doi.org/10.1080/13639811.2023.2276585

Encinas-Franco, J. (2022). The presidential kiss: Duterte's gendered populism, hypermasculinity, and Filipino migrants. *NORMA, 17*(2), 107–123. https://doi.org/10.1080/18902138.2022.2026107

Fraser, N. (2015). Legitimation crisis? On the political contradictions of financialized capitalism. *Critical Historical Studies, 2*(2), 157–189. https://doi.org/10.1086/683054

Grewal, I. (2022). Authoritarian patriarchy and its populism. In Cultures of Populism (pp. 122–141). Routledge. https://www.taylorfrancis.com/chapters/edit/https://doi.org/10.4324/9781003152606-9/authoritarian-patriarchy-populism-inderpal-grewal

Güçler, A. (2020). Nations and nationalism. In W. Leal Filho, A. Azul, L. Brandli, P. Özuyar, & T. Wall (Eds.), Peace, justice and strong institutions: Encyclopedia of the UN Sustainable Development Goals. Cham: Springer. https://doi.org/10.1007/978-3-319-71066-2_30-1

Gunnarsson Payne, J. (2023). Feminism and populism: Strange bedfellows or a perfect match? Etica & Politica / Ethics & Politics, 25(2), 269–283. https://sites.units.it/etica/2023_2/GUNNARSSONPAYNE.pdf

Hadiz, V. R. (2018). Imagine all the people? Mobilising Islamic populism for right-wing politics in Indonesia. *Journal of Contemporary Asia, 48*(4), 566–583. https://doi.org/10.1080/00472336.2018.1433225

Hatherell, M., & Welsh, A. (2019). Populism and the risks of conceptual overreach: A case study from Indonesia. *Representation, 56*(1), 53–69. https://doi.org/10.1080/00344893.2019.1663904

Hatherell, M., & Welsh, A. (2021). The technocratic national narrative in Indonesia. In The struggle for the national narrative in Indonesia (pp. 21–40). Singapore: Palgrave Pivot. https://doi.org/10.1007/978-981-16-3811-4_2

Heinemann, I., & Stern, A. M. (2022). Gender and far-right nationalism: Historical and international dimensions. *Journal of Modern European History, 20*(3), 311–321. https://doi.org/10.1177/16118944221110721

Herschinger, E. (2012). 'Hell is the other': Conceptualising hegemony and identity through discourse theory. *Millennium, 41*(1), 65–90. https://doi.org/10.1177/0305829812449501

Hundle, A. K., Szeman, I., & Hoare, J. P. (2019). What is the transnational in transnational feminist research? *Feminist Review, 121*(1), 3–8. https://doi.org/10.1177/0141778918817525

Kabullah, M. I., & Fajri, M. N. (2021). Neo-Ibuism in Indonesian politics: Election campaigns of wives of regional heads in West Sumatra in 2019. *Journal of Current Southeast Asian Affairs, 40*(1), 136–155. https://doi.org/10.1177/1868103421989069

Katsambekis, G. (2020). Constructing 'the people' of populism: A critique of the ideational approach from a discursive perspective. *Journal of Political Ideologies, 27*(1), 53–74. https://doi.org/10.1080/13569317.2020.1844372

Kociatkiewicz, J., & Kostera, M. (2018). After retrotopia? The future of organizing and the thought of Zygmunt Bauman. *Scandinavian Journal of Management, 34*(4), 335–342.

Kølvraa, C. (2017). The discourse theory of Ernesto Laclau. In R. Wodak & B. Forchtner (Eds.), The Routledge handbook of language and politics (pp. 96–108). Routledge. https://www.taylorfrancis.com/chapters/edit/https://doi.org/10.4324/9781315183718-8/discourse-theory-ernesto-laclau-christoffer-k%C3%B8lvraa

Kusaka, W. (2017). Bandit grabbed the state: Duterte's moral politics. Philippine Sociological Review, 65, 49–75. http://www.jstor.org/stable/45014309

Kwon, M., & Valdez, K. (2024). Sarcasm or sexism? Media framing of Duterte's misogynistic speeches. *Asian Journal of Women's Studies, 30*(2), 85–109. https://doi.org/10.1080/12259276.2024.2367809

Laclau, E. (1996). The death and resurrection of the theory of ideology. *Journal of Political Ideologies, 1*(3), 201–220. https://doi.org/10.1080/13569319608420738

Laclau, E. (2005). *On populist reason.* Verso.

Laguilles-Timog, R. A. (2020). Populism, patriarchy, protest: Feminist issues, responses, and actors during the first three years of the Duterte administration. *Review of Women's Studies, 30*, 87–106.

Löffler, M., Luyt, R., & Starck, K. (2020). *Political Masculinities and Populism. NORMA, 15*(1), 1–9. https://doi.org/10.1080/18902138.2020.1721154

Love, N. S. (2020). Shield maidens, fashy femmes, and tradwives: Feminism, patriarchy, and right-wing populism. *Frontiers in Sociology, 5*, Article 619572. https://doi.org/10.3389/fsoc.2020.619572

Maftuhin, A. (2023). Islamic law, disability, and women in Indonesia: The cases of Nahdlatul Ulama and Muhammadiyah. *Journal of Disability & Religion, 28*(1), 13–27. https://doi.org/10.1080/23312521.2023.2255860

Mahmood, S. (2006). Feminist theory, agency, and the liberatory subject: Some reflections on the Islamic revival in Egypt. Temenos-Nordic Journal for the Study of Religion, 42(1). https://doi.org/10.33356/temenos.4633

Maizunati, N. A., & Sulistyaningrum, E. (2019, August). Impact evaluation of Program Keluarga Harapan (PKH): Indonesia conditional cash transfer program on iron supplements consumption on pregnant women in Indonesia. In First International Conference on Administration Science (ICAS 2019) (pp. 35–41). Atlantis Press. https://www.atlantis-press.com/proceedings/icas-19/125916442

Malik, A. (2023). New variants of ultra-conservative Islamic schools in Indonesia: A study on Islamic school endeavor with Islamic group movement. *Power and Education, 16*(1), 14–28. https://doi.org/10.1177/17577438231163042

Marwah, S. (2019). Reading women participations on populism politics. Politik Indonesia: Indonesian Political Science Review, 4(2), 255–273. https://doi.org/10.15294/ipsr.v4i2.17053

Mendoza, R. U., & Jaminola, L. M. (2020). Is Duterte a populist?: Rhetoric vs. reality. Horizons: Journal of International Relations and Sustainable Development, 15, 266–279. https://www.jstor.org/stable/48573652

Mense-Petermann, U., Welskopp, T., & Zaharieva, A. (Eds.). (2022, May 5). In search of the global labor market. Leiden, The Netherlands: Brill. https://doi.org/10.1163/9789004514539

Mény, Y., & Surel, Y. (2002). The constitutive ambiguity of populism. In Y. Mény & Y. Surel (Eds.), Democracies and the populist challenge (pp. 1–21). London: Palgrave Macmillan. https://doi.org/10.1057/9781403920072_1

Mietzner, M. (2014). Indonesia's 2014 elections: How Jokowi won and democracy survived. *Journal of Democracy, 25*(4), 111–125. https://doi.org/10.1353/jod.2014.0073

Mietzner, M. (2020). Rival populisms and the democratic crisis in Indonesia: Chauvinists, Islamists and technocrats. *Australian Journal of International Affairs, 74*(4), 420–438. https://doi.org/10.1080/10357718.2020.1725426

Mills, C. (2000). Efficacy and vulnerability: Judith Butler on reiteration and resistance. *Australian Feminist Studies, 15*(32), 265–279. https://doi.org/10.1080/08164640050138761

Mudde, C., & Kaltwasser, C. R. (2015). Vox populi or vox masculini? Populism and gender in Northern Europe and South America. *Patterns of Prejudice, 49*(1–2), 16–36. https://doi.org/10.1080/0031322X.2015.1014197

Muhtadi, B. (2025). Collective memory, democratic ambivalence, and authoritarian notions of democracy: Explaining the rise of Prabowo Subianto. Journal of Current Southeast Asian Affairs, 0(0). https://doi.org/10.1177/18681034251337763

Navera, G. S. (2021). The president as macho: Machismo, misogyny, and the language of toxic masculinity in Philippine presidential discourse. In O. Feldman (Ed.), When politicians talk (pp. 209–226). Springer. https://doi.org/10.1007/978-981-16-3579-3_11

Novio, E. B. C. (2022). Marcos presidency and the challenges to journalists and educators in the Philippines. *Media Asia, 50*(1), 124–127. https://doi.org/10.1080/01296612.2022.2104489

Nurmila, N. (2020). New grounded feminist approach to Islam in Indonesia: A textual analysis of Rahima and Fahmina's publications. Journal of Asian Social Science Research, 2(1), 25–52. https://doi.org/10.15575/jassr.v2i1.11

Ostiguy, P., & Moffitt, B. (2020). Who would identify with an "empty signifier"?: The relational, performative approach to populism. In F. Panizza (Ed.), Populism in global perspective (pp. 47–72). Routledge. https://www.taylorfrancis.com/chapters/edit/https://doi.org/10.4324/9781003110149-4

Papaioannou, K., Slewe, S., Pantazi, M., & van Prooijen, J. W. (2025). "Dissatisfied democrats, but democrats nonetheless?" Unraveling the democratic paradox between populism and preference for alternative political systems. Political Psychology. https://doi.org/10.1111/pops.70009

Parcon, I. C. R. (2021). Understanding Dutertismo: Populism and democratic politics in the Philippines. *Asian Journal of Social Science, 49*(3), 131–137. https://doi.org/10.1016/j.ajss.2021.03.001
Pratt, G. (2009). Circulating sadness: Witnessing Filipina mothers' stories of family separation. *Gender, Place & Culture, 16*(1), 3–22. https://doi.org/10.1080/09663690802574753
Rašković, M., Haynes, K. T., & Vangeli, A. (2024). The emergence of populism as an institution and its recursive mechanisms: A socio-cognitive theory perspective. *Journal of International Business Policy, 7*, 19–40. https://doi.org/10.1057/s42214-023-00164-1
Rinaldo, R. (2011). Muslim women, moral visions: Globalization and gender controversies in Indonesia. *Qualitative Sociology, 34*, 539–560. https://doi.org/10.1007/s11133-011-9204-2
Sanders, R., & Jenkins, L. D. (2022). Control, alt, delete: Patriarchal populist attacks on international women's rights. *Global Constitutionalism, 11*(3), 401–429. https://doi.org/10.1017/S2045381721000198
Sauer, B. (2020). Authoritarian right-wing populism as masculinist identity politics: The role of affects. In G. Dietze & B. Roth (Eds.), Right-wing populism and gender: European perspectives and beyond (pp. 23–40). transcript Verlag.
Sauer, B. (2024). Chapter 12: Women, gender and right-wing authoritarian populism. In Drivers of authoritarianism. Cheltenham, UK: Edward Elgar Publishing. https://doi.org/10.4337/9781035324705.00022
Sengul, K. (2019). Populism, democracy, political style and post-truth: Issues for communication research. *Communication Research and Practice, 5*(1), 88–101. https://doi.org/10.1080/22041451.2019.1561399
Spierings, N., Zaslove, A., Mügge, L. M., & de Lange, S. L. (2015). Gender and populist radical-right politics: An introduction. *Patterns of Prejudice, 49*(1–2), 3–15. https://doi.org/10.1080/0031322X.2015.1023642
Stopler, G. (2021). The personal is political: The feminist critique of liberalism and the challenge of right-wing populism. *International Journal of Constitutional Law, 19*(2), 393–402. https://doi.org/10.1093/icon/moab032
Thomassen, L. (2019). Discourse and heterogeneity. In T. Marttila (Ed.), Discourse, culture and organization (pp. 33–56). Cham: Palgrave Macmillan. https://doi.org/10.1007/978-3-319-94123-3_3
Tuğal, C. (2023). Three routes to autocratic rule: Market reforms, politics, and masculinist performance in the making of right-wing regimes. Journal of Right-Wing Studies, 1(1). https://doi.org/10.5070/RW3.1497
Webb, A., & Curato, N. (2019). Populism in the Philippines. In D. Stockemer (Ed.), Populism around the world (pp. 57–76). Cham: Springer. https://doi.org/10.1007/978-3-319-96758-5_4
Webber, D. (2006). A consolidated patrimonial democracy? *Democratization in Post-Suharto Indonesia. Democratization, 13*(3), 396–420. https://doi.org/10.1080/13510340600579284
Yuval-Davis, N. (2004). Gender and nation. In N. Yuval-Davis, Women, ethnicity and nationalism (pp. 30–40). Routledge. https://www.taylorfrancis.com/chapters/edit/https://doi.org/10.4324/9780203169582-5/gender-nation-nira-yuval-davis
Yuval-Davis, N. (2006). Intersectionality and feminist politics. *European Journal of Women's Studies, 13*(3), 193–209. https://doi.org/10.1177/1350506806065752

Chapter 12
Women in the Media Spaces: Negotiating Inequalities and Power Struggle in a Neoliberal World

Caroline C. Netto and M. Maya

Abstract The neoliberal economy has significantly transformed the nature and meaning of work across sectors by deepening existing inequalities through the internationalisation of labour and shifts in work culture. Women were the worst victims of such a disruptive shift in work culture. The media industry is one sector that had a profound impact through digitalisation, the growth of satellite channels and the visual media revolution. With the demand for emerging visual media, the work culture and the skills of media personnel were redefined. On one hand, the visual media attracted many women to take up media journalism as a prospective career as it was perceived as a glamorous career with immense visibility and popularity. It redefined their ideas of courage, freedom and femininity. On the other hand, the women in the media struggle to keep up with the demands of the industry in terms of their work timings, nature of work and to negotiate with the power structure. In a patriarchal system, the cultural conditioning of society and family responsibilities also affect the well-being of women. This is a qualitative study using narrative method and in-depth interviews were conducted with seven women media professionals working in different media platforms in Kerala, South India. The research objective was to understand how work in media was redefined in a neoliberal context and examine its implications for women in media. Through a phenomenological lens, researchers have explored how 'successful' women media professionals navigated through their everyday challenges both at work and in their private spaces.

Keywords Women in media · Neoliberal economy · Power structure · Gender inequality · Work culture · Women in workplace · Work-life balance · Feminine identity · Visual media · Intersectionality · Economic inequality

---

C. C. Netto (✉) · M. Maya
Christ University, Bangalore, India
e-mail: nettocaroline89@gmail.com

M. Maya
e-mail: maya.m@christuniversity.in

C. C. Netto
Independent Researcher, Bengaluru, Karnataka, India

H. Adam and F. A. Malik (eds.), *The Political Economy of Gender*,
https://doi.org/10.1007/978-981-92-2785-3_12

1 Introduction

Trickle-down theories assumed that economic growth would automatically result in inclusive development. However, unequal distribution of economic resources across sections of society is still a reality. Although women made inroads into the male-dominated territories of the workforce, each profession remains a contested area where power struggle plays a great role in determining who gets what. Structural aspects and hierarchical organisation of societies result in women experiencing economic inequality which is reflected through female workforce participation, glass ceiling effect, job insecurity, job segregation and gender pay gap. Entry into a profession does not result in both males and females getting the same positions and privileges. In their studies on women in medicine and engineering, scholars like Bonner (1992) and Mcilwee (1992) discuss how women were getting lower-paying and less prestigious positions. They also examined the ways in which organisations uphold the traditional values in their workplace culture and ideologies. This is reflected in other professions as well.

A significant number of women began to enter medical and engineering professions by around the 1970s. Journalism was another elite profession where male domination was clearly practised. A study on media and gender in the Asian and Pacific regions by the International Federation of Journalists (IFJ) in 2015 (Seul, 2018) indicated that media is still a male-subjugated industry. Media groups were reluctant to provide leadership roles to women in the editorial and non -editorial departments due to the influence of gendered socialisation which categorized women as homemakers and inherently incapable (Joshi & Maniar, 2006). In the 1970s and 1980s women in print media generally were not allowed to work late. In India, institutional support for women media professionals remains inadequate, with limited provisions for workplace safety, transportation, and maternity benefits.

The increasing number of women in media (Black & Juhn, 2000) can be partially attributed to the expansion of media and communication courses at the tertiary level, and the growing appeal of audiovisual journalism. However, the professional lives of women in media must be examined through a deeper understanding of how gender operates within neoliberal workspaces.

This study addresses the critical gap in understanding how neoliberalism has reshaped the work culture in media and the implications it has for women professionals. While media appears to offer visibility and empowerment, it often reinforces gendered hierarchies and exclusions. This study explores the everyday life experiences of women in the media and how they balance their professional roles and personal responsibilities in a patriarchal structure.

The study also analyses how neoliberalism has influenced the nature and organisation of work in the media industry and contributes to the literature on gender and work in the context of the media industry in India. The narratives of women media professionals highlight the challenges of the demands of the workspace and the empowerment. It offers critical insights for policy makers, media organisations, and gender scholars to reimagine more inclusive and supportive work environments in the media sector.

2 Methodology

This study adopts a qualitative, phenomenological approach to explore the lived experiences of women media professionals in Kerala, South India. The Kerala Model of Development—marked by high female literacy rate, high rate of women's higher education, and favourable gender development indices—offers a significant backdrop to examine the paradoxes of women's empowerment in the media industry.

A narrative method was employed to elicit in-depth personal accounts, using a semi-structured interview guide. Seven women working across visual and print media platforms were selected through purposive sampling to capture diverse professional trajectories and institutional contexts. The thematic analysis focused on how participants construct meaning around power, gender, resistance, and autonomy in their professional lives. Ethical protocols were strictly followed. Informed consent was obtained, confidentiality assured, and pseudonyms used. Reflexivity addressed the influence of positionality on data collection and data analysis processes.

3 Proliferation of Electronic Media and Satellite Television in India

The history of the television industry in India dates back to the 1960s. The second phase of evolution began with the introduction of the Satellite Instructional Television Experiment (SITE) project in 1975 which brought developmental and educational programmes to the rural audience.

Television broadcasting remained largely a monopoly of the government till the landmark supreme court judgment in 1995 in the case the Union Government Vs Cricket Association of Bengal. Justice P.B. Sawant and Justice S. Mohan declared "The airwaves or frequencies are a public property." This led to the liberalisation of the Television broadcast sector. The entry of private players opened up a wide range of programmes, news and entertainment (Suresh, 2023). This legal shift facilitated the entry of private media enterprises, significantly altering the landscape of Indian television (Mehta, 2008; Suresh, 2023; Wildermuth, 2005).

In Kerala, Doordarshan Kendra was established in Thiruvananthapuram in 1985, but regular Malayalam-language programming only commenced in 1994 with the advent of regional satellite broadcasting. The expansion of the Malayalam visual media industry began in the 1990s with the emergence of private channels. Asianet, launched in 1993, became the first regional private channel, followed by Surya TV in 1998 under the Sun Network. These early channels predominantly focused on entertainment content such as serials and films, with limited attention to daily news broadcasts.

A pivotal transformation in Indian television history was with the onset of satellite-based commercial news broadcasting in the early 2000s. This development expanded the number of television news channels across India. By 2014, over 400 news channels were operational, signifying a marked transition from state-controlled news dissemination to a competitive, commercially driven media environment (Suresh, 2023).

The liberalised media economy led to intensified competition among private broadcasters, with significant emphasis placed on audience ratings. Programmes were increasingly designed to enhance Television Rating Points (TRP) and rankings provided by the Broadcast Audience Research Council (BARC). Consequently, the nature of television content—especially news—shifted from information dissemination to sensationalism and spectacle.

4 Gendered Nature of Work in Neoliberal Media Industries

Impact of globalization and liberalisation on the gendered self has been explored among the Indian women journalists working in the English speaking television newsrooms. The post feminist rhetoric makes women apolitical by emphasizing the notion of 'equality' and there is almost no space for collective resistance against sexism (Kanagasabai, 2019). The Network of Women in Media, India (NWMi), as an informal platform supports Indian women working in media. A newer way of protest is the effective use social media platforms to discuss instances of sexism, sexual harassment and gender discrimination at workplace (ibid).

Kanagasabai (2019) critically examined the intersection of age, gender and neoliberalism in shaping the lived experiences of women journalists in the Indian English language Television industry. This study highlights the subtle forms of sexism, the gendered expectations on their appearance and the barriers in career progression, particularly for the younger women. It often puts the burden of coping with the competition on the individual rather than pushing for structural changes to address gender inequalities. This work contributes significantly to the literature by foregrounding the often-overlooked generational dimensions of gendered labor in media spaces. This study critically situates the newsroom within a broader neoliberal context, where media organizations prioritize speed, sensationalism, and profit over ethics and inclusivity.

Women also began to use public platforms to challenge gendered ageism (Ross, 2023). Studies from the developed countries show that opportunities for women in the media are also affected by ageism. Based on the testimonials from 24 women media professionals in the United Kingdom who self identified themselves as 'older', Ross (2023) discusses routinized micro aggression and the practice of non renewal of contracts once women crosses their 40 s and lack of promotions. Women are pushed out of the front-of-camera roles after their 40 s and many women experience the death of their professional identity. The 'available-all hour' ethos also significantly affects the work-life balance of women who have caring responsibilities. This needs to be read alongside North's (2016) study among Australian television industry, where it was found that women who are in the decision-making roles are those having no children.

Louis North (2009) highlights the impact of neoliberal restructuring of the media industry. Her study among the journalists in the Australian print media examines how neoliberalism intensified workload and ethical pressure for marginalised women.

Ammu Joseph (2004), critically examined the systemic barriers faced by women in the Indian media industry. Her study highlights the underrepresentation of women in leadership roles, exclusion from decision making roles which limits their career progression, confinement of women to "soft" news and experiences of sexual harassment. that signifies the gendered nature of the media content. These have negative implications on women's participation and retention in the media industry.

There are many studies from Africa that examine the struggle of women in the media. Mwananjela (2022) explored the lived experience of women journalists in Media in Tanzania and argues that in a media industry, where systems and structures are patriarchal, women are underrepresented in decision-making process and confined to managing 'soft news'. Zviyita and Mare (2024) explore instances of online gender based violence experienced by women journalists from Namibia. The lack of structural support results in self censorship and retreating from the public sphere. Authors thus highlight the consequences of underreporting of specific challenges faced by women journalists and attribute it to the prevailing patriarchal, gendered norms. In a similar study, Alade (2025) discusses the subtle ways in which sexism and bias affect the career progress of women journalists.

Mahadeen (2022) examined the challenges faced by women media professionals in Jordan. Through a qualitative analysis, the study highlights challenges like sexual harassment, unequal pay, and restricted career progression. A similar study in the male dominated conventional society of Kuwait, Dashti and Mesbah (2015) analysed the perceptions of 237 female media professionals to understand their perceptions. Although they felt empowered through education and changed lifestyle, societal and cultural factors were detrimental to their empowerment. All these studies reiterate the gendered nature of work in neoliberal media industries.

5 Media as a Glamorous but Precarious Career

The proliferation of private media houses and the expansion of journalism education contributed to an increased presence of women in the early phases of media careers. Journalism, especially in the visual media, has been increasingly perceived as a creative and glamorous profession offering high visibility and social recognition (Josephi & Alonso, 2021). For many women, this visibility was both empowering and burdensome.

> ... because of the visibility we get we are considered celebrities at one time, but we are not celebrities. If we go somewhere, we will be recognized... our family might be proud of us (Participant A).

However, the perception of glamour often obscures the structural challenges embedded in the profession. Despite growing numbers of women enrolling in journalism courses, their long-term participation in the workforce remains limited, with a sharp decline observed after the early career phase.

6 Mid-Career Dropout and Gendered Career Trajectories

While women's entry into journalism has increased, their retention in the field shows a significant gender gap. The majority of women journalists are concentrated in the 25–34 age group, but there is a sharp drop in the 34–44 age group. This attrition is often linked to marriage, motherhood, and the struggle to balance professional demands with domestic responsibilities.

Studies show that India has seen a nearly 40 percent drop in female workforce participation (Josephi & Alonso, 2021), reflecting how deeply entrenched patriarchal norms intersect with neoliberal work cultures.

> The absence of extended familial support, poses a significant challenge… Unlike our male counterparts, we are constrained in our ability to devote time to further study or professional reading—both of which are essential for our career advancement. If we were unmarried or did not have children, perhaps more time could be dedicated to these pursuits. ..time is a scarce resource… —after my office hours, my second shift starts at home. It is not that female anchors are not talented or not as dedicated as their counterparts (Participant A).

The reorganisation of media into a competitive, ratings-driven industry has intensified the pace of work, introducing irregular shifts, high performance expectations, and job insecurity. This restructuring makes it increasingly difficult for women to maintain a work-life balance, particularly in the absence of family or institutional support systems.

> We cannot grow in this career without adequate support from our family. I am even considering switching to teaching or any government jobs… I am not sure how many men in my community would be open to marry me because of my career (Participant G).

Many women in the early stages of their careers are already considering alternative professions that offer greater stability and predictability. The pressure to perform in a hyper-competitive environment, without adequate support, leads to burnout and career dissatisfaction.

7 Work-Life Balance and Role Constraints in the Media Industry

The persistent gender gap in workforce participation in the media industry underscores the urgent need for gender mainstreaming in journalism education (Bamezai et al., 2020). Integrating gender perspectives into media curricula is crucial for enabling future journalists to critically engage with the gendered power dynamics that operate from within newsrooms to the content disseminated to the public (North, 2010). Such an approach can foster a more reflexive and equitable professional culture in media institutions.

A significant shift has occurred in the norms regulating working hours within the media industry, particularly with the adoption of shift-based systems. While these changes are framed as flexible management practices aimed at maximizing productivity in neoliberal economies, they often redefine normative expectations around working hours. Instead of promoting genuine flexibility, they can result in heightened stress, instability, and psychological strain for workers (Telford & Briggs, 2022).

The narratives of our participants illustrate how these changing work structures intersect with gendered expectations in complex ways. Our participant A shared how she navigated irregular work schedules and caregiving responsibilities. Despite working in the same organization as her husband, the burden of childcare, particularly when her child was unwell, fell disproportionately on her. She devised her own strategy by taking unconventional split shifts, a practice not formally supported by the organization, at great cost to her health and well-being.

> I began my workday as early as 5:00 AM and continued until 9:00 AM to accommodate my husband's office schedule, as he needed to report to work by 9:00 AM. At the time, we were living nearby, which made this arrangement somewhat manageable. However, when my son fell ill, the situation became far more challenging, leaving me with no opportunity to rest. I would return for another shift from 8:00 PM to 12:00 AM. Although our organisation did not have a system for split shifts, I negotiated a special arrangement with management, without which I would not have been able to continue working. In doing so, I severely compromised my own health, sleeping only between 1:00 AM and 4:00 AM, with no time for rest during the day (Participant A).

Such accounts reveal how deeply entrenched gender roles and societal expectations continue to shape women's experiences in the workplace. The prevailing norms regarding 'normal' working hours often conflict with the multiple roles women are expected to perform at home, constraining their career choices and personal aspirations. The media industry, in its gender-neutral framing, frequently overlooks the unequal burden of care work, making it difficult for women to thrive professionally.

> I am passionate about filmmaking and have close friends who invited me to collaborate as an assistant on their projects. However, I am unable to commit to extended periods away from home—such as two-month shoots—due to the responsibilities expected of me as a wife and mother. Sometimes, these expectations become burdensome, leaving little room to pursue my own aspirations (Participant D).

The dilemma of prioritising between family and career was a recurring theme among various participants. This highlights the significance of institutional support for healthy work-life balance. Projecting media as a gender neutral profession has obscured the caregiving responsibilities of women in a patriarchal society, thus forcing many women to opt for career breaks or exiting the profession. This imbalance adds on further to the growing gender disparity in media workforce participation.

> Taking a career break was the most difficult compromise I made. Although I experienced a deep sense of despondency, I prioritised my children's well-being over my professional aspirations… I set aside all my personal and professional dreams, ... My decision was met with strong resistance, particularly from my mother, who had also been compelled to leave her job to care for us found it emotionally difficult to accept my choice. That period was marked by intense emotional stress and internal conflict (Participant A).

These narratives reflect how personal agency is often undermined by structural and cultural expectations, reinforcing the need for policy-level interventions and institutional reforms that support women's sustained participation and growth in the media sector.

8 Gender Stereotyping and Limited Access to Professional Opportunities

One of the key challenges of women in the media industry is the persistence of gender stereotypes that shape perceptions of professional competence and limit access to career-enhancing opportunities. The gendered nature of news production in Indian media, particularly in the Malayalam television industry, is reflected in both vertical and horizontal segregation. Vertical segregation refers to women's underrepresentation in decision-making roles, while horizontal segregation manifests through gendered divisions of reporting tasks (North, 2014).

Women journalists are frequently assigned to cover 'soft news' beats such as entertainment, health, education, and lifestyle, whereas men dominate the "hard news" domains of politics, economics, and crime reporting. The distinction between hard and soft news is not just a journalistic classification but a hierarchical one, where soft news is often devalued in terms of professional prestige and influence.

> Political and business news are for men. Even if we prove ourselves, we are still given less visible assignments. We're called in for softer stories, or women's issues—hardly the political debates on prime time (Participant B).

This division has significant implications for women's career progression, particularly in an industry increasingly driven by TRP (Television Rating Point) metrics. Editorial boards, operating under intense commercial pressure, often resist assigning prime-time political coverage to women, fearing potential losses in viewership.

> A man in this profession is perceived as a journalist by society. But a woman doing the same job is viewed as a 'news anchor' or a 'programme presenter'. The public sees us as closer to soap opera stars than journalists (Participant E).

The cumulative effect of these stereotypes and structural biases is the systemic exclusion of women from editorial leadership and decision-making roles. Despite increasing numbers of women entering the media industry, few rise to executive positions in television journalism in Kerala.

> If you look at the Malayalam visual media industry today, there's just one woman executive editor. It's not because women aren't capable. That's how patriarchy operates in this industry (Participant C).

This underrepresentation is not only a reflection of individual bias but a structural issue rooted in patriarchal attitudes within media institutions. Media organisations remain reluctant to risk breaking gender norms, thereby denying women journalists the opportunity to demonstrate their capabilities in high-stakes or high-visibility contexts.

Despite their growing presence, women continue to be excluded from decision-making and managerial positions in the media industry. Women in the media industry continue to encounter a hostile organizational culture, particularly when seeking opportunities that involve risk-taking, leadership, and autonomy. Structural constraints—rooted in patriarchal ideologies—impede their professional growth and diminish their access to decision-making roles (Sarikakis, 2014). The work culture remains male-dominated and often unresponsive to the specific needs of women employees. Structural exclusion from leadership roles limits women's ability to influence institutional culture and policy.

The industry, as narrated by participants, remains largely unreceptive to the upward mobility of women, instead reserving power and support for male professionals. Women's lack of access to administrative and managerial positions and male domination in the workspace construct a work culture insensitive to the needs and problems of women. Participant E succinctly described the emotional and structural dimensions of power within media organizations:

> Power operates as an emotional and symbolic construct within the media workspace... organisational culture does not actively create space for women's advancement. The institutional system tends to support and favour men, reinforcing patriarchal norms... women must constantly prove their competence in order to access leadership roles. However, such opportunities are frequently denied. They are hesitant to take risks by assigning prominent roles to emerging women professionals, driven by the fear that a lack of immediate audience acceptance could negatively affect ratings and competitive positioning (Participant E)

The systemically embedded belief that women are less capable of occupying leadership roles reinforces gendered power hierarchies and contributes to women's underrepresentation in key editorial and managerial positions. Risk-aversion among organizational decision-makers, driven by market competitiveness and audience reception, further restricts women's access to high-stakes responsibilities, regardless of their experience or demonstrated capabilities.

Women journalists who excel in their profession are met with a culture of professional jealousy, character assassination, and sexualized accusations—particularly when women transgress gendered boundaries or excel in male-dominated news beats. Participant F described the hostile reception of women's success in the field:

> As women in this profession, our work is often not taken seriously. I have personally encountered—and heard from numerous colleagues—that when a female journalist secures an exclusive story, her achievement is frequently attributed to alleged sexual favours rather than professional competence… It reflects a deeply ingrained perception that women who attain career success must have compromised themselves in some way. Such assumptions are rarely, if ever, directed at men, whose professional advancements are presumed to be based solely on merit (Participant F).

This deeply ingrained misogyny illustrates how women's professional achievements are frequently undermined by insinuations of sexual impropriety. The tendency to attribute women's success to perceived moral compromises, rather than competence, reflects a broader culture of patriarchal control and delegitimization. It reveals the gendered double standards that women must navigate, where career advancement is often viewed with suspicion, and merit is overshadowed by gendered stereotypes.

9 Sexual Objectification and Gendered Violence in the Media Workplace

Sexual objectification and symbolic violence against women are growing concerns in the media industry (Menéndez-Menéndez, 2014), reflecting deeper patriarchal structures embedded in professional environments. The very nature of journalistic work—requiring irregular hours, travel with male colleagues, and public visibility—places women in vulnerable positions. These experiences are not merely incidental but are symptomatic of the unequal gender power relations that persist in newsroom cultures (De Vuyst, 2017).

Women journalists often find themselves navigating male-dominated spaces where their presence is sexualised, and their professional identity is undermined. The media workplace, thus, becomes a site where gendered hierarchies are reinforced through both overt and covert forms of discrimination, including the trivialization of women's capabilities and the normalization of harassment.

> At the end of the day, no matter how well you interact, …, you're still just a body. That's the trend, and it's getting worse. With social media, this objectification and bullying become more rampant. If a woman voices an opinion, she's immediately targeted (Participant A).

This everyday experience of objectification constitutes one of the factors contributing to the gender gap in workforce participation. Women who enter the media industry often face burnout, fear of harassment, and emotional fatigue, leading to early exits or career stagnation. The lack of institutional mechanisms to protect and support women in these environments further exacerbates the issue. Without a critical transformation in workplace culture and accountability structures, the media industry risks continuing as a space where gender inequality is deeply entrenched.

10 Gendered Power Dynamics, and Resistance in the Media Industry

Political institutions in India maintain intricate ties with media organizations (Rajagopal, 2017), and the political allegiances of media houses significantly influence the production and framing of news content. For women professionals in the media industry, this alignment necessitates a constant negotiation with entrenched power hierarchies, especially for those aspiring to advance within these politically entangled structures.

Women journalists are not passive in these power dynamics. They develop personal strategies to challenge the systemic inequalities and assert their agency. They confront the institutional authority directly and indirectly when they are denied due recognition for their expertise.

> I was not given responsibilities and opportunities according to my experience. It has impacted my career growth and, consequently, my personal self esteem and personal well-being. I've expressed my concerns to my superiors, highlighting that my current role does not adequately utilize my experience and potential. I've communicated that I may need to explore other career paths if I don't see a pathway for further development (Participant A).

This act of negotiation was a means of asserting their professional worth and reclaiming self-identity and self-esteem. These are acts of everyday resistance to the marginalisation they experience in the media spaces by challenging the structural forces that delegitimize women's cultural and gender capital.

In sum, the findings underscore the intersection of structural inequality, symbolic violence, and gendered norms in shaping women's professional experiences in the media. Despite these constraints, women continue to assert their agency through both overt and subtle forms of resistance, challenging the deeply embedded patriarchal systems that govern the industry. These finding demonstrate that the subjective experience of women from the global south needs to be viewed in the larger framework of cultural, social and economic elements.

11 Discussion

This study contributes to the existing scholarship on gender and power in journalism by foregrounding the everyday experiences of women media professionals in India. In doing so, it interrogates how gendered inequalities are maintained and reproduced through the institutional and cultural logics of the media industry. Djerf-Pierre's (2007) analysis of journalism in Sweden outlines the interlocking influence of political, economic, and professional forces in shaping the field, while also identifying how journalistic capital is gendered and masculinity is aligned with prestige and authority. The findings of this study align with and extend these insights into the Indian context, revealing how masculine norms and power structures underpin not only newsroom hierarchies but also the symbolic valuation of what constitutes 'good' journalism.

While discussing gender and power in journalism in the context of Sweden, Djerf-Pierre (2007) argues how the field of journalism is defined by the nexus between political, economic and professional forces. The study also highlights the position of men and women within the industry; the forms of 'capital' accumulated by each of these binaries and the gendered perceptions on what is 'good' journalism. Prestige and power around the industry is associated with masculinity and this is reflected in the practices. The present study aligns with the findings of this study. As a masculine industry, media ensures systems, structure, traditions and a working environment that perpetuates gender inequality.

Pierre Bourdieu's (Bourdieu, 2006; Power, 1999) theories of field, habitus and capital can be used to understand the structure of the field of media. Media industry operates as a field where professionals compete for recognition, prestige and acknowledgement. The governing rules, norms and traditions in the industry support a traditional hierarchy where men outnumber women in key positions and a shared understanding of handing of 'hard news' as a male's responsibility. These deeply entrenched dispositions also create a self image for women professionals about their roles and limited career goals. Thus, we can say that the field is structured to make the media industry more accessible and supportive to men and there exists a gendered habitus. A woman professional's position in the media industry is also related to her access to the economic, social, cultural and symbolic capital. Gender pay gap (economic capital), male-dominated narratives on accomplished media professionals (symbolic capital) and the stereotypical images on feminine characteristics as weak in being assertive or risk taking (cultural capital) shapes the personal and professional images of women in the media industry. Access to social capital is very critical for any media professional. Networking opportunities, mentoring and informal networking are male dominated and many a time women cannot access influential networking opportunities. Informal meetings over social drinks usually occur outside of office hours and men take advantage of the situation. Data also shows the way in which the society and the industry looks at a woman who could excel in her profession - the lens of seduction and not on her merit and social capital.

The scenario can also be further understood through the lens of Amartya Sen's capability framework which focuses on people's capabilities and functionings. While education and training enables women to equip themselves with the skills to work in media settings, lack of adequate policies to ensure equal pay, protection against discrimination and maternity and child care support hinders them to succeed in their profession. Equally significant is the prevailing cultural norms that identify 'good media journalism' through a male gaze. Access to technology and networking opportunities are other factors that enhance the functioning of female media professionals. In essence we can say that structural factors play a critical role in defining the success of women media professionals.

Joan Acker (Acker, 1990) argues that gender differences in organisational culture are due to structural factors and not personal characteristics. The neoliberal economies portray a gender-neutral and disembodied organisational structure.

However, this is a strategy of control and image building. In actuality, organisational structures are deeply embedded within the masculine lens of gender differences. The portrayal of a gender -neutral organisational structure compels women to excel in their profession with their individual merit by completely negating the support systems at the familial, organisational and societal levels to achieve the goals. Lumsden (1995) examines this paradox in the context of women journalists. This stands very relevant in the context of this study also. Media industry in India is grappling with the neoliberal trends of increasing commercialisation, corporatisation (Chadha, 2017) and is a heavily politicised arena. Politicisation of ownership determines the kinds of news to be produced and controlled. The work culture and 'who does what' in the industry is influenced by these currents. Women hardly find a place in the decision making or leadership positions and thus the need for any support systems for women professionals is subsumed under the trope of gender neutral, merit based ecosystem.

12 Conclusion

The phenomenological exploration of the everydayness of women working in media highlights the changing organisational culture in the neoliberal era and the impact of it on women. The gender-neutral and disembodied organisational structure operate subtly and suppress women's career advancement in a very subtle way. The neoliberal structures obscures the gendered realities of work, leaving limited institutional support amidst gender discrimination and glass ceiling.

The study explored how patriarchal structures operate in the media industry and the gendered nature of access to professional capital. The everyday experiences of women journalists shows how they resist, negotiate and contest these structural inequalities. The narratives highlight the micro-level realities of reproduction of power and challenges of women in the media spaces. It foregrounds the significance of micro narratives in understanding structural inequalities.

The research contextualises the lived experience of Indian women journalists within the theoretical frameworks of Bourdieu and Sen. It adds on to the discourses on gender power dynamics in the media industry and explores how neoliberalism shapes the gendered subjectivities in the workplaces.

As a way forward the further studies can interrogate the intersections of caste, class, religion and regional differences with gender in producing structural inequalities in the media spaces. Comparative studies can analyse the diversity of experiences, the various challenges and strategies of women. The studies that engage with policy frameworks and organisational practices can facilitate equitable and inclusive media workspaces. The study also underscores the need for a structural change by adopting proactive measures by the media industry to support women in their organizations.

References

Acker, J. (1990). Hierarchies, jobs, bodies: A theory of gendered organizations. *Gender & Society, 4*(2), 139–158.

Agrawal, B. C., Joshi, S. R., & Sinha, A. K. (Eds.). (1986). *Communication Research for Development: The ISRO Experience*. Concept Publishing Company.

Alade, M.O. (2025). Gendered threats and attacks in and outside the newsroom: Nigerian female journalists' experiences with harassment. In *Patterns of Harassment in African Journalism* (pp. 67–87). Routledge.

Bamezai, G., Roy, A., Roy, A., & Chhetri, S. (2020). Gender mainstreaming as an essential part of journalism education in India. *World of Media. Journal of Russian Media and Journalism Studies* (3), 1–33.

Black, S. E., & Juhn, C. (2000). The rise of female professionals: Are women responding to skill demand? *American Economic Review, 90*(2), 450–455.

Bollinger, L., & O'Neill, C. (2008). *Women in media careers: Success despite the odds*. University Press of America.

Bonner, T. N. (1992). *To the ends of the Earth: Women's search for education in medicine*. Harvard University Press.

Bourdieu, P. (2006). The structures of the habitus. In *Anthropology in theory: Issues in epistemology* (pp. 407–416).

Chadha, K. (2017). The Indian news media industry: Structural trends and journalistic implications. *Global Media and Communication, 13*(2), 139–156.

Chaudhuri, M. (2017). *Refashioning India: Gender*. Media and a Transformed Public Discourse. Orient BlackSwan.

Dashti, A. A., & Mesbah, H. (2015). The perceptions of female media professionals in Kuwait about their job: An empowerment perspective. *Feminist Media Studies, 16*(2), 276–292.

De Vuyst, S. (2017). Shifting gender gaps in journalism? A longitudinal study on gender segregation in a converging media environment. *Catalan Journal of Communication & Cultural Studies, 9*(2), 249–263.

Djerf-Pierre, M. (2007). The gender of journalism: The structure and logic of the field in the twentieth century. *Nordicom Review,* 28.

Joseph, A. (2004). Working, watching, and waiting: Women and issues of access, employment, and decision-making in the media in India. In K. Ross & C. M. Byerly (Eds.), *Women and media: International perspectives* (pp. 149–167). Blackwell Publishing.

Josephi, B., & Alonso, M. O. (2021). Testing the connection between tertiary journalism education and the rising number of female journalists. *Journalism Practice, 17*(5), 1098–1113.

Joshi, U., Pahad, A., & Maniar, A. (2006). Images of women in print media—a research inquiry. *Indian Media Studies Journal, 1*(1), 39–51.

Kanagasabai, N. (2019). In the silences of a newsroom: Age, generation, and sexism in the Indian television newsroom. In *An intergenerational feminist media studies* (pp. 107–121). Routledge.

Lumsden, L. (1995). "You're a tough guy, mary—and a first-rate newspaperman": Gender and women journalists in the 1920s and 1930s. *Journalism & Mass Communication Quarterly, 72*(4), 913–921.

Mahadeen, E. (2022). *Female media professionals: Potential and limitations*, pp. 39–68 (2022).

Mcilwee, J. S. (1992). *Women in engineering: Gender*. Power and Workplace Culture. State University of New York Press.

Mehta, N. (2008). *Television in India: Satellites*. Politics and Cultural Change. Routledge.

Menéndez-Menéndez, M. I. (2014). Cultural industries and symbolic violence: Practices and discourses that perpetuate inequality. *Procedia - Social and Behavioral Sciences, 161*, 64–69.

Mwananjela, S. J. (2022). Gender equality; Lived experiences of women in the media industry in Tanzania. *International Journal of Research and Innovation in Social Science, 06*(08), 734–738.

North, L. (2009). Gendered experiences of industry change and the effects of neoliberalism. *Journalism Studies, 10*(4), 506–521.

North, L. (2014). The gender of "Soft" and "Hard" News: Female journalists' views on gendered story allocations. *Journalism Studies, 17*(3), 356–373.
North, L. (2016). Still a 'blokes club': The motherhood dilemma in journalism. *Journalism, 17*(3), 315–330.
North, L. (2010). The gender 'problem' in Australian journalism education. *Australian Journalism Review,* 32(2). https://papers.ssrn.com/sol3/papers.cfm
Power, E. M. (1999). An introduction to Pierre Bourdieu's key theoretical concepts. *Journal for the Study of Food and Society, 3*(1), 48–52.
Rajagopal, A. (2017). On media and politics in India: An interview with Paranjoy Guha Thakurta. *South Asia: Journal of South Asian Studies, 40*(1), 175–190.
Rao, S. (2009). Glocalization of Indian Journalism. *Journalism Studies, 10*(4), 474–488.
Robeyns, I. (2003). Sen's capability approach and gender inequality: Selecting relevant capabilities. *Feminist Economics, 9*(2–3), 61–92.
Ross, K. (2023). Gendered agism in the media industry: Disavowal, discrimination and the pushback. *Journal of Women & Aging, 36*(1), 61–77.
Sarikakis, K. (2014). Power, patriarchy, profit: Barriers to gender mainstreaming in media policy. In *Media and gender: A scholarly agenda for the global alliance on media and gender* (pp. 66–69).
Sen, A. (1999). *Development as freedom.* Oxford University Press.
Seul, S. (2018). A History of the international movement of journalists: Professionalism versus politics. *European Journal of Communication, 33*(2), 234–236.
Suresh, K. G. (2023). Emerging trends of regional news channels in India: A comparative study of Kerala and Uttar Pradesh. Unpublished PhD Thesis, Manav Rachna International Institute of Research and Studies, Faridabad.
Telford, L., & Briggs, D. (2022). Targets and overwork: Neoliberalism and the maximisation of profitability from the workplace. *Capital & Class, 46*(1), 59–76.
Vartika. (2022). Understanding gender and organizations: A literature review. In *Leading with diversity, equity and inclusion: Approaches, practices and cases for integral leadership strategy* (pp. 167–181).
Wildermuth, N. (2005). *A Cultural Economy of Satellite Television in India (Doctoral dissertation).* Film & Media Studies, University of Copenhagen.
Zviyita, I., & Mare, A. (2024). Same threats, different platforms? Female journalists' experiences of online gender-based violence in selected newsrooms in Namibia. *Journalism, 25*(4), 779–799.

Caroline C. Netto is an independent researcher based in Bangalore with a Ph.D. and M.Phil. in Public Health and a Master's in Sociology from Jawaharlal Nehru University, New Delhi. She has taught Sociology at the university level and worked as a research consultant with leading organisations. Her expertise spans gender, health, well-being, social inequalities, and qualitative research. Her doctoral work examined the social construction of professional women's well-being within the economic, political, and socio-cultural contexts of Kerala. With an interdisciplinary approach, her research reflects a commitment to critical inquiry and socially responsive scholarship in health equity, gender justice, ecology, and public health.

M. Maya is a sociologist and an Associate Professor in the Department of Sociology, Christ University, Bangalore. Her teaching and research interests intersect across critical domains such as indigenous communities, ecology and conservation, education, health, and participatory development. Her doctoral research examined the ways in which indigenous communities navigate participatory development frameworks in India. Her current research project is on the socio-economic and spatial transformations of urban peripheries in Bangalore. She has also published extensively on teaching-learning practices in higher education.

Chapter 13
Reimagining Gender Roles: The Politics of Femininity in the Global South

Ishika Jaiswal

Abstract This study analyses how right-wing populist governments in the Global South have politicized femininity to promote patriarchal nationalism, manifesting it as an instrument of ideological repression and enforcing gendered standards to consolidate power. In line with feminist political theory, postcolonial studies, and populism research, the study analyzes how women are made pivotal to nationalistic discourses, moral economies, and populist statecraft. Drawing from case studies of India, Brazil, El Salvador, Indonesia, Ethiopia, Pakistan, Sri Lanka, Mexico, and the Philippines, the study finds that femininity is not merely a cultural construct or personal identity but a politically contested and constructed subject. The major patterns identified include idealizing womanhood with nationalism, silencing feminist resistance, and employing legal and technological resources to monitor and discipline gender-nonconforming subjects. Each nation with specific yet intersecting configurations of gendered populism encompasses disguised cultural idealism, witnessing evangelical and misogynist populism, integrated conservatism, militarized patriarchy, and performative paternalism. These gendered imaginaries are not random byproducts but conscious tools of populist rule, inscribed through legislation, media rhetoric, religious vocabularies, and violence legitimized by the state. Channelling these spaces, femininity is disciplined, mobilized, moralized, monitored, and called upon as an icon of purity, sacrifice, and tradition, yet women's agency is cut short. Femininity, as both a contested and constructed space, is still a crucial site where the future of democracy and social justice in the Global South is under active negotiation.

Keywords Gender roles · Global south · Political ideology · Cultural idealism · Performative paternalism · Feminism · Gender-based violence · Authoritarianism · Intersectionality · Populism

I. Jaiswal (✉)
Former Faculty of Economics, Indian Institute of Management Sambalpur, Sambalpur, Odisha, India
e-mail: ishikajais.2@gmail.com

H. Adam and F. A. Malik (eds.), *The Political Economy of Gender*,
https://doi.org/10.1007/978-981-92-2785-3_13

1 Introduction

The Global South has experienced an increased presence of right-wing populist governments over the past decade that reimagine democratic institutions, political culture, and the parameters of belonging. Characterized by authoritarian strongman rule, anti-elite populism, and claims to represent "the real people," populism is fueled by the invention of internal enemies and national messiahs. Less well understood, however, is how gender, and particularly femininity, is made a central concern of these populist discourses. Rather than a marginal or symbolic issue, the representation and governance of femininity are instrumental in the project of authoritarian consolidation, the demarcation of national identity, and the institution of heteropatriarchal norms. This study explores femininity as a space of political contention—an arena where moral concerns, cultural uncertainties, and exclusionary rule come together in the populist imagination. Right-wing populism in the Global South is not merely reacting to economic grievances or political disillusionment but to an experienced crisis of identity. Consequently, populist politicians habitually invoke women's identities and reproductive roles as spaces for national purity or corruption (Farris, 2017). Whether portrayed as bearers of tradition or as agents of disruptive westernized modernity, feminine subjects are recruited into regimes of ideology that centralize particular norms of gender. The nation is imagined as feminine with the need for protection and simultaneously policed for deviance. This ambivalence is exactly why femininity proves to be such a powerful and versatile trope in right-wing populist enterprises.

Drawing on feminist scholarship and emphasizing the close relationship between nationalism and gender, this study positions femininity not as a passive recipient of state power but as an active location where political meaning is made and challenged. Women are integral to the symbolic reproduction of the nation biologically, culturally, and morally (Butler, 2020). Femininity is a battleground for moral regulation, cultural legitimacy, and disciplinary authority within right-wing populist regimes. Populist forces instrumentalize femininity to promote a masculinist state apparatus that sanctifies patriarchal family forms, suppresses feminist and queer activism, and practices moral panic as a form of governance (Ahmed, 2014; Banet-Weiser, 2018). Such instrumentalization is seldom homogeneous but rather mirrors the local political, religious, and cultural contexts within which populism emerges. In India, for example, Hindutva ideology both makes the Hindu woman a goddess and a gatekeeper of caste honour (Sahu, 2023). In Brazil, Bolsonaro's populism invokes evangelical Christian values and toxic masculinity to demonize feminists, queer identities, and sexual minorities (Reyes et al., 2022). In the same vein, Philippine President Duterte has utilized hypermasculine rhetoric and public misogyny to perform political claims of dominance, pronouncing a patriarchal regime of violence where women are demeaned and mythologized (Navera, 2021). In El Salvador, Bukele's populism merges digital surveillance with religious moralism to govern women's reproductive lives and provide cover for carceral rule (Ugarte et al., 2023). Indonesia's populist shift has drawn upon Islamic morality campaigns and limiting laws re-inscribing patriarchal codes of practice in the post-reform period (Ramadhani, 2023; White et al., 2023). The varying national backgrounds result in an agreed-upon logic that the regulation of femininity is foundational for the regulation of the nation. All such populist tactics are united by appealing to moral dualisms such as purity and impurity, traditionalist and modernism, and protector and enemy. Here, women are either portrayed as nationalist heroines or as cultural order traitors. Official femininity is usually rooted in religious orthodoxy, traditional family values, and circumscribed public agency. Departures from this norm, feminist activism, LGBTQ visibility, and egocentric vision, are not only read as political opposition but as threats to the very existence of the moral fibre of society (Phipps, 2020). This dynamic renders femininity a field of high political contention, where body behaviours, standards of dress, reproductive choices, and even public speaking are required to be regulated in the interest of cultural preservation. Yet femininity is more than a place of repression and is a tool of resistance.

In this connection, this study employed a comparative, intersectional approach to examine ways in which right-wing populist regimes in countries such as India, Brazil, El Salvador, Indonesia, Ethiopia, Pakistan, Sri Lanka, Mexico, and the Philippines organize, govern, and contest femininity. It establishes the symbolic and material form of gendered populist governance and maps lines of feminist counter-resistance that follow. In so doing, it fills the gap in feminist international political economy by showing how femininity becomes a crucial battleground in the political reorganization of the Global South.

2 Significance

Across the Global South, women and gender minorities are mobilizing against the illiberal tides of right-wing populism. These resistances tend to work at the intersections of gender, class, religion, and ethnicity, creating new solidarities that contend with both patriarchal nationalism and neoliberal exclusion. In this regard, this research holds significance in certain ways. It bridges the gap between critical feminist and populism studies by examining how femininity enables both domination and resistance in contemporary political regimes apart from providing a comparative lens across diverse Global South context that puts a nuanced understanding avoiding over-generalization based on Western-centric models on the table for discussion. Additionally, it illuminates the intersectionality of feminist struggles, revealing how the gender governance is entwined with other social dimensions. It also offers policy-relevant insight into how state laws, education, and digital rights shape gendered citizenship, contributing to international debates on gender justice. This study is significant to define how right-wing populist regimes in the Global South instrumentalize femininity as both a site of political control and resistance. The study analyses how do current forms of populist governance deploy femininity in the (re)production of national identity, morality, and state power across diverse contexts in selected nations and how do local factors shape these dynamics. In addition, it examines how do feminist movements and everyday resistances counter and reconfigure state-driven politics of femininity in these settings considering the intersectionality, especially the interplay of gender religion, and sexuality, that informs both the operation of authoritarian populist power and feminist resistance. Therefore, the study has following three broader objectives:

- The study theorises femininity as an active, contested political terrain under right-wing populism.
- The study compares national country-specific cases to reveal patterns and divergences in the governance of femininity.
- The study illustrates how feminist and intersectional mobilizations disrupt or subvert dominant patriarchal-nationalist scripts.

3 Review of Literature

The gendered dynamics of right-wing populism in the Global South intersect feminist political economy, intersectionality, and scholarship on authoritarian populism through an interdisciplinary theoretical perspective. These dynamics define how femininity is mobilized and regulated to reinforce political power, cultural dominance, and economic restructuring. This section reviews the available literature to understand how right-wing populist movements use femininity to reinstate national identity, impose heteropatriarchy, and controls resistance.

3.1 Feminism in Political Economy and the Gendered State

Feminism in political economy counters the conventional politico-economic dichotomy by focusing on how gender relations frame both markets and states. According to this perspective, the state is not neutral, thereby constructing the gendered power relations, and is being constructed by patriarchal norms. Feminist researchers have established that economic crises and neoliberal transitions tend to restructure gender roles in ways that complicate the burden on women through both paid and unpaid labour (Elson, 2017). These changes do not happen in isolation but are mediated through politically instrumental, culturally specific ideologies of femininity. In the Global South, state welfare rollback, privatization of social services, and labour informalization have disproportionately impacted women, especially those from marginal, caste, and class positions (Razavi, 2007a, 2007b). Populist regimes mobilize these insecurities using a romanticized picture of secure families and gender stratification, protecting exchange for compliance. The cult figure of the self-sacrificing nation-woman becomes pivotal to the populist political economy. She is hailed in nationalist discourse, but at the same time, overworked, marginalized, and deprived of bodily autonomy.

3.2 *Intersectionality and Politics of Belonging*

Intersectionality is a crucial parameter to comprehend the interaction of gender with demographics of class, caste, religion, and sexuality in complicated settings and context-dependent cases (Crenshaw, 1989). Instead of positing femininity in general, intersectional theory puts in the center the differential lives of women and gendered minorities according to intersecting systems of oppression. In right-wing populist discourses, this implies that state narratives regarding femininity are not unanimously defined. They valorize and demonize selectively various groups of women for building upon majoritarian support. For example, in Brazil, "gender ideology" moral panic creates a binary opposition between the 'good' Christian mother and the 'deviant' feminist or queer activist (Reyes et al., 2022). Such narratives create sharp boundaries around who is part of the nation and who poses a threat, and often have legal and violent ramifications. These processes within the "politics of belonging" are a discursive and material construction of national boundaries (Yuval-Davis, 2011, 2006). Belonging encompasses not merely citizenship but also cultural legitimacy and moral deservingness. Populist governments use this frame to exclude individuals who threaten heteronormative, patriarchal, or religious norms from complete national membership. Femininity then serves as the signal of inclusion or exclusion based on how it sits within the prevailing script of ideology.

3.2.1 Authoritarian Populist Moral Governance

Right-wing populism in the Global South increasingly overlaps with authoritarianism, creating regimes that concentrate power, constrain civil rights, and repress opposition. These regimes tend to act through what is called "moral governance," where the deployment of codes of the norm disciplines bodies and governs conduct (Foucault, 2007). Women and gender minorities are the ultimate victims of such moral governance because they threaten the figure of imagined purity and homogeneity of the nation. Populist authoritarianism resorts to gendered moralities to legitimate surveillance, censorship, and even violence exercised by the state. The leadership regimes in the Philippines and Brazil employed overtly misogynistic rhetoric as a performative tactic for mobilizing their constituency and expressing contempt for liberal democratic values (Navera, 2021). These discourses are not so much rhetorical as they have real-world consequences, like budget cuts to gender equality initiatives, greater impunity for gender violence, and legal limitations on reproductive and LGBTQ rights. Importantly, moral governance is frequently framed in terms of protection. The state presents itself as the benevolent protector of women, requiring safeguards from external and internal threats. This securitizing logic of protection is paradoxically profound, calling for surveillance, control, and force against the women as the declared protected subjects (Brown, 2019). Here, femininity is a weapon of securitization to legitimize authoritarianism.

3.2.2 Nationalism and the Affective State

Populist nationalism is not only a rational retaliation to politico-economic conditions but also an affective enterprise. Emotions, being a key driver, determine how individuals become attached to national imaginaries (Ahmed, 2014). Fear, nostalgia, pride, and disgust are enlisted to produce public policy and collective identities. The femininity in the emotional economy exists both as an object and a trench to channelise feelings. Nostalgia for patriarchy persistently underlies the impactful pull of right-wing populism. The idealized figure of the obedient housewife or sacrificial mother provokes a nostalgia for 'simpler times' that never actually existed but hold symbolic force (Banet-Weiser, 2018). Such impactful narratives are further amplified by digital media, religious entities, and educational institutions in perpetuating the gendered bases of the populist state. The state, in this case, does not simply exist as a legal or economic instrument but as an "affective state" (Laszczkowski & Reeves, 2018), manipulating public emotions to justify its power. Femininity is the site of this manipulation, bearing both idealized national virtues and feared transgressions. This is the emotional terrain that has to be traversed in order to chart the durability and appeal of gendered populism.

Therefore, the literature draws on feminist political economy, theories of populism, and gendered nationalism. It makes the case that gender, particularly femininity, is not peripheral but foundational to state and nation-building processes under authoritarian-populist rule. The literature highlights how women's bodies, roles, and representations are co-opted in nation-making and how "moral panic" and patriarchal discipline underpin populist governance, helping to create an "insider/outsider" dynamic both within and across nations. Also, the intersectionality is used here not only as an interpretive tool but as a means to understand the differentiated impact of, and response to, state power on marginalized women and non-binary people.

4 Data and Methodology

This study utilizes a case study approach, and the methodological framework analyzes nine Global South nations in which right-wing populist governments have used gendered rhetoric to redefine femininity and impose nationalist imaginaries from 2014 to 2024. The country-specific cases are based on purposive sampling to reflect diverse forms of right-wing populism and varieties of nationalism, religion, and regime type within the Global South. Each country was chosen because of the presence of a recent or ongoing populist regime with a visible gendered discourse along with the documented feminist mobilization and/or policy responses. The study utilizes various secondary sources including journal articles, books, government reports, policy documents as well the reports released by non-governmental and international organization from time to time. Further, the principle of intersectionality guides both data selection and interpretation while the comparative analysis used intersectionality as a lens to assess similarities and differences in managing femininity by the populist regimes and the specific forms of resistance that emerge. Intersectionality was employed as a leading principle in selecting case studies and sources of data for the nine Global South countries. This guaranteed inclusion of different varieties of right-wing populism and nationalist varieties, religious forms, and regime types, with priority on reported gendered discourses and feminist movements determined by intersecting social identities. Intersectionality helps in interpretation by parallelism and variability among the approaches selected populist regimes adopted to define femininity and the peculiar resistance that is witnessed. The study accounts for the intersectionality of gender, religion, and sexuality resulting in varying effects and responses for gender minorities and marginalized women under populist rule. The study revolves around the aspects that exemplify how women's bodies, roles, identities, preferences, and rights are deliberately placed at the heart of moral panics, cultural protectionism, and patriarchal domination. Each example consists of context, populist gendered tactics, and civil society or feminist reactions.

5 Analysis—Femininity and Right-Wing Populism in the Global South

5.1 India: Hypermasculinity and the Protector Paradigm

With the NDA-led government in 2014, the Hindu woman is significantly represented as a symbol of purity, sacrifice, and motherhood within right-wing nationalist rhetoric that epitomizes an idealized figure. Indian Hindu women hold a contradictory position within the populist Hindutva approach, which glorifies them as guardians of national culture while subordinating them through patriarchal domination. The government and governance proclaim to "protect" Hindu women by controlling their mobility, choices, and relationships instead of promoting their decisional autonomy. Feminist scholars believe these narratives help maintain gender hierarchies and presents an intensely exclusionary nationalism simultaneously (Pande, 2022; Singh & Parihar, 2024). Despite this, numerous Hindu women participated in movements, earning symbolic power while remaining bound to patriarchal scripts. The movements, such as #MeToo India Movement against sexual harassment at work, Anti-Rape protests against gender violence, Farmers' protests with large rural women participation, and Protests for environmental protection as well as women's land rights by Indian women from 2019 to 2024, provide a historically counter-narrative to state-centric constructs of womanhood (Chakrabarti, 2022; Rathnam, 2024; Kumar, 2021; Nanditha, 2022; Pan, 2023). Therefore, protection is a tool of control, disguised by the language of reverence and national pride. The well-performed resistance was not symbolic but performative, and feminism calls for equal opportunity and rights.

5.2 Brazil: Bolsonaro's Gender Backlash

In Brazil, Jair Bolsonaro's presidency (2019–2023) brought a surge in patriarchal nationalism infused with evangelical Christian ideology. Bolsonaro's homophobic and misogynist discourse and attacks on LGBTQ+ rights formed the pillars of his populist agenda. Femininity was reimagined through patriarchal family structures, motherhood as described through religion, and conformity to traditional norms. Programs on gender identity were defunded, and "gender ideology" was framed as a left-wing plot to obliterate Brazilian people (Corrêa, 2020). Feminist mobilization outraged through the #EleNão ("Not Him") movement and Black feminist mobilizations, thereby highlighting intersectionality (Yuval-Davis, 2011; Barbosa & Casarões, 2022; Reyes et al., 2022).

5.3 El Salvador: Criminalization of Reproductive Rights

In El Salvador, populist President Nayib Bukele's authoritarian drift has reinforced state's control over women's reproductive lives announcing the nation's absolute ban on abortion. Presented as "protecting life," the policy is an indication of punitive moral nationalism (Ugarte et al., 2023), where particularly poor, rural, and local women are jailed for obstetric emergencies errantly labelled as abortions. The regime constructs femininity as identical to maternity, eroding bodily autonomy (Center for Reproductive Rights, 2022). Feminist NGOs and global human rights pioneers resisted this moral absolutism, but repression and online surveillance have made it dangerous (UN Women, 2024).

5.4 Indonesia: Political Islam, Respectable Femininity, and Social Sanctions

The Joko Widodo government of Indonesia has witnessed growing Islamist populism under nominally secular rule. Dress standards, public behaviours, and feminism are increasingly governed by local Sharia-based regulations, especially in provinces like Aceh (Ramadhani, 2023; White et al., 2023). Veiling is presented as national moral duty, and unmarried women can go to school, travel, and enjoy nightlife, but in a strictly controlled manner. Gender is invoked in anti-LGBTQ legislation and social media shaming campaigns enforcing reasonably satisfactory femininity (Bratton, 2018) and the Indonesian feminists used digital media to oppose moral policing and adopt pluralism (Rinaldo, 2019).

5.5 Ethiopia: Militarized Masculinity and Ethno-Nationalist Gender Scripts

Prime Minister Abiy Ahmed's Ethiopia has seen militarization of politics and ethnic conflict, where gender is compromised and weaponized. Sexual violence by state and allied forces during war in Tigray is one of the instances whereby women's bodies are utilized as metaphors for national domination and degradation (Amnesty International, 2022). Women's appointments to prominent government seats, such as the presidency, however, points out strong patriarchal settings. Femininity is either romanticized in nationalist iconography or repressed in war and sacrifice narratives. Abuses have been documented by women's rights groups and transitional justice lobbied for, although repression is still high.

5.6 Pakistan: Honour, Surveillance, and Religious Nationalism

In Pakistan, the state and Islamic populists appeal to 'honour' as a foundation of national and family respectability. Women's freedom of movement, education, and dress are closely monitored, and honour killings and legal discrimination remained despite global condemnation (Zia, 2020). Populist leaders often frame women who protest or challenge norms, like those in the Aurat March, against Islamic and national values (Imran & Munir, 2018; Khan, 2023). Social media campaigns, such as #MeraJismMeriMarzi ("My Body My Choice"), ignited the national debates on bodily autonomy, however, it experienced backlash using fatwas and legal threats.

5.7 Sri Lanka: Ethno-Religious Purity and Femininity

Sinhalese-Buddhist right-wing nationalism in Sri Lanka has used femininity as a site of nationalist complaint and cultural memory. Post-war mythology turns Sinhala women into martyrs' mothers or war widows, making them icons of ethno-religious purity (Koens & Gunawardana, 2021), and the migrant women as 'foreign' or aberrant, especially where the dress code comes under discussion. Women's NGOs have resisted with peacebuilding and interfaith solidarity, but surveillance and stigma persisted (Tripathi, 2019).

5.8 *Mexico: Machismo Populism and the Feminicide Crisis*

The President of Mexico, Andrés Manuel López Obrador, has consistently downplayed the scale of gender-based violence, positioning feminist protests as elite or foreign-influenced. In the face of surging rates of feminicide, the government's response has been bland and reactive. Women's movements have organized large-scale protests, such as the #UnDíaSinNosotras ("A Day Without Us") strike, for state responsibility. Populist rhetoric names feminists as destabilizers rather than rightful claimants of rights, effectively vindicating patriarchal myths. Femininity in this context is contested space between symbolic motherhood and political annoyance.

5.9 *The Philippines: Duterte's Vulgar Populism and the Performance of Gender*

Under Rodrigo Duterte, the Philippines was treated to a hypermasculine political spectacle that objectified, insulted, and mocked women. Duterte's jokes on rape, menstruation, and female opposition leaders made misogyny seem mundane as populist charm (Navera, 2021). Femininity was demeaned and commodified, and women were glorified as caregivers or enablers of "strongmen," while detractors were labeled "bitches" or turncoats. In spite of this, campaigns like #BabaeAko ("I Am Woman") flew off the ground, counter narrating Duterte's through satire, online protest, and feminist coalition-building.

6 Negotiating the Narrative—Resistance and Reclamation

Even as right-wing populist regimes across the Global South strive to discipline and define femininity in a restrictive and instrumentalized manner, feminist movements continue to counter with stories, fostering resistance at global level. This section discusses how gender minorities and women in India, Brazil, El Salvador, Indonesia, Ethiopia, Pakistan, Sri Lanka, Mexico, and the Philippines resist the redefinition of gender roles, mostly taking back femininity as a space of collective empowerment, agency, and dissent.

6.1 *Intersectional Feminist Resistance*

The return of feminist mobilization in these nations is principally based on intersectional convention. Feminist movements are more and more defined by a consciousness of intersecting axes of oppression of gender, race, class, caste, religion, and sexuality. In India, the #MeToo movement and anti-rape protests at different points of time represented the intersection of gender-based resistance (Singh & Parihar, 2024). Women's bodies were politically asserted as spaces, contesting public space against patriarchal norms as well as authoritarian nationalism. Likewise, in Brazil, the #EleNão ("Not Him") movement rallied millions against Bolsonaro's misogynistic and authoritarian language. These movements channelized the histories of Afro-Brazilian, Indigenous, and LGBTQ+ activism to create a mass feminist front, leveraging online resources and street action to combat patriarchal and neoliberal authoritarianism (Barbosa & Casarões, 2022; Reyes et al., 2022).

6.2 Digital Feminism and Networked Solidarity

Digital media platforms have become important sites of resistance. Mexican and Philippine feminist activists have employed hashtags, memes, and social media campaigns to make protests against gender-based violence and authoritarian misogyny viral. Campaigns like #NiUnaMenos and #BabaeAko points out he state complicity in violence against women and hold the government publicly accountable (Navera, 2021; UN Women, 2024). In El Salvador and Pakistan, where protest is limited by state surveillance and repression, digital feminist campaigns provided comparative safety and magnified reach. Pakistani feminist initiatives such as Aurat March have used Instagram and Twitter to construct transnational feminist alliances, subvert religious orthodoxy, and organize around bodily autonomy in the face of ongoing threats from right-wing and state forces (Zia, 2022).

6.3 Reclaiming Feminine Symbols and Cultural Practices

At times, the reclaiming of religious and cultural heritage is an effective antidote to right-wing hijackings of femininity in the Global South and is not necessarily oppositional in Western liberal ways. In Indonesia, Muslim feminists dispute both Islamist and nationalist patriarchies through reinterpretation of religious scriptures, intending to achieve gender justice (Bratton, 2018). They decolonize feminism by using local knowledge and spiritual resources. In Sri Lanka and Ethiopia, motherhood, elder women's roles, and leadership in the community are rearticulated as traditionally held practices that challenge imposed norms of gender. Ethiopian women's organizations involved in peacebuilding and community resilience, for example, underscore traditionally feminine roles not as subordinate or passive, but as politically critical to post-conflict nation-building (Hadis et al., 2021).

6.4 Institutional Advocacy and Policy Interventions

Resistance also appears in institutionalized actions. The bureaucrats, academicians, and lawyers in India, Sri Lanka, and Mexico advocate for legal change and gender-sensitive policy. Although, they work in the patriarchal settings in government organizations, they initiate reform via channels of litigation and advocacy. Feminist politicians in Mexico have used legislative authority to enact gender equality and reproductive rights despite religious conservatism (Reyes et al., 2022). In Sri Lanka, feminist movements during and after the war push for transitional justice, aiming to prioritize women's experiences in peace negotiations and processes of memorialization (Tripathi, 2019). Such efforts illustrate that resistance is not just about protest and performance but also the slow, painstaking work of reforming institutions.

Across all of these contexts, what is important is a rich tapestry of affective solidarities where affective connections are made through the shared experience of dispossession, violence, and hope (Berlant, 2011). International groups like the Global South Women's Forum and regional groups like DAWN (Development Alternatives with Women for a New Era) collaboratively work to manage the local dynamics in a globalized manner with autonomy and differentiation (Dengler & Seebacher, 2019). Feminist opposition is not the definition opposite of the populist endeavour, but its negation, where populism constricts identity, feminism broadens it; where it mythologises the past, feminism envisions the future; where it suppresses, feminism roars, diversely, and with intent.

7 Findings: Femininity Under Populism

This study advocates that the right-wing populist regimes throughout the Global South institutionally instrumentalize femininity as a fundamental site of political domination, symbolic representation, and moral rule. Far from being a passive or a political category, femininity proves to be a highly contested and dynamic terrain which is idealized, regulated, degraded, and resisted all at once. Within populist discourses, the woman is a flexible symbol of a sacrificing mother, keeper of culture, vulnerable body in need of state protection, and, on the other hand, feminist, queer, or sexually independent subject as a national threat. Through these binary figurations, femininity is deployed as a device to buttress patriarchal state power and moral authority. From India's Hindutva mobilizations to Brazil's evangelical anti-gender politics, from El Salvador's criminalization of procreation to the Philippines' state misogyny, populist governments have used emotional, cultural, and legal means to discipline gender nonconformity and silence feminist resistance. Femininity here is not merely about personal identity or social role; rather, it is at the center of the state's project to determine who belongs and who does not. It is the ground upon which more expansive ideological struggles concerning nationalism, morality, and state legitimacy are fought. Femininity is not simply a space of control but also resistance and reinvention. Feminist struggles across the Global South are reclaiming feminine icons in creative forms, mobilizing intersectional solidarities, and transgressing hegemonic scripts all alike through grassroots activism as well as social media campaigns. Whether by means of the #MeToo resistance, the #EleNão imagination, or women legislatures' institutional work in Mexico and Sri Lanka, these struggles are producing eye-opening counter-narratives that counter the populist-authoritarian state. Construing femininity as a political space requires an interdisciplinary analytical framework that appropriates feminist political economy, intersectionality, affect theory, and critical populism studies (Berlant, 2011; Yuval-Davis, 2011). This is to better understand how gendered the scaffolding of right-wing populist rule is, and how crucial feminist resistance is to any dream of democratic rebirth and nationhood on inclusive terms.

8 Conclusion and Policy Recommendations

Femininity under a Democratic Imperative in confronting the global rise of right-wing populism makes it clear that resisting gendered authoritarianism is not a secondary issue but is central to the democratic project itself. Populist regimes understand this well, which is why they invest heavily in regulating femininity, moralizing gender norms, and suppressing feminist dissent. The struggle for gender justice is therefore inextricable from the struggle for democracy, pluralism, and human dignity in the Global South. In confronting femininity not as an apolitical identity but as a political construction, this study uncovers the stakes of gendered populism and the imperative need for holistic, intersectional, and transnational forms of resistance. Feminist movements provide not just critique but also a vision for reimagining what nationhood, citizenship, and justice can be outside of patriarchal scripts. Therefore, they need to be in the foreground of policy, scholarship, and global solidarity work to protect the futures of democracy in the twenty-first century. Considering the Gender-Just Democratic Futures, the following policy suggestions are made for feminist scholars, civil society organizations, policymakers, and global organizations devoted to rolling back gendered authoritarianism and consolidating democratic pluralism within the Global South.

8.1 Legal Reforms to Secure Bodily Autonomy and Expression

The need of the hour is codification and enforcement of protections for reproductive rights, sexual freedom, and gender identity, including decriminalizing abortion, safeguarding inter-caste marriages, and legal recognition of LGBTQ+ people in countries. Removing such morality laws that criminalize consensual activities, regulate dress codes, or limit gender expression, especially those based on religious fundamentalism or colonial heritage, will grant autonomy and freedom of expression. Also, creating autonomous bodies to probe rights abuses, especially in areas where state actors are involved in gender-based repression, will help marginalized women to raise their voices loud and clear.

8.2 Institutionalizing and Promoting Gender-Sensitive Governance

It is imperative to enforce gender equality in political representation in terms of electoral quotas and leadership pipelines so that intersectional inclusion is celebrated across caste, class, religion, and ethnicity. In addition, ensuring gender-responsive budgeting and planning in all ministries and local governments to prioritize care infrastructure, education access, and economic inclusion, as well as enhancing civilian oversight of the military and police, especially in conflict-affected regions where security operations include sexual violence and surveillance of women, will help in gender-sensitized governance. Moreover, promoting freedom of association and expression for women's rights organizations, and protecting activists from online monitoring, random detention, or propaganda campaigns, along with providing core funding and emergency legal support to feminist NGOs, refuges, and lobby groups under attack in regimes of repression will inspire and empower them.

8.3 Investing in Gender-Inclusive Digital Rights

Addressing the gendered aspects of digital authoritarianism through regulation of online harassment, doxing, and algorithmic bias, particularly where hate is state-enabled online, supporting digital literacy campaigns to enable women and gender minorities to use and shape online spaces safely, and ensuring platform accountability from technology companies based in the Global South are the key proactive measures that must be taken to avert the utilization of social media for gender-based violence or distorted information.

8.4 Enlarging Intersectional Civic Education

Updating national curricula to include gender justice, feminist history, and pluralistic values, particularly in the nations where populist governments have censored or distorted gender discourse, and encouraging critical media literacy among young people to identify misogynistic populism, state propaganda, and gender stereotyping in political rhetoric and entertainment media can assist in the recovery and reinterpretation of traditions in a manner that upholds gender equity and social justice.

8.5 *Promoting Transnational Feminist Networks and South-South Solidarity*

Enabling cross-border feminist activist research exchanges, scholar visits, and legal strategist meetings to exchange data, legal precedents, and movement-building strategies, funding Global South feminist research and documentation, acknowledging data sovereignty and narrative power are essential to contesting Western-hub-centric paradigms as well as populist misrepresentations alike. Additionally, forming regional feminist solidarities will assist in resisting together common threats like religious fundamentalism, carceral populism, and neoliberal co-optation. The existing alliances such as South Asia's South Asia Feminist Alliance (SAFA) on anti-fundamentalism, caste, secular rights; Latin America's Articulación Feminista Marcosur (AFM) on reproductive rights, anti-violence, justice; and Africa's African Feminist Forum (AFF) on sexual rights, feminist leadership, decolonization, are doing inspirational work.

Lastly, the scope of the study can be expanded to other countries using a different sampling technique. In case of comparative analysis, the depth of the case studies varies across the selected units of study depending upon the availability and richness of the documentation. Moreover, the study can conduct on-field interviews in future to capture the experiences and resistance that could not be included otherwise.

References

Ahmed, S. (2014). *The cultural politics of emotion* (2nd ed.). Edinburgh University Press.

Amnesty International. (2022). *Ethiopia: Survivors of sexual violence in Tigray left without justice or support*. https://www.amnesty.org

Banet-Weiser, S. (2018). *Empowered: Popular feminism and popular misogyny*. Duke University Press.

Barbosa, R., & Casarões, G. (2022). Statecraft under god: Radical right populism meets Christian nationalism in Bolsonaro's Brazil. *Millennium: Journal of International Studies, 50*(3). https://doi.org/10.1177/03058298221110922

Berlant, L. (2011). *Cruel optimism*. Duke University Press.

Bratton, M. (2018). Shari'a law and modern Muslim ethics. *Journal of Contemporary Religion, 33*(2). https://doi.org/10.1080/13537903.2018.1473212

Brown, W. (2019). *In the ruins of neoliberalism: The rise of antidemocratic politics in the west*. Columbia University Press.

Butler, J. (2020). *The force of nonviolence: An ethico-political bind*. Verso.

Center for Reproductive Rights. (2022). *El Salvador's criminalization of abortion*. https://reproductiverights.org

Chakrabarti, P. (2022). Dissenting bodies, disruptive pandemic: Farmers' protest and Women's participation in mass mobilisation in India. *Wagadu: Journal of Transnational Women's and Gender Studies, 24*(1).
Corrêa, S. (2020). Forward. Anti-gender politics in Latin America: Summaries of country case studies. In S. Correa (Ed.), *Brazilian Interdisciplinary AIDS Association* (pp. 10–20). ISBN 978-65-87854-04-5.
Crenshaw, K. (1989). *Demarginalizing the intersection of race and sex* (Vol. 1, pp. 139–167). University of Chicago Legal Forum.
Dengler, C., & Seebacher, L. M. (2019). What about the global south? Towards a feminist Decolonial degrowth approach. *Ecological Economics, 157*. https://doi.org/10.1016/j.ecolecon.2018.11.019
Elson, D. (2017). Recognize, reduce, and redistribute unpaid care work: How to close the gender gap. *New Labor Forum, 26*(2), 52–61.
Farris, S. R. (2017). *In the name of women's rights: The rise of femonationalism*. Duke University Press.
Foucault, M. (2007). In M. Senellart (Ed.), *Security, territory, population: Lectures at the Collège de France 1977–78*. Palgrave Macmillan.
Hadis, S., Tesfaye, M., & Hailu, S. (2021). Woman in conflict resolution and peace building in Ethiopia: Rhetoric or reality? A call for reconsideration. *Abyssinia Journal of Business and Social Sciences, 6*(1).
Imran, R., & Munir, I. (2018). Defying marginalization: Emergence of women's organizations and the resistance movement in Pakistan: A historical overview. *Journal of International Women's Studies, 19*(6).
Khan, Z. (2023). Gender segregation & women's rights in Muslim societies: de-constructing feminist opposition to spatial boundaries through the lens of feminist documentary film. *Continuum, 37*(5). https://doi.org/10.1080/10304312.2023.2287969
Koens, C., & Gunawardana, S. J. (2021). A continuum of participation: Rethinking Tamil women's political participation and agency in post-war Sri Lanka. *International Feminist Journal of Politics, 23*(3). https://doi.org/10.1080/14616742.2020.1734043
Kumar, A. (2021). Sexual violence against Dalit women: An analytical study of intersectionality of gender, caste, and class in India. *Journal of International Women's Studies, 22*(10).
Laszczkowski, M., & Reeves, M. (Eds.). (2018). *Affective states: Entanglements, suspensions, suspicions*. Berghahn Books.
Mena Ugarte, S. C., Rodríguez Funes, M. V., & Viterna, J. (2023). Maternal morbidity under an absolute abortion ban: Insights from a 6-year case series of fatal fetal malformations in El Salvador. *AJOG Global Reports, 3*(1). https://doi.org/10.1016/j.xagr.2022.100147
Nanditha, N. (2022). Exclusion in #MeToo India: Rethinking inclusivity and intersectionality in Indian digital feminist movements. *Feminist Media Studies, 22*(7). https://doi.org/10.1080/14680777.2021.1913432
Navera, G. S. (2021). The president as macho: Machismo, misogyny, and the language of toxic masculinity in Philippine presidential discourse. In *When politicians talk: The cultural dynamics of public speaking*. https://doi.org/10.1007/978-981-16-3579-3_11
Pan, A. (2023). Gender, caste and subjectivity: Revisiting the #MeToo movement in India. *Feminist Encounters, 7*(1). https://doi.org/10.20897/femenc/12881
Pande, M. (2022). Gendered analysis of Hindutva imaginaries: Manipulation of symbols for Ethnonationalist projects. *Journal of Modern European History, 20*(3). https://doi.org/10.1177/16118944221110725
Phipps, A. (2020). *Me, not you: The trouble with mainstream feminism*. Manchester University Press.
Ramadhani, F. N. (2023). How gender orders and Islamic influence affect Women's participation in Indonesian politics? *JILS (Journal of International and Local Studies), 7*(2). https://doi.org/10.56326/jils.v7i2.2914

Rathnam, R. (2024). Remapping the connections between feminism and secularism: A study of the women's movements in India and their engagements with religion. *Asian Journal of Women's Studies, 30*(3), 227–254. https://doi.org/10.1080/12259276.2024.2392945
Razavi, S. (2007a). *The political and social economy of care in a development context: Conceptual issues, research questions and policy options.* UNRISD.
Razavi, S. (2007b). The Political and Social Economy of Care in a Development Context. Conceptual Issues, Research Questions, and Policy Options. *Gender and Development Programme*, (3).
Reyes, E. D., Ramírez, C. Q., & Wolff, C. S. (2022). Anti-gender populism in Latin America: The cases of Mexico and Brazil. *Journal of Human Security, 18*(2). https://doi.org/10.12924/johs2023.18020047
Rinaldo, R. (2019). The women's movement and Indonesia's transition to democracy. In T. Dibley., & M. Ford (Eds.), *Activists in transition: Progressive politics in democratic Indonesia* (Ithaca, NY, 2019; online edn, Cornell Scholarship Online, 21 May 2020). Retrieved July 15, 2026, from https://doi.org/10.7591/cornell/9781501742477.003.0008
Sahu, S. (2023). *Unfolding feminism in India: The women's movement in India.* https://doi.org/10.4324/9781003275411-9.
Singh, P., & Parihar, G. K. (2024). The Hindutva brand of populist politics and the women question. *Political Studies Review, 22*(1). https://doi.org/10.1177/14789299221146695
Tripathi, P. (2019). Women and politics of peace: South Asian narratives on militarization, power and justice. *Contemporary South Asia, 27*(2). https://doi.org/10.1080/09584935.2019.1609791
United Nations Women. (2024). Intensification of efforts to eliminate all forms of violence against women and girls: Technology-facilitated violence against women and girls: Report of the Secretary-General (A/79/500). United Nations. https://www.unwomen.org/en/digital-library/publications/2024/10/intensification-of-efforts-to-eliminateall-forms-of-violence-against-women-report-of-the-secretary-general-2024
White, S., Warburton, E., Hendrawan, A., & Aspinall, E. (2023). Voting against women: Political patriarchy, Islam, and representation in Indonesia. *Politics and Gender, 20*(2), 391–421. https://doi.org/10.1017/S1743923X23000648
Yuval-Davis, N. (2006). Belonging and the politics of belonging. *Patterns of Prejudice, 40*(3). https://doi.org/10.1080/00313220600769331
Yuval-Davis, N. (2011). *The politics of belonging: Intersectional contestations.* SAGE Publications.
Zia, A. S. (2020). Who is afraid of Pakistan's Aurat March? *Economic and Political Weekly, 55*(8).
Zia, A. S. (2022). 'My body, Allah's choice': Islamic Laws and Sexual autonomies in Pakistan. *Australian Journal of Asian Law, 23*(2).

Ishika Jaiswal served as an Assistant Professor in Economics at the Indian Institute of Management (IIM) Sambalpur. She holds a doctorate in applied economics from the University of Lucknow. Her research areas include Labor Economics, Emerging Issues in the Indian Economy, Behavioural Economics and Sustainability. She has co-authored a textbook titled "Indian Economy" and authored a research book titled "Demographic Transition in Major Indian States". She actively publishes research papers in several national and international journals and has presented her work in various conferences and doctoral colloquiums at national and international levels. She is also associated with several reputed journals as a reviewer.

Part IV
Voice, Violence, and Visibility

Chapter 14
Climate Crisis and Gender-Based Violence: Ecofeminist Perspectives on Power and Politics in the Global South

Tanni Ganguly and Aaratrika Pandey

Abstract Climate change has a disproportionate impact on women and marginalized communities, exacerbating existing structural inequalities and contributing to increased gender-based violence (GBV) in both migratory scenarios and climate-based environments. This chapter analyzes the association between ecofeminism and GBV, highlighting the shared causes of environmental damage and patriarchal oppression. Ecofeminism is theoretical and activist framework that emphasizes the linked exploitation of nature and women by gender hierarchy, capitalist and colonial regimes. This write up explores important concepts of ecological feminism philosophy, emphasizing on how the oppression of women and the exploitation of nature have ideological footings. It looks on how environmental crises including climate change, droughts, floods, water scarcity, and extractive industries exacerbate hazards for women, especially in marginalized and climate vulnerable communities. This chapter delves into the deeper political economics of gender in the global south, underlining how intersectional power structures heighten climate related vulnerabilities. It addresses how economic extraction, gender subordination, and imperial legacies contribute to GBV as both an indication and a structural control mechanism. Drawing on verified case studies from the global south, It shows how climate-induced stressors cause relocation, trafficking, sexual assault and domestic abuse making GBV a symptom and a tool for environmental and social control. It addresses the power of community-led resistance, which is founded on Indigenous knowledge, grassroots organizing and feminist care ethics. Finally, this chapter seeks to connect ecofeminism with climate-related GBV to expose their roots. It's outcome is a call for gender-sensitive climate justice and sustainable futures.

Keywords Gender-based violence · Ecofeminism · Climate crisis · Political economy · Global South · Feminist theory · Environmental justice · Patriarchy · Intersectionality

---

T. Ganguly (✉) · A. Pandey
School of Law, Manav Rachna University, Faridabad, India
e-mail: tanniganguly2423@gmail.com

A. Pandey
e-mail: pandeyaaratrika0003@gmail.com

H. Adam and F. A. Malik (eds.), *The Political Economy of Gender*,
https://doi.org/10.1007/978-981-92-2785-3_14

1 Introduction

Climate change is leading to more regular, severe, and prolonged natural disasters. However, not all calamities are the result of changing the climate. Human-caused climate change is responsible for around two-thirds of extreme weather events, according to available evidence (Allen, 2003). Climate change affects entire communities, but women and girls suffer the most (UN Women, 2014). Because of their traditional responsibilities, women rely largely on natural resources. Feminist environmental principles are crucial in tackling gender-based violence (GBV) and environmental degradation, as they are linked to patriarchy and capitalism as basic causes. In global south, this is advancing into a matter demanding urgent attention.

Numerous studies have shown that in South Asia natural calamities have increased women's vulnerability to sexual and gender-based violence (SGBV). They experience lack of protection and mental trauma (Desai & Mandal, 2021). In India, increase in annual mean temperature by 1 °C led to 8% rise in physical violence and 7.3% sexual violence on women by their intimate partner (Zhu et al., 2023). Following the 2011 floods in Pakistan, in a 2012 Protection Rapid Assessment communities surveyed stated that some women and girls were subjected to incidents of GBV, including exacerbated domestic abuse, forced marriage, early marriages, and exchange marriages (Irish Consortium on Gender Based Violence, 2022). Disasters have far-reaching consequences for human populations. Between 2000 and 2019, the United Nations Office for Disaster Risk Reduction (UNDRR) reported 7348 catastrophic disasters worldwide, resulting in 1.23 million deaths and affecting 4.2 billion people. According to the Sixth Assessment Report of the Intergovernmental Panel on Climate Change: Working Group 2, extreme weather events increase the risk of GBV, harassment, sexual violence, and trafficking for women and girls.

There is evidence linking increased rates of GBV against women and girls to disasters. Victims of GBV after a disaster, regardless of whether it has been heightened or caused by climate change, require legal recognition, protection, and support services. Gender mainstreaming in climate change science follows the 1995 Beijing Platform and Declaration, which identified 12 important socioeconomic areas that require immediate action to achieve equal opportunities for men and women. Gender mainstreaming refers to infusing a gender perspective into political responses to reduce gender inequities through systemic processes (Alston et al., 2014). Research from the global south has primarily focused on forced or underage marriage and gender-based violence (GBV) among individuals displaced after disasters. In 2015, the International Federation of Red Cross Societies conducted a global survey in nine countries, including Bangladesh, Bosnia-Herzegovina, El Salvador, Haiti, Malawi, Myanmar, Namibia, Romania, and Samoa.

A comprehensive examination of major areas of international law reveals no international legal instrument dealing with SGBV against women during and after climate change-induced disasters (UN Women, 2014). This is especially concerning given the accumulating evidence that climate change contributes to the worsening of SGBV against women and girls. The texts of three specific climate change accords

(1992 UNFCCC, 1997 Kyoto Protocol, and 2015 Paris Agreement) do not address this topic. This chapter emphasises the importance of recognizing, listening to, and providing appropriate help to persons facing violence after disasters. Our aim to look at how GBV give an address in the context of climate crisis by the international instruments.

The study's goals and methodology are discussed after a review of essential ecofeminist theory and research on GBV in relation to the changing climate. It explains how an extractive structures and patriarchy influence gendered violence and adverse ecological effects through selected case studies from the Global South.

2 Review of the Literature on Ecofeminist Theories, Climate Change, and Gender Vulnerabilities

The idea that environmental exploitation and women's oppression are not isolated incidents but rather intentional in overlapping oppressive structures such as colonizing practices, capitalist framework, and male supremacy is the main point of concern. An essential aid for understanding the complex connections between ecological degradation and GBV, significantly in the Global South, is the ecofeminist model. This section explores the core concepts of ecofeminism, including its historical foundations, the conceptual links between environmental damage and gendered oppression.

As a theoretical and activist framework, ecofeminism shows how the same structures of dominance give rise to both environmental destruction and the exploitation of women. It questions dualistic thinking that separates men from women, culture from biology, and humans from nature, claiming that these dichotomies are created and used as weapons to maintain power structures (Maathai, 2004). Ecofeminism is gaining theoretical foothold in fields including public health, Sociology, philosophy, ecology, and science (Seager, 2003). It argues that (Thompson & MacGregor, 2017), marginalized groups share similar ideas that justify environmental exploitation and degradation. According to this viewpoint, environmental degradation is a sociopolitical issue rather than an ecological one; an reflection of deep-seated inequalities that appear both environmentally and interpersonally (Radel & Schmook, 2024).

2.1 *Foundations of Ecofeminist Thought*

Françoise d'Eaubonne, a French feminist, coined the term "ecofeminism" in 1974 to highlight the connection between women's enslavement and nature's exploitation. It emphasises women's potential to drive the ecological revolution. Developed from the combination of ecology Ecofeminism argues that "non-human nature and the undue domination of nature" are feminist issues (Warren, 1997). According to

Karen Warren, feminists aim to eliminate masculine gender dominance and privilege, sometimes known as sexism. However, their opinions may differ. At its core, ecofeminism stems from the belief that women engage with the environment in a "spiritual, nurturing, and intuitive manner" (James, 1996).

A broad understanding of ecofeminism encompasses the idea that "the mentalities and actions leading to the subordination of women by men are directly tied to the plundering of the natural environment" (Jacobs, 2014). Women are often viewed as objects for men due to their presumed "closeness to nature" and humanity-bridging roles. To oppose injustice that affects both women and the environment, it's important to apply feminist and ecological ideas, as the two are inextricably linked (George & Ahmed, 2023). Ecofeminism includes several threads, including social, cultural, and liberal ecofeminism (Fawole, 2008). Liberal ecofeminism seeks to transform humanity's connection with nature by enacting laws that regulate exploitative relationships with the environment. Cultural ecofeminism, on the other hand, criticises patriarchy and provides alternatives that strive to liberate both women and the environment. Social ecofeminism (Faria & Jenkins, 2024) is a criticism of the capitalist system that investigates how patriarchal dynamics in reproductive relationships and capitalist modes of production contribute to men's subordination of women and nature.

According to Chigumira It intentionally promotes positions that are frequently marginalized or removed from dominant narratives, such as the voices of Chipko women, in order to foster a truly global awareness of how dominating structures contribute to the exploitation of both women and the environment (Chigumira, 2025). Warren defines (Warren, 1988) ecofeminism as intrinsically contextual, inclusive, and structurally pluralistic, acknowledging that ethical and political responses to oppression must be grounded in the lived experiences of those most affected.

Ecofeminists, building on this inclusive and contextual foundation, present an alternative worldview based on interdependence, care, mutual respect, and ecological balance (Shiva, 1988). This relational ethic challenges conventional paradigms that regard nature and human labour, particularly women's labour, as commodities to be exploited for profit (Weatherill, 2024). Unlike extractive, profit-driven paradigms, ecofeminism emphasises the critical role that women, particularly in the Global South, play as ecosystem caretakers and stewards of traditional ecological knowledge. Their strong connections to land, water, seeds, and local biodiversity are not only essential for sustainable living, but also for communal resiliency (Kostecka, 2025). These contributions, however, are typically disregarded, discounted, or co-opted by patriarchal and capitalist frameworks that routinely exclude women from decision-making and resource access (Mies & Shiva, 1993).

2.2 *Patterns of Domination: How Patriarchy, Capitalism, and Colonialism Interwine*

Ecofeminism provides a robust analytical paradigm for understanding how environmental degradation and GBV are structurally related. The existing traditional institutions work together to establish what Karen Warren (2000) refers to as the "logic of domination," a worldview that justifies the exploitation, control, and subjection of both women and the Earth.

Patriarchy is a sociopolitical structure that emphasises male power while subordinating women in cultural, legal, and institutional contexts. It is based on inflexible dualisms-man, woman, culture, nature, reason and emotion, which have long been used to connect women with the natural world, labelling both as illogical, passive, and in need of control (Ortner, 1974). This symbolic alignment has justified the dominance of women and nature alike, obscuring their contributions within dominant paradigms. Women's unpaid labour in caregiving, agriculture, and home economics is routinely devalued, much like the environmental services offered by forests, rivers, and biodiversity, which are frequently taken for granted. In climate-vulnerable areas, patriarchal ideas manifest in actual, violent ways. Women bear a disproportionate share of the burden of collecting food, water, and fuel, all of which are increasingly endangered by environmental degradation (Dankelman, 2010).

Nonetheless, their perspectives are largely neglected from environmental policies and disaster management. The effects are severe: women are more likely to die, be displaced, or experience GBV during extreme weather events due to their socially defined roles, mobility limits, and lack of access to information and resources (Neumayer & Plümper, 2007). Furthermore, female environmental defenders who oppose ecological degradation, which includes Indigenous land protectors in Latin America or anti-mining activists in South Asia, endure persecution, criminalization, and even assassination.

Capitalism exacerbates these disparities by commodifying both nature and human labor. In the Global South, this logic has been exacerbated by neoliberal development policies that prioritize large-scale infrastructure, industrial agriculture, and resource extraction over local lives and ecological sustainability (Moore, 2015). Women's informal and subsistence labour, particularly in food production and water management, is economically invisible, further marginalising them in environmental and economic policies (Mies & Shiva, 1993).

There are numerous examples of women being displaced from communal lands in East Africa and Southeast Asia as a result of land seizures for bio-fuel cultivation or export-oriented agriculture (Borras & Franco, 2012). These enclosures not only endanger women's survival and food security, but they also undermine their traditional ecological expertise. Climate mitigation efforts, such as carbon offsetting or afforestation programs under REDD+, have also been accused of displacing Indigenous populations, particularly women, by converting forests into financial assets while failing to address underlying issues of access and equity (Lohmann, 2012).

The territorial expansion of gender hierarchy is violently changing Indigenous environments and social systems to serve imperial objectives. Colonial regimes implemented Western legal codes, commercialized community lands, and abolished matrilineal governance institutions, effectively displacing women from their traditional duties as environmental guardians (Merchant, 1980). Traditional cultures that saw nature as sacred and interrelated were discarded as "primitive" and supplanted by extractive, resource-driven approaches to land usage (Federici, 2004).

These legacies still have an impact on environmental governance and the climate today. Top-down, mechanistic approaches of today usually prioritize so-called "universal" empirical reasoning over female perspectives and Indigenous knowledge. Despite being directly affected by climate change and environmental degradation, women particularly Indigenous and rural women are disproportionately excluded from decision-making processes concerning land, water, and natural resource governance (Castañeda Carney et al., 2020). Furthermore, environmental conflicts disproportionately affect Indigenous women, who are frequently the frontline defenders of ecosystems but face the greatest threats from militarized resource extraction, forced displacement, and governmental or industrial brutality (Simpson, 2017).

All things considered, colonialism, capitalism, and patriarchy function as interwoven systems that perpetuate gendered and environmental injustice rather than as distinct entities. They work together to create an underlying web that supports GBV and ecological deterioration. It demands that these interconnected systems be dismantled and replaced with frameworks based on sustainability, justice, care, and the leadership of those most impacted, mainly women in the Global South.

2.3 *Gendered Dimensions of Vulnerability in Climate Change Discussion*

Early versions of ecofeminism were not without criticism, despite providing important insights into the intertwined dominance of women and nature. The first ecofeminist schools of thought concentrated on essentialist discourses arguing that women and nature are bound together biologically. Such ecofeminist theories emerged during the feminist and environmentalist movements in the 70s and 80s.

Intellectuals such as Carolyn Merchant (1980) and Vandana Shiva (1988) strove to highlight women's "natural" affinity with the Earth due to their roles in reproduction and nurturing. While this paradigm effectively countered masculinist and mechanistic perspectives, it too risked promoting gender stereotyping by making women's associations with emotion, care, and conservation "normal." Bina Agarwal (1992), for example, criticized the essentialist ecofeminism for not considering the caste, economic, and regional inequalities affecting women's control and access to diversity in nations such as India.

Rocheleau et al. (1996) made an even stronger argument against essentialist binary thinking and in favor of a feminist political ecology that analyzes the intersections of gender, class, and local power relationships in environmental conflicts. This criticism wave enabled ecofeminism to be subjected to a deeper philosophical transformation. Contemporary ecofeminists employ (Ayeb-Karlsson et al., 2023) theory of intersectionality in order to state that women's environmental experiences cannot be isolated, independently of other axes of identity and oppression such as race, class, sexuality, and colonial past. As some scholars, such as Radcliffe (2015), argue, the intersection of land appropriation, rationalization, and state indifference leads to environmental degradation and gender violence towards Indigenous women, particularly in the Global South.

Thus, rather than criticising Indigenous, communal, and relational worldviews, decolonial ecofeminism re-centers them. Feminist movements led by women in climate-vulnerable areas, like the Chipko movement in India or land and water defenders across Latin America, are prime examples of ecofeminism in action. In addition to defending the environment, these movements attempt to assert relationships, survival, and sovereignty in resistance to settler colonial and ecological exploitative institutions (Simpson, 2017).

2.4 *Evolution of Ecofeminism: Intersectional Criticisms and Philosophical Transitions*

Climate change is increasingly being recognized as a source of social inequality that disproportionately affects already marginalized people. Gender-based vulnerability has emerged as a major concern in this discussion. An increasing amount of scholarly study emphasises that not everyone is equally impacted by climate-related disasters, which can range from droughts and floods to long-term environmental degradation.

Because of widespread gender norms, restricted political agency, mobility impairments, and unequal access to resources, women suffer more drastically, particularly in the Global South (Alston, 2013; Dankelman, 2010). Various research has established a link between gender violence (GBV) and environmental distress caused by climate change. Sexual violence, domestic violence, child marriage, and human trafficking are more probable in times of food insecurity, scarcity of resources, and displacement (Alston et al., 2014; Neumayer & Plümper, 2007). For example, studies after disasters like the 2004 South Asian tsunami and Cyclone Sidr in Bangladesh illustrate how patriarchal culture and poor facilities exposed women to GBV in shelters and camps (Ahmed et al., 2019).

In addition, within the context of climatic catastrophes, feminist critiques highlight crisis-boundaries and the deficiencies of international law in dealing with GBV (Drucza, 2023). Otto calls for the integration of GBV concerns into frameworks of disaster response and advocates 'un-crisis' thinking in an effort to stimulate proactive legal reform and interaction with marginal voices (Otto, 2014). Among the first to theorize the systemic connection between environmental damage and women's oppression were ecofeminist academics. Authors contends that the same patriarchal and capitalist logics that place a higher priority on dominance, profit, and control are responsible for both the marginalization of women and the destruction of the environment (Serraglio, 2024). Similar to this, It has been examined how scientific rationalism of the Enlightenment era viewed nature as passive and lifeless, paralleling the oppression of women in newly emerging capitalist society (Hailemariam et al., 2023).

These seminal works laid the groundwork for Eco-critique by demonstrating the ideological and historical connections between gender-based exploitation and environmental degradation. But early ecofeminism has also come under fire for depicting women as naturally compatible with ecological processes or as essentialising their relationship to nature. Agarwal (1992) and other scholars contend that this viewpoint disregards caste, economic, and cultural contexts, especially in the Global South, where women's ecological responsibilities are frequently determined more by material need than by spiritual affinities. The "feminist environmentalism" (Ramcilovic-Suominen, 2025) emphasizes the value of examining power relationships and resource control as opposed to depending solely on essentialist narratives.

Expanding on this critique, feminist political ecologists like Rocheleau et al. (1996) developed a more intersectional approach, highlighting that gender relations are rooted in specific social and ecological circumstances. They emphasize how women's experiences with environmental degradation differ based on ethnicity, geography, and economic status. This method was essential in redefining environmental justice through a relational and place-based lens, focusing on everyday behaviors, informal economies, and community resilience (Mack & Na'puti, 2025). Other contemporary work (Rigon, 2025) combines intersectionality into climate and environmental studies, suggesting that climate change interacts with numerous systems of oppression, including racism, classism, colonialism, and ableism. Scholars like Gaard and Gruen (2015) underline the necessity for ecofeminist frameworks to engage with queer theory, critical race theory, and Indigenous knowledge systems to prevent reproducing hierarchies within feminist discourse itself.

There is also rising concentrate on postcolonial and decolonial critiques of environmental governance. Scholars like Magalhães Teixeira (2024) and Radcliffe (2015) have called attention to how experiences of land dispossession, epistemicide, and forced labor have disproportionately afflicted Indigenous women and colored groups. These studies caution against gender-inclusive climate policies that are designed within Eurocentric or neoliberal frameworks, claiming that such approaches typically utilize gender while failing to dismantle the structures of violence that cause climate vulnerability in the first place.

Even with growing awareness, there are still a number of significant gaps in the literature. First, although the gendered effects of climate change have been well documented, little research has been done on GBV as a systemic instrument of environmental control that is used to stifle opposition or displace women from leadership and land (Hackfort, 2025). Second, there has been little attention paid to the experiences of queer, trans, and gender-diverse individuals in areas impacted by climate change, with the majority of empirical research concentrating on cisgender women

(Sultana, 2022). Third, although Indigenous and grassroots women's contributions to environmental activism are typically praised, global environmental governance venues such as the UNFCCC tend to overlook or tokenize their political demands (MacGregor, 2010).

The literature assessment concludes that climate change is gendered by nature since it exacerbates structural inequality and disproportionately impacts vulnerable groups, especially women and Indigenous communities. The scholarly contributions of intersectional and decolonial frameworks, ecofeminism, and feminist political ecology have been crucial in revealing the intricate relationship between gender-based oppression and environmental degradation. These theoretical stances have posed a challenge to prevailing narratives that ignore or simplify the sociopolitical aspects of climate vulnerability. More community-led, politically involved, and context-specific research that prioritizes the perspectives and experiences of those most impacted is still urgently needed. This chapter aims to bridge this gap by highlighting resistance strategies coming from the Global South and evaluating the gendered political economy of climate-induced violence through an ecofeminist lens.

3 Objectives of the Study and Thematic Scope

The primary objective of this chapter is to critically analyze, from an ecofeminist perspective, the connections between GBV and the climate catastrophe, especially in the sociopolitical contexts of the Global South. The study aims to examine how environmental degradation perpetuates structural forms of violence against women and marginalized communities and exacerbates already-existing gender disparities, drawing on diverse research and intersectional and decolonial ecofeminist theory. In particular, this chapter's purposes are:

1. To gaze into the structural connection between the escalation of gender-based violence and climate-induced environmental degradation, with an emphasis on resource scarcity, ecological conflict, and displacement in the Global South.
2. To investigate how women's and indigenous individuals people' lived experiences in climate-vulnerable areas are shaped by intersecting systems of power that promote gendered oppression and environmental exploitation.
3. In order to combat gendered violence and environmental injustice, it is important to examine and emphasize the contributions of feminist, Indigenous, and community-led resistance strategies to alternative forms of ecological care, resilience, and justice.
4. To support the development of a gender-sensitive, ecofeminist framework for environmental governance and climate policy that places a higher priority on fairness, sustainability, and the lived realities of those most affected by the climate disaster.

In order to promote scholarly and policy discourse, the chapter emphasises resistance strategies grounded in the leadership and lived experiences of communities in the Global South, while also offering an intersectional understanding of the relationship between gender, violence, and climate change.

4 Methodology

Using a qualitative, interpretive approach that is both theoretical and case-driven, this chapter reflects the multifaceted nature of ecofeminist research. This analysis, based on an ecofeminist political economy, is critically examining the interrelations among GBV, climate change, and hierarchical power structures, against the backdrop of climate-vulnerable countries in the Global South. The research employs secondary data, such as case studies, institutional documents, peer-reviewed scholarly articles, and feminist and Indigenous peoples' testimonies who are spearheading environmental movements, in lieu of primary data collection. The sources serve as markers and instruments of environmental control, revealing the ecological and political factors contributing to sexual violence, human trafficking, displacement, and other types of GBV. Intersectionality is an essential research strategy for analyzing how geography, gender, race, class, and indigeneity intersect to produce elevated environmental threats and vulnerabilities. Two case studies, one from South Asia and one from Latin America, have been chosen specifically to illustrate geo-cultural differences in eco-gendered violence while also emphasizing structural similarities in inequalities. Thematic analysis was made concrete through engagement of relevant secondary sources to determine repeating patterns of environmental damage, gender exclusion, and resistance by communities. This allowed for intentional synthesis of ideas such as Indigenous knowledge and feminist care ethics. The utilization of secondary data alone restricts direct understanding of lived experiences and might miss nascent grassroots voices. Examples of ethical practice include upholding academic integrity, upholding the intellectual sovereignty of marginalized groups, and ensuring that lived experiences are accurately represented without essentialism or exploitation.

5 Results and Discussion: Case Studies from the Global South

To show how gender-based violence erupts in climate crisis contexts, this section offers two case studies. Drawing on intersectional political economics and ecofeminist concepts, it examines how situations of gendered violence, especially in the Global South, are co-produced through capitalist exploitation, patriarchal domination, and ecological degradation. Rather than being an accidental consequence, GBV functions as an effect and tool of structural power in both settings, attempting to limit access to land, labor, and environmental knowledges (Lugones, 2007; Shiva, 1988).

5.1 Case Study 1: South Asia's Displacement, Climate Migration, and GBV

South Asian countries like Bangladesh, India, and Nepal, climate-related calamities including floods, cyclones, droughts, and river erosion frequently root out communities. These displacements increase women's vulnerability to sexual violence, human trafficking, domestic abuse, and early marriage, especially in overcrowded shelters or informal settlements with poor infrastructure (Ahmed et al., 2019; Alston et al., 2014; Neumayer & Plümper, 2007). During disasters like Cyclone Sidr (2007) and Cyclone Aila (2009) in Bangladesh, women faced increased sexual harassment in shelters and limited access to reproductive healthcare and humanitarian aid (Castañeda Carney et al., 2020; Rashid & Michaud, 2000). These trends have their roots in gendered societal systems that deny women agency and exclude them from climate adaption planning. Patriarchal norms, discriminatory legal systems, and institutional neglect, according to feminist political ecology (Rocheleau et al., 1996), create vulnerability socially and politically. Additionally, displacement weakens traditional community safety mechanisms and creates dependency, especially for women from low-income, Dalit, or Indigenous backgrounds who already suffer increased marginalisation (Agarwal, 1992). Due to a continuing gender-blindness in institutional responses, these intersecting vulnerabilities are rarely addressed in national climate adaptation plans or disaster risk frameworks (Arora-Jonsson, 2011; MacGregor, 2010).

5.2 Case Study 2: Eco-Gendered Violence, Indigenous Resistance, and Extractivism in Latin America

Discrimination against people and environmental degradation have increased throughout Latin America as a result of the growth of extractive industries, such as mining, oil drilling, and large-scale farming, especially in Indigenous lands. Whole communities are uprooted, and systematic violence against women results from these businesses, which are frequently backed by corporate and state players and enforced by militarised security (Global Witness, 2021). Indigenous women who have opposed environmental damage have faced harassment, criminalisation, and assassination in nations such as Colombia, Peru, and Honduras. One example of the perils encountered by Indigenous environmental defenders is the assassination of Berta Cáceres, a Lenca leader who opposed the Agua Zarca dam in Honduras (Global Witness, 2021; Simpson, 2017). This is what Lugones (2007) calls the "conviviality of gender" where colonial and capitalist logic commodities bodies and land and enforces rigid gender norms. GBV is an instrument of dispossession and silence in these environments, undermining Indigenous self-governance and shattering communal resistance (Castañeda Carney et al., 2020; Radcliffe, 2015). Amidst these dangers, indigenous women have spearheaded powerful movements based on ecofeminist principles, community sovereignty, and Indigenous epistemologies. These movements range from anti-extractivist protests in Ecuador's Amazon to ecological action by Maya women in Guatemala and represent feminist reappropriation of land and life and ecological resistance (Simpson, 2017). They problematize Western understandings of climate mitigation and "green growth," which typically follow extractive practices under pseudonyms like carbon markets or enclosures for conservation (Lohmann, 2012; Sultana, 2022).

5.3 Discussion: GBV as an Ecological Tool of Exploitation and Outcome

Together, these examples illustrate that GBV in climatically affected regions is an intentional and structural consequence of cross-cutting structures of power, not an inadvertent result of environmental pressure. Both instances, gendered violence exercises control over natural resources and women's bodies and work, especially where those women are fighting against exploitation. These case studies also reveal the revolutionizing potential of Indigenous and women's resistance against structural and environmental exploitation. Instead of merely opposing ecological degradation, these groups go ahead to reconceptualize sustainability ideas using epistemologies predicated on caring ethics, reciprocity, and relational relatedness.

6 Implications for Policy: A Pathway to Intersectional Environmental Justice

Climate change and gender-based violence have together revealed deep weaknesses in existing legal and environmental governance institutions. Most national and international policy remains to treat women as a homogeneous category, rendering invisible structural causes of gender-based violence and withholding feminist or Indigenous perspectives from decision-making, even as there is increasing global recognition of gendered climate vulnerability. As seen in an ecofeminist critique, addressing the intersection of gender, climate change, and violence requires not only the incorporation of policy but also a necessary re-imagination of the conception and practice of environmental justice.

6.1 Critiquing Current Frameworks

The only convention to come out of the 1992 Rio Earth Summit that did not acknowledge gender in any way was the UNFCCC, which reflected a worldview from the 1950s. Gender was not acknowledged in the 1997 Kyoto Protocol, which established legally bound emission commitments to operate from 1997 to 2020. Prior to the 2015 Paris Agreement, gender was not acknowledged in the "hard" instruments of the international climate policy. While Articles 7(5) and 11(2) contain non-binding wording like "acknowledge" and "consider," making gender concerns optional rather than required, the preamble only invites parties to take human rights and gender equality into consideration. This flimsy wording suggests that gender is not actually given priority in climate policy. Although the relationship between climate disasters and higher rates of GBV is acknowledged in a number of international human rights agreements, this acknowledgement is still dispersed and mostly limited to specialized publications. The Human Rights Council's Analytical Study on Gender-Responsive Climate Action, CEDAW General Recommendation No. 37, and other soft-law guidelines emphasize how poverty, economic stress from disasters, and institutional breakdown increase the likelihood of GBV, including child marriage and domestic abuse (CEDAW, 2018; Human Rights Council, 2019).

Gender language has long been incorporated into international agreements such as the United Nations Framework Convention on Climate Change (UNFCCC), the Convention on the Elimination of All Forms of Discrimination Against Women (CEDAW), and climate adaptation mechanisms such as REDD+ (Reducing Emissions from Deforestation and Forest Degradation). Scholars argue, however, that these frameworks frequently take a technocratic or instrumentalist approach to gender, depicting women as victims or useful tools for achieving environmental goals rather than political actors with agency, knowledge, and rights (Arora-Jonsson, 2011; MacGregor, 2010). Despite data linking ecological stress to increased violence and exploitation, few frameworks address GBV as a climate-related concern (Castañeda Carney et al., 2020). Furthermore, by emphasising market-based solutions such as carbon trading, green finance, and public-private partnerships, mainstream development and climate resilience strategies usually marginalise female movements and Indigenous communities. While ignoring traditional ecological knowledge, community land practices, and collective decision-making frameworks, these techniques often replicate the same extractive logics that propel environmental degradation and migration (Radcliffe, 2015).

6.2 Policy Recommendations

The following policy paths are suggested to transition to a more transformative and inclusive environmental governance system:

1. Include GBV prevention in frameworks for climate policy: GBV must be specifically addressed as a massive risk in catastrophe risk reduction and climate adaptation plans, particularly in situations involving displacement. This entails providing gender-responsive early warning systems, safe shelter infrastructure, and access to justice and psychosocial support.
2. Focus on relational worldviews and feminist care ethics: An ethic of caring that prioritizes ecological balance, community well-being, and interdependence over profit-driven strategies must be adopted by environmental governance. Women's mental endurance and unpaid labour in Environmental stewardship should be acknowledged by policy.
3. Acknowledge and formalize Indigenous and local knowledge systems: Indigenous communities' sovereignty and ecological wisdom, especially those led by women, should be upheld by laws and regulations.
4. Employ intersectional policy prisms: Law and policy interventions should account for how gender, race, caste, indigeneity, disability, and class all intersect to determine climate vulnerability. As a diagnostic tool, intersectionality must also function as a principle of inclusive and situation-specific policymaking.
5. Support grassroots feminist movements: Women's environmental groups need constant support and legal safeguarding, particularly in areas where activists are under attack or prosecution. Grassroots movements disrupt exploitative models by creating alternative systems while also fostering local resiliency.

In short, it is necessary to transform the epistemic underpinnings of environmental regulation to combat the intersection of GBV and climate change that requires greater than policy change. Policymakers have the capacity to dismantle the inequalities that drive gendered violence and environmental ruination by incorporating these frameworks into regulatory and legal frameworks.

7 Limitations

Although this chapter is an extensive analysis of ecofeminism and GBV due to climate change in the Global South, it only discusses a limited number of case studies that might not encompass every situation. Some intersectional issues, such as disability, caste, and sexual orientation, are handled only to a certain extent. The discussion is qualitative in nature rather than quantitative. Climate policies and social patterns are changing quite fast, which could impact future use. In spite of these limitations, the chapter stresses the vital connection among gender, environmental justice, and community-based resilience.

8 Conclusion

In sum, this chapter has highlighted the entrenched and structural linkages between gender-based violence and climate disasters, especially in the situations of the Global South. Through taking an ecofeminist perspective, it is now apparent that GBV is not a residual or peripheral consequence of ecocrises but a targeted mechanism associated with deep-seated structures of traditional male dominating acts. These overlapping systems continue environmental exploitation while supporting gendered hierarchies that disproportionately affect women, Indigenous women, and other populations of concern. These examples from Latin America and South Asia show how climate change exacerbates the vulnerabilities and limits access to essential resources, security, and justice for already marginalized groups of people. In addition, existing legal schemes and institutional responses are still lacking and often do not account for the gendered aspects of environmental disasters. Tokenistic involvement of women in environmental decision-making also cripples the process of actual change. But amidst these crises, ecofeminist praxis provides an empowering and optimistic counter-narrative. By prioritizing justice, reciprocity, community sovereignty, and indigenous knowledge, ecofeminism locates women as active ecological guardians and political subjects rather than as passive victims. Theirs is the leadership that is needed to build just and sustainable futures that challenge and deconstruct structural oppression. Finally, meeting the intertwined crises of GBV and climate catastrophe requires a radical rethinking of social, political, and economic relations that centers the voices and experiences of marginalized people, and is determined to construct more equitable and sustainable environmental futures for everyone.

References

Agarwal, B. (1992). The gender and environment debate: Lessons from India. *Feminist Studies, 18*(1), 119–158.

Ahmed, A. U., Appadurai, A. N., & Neelormi, S. (2019). *Climate-induced migration and gender-based violence in South Asia.* International Centre for Climate Change and Development (ICCCAD).

Allen, M. R. (2003). Liability for climate change. *Nature, 421*(6926), 891–892.

Alston, M. (2013). Women and adaptation. *Wiley Interdisciplinary Reviews: Climate Change, 4*(5), 351–358.

Alston, M., Whittenbury, K., Haynes, A., & Godden, N. (2014). Are climate challenges reinforcing child and forced marriage and dowry in Bangladesh? *Women's Studies International Forum, 47*, 137–144.

Arora-Jonsson, S. (2011). Virtue and vulnerability: Discourses on women, gender and climate change. *Global Environmental Change, 21*(2), 744–751.

Ayeb-Karlsson, S., Kniveton, D., & Cannon, T. (2023). Gender and ecosystem-based adaptation to climate change. *Springer Climate, 1*(1), 1–10.

Borras, S. M., & Franco, J. C. (2012). Global land grabbing and trajectories of agrarian change: A preliminary analysis. *Journal of Agrarian Change, 12*(1), 34–59.

Castañeda Carney, I., Sabater, L., Owren, C., & Boyer, A. E. (2020). *Gender-based violence and environment linkages: The violence of inequality*. International Union for Conservation of Nature (IUCN).
CEDAW. (2018). *General recommendation No. 37 on the gender-related dimensions of disaster risk reduction in the context of climate change*. UN Committee on the Elimination of Discrimination Against Women.
Chigumira, E. (2025). Climate change and the feminization of poverty in Africa: Insights from rural Zimbabwe. *Journal of Black Studies, 56*(1), 102–119.
Dankelman, I. (Ed.). (2010). *Gender and climate change: An introduction*. Earthscan.
Desai, B. H., & Mandal, M. (2021). Role of climate change in exacerbating sexual and gender-based violence against women: A new challenge for international law. *Environmental Policy and Law, 51*(3), 147–160.
Drucza, K. (2023). *Centering gender in the era of digital and green transition* (1st ed.). Springer Nature.
Faria, C., & Jenkins, K. (2024). Feminist approaches to environmental politics. *Contemporary Political Theory, 24*, 81–97.
Fawole, O. I. (2008). Economic violence to women and girls: Is it receiving the necessary attention? *Trauma, Violence, & Abuse, 9*(3), 167–177.
Federici, S. (2004). *Caliban and the witch: Women, the body and primitive accumulation*. Autonomedia.
Gaard, G., & Gruen, L. (2015). Ecofeminism. In D. Keller (Ed.), *Environmental ethics: The big questions* (pp. 332–345). Wiley-Blackwell.
George, N., & Ahmed, S. (2023). Climate justice, gender and activisms. *Agenda: Empowering Women for Gender Equity, 37*(1), 1–12.
Global Witness. (2021). *Last line of defence: The industries causing the climate crisis and attacks against land and environmental defenders*. Global Witness.
Hackfort, S. (2025). Nature, care, and (re)productivity: Feminist perspectives on sustainability and the bioeconomy. *Feminist Review, 126*(1), 1–17.
Hailemariam, A., Kalsi, J. K., & Mavisakalyan, A. (2023). Climate change and gender equality. In *The Palgrave handbook of global social problems* (1st ed., pp. 1–15). Palgrave Macmillan.
Human Rights Council. (2019). *Analytical study on gender-responsive climate action for the full and effective enjoyment of the rights of women* (A/HRC/41/26). United Nations.
Irish Consortium on Gender Based Violence. (2022). *Gender, climate and security: Policy brief*. Irish Consortium on Gender Based Violence.
Jacobs, A. (2014). Psychoanalysis and feminist theory. In D. Richardson & V. Robinson (Eds.), *The SAGE handbook of feminist theory*. SAGE Publications.
James, B. (1996). Is ecofeminism relevant? *Hecate, 22*(1), 8–26.
Kostecka, J. (2025). Ecofeminism as a perspective of studying 21st-century sustainability challenges. *In sustainable development and environmental justice*. Springer Nature.
Lohmann, L. (2012). Financialization, commodification and carbon: The contradictions of neoliberal climate policy. *Capitalism Nature Socialism, 23*(4), 84–101.
Lugones, M. (2007). Heterosexualism and the colonial/modern gender system. *Hypatia, 22*(1), 186–209.
Maathai, W. (2004). *The green belt movement: Sharing the approach and the experience*. Lantern Books.
MacGregor, S. (2010). A stranger silence still: The need for feminist social research on climate change. *The Sociological Review, 57*(S2), 124–140.
Mack, J., & Na'puti, T. (2025). Decolonial ecofeminism: A paradigmatic contribution to critical research of gender, ecology and coloniality. *Gender, Place and Culture, 32*(1), 1–15.
Magalhães Teixeira, B. (2024). Room to grow and the right to say no: Theorizing the liberatory power of peace in the Global South. *Geopolitics, 29*(5), 1724–1756.
Merchant, C. (1980). *The death of nature: Women, ecology, and the scientific revolution*. Harper & Row.

Mies, M., & Shiva, V. (1993). *Ecofeminism*. Zed Books.
Moore, J. W. (2015). *Capitalism in the web of life: Ecology and the accumulation of capital*. Verso.
Neumayer, E., & Plümper, T. (2007). The gendered nature of natural disasters. *Annals of the Association of American Geographers, 97*(3), 551–566.
Ortner, S. B. (1974). Is female to male as nature is to culture? In M. Z. Rosaldo & L. Lamphere (Eds.), *Woman, culture, and society* (pp. 67–87). Stanford University Press.
Otto, D. (2014). Remapping crisis through a feminist lens. In S. Kouvo & Z. Pearson (Eds.), *Feminist perspectives on contemporary international law: Between resistance and compliance* (pp. 78–96). Hart Publishing.
Radcliffe, S. A. (2015). Dilemmas of difference: Indigenous women and the limits of postcolonial development policy. *Gender, Place and Culture, 22*(2), 215–232.
Radel, C., & Schmook, B. (2024). Gender-based climate (in)justice: An overview. *Environmental Science & Policy, 162*, 103814.
Ramcilovic-Suominen, S., Giuntoli, J., Oliver, T., & Mehta, L. (2025). How can relational, decolonial and feminist approaches inform the EU bioeconomy? *Sustainability Science, 20*, 649–657.
Rashid, S. F., & Michaud, S. (2000). Female adolescents and their sexuality: Notions of honour, shame, purity and pollution during the floods. *Disasters, 24*(1), 54–70.
Rigon, A. (2025). A review of intersectionality and climate change and the potential of intersectional participatory methods and storytelling to co-produce climate justice. *Climate and Development, 17*, 892–904.
Rocheleau, D., Thomas-Slayter, B., & Wangari, E. (1996). *Feminist political ecology: Global issues and local experiences*. Routledge.
Seager, J. (2003). Rachel Carson died of breast cancer: The coming of age of feminist environmentalism. *Signs: Journal of Women in Culture and Society, 28*(3), 945–972.
Serraglio, D. A. (2024). Women on the move? Mainstreaming gender in policies for climate-induced displacement. *Climate and Development, 16*(4), 1–15.
Shiva, V. (1988). *Staying alive: Women, ecology and survival in India*. Zed Books.
Simpson, L. (2017). *As we have always done: Indigenous freedom through radical resistance*. University of Minnesota Press.
Sultana, F. (2022). The unbearable heaviness of climate coloniality. *Political Geography, 99*, 102638.
Thompson, H., & MacGregor, S. (2017). Introduction: Gender and green governance. In S. MacGregor (Ed.), *Routledge handbook of gender and environment* (pp. 1–14). Routledge.
UN Women. (2014). *World survey on the role of women in development 2014: Gender equality and sustainable development*. United Nations.
UN Women. (2018). *Gender equality in the 2030 agenda for sustainable development*. UN Women.
UNFCCC. (2015). *Paris Agreement*. United Nations Framework Convention on Climate Change.
Warren, K. J. (1988). Feminism and ecology: Making connections. *Environmental Ethics, 10*(1), 3–20.
Warren, K. J. (1997). *Ecofeminism: Women, culture, nature*. Indiana University Press.
Warren, K. J. (2000). *Ecofeminist philosophy: A western perspective on what it is and why it matters*. Rowman & Littlefield Publishers.
Weatherill, C. K. (2024). Resisting climate change vulnerability: Feminist and decolonial perspectives from the Pacific. *Feminist Review, 126*(1), 1–17.
Zhu, Y., He, C., Bell, M., Zhang, Y., Fatmi, Z., Zhang, Y., Zaid, M., Bachwenkizi, J., Liu, C., Zhou, L., Chen, R., & Kan, H. (2023). Association of ambient temperature with the prevalence of intimate partner violence among partnered women in low-and middle-income South Asian countries. *JAMA Psychiatry, 80*(9), 952–961.

Tanni Ganguly is a Ph.D. Scholar at the School of Law, Manav Rachna University, Haryana, India. She holds an LL.M. in International Law from South Asian University, New Delhi, and an LL.B. (Hons.) from Daffodil International University, Dhaka, Bangladesh. Her research focuses on gender justice, climate change, and environmental law, with particular emphasis on ecofeminist perspectives in the Global South. She has published scholarly work on gender-based violence, sustainability, and human rights. Her research adopts an interdisciplinary and comparative approach, seeking to advance legal scholarship at the intersection of climate justice, gender equality, and social equity through inclusive and rights-based legal discourse.

Dr. Aaratrika Pandey is an Assistant Professor of Law at the School of Law, Manav Rachna University. She holds a B.A. LL.B. (Hons.) from Jamia Millia Islamia, New Delhi, an LL.M. from Tata Institute of Social Sciences (TISS), Mumbai, and a Ph.D. from National Law University Odisha. Her academic and research pursuits are rooted in interdisciplinary and socio-legal inquiry, with particular interests in gender studies, feminist jurisprudence, child psychology, climate justice, artificial intelligence, and emerging technologies. Through her research and publications, she examines the intersections of law, society, technology, and identity, engaging with questions of equity, inclusion, and social justice. Her work reflects a commitment to advancing critical research and fostering a nuanced understanding of contemporary legal and societal challenges.

Chapter 15
Ecofeminist Resistance in the Margins: Women's Environmental Struggles in Contemporary Indonesia

Iradhad Taqwa Sihidi, Salahudin, Naila Febrina Akmalia, and Muhammad Januar Galang

Abstract The issue of environmental degradation in Indonesia is increasing along with the expansion of extractive industries that destroy the living space of local communities. The impact of this damage is most strongly felt by women in marginalized areas who depend directly on land, forests and the sea for their survival. This article aims to analyze the forms of ecological resistance carried out by women in five marginalized areas of Indonesia, namely Kendeng, Kodingareng, Mollo, Lake Toba, and Sengah Temila, in the face of extractive industry expansion and environmental crisis. This article will compare women's resistance strategies in these five locations rooted in local knowledge, spirituality, and community solidarity, and assess their contribution to social-ecological transformation. This article employs an ecofeminist framework alongside a qualitative desk-based research methodology to investigate the intricate relationship among women's corporeal experiences, their habitats, and the natural environment, both in a symbolic and practical context, in the ongoing fight against ecological inequity. The findings indicate that various forms of resistance, including weaving practices, engaging in forest stewardship, delineating customary territories, and establishing community organizations, represent tangible manifestations of ecofeminism that serve to enhance women's political agency. These findings substantiate the assertion that the women's movement in marginalized regions not only contests the patriarchal and capitalist structures that pervade the developmental paradigm in Indonesia but also proposes an alternative developmental model that is both ecologically equitable and gender-inclusive.

I. T. Sihidi (✉) · Salahudin · N. F. Akmalia
Department of Government Studies, Universitas Muhammadiyah Malang, Malang, Indonesia
e-mail: iradhad@umm.ac.id

Salahudin
e-mail: salahudinmsi@umm.ac.id

M. J. Galang
Department of Politics and Government, Universutas Gadjah Mada, Yogyakarta, Indonesia
e-mail: muhjanuargalangrivaldan@mail.ugm.ac.id

H. Adam and F. A. Malik (eds.), *The Political Economy of Gender*,
https://doi.org/10.1007/978-981-92-2785-3_15

Keywords Ecofeminism · Women's movement · Ecological resistance · Gender violence · Environmental justice · Local knowledge · Community solidarity · Extractive industry · Marginalized areas · Indonesia

1 Introduction

Environmental challenges in Indonesia persist as a significant issue in the context of numerous extensive development initiatives that often lead to ecological deterioration (Alamgir et al., 2019; Ambarwulan et al., 2021; Padmanaba et al., 2023; Pujiati et al., 2023). Projects such as mining, reclamation, and large-scale land clearing often have a direct impact on local communities living around the area (Huang & Ge, 2024; Toumbourou et al., 2020; Werner et al., 2023). Among the most affected groups are women, whose role in the day-to-day management of natural resources makes them the first to experience the impacts of environmental damage (Glynn & Maimunah, 2021, 2023). However, women are not only victims, but also important actors in fighting ecological injustice (Gazing Wolf, 2024).

Women's resistance to the environmental crisis demonstrates distinctive forms of resistance, distinct from the masculine and formal models of mainstream social movements (Deckard, 2024; Pena, 2022). In various regions of Indonesia, women have demonstrated the capacity to organize action, preserve collective memory, and mobilize local values and spirituality in challenging state and corporate power (Glynn & Maimunah, 2021; Lynch & Turner, 2021; Sulistyati, 2023). Their resistance is motivated not only by ecological interests but also by a commitment to the sustainability of their communities. Thus, the women's movement is a manifestation of an ecological politics that is rooted, contextual, and grounded in the survival of their generations (Petrova, 2024).

In this context, the ecofeminist approach offers a powerful theoretical framework for understanding the connection between the domination of nature and gender inequality. Ecofeminism views environmental exploitation and women's subordination as having the same ideological and structural roots, namely patriarchy and capitalism (Ali & Sasani, 2024; Silberzahn, 2024). Consequently, the efforts of women to preserve the environment constitute not merely an ecological endeavor but also a manifestation of political and cultural emancipation (Glynn & Maimunah, 2021, 2023; Lynch & Turner, 2021; Sulistyati, 2023; Toumbourou et al., 2020). This perspective is especially pertinent when analyzing the women's movement in Indonesia's peripheral regions, where opposition frequently emerges against extractivism (the large-scale exploitation of natural resources), the safeguarding of customary land (territories governed by indigenous laws and traditions), and the practices associated with spiritual ecology (the cosmological and ritualistic engagements with the natural world).

This research investigates five regions as illustrative case studies: the Kendeng Mountains (Central Java), Kodingareng Island (South Sulawesi), the Lake Toba region (North Sumatra), Mollo (East Nusa Tenggara), and Sengah Temila District

(West Kalimantan). The rationale for selecting these regions lies in their geographical heterogeneity, the variety of ecological challenges encountered, and the distinct strategies employed by women's movements within differing contexts. Through a comparative approach, this study seeks to understand patterns of resistance that emerge in specific local conditions, yet have national resonance. These five cases also demonstrate how women from diverse cultural backgrounds construct strong, connected, and consistent ecological narratives.

2 Literature Review

Ecofeminism, as a theoretical approach, emerged in the late 1970s and early 1980s as a response to the environmental crisis, which was seen as intersecting with gender inequality (Alice et al., 2024; Anjum, 2020; Merchant, 2022). Notable theorists such as Vandana Shiva and Maria Mies claim that the degradation of the natural environment is inextricably linked to the subjugation of women, with both issues emerging from the interconnected dynamics of patriarchy and capitalism. Within this framework, the corporeal existence of women and the environment are regarded as mere commodities, subjected to exploitation for the purpose of economic profit (Kozhisseri & Rajan, 2020; Valero et al., 2024; Wichterich, 2024). Ecofeminism integrates the interrelated issues of ecological degradation and gender-based oppression within a cohesive paradigm of resistance (Deckard, 2023; Oksala, 2018).

Two predominant strands exist within the framework of ecofeminism: spiritual ecofeminism and materialist ecofeminism. The spiritual strand accentuates the intrinsic connection between women and nature through the motifs of fertility, motherhood, and indigenous rituals (Liu, 2024). In contrast, materialist ecofeminism prioritizes the examination of socio-political dynamics that contribute to disparities in the distribution of resources and decision-making authority (Tokay, 2025). Both paradigms are equally pertinent in the analysis of women's movements in Indonesia, which frequently integrate spiritual practices alongside political advocacy.

Prior investigations have indicated that women occupy a pivotal position in environmental movements, especially in regions acutely affected by ecological degradation. In the Southeast Asian context, particularly in Indonesia, women's resistance to mining, land reclamation, and palm oil plantation projects often occurs through informal networks and strong indigenous communities (Astono et al., 2024; Elmhirst et al., 2017; Parastasia, 2024). However, most of these studies focus on cases in a single location, leaving a limited body of research that explores the spiritual and symbolic dimensions of women's resistance in a comparative, cross-regional manner. This study shows that spirituality is not only a cultural expression but also a political strategy rooted in women's everyday lives.

3 Importance of the Study

This study is important because it examines women's ecological resistance in five marginalized regions of Indonesia, namely Kendeng, Kodingareng, Lake Toba, Mollo, and Sengah Temila, in order to understand how they confront extractivism through locally rooted and gendered strategies. The objective of the study is to identify both shared patterns and unique forms of women's agency in these struggles. By comparing these cases, the research emphasizes the role of local knowledge, spiritual ecology, and everyday care practices. The findings enrich ecofeminism literature and provide strategic input for advocacy on ecological justice and the protection of customary land and traditional living spaces.

4 Methods

This study uses a qualitative approach through library research to examine various forms of ecological resistance carried out by women in five regions of Indonesia: Kendeng Mountains (Central Java), Kodingareng Island (South Sulawesi), Keerom Regency (Papua), the Lake Toba area (North Sumatra), Mollo (East Nusa Tenggara), and Sengah Temila District (West Kalimantan). The selection of these locations is based on geographical diversity, types of ecological threats, as well as the plurality of cultures and forms of movements that represent the complexity of women's struggles in the environmental context in Indonesia. Data were gathered from a multitude of secondary sources, encompassing reports issued by civil society organizations, articles published in academic journals, media documentation, and other pertinent publications.

To fortify the analytical framework, this investigation conducted methodical inquiries on Scopus and Google Scholar (2017–2025) using the terms "ecofeminism" and "ecofeminism in Indonesia." Only scholarly articles that have undergone peer review were incorporated, whereas irrelevant materials were systematically omitted. The chosen publications were thematically categorized into classifications such as spiritual resistance, material resistance, symbolic narratives, and collective action, which were subsequently synthesized into overarching themes.

The examination of data was conducted using an ecofeminist paradigm as the primary theoretical framework for elucidating the correlation between gender disparities and environmental degradation. This scholarly inquiry examines how women express their ecological experiences through symbolic narratives, spiritual engagements, and community-oriented collective initiatives. The methodological approach employed was thematic analysis, which enabled the identification of patterns of resistance, manifestations of structural violence encountered, and advocacy mechanisms utilized. Through this methodological lens, the investigation aims to capture the political, cultural, and symbolic dimensions inherent in women's movements as they respond to ecological threats within their respective localities.

5 Results and Discussions

5.1 Kendeng, Central Java: Women's Ecological Resistance in the Context of Karst Ecosystems and Local Wisdom

The ecological resistance movement initiated by women in the Kendeng Mountains of Central Java commenced with profound apprehension regarding the environmental hazards posed by plans to exploit the karst region by a cement mining corporation (Fitri & Akbar, 2017). Approximately in 2005, the local populace became aware of proposals to establish a cement manufacturing facility by PT Semen Gresik, which PT Semen Indonesia subsequently expanded. The Kendeng karst region transcends mere geological significance; it functions as a crucial groundwater reservoir, serving as the primary source of sustenance for thousands of inhabitants, particularly those engaged in agriculture. As the mining initiative commenced, the women of Kendeng, who rely daily on the ecosystem's viability for activities such as laundering, agriculture, culinary practices, and child-rearing, perceived that not only was the natural environment imperiled, but also the sustainability of their own livelihoods.

In 2014, the resistance movement began to take concrete form with the establishment of struggle tents at the designated mining sites. Women, who became known as "Srikandi Kendeng," took a central role, standing guard for months, becoming symbols of the struggle for land and water. Unlike confrontational forms of protest, they chose a nonviolent approach, sitting together in the streets, performing spiritual rituals, singing traditional songs, and reciting dhikr, as a form of affirmation of local identity and values. This approach demonstrated the movement's moral and spiritual strength, which far transcended mere economic demands (Fitri & Akbar, 2017).

Within the framework of ecofeminism, this movement not only rejects environmental damage but also challenges the patriarchal system that objectifies nature and women's bodies. Kendeng women frame land and water as "Mother Earth"—a living entity that gives life and should be respected, not exploited. This view aligns with the thinking of Vandana Shiva and Maria Mies, who position women as ecological subjects with a cosmological and historical closeness to nature (Trujillo, 2021). In the Kendeng context, women are not only victims of ecological damage but also active agents who resist masculine forms of development that displace local knowledge and subsistence-based life systems.

The culmination of this symbolic resistance occurred in March 2016 and again in 2017, when nine Kendeng women cemented their feet in front of the State Palace in Jakarta. This action was not only a powerful visual act of resistance, but also a statement of courage and spiritual attachment to the land, which they considered part of their own bodies. This act was a metaphor that if the earth were cemented, they too would be "imprisoned." This movement not only targeted the government but also prompted public reflection on the power dynamics between the state, corporations, and the general public.

On numerous occasions, Kendeng women have stated that their struggle is not for money or replacement projects, but for water, for rice fields, and the sustainability of their children and grandchildren. This demonstrates that the development narrative, which has historically been based solely on economic growth, is being challenged through a narrative of life rooted in local wisdom. This is where ecofeminism emerges as an ideological force that challenges the dichotomy between humans and nature, as well as between men and women, and between development and conservation. They are not simply protesting but also proposing a more equitable model of the relationship between humans and the earth.

However, this struggle did not go without pressure. Although the Supreme Court initially revoked the environmental permit for the cement project, the local government subsequently issued a new permit, further sparking resistance. When Patmi, a Kendeng activist, died after the second cement project in March 2017, public sympathy spread, but it also demonstrated the heavy price women pay for maintaining their living space. Their resistance symbolized that change does not come from elites, but from the communities directly impacted.

The Kendeng women's movement ultimately teaches that ecological struggle is not just about the environment, but also about social justice, spirituality, and local knowledge. They refuse to be categorized as "development-ignorant," instead demonstrating that their understanding of land and water goes far beyond the numbers in an Environmental Impact Assessment (AMDAL) report. By publicly manifesting their physical presence, vocal expressions, and spiritual beliefs within communal and legislative arenas, the women of Kendeng are systematically dismantling the entrenched power dynamics that have historically marginalized them.

This examination elucidates that the resistance exhibited by Kendeng women embodies a form of spiritual ecofeminism, which intricately weaves together the symbolism of the body, sacred religious practices, and the cosmological reverence for "Mother Earth" as the fundamental source of existence. The act of foot cementing, alongside dhikr and traditional musical expressions, transcends mere symbolic gestures; it serves as a profound affirmation of the notion that nature constitutes a sentient being, which ought not to be commodified. Concurrently, this movement critiques the patriarchal capitalist framework that dismisses indigenous knowledge in preference for resource-extractive enterprises. This spiritual form of resistance signifies a counter-narrative to the masculinist and exploitative developmental discourse that has predominated environmental policy in Indonesia.

Viewed through the prism of ecofeminism, this movement epitomizes the pinnacle of grassroots resistance: an integration of corporeal identities, the natural world, and local communities in a cohesive struggle. They not only protect water, but also preserve memories, generations, and values. In a world dominated by the logic of extraction and capitalism, the women of Kendeng stand as the last bastion of hope for life. As they say in their song: "Ibu Bumi wis maringi, Ibu Bumi dilarani, Ibu Bumi kang ngadili", Mother Earth has given, Mother Earth has been hurt, and Mother Earth will judge.

5.2 *Kodingareng Island, South Sulawesi: Collective Action by Coastal Women Against Maritime Extractivism*

The women's resistance movement on Kodingareng Island, South Sulawesi, began in mid-2020 when a mining vessel owned by PT Boskalis began mining sea sand in traditional fishing grounds. This mining activity has caused seawater to become murky, drastically reducing catches and disrupting the coastal ecosystem on which the community relies. Women, who manage the fishermen's catch and maintain households daily, are the ones most affected. This unrest has given rise to a realization that they cannot remain silent, and women are beginning to build collective strength to resist this exploitation.

Initial resistance took the form of direct action at sea, when the women of Kodingareng intercepted a mining vessel using a small boat. They also held demonstrations at the governor's office, the Regional People's Representative Council (DPRD), and even in Jakarta, carrying banners and posters expressing their plight (Chandra, 2022; Satizábal et al., 2024; Strange, 2020). This demonstration was peaceful yet courageous, often confronting security forces or battered by high waves. The actions of the Kodingareng women represent the ecological political courage of a group previously considered subordinate to the development process.

From an ecofeminist perspective, this resistance demonstrates that the relationship between women and nature is not merely symbolic, but based on concrete experiences as guardians of life. The marine and coastal environments represent not only economic domains but also social and spiritual realms that are essential to the existence of the women from Kodingareng. When the marine ecosystem is compromised, its communal structure is significantly destabilized. Consequently, their opposition is not merely a response but rather a manifestation of an ecological identity that has been cultivated over numerous generations. They do not simply oppose mining activities but also contest the patriarchal framework of development that categorizes both nature and women as mere resources for exploitation.

The Kodingareng women's movement has consequently evolved into a more structured entity through the establishment of local forums and organizations. In 2022, they convened a women's congress, appointed leaders, and devised a collective agenda that encompassed issues such as coastal zoning, waste management, and strategies for addressing the climate crisis. This initiative exemplifies that their struggle extends beyond mere resistance and includes the pursuit of social transformation. They are progressively asserting autonomy in decision-making, thereby occupying the space that was previously abandoned by the state.

On the other hand, the women of Kodingareng are facing an economic crisis due to sea damage that has eliminated their primary livelihood. To survive, they develop household economics such as producing dried fish and shredded fish, forging debt solidarity within their families, and even encouraging their husbands to migrate. These strategies demonstrate not only resilience but also creativity in building local economic resilience. In times of crisis, they are the ones who support the stability of their families and communities.

Environmental Vehicle Indonesia (Walhi) South Sulawesi noted that the state has neglected to protect both environmental rights and the economic rights of coastal residents (Chandra, 2023; Matalatta et al., 2021; Sabar & Asisah, 2023). Amidst a policy vacuum and the absence of government accountability, the women of Kodingareng have emerged as key actors in responding to the climate crisis and ecological destruction. Their struggle transcends advocacy, it becomes a form of grassroots political education, born from the very bodies directly impacted by resource exploitation. This signifies that change does not come solely from elites, but from the courage of organized communities.

This movement also touches on human rights, as mining practices and environmental degradation have been proven to trigger violations of women's rights. Many women experience psychological distress, lose safe spaces, and are forced to bear a disproportionate economic burden. In this context, ecofeminism encompasses not only nature but also social justice and the redressing of unequal power relations. When the women of Kodingareng speak out and act, they are correcting the course of development that has marginalized the rights of local communities.

The resistance of Kodingareng women reflects materialist ecofeminism, as the main focus is on maintaining access to marine resources as the basis of the economic, social and identity of coastal communities. The formation of community forums, zoning advocacy, and women's congresses demonstrate political-structural strategies to resist state and corporate power. In the framework of ecofeminism, this action is a rejection of maritime patriarchal capitalism that makes the sea a commodity and positions women only in the domestic sphere, not as decision-making actors in coastal governance.

Ultimately, the Kodingareng women's movement demonstrates that ecofeminist resistance doesn't always require grand theories, but grows from concrete, everyday experiences. They challenge the state, corporations, and patriarchal structures in their own ways, through collective action, community solidarity, and a steadfast commitment to protecting the ocean as their home. In a world facing a growing climate crisis and a moral crisis of development, the women of Kodingareng emerge as a clear and strong voice from the country's margins. A voice that proclaims that the ocean is not merely sand and a commodity, but a life-giving mother that must be protected.

5.3 Lake Toba, North Sumatra: Advocacy by Batak Indigenous Women for Land Rights and Customary Territory

This resistance began in 1977 when the New Order government, through the Forestry Service, planted pine trees on the customary land of Siria Village, without the consent of the local community (Cusdiawan & Mudiyati Rahmatunnisa, 2023). Customary agricultural land, a source of livelihood and community identity, was suddenly rezoned without the participation of residents. The ina—Batak women, who traditionally have no land rights, were at the forefront of the fight against this land grab by occupying the land and temporarily halting the reforestation program.

Within an ecofeminist framework, the actions of the women represent an integrative reclaiming of women's bodies and the Motherland. They argue that when nature is destroyed, the social and spiritual well-being of the community is also compromised. By occupying land, Batak women demonstrate that the relationship between women and the Motherland is not just about economics, but also about identity, ancestral memory, and the preservation of community continuity.

Further action took place in December 1978 when the Forestry Service rebuilt a reforestation hut. The ina group destroyed the hut and equipment as a form of anger against the oppression of customary and state structures that excluded their voices. A major conflict ensued; the military arrested several residents, and women took to the streets in a collective demonstration of around 200 people.

During the conflict, Batak women developed ecological and ecofeminist survival strategies. They constructed narratives of opposition to dispossession through bodily symbolism: covering their mouths together when detained, answering their names in unison as a form of anonymous solidarity, and refusing to submit to the stifling patriarchal structure. This demonstrates that resistance is not merely physical, but also spiritual and a collective identity (Lumbanbatu, 2025; Simangunsong, 2024).

The struggle continues with more symbolic yet strategic actions. In July 2022, indigenous Tano Batak women held a floating banner on Lake Toba during the W20 Summit, displaying the message "North Sumatran Women Against Deforestation". This action highlights the direct connection between the rights of indigenous women and the preservation of forests and spiritual ecologys, which are under constant threat from corporations like Toba Pulp Lestari (TPL).

From an ecofeminist perspective, this initiative substantiates that Indigenous women are not mere instruments of development but rather active agents in the defense of their own territories. They assert their roles as ethical stewards of ancestral land, water, and forests, which have a significant influence on the community's sustainability. From the viewpoints of Vandana Shiva and Maria Mies, this collective demonstration signifies a repudiation of patriarchal industrialization that neglects indigenous knowledge and the rights of women (Trujillo, 2021).

The Batak indigenous women's movement in Lake Toba exemplifies a synthesis of spiritual and materialist ecofeminist ideologies. The occupation of lands and demonstrative public actions elucidate a profound spiritual connection to ancestral territories, integral to their collective identity, alongside a systematic resistance against corporations that appropriate customary lands. The floating banner demonstration on Lake Toba during the W20 event exemplifies the intersection between the rights of indigenous women and the preservation of ecosystems, while simultaneously serving as a poignant critique of patriarchal capitalism that marginalizes women's participation in the governance of natural resources. The Batak women of Lake Toba present a notable case study, illustrating that ecological resistance and heightened identity consciousness are not merely derived from theoretical frameworks but are rather products of lived realities, influenced by the encroachments of development, land appropriation, and the marginalization of social structures. Through their valiant public demonstrations and community fortitude, they assert that ecological resilience is embodied by those who actively reinterpret the dynamics between humanity, nature, and authority.

5.4 Mollo, East Nusa Tenggara: Cultural Ecofeminism as a Strategy of Opposition to the Extractive Mining Sector

The indigenous women's movement in the Mollo region of East Nusa Tenggara began in response to the establishment of a marble mining corporation that secured an exploitation permit in 1994, without the local community's consent. This mining endeavor precipitated significant environmental degradation, manifesting in deforestation and the deterioration of water sources, thereby jeopardizing the sustainability of weaving traditions, which are intricately dependent on natural resources (Ernanda, 2023; Parastasia, 2024). The women of Mollo, who possess a profound spiritual and cultural affiliation with the natural environment, perceived an existential threat to their habitat. This circumstance gave rise to a collective consciousness aimed at safeguarding their ancestral lands and forests through non-violent actions spearheaded by the indigenous women's leader, Mama Aleta Baun.

The movement reached a pivotal point with an extended, peaceful demonstration that engaged approximately 150 women who were actively weaving at the site of the mine. In a display of solidarity, men assumed domestic responsibilities to bolster the women's resistance efforts (Desrianti, 2025). Weaving transcends mere cultural symbolism; it also serves as a mechanism of ecological resistance, underscoring the intrinsic connection between women's corporeal existence and the natural world. The women of Mollo embody a philosophical perspective wherein nature is an integral aspect of their identity, the land as flesh, the water as blood, and the forest as hair.

This form of resistance is also evident in various tangible expressions, such as obstructing corporate access and establishing inter-village solidarity networks. The act of weaving serves as a medium of communication and a representation of struggle, articulating the entitlements of indigenous populations to their land and a sustainable ecosystem. Through this cultural practice, the women of Mollo exemplify that resistance can be enacted in a peaceful, symbolic manner, grounded in local traditions, while simultaneously possessing substantial political efficacy.

The exit of numerous mining corporations from the Mollo region signified a pivotal success for this movement (Mandalika, 2024; Nelson, 2013). This outcome illustrates that collectively employed nonviolent strategies by women possess considerable transformative potential (Lubis et al., 2025; Tan & Jegalus, 2025). They are adept at undermining the hegemony of extractive capitalism through approaches that are deeply rooted in indigenous values and ecological spirituality. This further underscores that ecofeminist resistance strategies can serve as a viable alternative in confronting environmental challenges.

In the aftermath of this triumph, the women of Moll persisted in their advocacy. They established a collective aimed at bolstering the ongoing involvement of women in conservation efforts, sustainable agricultural practices, the mapping of indigenous territories, and community-based ecological education. This transition from a movement focused on resistance to one centered on enhancing community capacity exemplifies the evolution of ecofeminism from a merely symbolic endeavor to a sustainable, community-oriented framework for environmental stewardship. This initiative also facilitated the rejuvenation of women's leadership within the realm of natural resource management.

Theoretically, the Mollo women's movement corroborates the ecofeminist assertion that the subjugation of both nature and women is entrenched in analogous structural systems: patriarchy and capitalism. As stewards of the environment, women maintain not only a symbolic connection with nature but also engage in practical actions that uphold ecological equilibrium. By reviving traditional weaving practices and advocating for forest preservation, the women of Mollo demonstrate that sustainable living is grounded in women's wisdom and indigenous knowledge.

The weaving initiative at the mining site, spearheaded by Mama Aleta Baun, exemplifies a potent manifestation of spiritual ecofeminism, wherein weaving functions as a symbolic conduit that intertwines the corporeal presence of women with the natural environment. The philosophy that land, water, and forests are integral to their bodily existence invigorates resistance that is anchored in local cultural paradigms. Nevertheless, this endeavor encompasses a materialist aspect as it concurrently halts mining activities and safeguards livelihoods. By engaging in culture-based peaceful resistance, the women of Mollo contest the patriarchal capitalist paradigm that reduces nature to mere commodities.

This entire process demonstrates that women are not merely victims of the environmental crisis but also key actors in restructuring the relationship between humans and nature. The Mollo women's movement is a concrete manifestation of ecofeminist empowerment that upholds life, cares for the earth, and presents nonexploitative development alternatives. Through cultural work, spirituality, and collective action, Mollo women demonstrate that resistance to ecological injustice canbegin at the grassroots and grow into a force for sustainable change.

5.5 Sengah Temila, West Kalimantan: Reproduction of Local Knowledge and the Dayak Women's Movement in Customary Forest Conservation

The women's ecological resistance movement in Sengah Temila District, Landah Regency, began with the impact of the expansion of palm oil companies, which continued to encroach on the Dayak traditional area (Astono et al., 2024; Toumbourou & Dressler, 2021). Massive deforestation and land conversion have led to damage to water sources, the loss of forests on which communities rely for their livelihoods, and the erosion of traditional natural resource management practices based on local wisdom. Dayak women, who have played a central role in subsistence agriculture, forest medicine management, and traditional rituals, are beginning to experience the loss of living space, which is not only economically but also spiritually significant. When the local government and indigenous men, some of whom have compromised with corporations, are unable to respond to this crisis, women are rising and organizing themselves to defend their forests and customary lands.

These women initiated collective action by blocking access to land intended for clearing by companies and reviving traditional rituals and community-based forest management practices. They repudiated partnerships involving palm oil and land acquisition initiatives that failed to respect the rights of indigenous populations. In numerous instances, they encountered coercion from both authorities and corporations; nevertheless, they remained steadfast in their adherence to the principles of nonviolence and traditional ethical frameworks, which formed the bedrock of their activism. This form of resistance aimed not solely at safeguarding their habitats but also at preserving their ancestral legacies and ensuring the continuity of their descendants. Their opposition extends beyond mere physical protest, encompassing everyday practices that promote ecological sustainability, such as cultivating indigenous food crops, managing village forests, and passing on traditional knowledge to future generations. They enhance their negotiating leverage through inter-village women's networks, participation in village assemblies, and articulating their customary land rights within development planning frameworks. These endeavors exemplify tangible manifestations of ecological resistance that depend on women's reproductive and symbolic labor, a dimension that patriarchal development paradigms have overlooked.

From an ecofeminist standpoint, the women's movement in Sengah Temila embodies the intricate relationship between women's corporeality and the natural environment. The devastation of the forest signifies not only the loss of their economic means but also a diminishment of their cultural identity and spiritual ties. Women emerge as both symbols and pivotal figures in the resistance, perceiving nature not merely as a commodity for production but as a nurturing mother. This perspective stands in stark contrast to the rationale of capitalist development, which commodifies both nature and women as resources subject to exploitation.

Furthermore, these women's resistance contests the power dynamics that have systematically marginalized them from decision-making spheres concerning natural resource governance. Through the establishment of advocacy coalitions and learning communities, they cultivate alternative arenas that amalgamate indigenous knowledge with political consciousness. They build sustainability strategies not from the outside, but from within: through culture, local languages, and ritual practices. This is the core strength of the indigenous women's movement, they not only resist, but also create vibrant, rooted alternative systems.

Beyond being guardians of values and ecosystems, these women have successfully changed the narrative about who is considered the "owner of knowledge" in conservation. They demonstrate that food security, ecological resilience, and the preservation of traditions depend heavily on women's active roles. Amidst the climate crisis and agrarian conflict, their voices not only deserve to be heard but also lay the foundation for a more equitable and sustainable development.

The resistance strategies of Dayak women in Sengah Temila who reject palm oil partnerships, block company access, and revive traditional rituals are examples of spiritual ecofeminism, because rituals and local cosmology become the symbolic basis that unites women's bodies with the body of the forest as a source of life. At the same time, their actions also contain dimensions of materialist ecofeminism, because the rejection of land grabbing preserves food sources, maintains living space, and ensures the continuity of subsistence practices. By promoting peaceful resistance based on culture and daily reproductive work, Dayak Sengah Temila women at the same time challenge patriarchal capitalism that reduces forests to commodities and excludes women from decision-making, while showing that ecological and gender justice is only possible when local knowledge and women's roles are recognized as central to development.

The Dayak women's ecological movement in Sengah Temila is a living, rooted form of ecofeminism: linking ecological sustainability with women's liberation from structural subordination. By fulfilling the roles of stewards of the environment and advocates for social change, they contest the prevailing discourse that posits development as necessarily detrimental to the natural world and local communities. Conversely, they illustrate that authentic development transpires when the integrity of the environment, the richness of cultural heritage, and the dignity of individuals, particularly women, are upheld and accorded equitable treatment.

6 Conclusion and Recommendation

Ecological resilience manifested by women in Kendeng, Kodingareng, Mollo, Lake Toba, and Sengah Temila evidences that ecofeminism transcends mere theoretical discourse and embodies a pragmatic engagement deeply rooted in indigenous knowledge, communal solidarity, and spiritual principles. In various contexts, women actively resist extractivist practices that threaten their livelihoods, protect ancestral lands and traditional habitats, and express their opposition through spiritual ecology, which combines cosmological ideologies with ecological equity. These endeavors validate that women residing in marginalized regions are not merely passive casualties of environmental deterioration; rather, they are vital agents who propose alternative, life-sustaining paradigms of development.

The outcomes of this investigation hold significant ramifications for policy formulation and advocacy initiatives. Progressing beyond extractivist paradigms necessitates policy structures that acknowledge women's ecological expertise, uphold customary land entitlements, and rejuvenate traditions anchored in spiritual ecology.

Facilitating women's involvement in decision-making frameworks is imperative for promoting ecologically just and gender-equitable development in Indonesia. Concurrently, forthcoming research ought to examine the intergenerational dynamics within women's movements, the influence of digital networks on enhancing ecological resistance, and how localized ecofeminist practices can inform broader national and international environmental policies. By integrating practical ramifications with theoretical perspectives, this study emphasizes ecofeminism's capacity to inform transformative socio-ecological trajectories.

References

Alamgir, M., Campbell, M. J., Sloan, S., Suhardiman, A., Supriatna, J., & Laurance, W. F. (2019). High-risk infrastructure projects pose imminent threats to forests in Indonesian Borneo. *Scientific Reports, 9*(1), 140. https://doi.org/10.1038/S41598-018-36594-8

Ali, R., & Sasani, S. (2024). An ecofeminist study of Barbara Kingsolver's animal dreams and prodigal summer. *Research Journal in Advanced Humanities*. https://doi.org/10.58256/gb9j2575

Alice, C., Jebaselvi, E., & Mohanraj, K. (2024). The feminine face of environmental activism: An ecofeminist perspective. *Shanlax International Journal of Arts, Science and Humanities*. https://doi.org/10.34293/sijash.v12is2-july.7943

Ambarwulan, W., Nahib, I., Widiatmaka, W., Suryanta, J., Munajati, S. L., Suwarno, Y., Turmudi, T., Darmawan, M., & Sutrisno, D. (2021). Using geographic information systems and the analytical hierarchy process for delineating erosion-induced land degradation in the middle Citarum sub-watershed, Indonesia. *Frontiers in Environmental Science, 9*, 710570. https://doi.org/10.3389/FENVS.2021.710570

Anjum, T. (2020). Ecofeminism: Exploitation of women and nature. *International Journal of English and Literature, 5*(4), 846–848. https://doi.org/10.22161/IJELS.54.2

Astono, A., Muyassar, Y. R., & Wagner, I. (2024). Perempuan Dayak dalam Peran Menjaga Lingkungan Hidup Perspektif Ekofeminisme terhadap Hukum Lingkungan di Kalimantan Barat (Studi Kasus: Kecamatan Sengah Temila, Kabupaten Landak). *Arus Jurnal Sosial Dan Humaniora, 4*(1), 8–16. https://doi.org/10.57250/ajsh.v4i1.308

Chandra, W. (2022). *Strategi Perempuan Kodingareng Bertahan dalam Krisis*. Mongabay.Co.Id. https://mongabay.co.id/2022/07/07/strategi-perempuan-kodingareng-bertahan-dalam-krisis/.

Chandra, W. (2023). *Riset WALHI: Perubahan Iklim dan Tambang Pasir Laut Picu Terjadinya Pelanggaran HAM pada Perempuan di Sulsel*. Mongabay.Co.Id. https://www.mongabay.co.id/2023/12/01/riset-walhi-perubahan-iklim-dan-tambang-pasir-laut-picu-terjadinya-pelanggaran-ham-pada-perempuan-di-sulsel/.

Cusdiawan, & Rahmatunnisa, M. (2023). Indigenous peoples movement in maintaining living spaces perspective of recognition politics (study on indigenous peoples in Lake Toba). *PERSPEKTIF, 12*(1), 37–45. https://doi.org/10.31289/perspektif.v12i1.7946

Deckard, S. (2023). Social reproduction, struggle and the ecology of 'women's work' in world-literature. *Feminist Theory*. https://doi.org/10.1177/14647001231209901

Deckard, S. (2024). Social reproduction, struggle and the ecology of 'women's work' in world-literature. *Feminist Theory, 25*(2), 222–241. https://doi.org/10.1177/14647001231209901

Desrianti, F. (2025). Women' s resistance to the issue of appropriation of living space: An ecofeminist study. *Journal of Sociology Indicators of Sumatra, 04*(01), 383–390.

Elmhirst, R., Siscawati, M., Basnett, B. S., & Ekowati, D. (2017). Gender and generation in engagements with oil palm in East Kalimantan, Indonesia: Insights from feminist political ecology. *Journal of Peasant Studies, 44*(6), 1137–1159. https://doi.org/10.1080/03066150.2017.1337002

Ernanda. (2023). Challenging the patriarchal culture; feminist critical discourse analysis of the Indonesian environmental heroines. *Wacana, Journal of the Humanities of Indonesia, 24*(1), 4. https://doi.org/10.17510/wacana.v24i1.1173

Fitri, A. I., & Akbar, I. (2017). Gerakan Sosial Perempuan Ekofeminisme Di Pegunungan Kendeng Provinsi Jawa Tengah Melawan Pembangunan Tambang semen. *CosmoGov, 3*(1), 83. https://doi.org/10.24198/cosmogov.v3i1.12634

Gazing Wolf, J. (2024). Why we all lose when indigenous women suffer: An ecological perspective. *Frontiers in Ecology and the Environment*. https://doi.org/10.1002/fee.2717

Glynn, T., & Maimunah, S. (2021). Unearthing conscious intent in women's everyday resistance to mining in Indonesia. *Ethnography*. https://doi.org/10.1177/14661381211039372

Glynn, T., & Maimunah, S. (2023). Seeing empathy as resistance: A conjunctural photovoice study of women and mining in Indonesia. *Gender Place and Culture*. https://doi.org/10.1080/0966369x.2023.2228502

Huang, N., & Ge, L. (2024). Mining and indigenous communities in Southeast Asia: Examining the social impact of mineral development. *The Extractive Industries and Society*. https://doi.org/10.1016/j.exis.2023.101363

Kozhisseri, D., & Rajan, S. C. (2020). Unfolding nomadism? A feminist political ecology of sedentarization in the Attappady Hills, Kerala. *Journal of Political Ecology, 27*(1), 939–960. https://doi.org/10.2458/V27I1.23600

Liu, P. (2024). Laozi's ecofeminist ethos: Bridging ancient wisdom with contemporary gender and environmental justice. *Religions*. https://doi.org/10.3390/rel15050599

Lubis, S., Ali, M., & Ali, A. (2025). Decolonizing education and the green economy: Religious and indigenous resistance to extraction in Indonesia. *Journal of Religion, 1*(1), 16–30.

Lumbanbatu, H. A. (2025). The Batak Toba Tribe's cultural Capital in the Context of protecting natural resources from environmental threats. *Journal of Socio-Cultural Sustainability and Resilience*. https://doi.org/10.61511/jscsr.v2i2.2025.1493

Lynch, M., & Turner, S. (2021). Rocking the boat: Intersectional resistance to marine conservation policies in Wakatobi National Park, Indonesia. *Gender Place and Culture*. https://doi.org/10.1080/0966369X.2021.1971630

Mandalika, L. P. R. (2024). *Beyond religious crisis [Vrije Universiteit Amsterdam]*. https://doi.org/10.5463/thesis.980

Matalatta, Solihin, Ardianto, Y., J., & Karim, A. (2021). Environmental damage impact on economic losses in Sulawesi-south society. Saudi Journal of Economics and Finance, 5(2), 51–55. https://doi.org/10.36348/sjef.2021.v05i02.003.

Merchant, C. (2022). The death of nature: Production, reproduction, and the female. *Philosophical Literary Journal Logos, 32*(1), 191–222. https://doi.org/10.22394/0869-5377-2022-1-191-218

Nelson, J. C. (2013). Globalization and religious identity. *Millah, 12*(3), 23–50. https://doi.org/10.20885/millah.vol12.iss3.art2

Oksala, J. (2018). Feminism, capitalism, and ecology. *Hypatia: A Journal of Feminist Philosophy, 33*(2), 216–234. https://doi.org/10.1111/HYPA.12395

Padmanaba, M., Sloan, S., Watts, J. D., Irawan, S., Lee, J. S. H., Pasaribu, K. N., Wiratama, C. G., Watson, E., & Utami, N. P. (2023). Jurisdictional approaches to high conservation value area designation using regulatory instruments: An Indonesian pilot project. *Frontiers in Environmental Science*. https://doi.org/10.3389/fenvs.2023.1226070

Parastasia, C. (2024). Ekofeminisme Spritiualis pada Gerakan Perempuan Adat dalam Menolak Tambang Marmer di Mollo, Nusa Tenggara Timur. *Peradaban Journal of Religion and Society, 3*(1), 67–83. https://doi.org/10.59001/pjrs.v3i1.144

Pena, M. (2022). Resistencias ambientales y feminismos territoriales frente al extractivismo agroindustrial en Argentina, ¿qué nos ha dejado la pandemia? *Revista de Estudios Sociales, 80*, 57–74. https://doi.org/10.7440/res80.2022.04

Petrova, S. (2024). Ecofeminism–Historical Development and Perspectives. *Istoriya-History, 32*(6), 494–504. https://doi.org/10.53656/his2024-6-4-eco

Pujiati, A., Yanto, H., Handayani, B. D., Ridzuan, A. R., Borhan, H., & Shaari, M. S. (2023). The detrimental effects of dirty energy, foreign investment, and corruption on environmental quality: New evidence from Indonesia. *Frontiers in Environmental Science, 10*, 1074172. https://doi.org/10.3389/fenvs.2022.1074172

Sabar, H., & Asisah, N. (2023). Identifikasi Pelanggaran HAM dan strategi Bertahan Hidup Perempuan Kodingareng-Galesong dalam Menghadapi Perubahan Iklim. In *walhisulsel.or.id*.

Satizábal, P., Quinquillà, A., Franco, M., & Pedersen, C. (2024). *Ocean, water and fisher peoples' tribunals*.

Silberzahn, L. (2024). Care, ecology, and the crisis of eco-social reproduction: Politicizing more-than-human care. *Hypatia: A Journal of Feminist Philosophy*. https://doi.org/10.1017/hyp.2024.16

Simangunsong, T. (2024). *"Harusnya kami Tak lagi berjuang": Kisah Perempuan Batak yang Kembali Melawan Demi Tanah Adat*. Projectmulatuli.Com. https://projectmultatuli.org/harusnya-kami-tak-lagi-berjuang-kisah-perempuan-batak-yang-kembali-melawan-demi-tanah-adat/.

Strange. (2020). *Pronesiata-platform Berbagi karya literasi*. Pronesiata. https://www.pronesiata.id/homepage/detail/Esai/gerakan-perempuan-kodingareng-kesetaraan-gerakan-tanpa-teori-1613010629.

Sulistyati, M. (2023). Locality, equality, and piety: Pesantren ecofeminism movement in Indonesia. *Studia Islamika*. https://doi.org/10.36712/sdi.v30i2.25175

Tan, P., & Jegalus, N. (2025). The body as resistance: The naked body movement of women in Nusa Tenggara Timur as A political action from Hannah Arendt's perspective. *International Journal of Indonesian Philosophy & Theology, 6*(1), 18–34. https://doi.org/10.47043/ijipth.v6i1.86

Tokay, E. (2025). Toward an ecofeminist new materialism: Agency and action in a more-than-human world. *Hypatia: A Journal of Feminist Philosophy*. https://doi.org/10.1017/hyp.2024.97

Toumbourou, T. D., & Dressler, W. H. (2021). Sustaining livelihoods in a palm oil enclave: Differentiated gendered responses in East Kalimantan, Indonesia. *Asia Pacific Viewpoint, 62*(1), 40–55. https://doi.org/10.1111/apv.12265

Toumbourou, T., Muhdar, M., Werner, T., & Bebbington, A. (2020). Political ecologies of the post-mining landscape: Activism, resistance, and legal struggles over Kalimantan's coal mines. *Energy Research and Social Science, 65*, 101476. https://doi.org/10.1016/j.erss.2020.101476

Trujillo, M. L. N. (2021). Notes for a critical and ecological view of patriarchal capiltalism in the web of life. *Capital & Class, 45*(1), 21–32. https://doi.org/10.1177/0309816820929115

Valero, S. D., Kaul, S., Billi, L., Encarnacion, J., & Olofsson, S. (2024). Curbing the crises, gauging the gap: Measuring the nexus between gender and the environment. *Environmental Research*. https://doi.org/10.1088/2752-5295/ad91d8

Werner, T., Toumbourou, T., Maus, V., Lukas, M. C., Sonter, L. J., Muhdar, M., Runting, R. K., & Bebbington, A. (2023). Patterns of infringement, risk, and impact driven by coal mining permits in Indonesia. *AMBIO: A Journal of the Human Environment*. https://doi.org/10.1007/s13280-023-01944-y

Wichterich, C. (2024). Feminist critique of bioeconomies: Paradigm struggles toward a caring economy. *Sustainability: Science, Practice and Policy, 21*(1), 2435646. https://doi.org/10.1080/15487733.2024.2435646

Iradhad Taqwa Sihidi Master's degree in Political Science from the Department of Politics and Government, Universitas Gadjah Mada, Yogyakarta, and Bachelor's degree in Government Studies from the University of Muhammadiyah Malang. Currently serves as Lecturer at the Department of Government Studies, University of Muhammadiyah Malang, Indonesia. Research interests include political parties and elections, digital democracy, green democracy, and civil society, with active publications in national and international reputable journals and conference.

Salahudin Ph.D. in Political Science from Universitas Muhammadiyah Yogyakarta, Indonesia, with a Master's degree in Political Science from Khon Kaen University, Thailand, and a Bachelor's degree in Government Studies from the University of Muhammadiyah Malang. Currently serves as Lecturer at the Department of Government Studies, University of Muhammadiyah Malang, Indonesia. Research interests include local public finance politics, particularly green budgeting, with numerous publications in reputable international journals and presentations at international conferences.

Naila Febrina Akmalia is a research scholar in Government Studies at the University of Muhammadiyah Malang, Indonesia. Research interests focus on green politics and its contemporary developments.

Muhammad Januar Galang a graduate of the Department of Government Studies, Universitas Muhammadiyah Malang, Indonesia, and currently enrolled in the Master's Program at the Department of Politics and Government, Universitas Gadjah Mada, Yogyakarta. Research interests include politics, environmental issues, and gender studies.

Chapter 16
Global Capitalism and Female Precarity in India and Bangladesh Workforce

Anna Bashir, Abhilash Aggarwal, and Mehvish Mehraj

Abstract Global Capitalism has opened doors for women throughout the globe, offering jobs in export driven industries since 1990's, especially in India and Bangladesh. The dual impact of opportunities and exploitation upon women workers in the nations driven by Colonial Legacies and neoliberal policies, channeling women into low-wage and precarious roles is much evident, while intersectional vulnerabilities, patriarchal norms and capitalist strategies have amplified these exploitation, with pervasive harassment at hazardous workplaces fueled by global supply chain (GCS) demands. Grounded in feminist political economy and intersectional analysis, we expose the deliberate feminization of labor as a corporate strategy, where transnational organizations exploit myths of 'docility' and 'nimble fingers' to trap women in starvation-wage employment. This study undertakes a rigorous examination of capitalism's exploitative structures that perpetuate gendered subordination, exposing the interplay between transnational capital, state policies and patriarchal norms. It analyses the role of global capitalism in configuring labor conditions for women in India and Bangladesh, while proposing targeted policy reforms to mitigate gendered inequities in employment. Challenging the 'triple entanglement' of oppression that fosters a cycle of female vulnerability, encompassing eroded economic, corporeal and social entitlements, this article advocates for profound structural transformations, including the expansion of formal employment opportunities, the valuation of unpaid care work, the promotion of digital literacy and the enhancement of family support mechanisms. Expanding maternity and family benefits like paternity leaves, bolstering workplace oversight, developing skills among rural women, promoting formalized labor through vocational training, recognizing and redistributing uncompensated care services and strengthening labor unions for collective bargaining are

A. Bashir (✉)
School of Law, University of Kashmir, Srinagar, India
e-mail: annabashir@uok.edu.in

A. Aggarwal (✉)
School of Law, CHRIST (Deemed to be University), Bangalore, India
e-mail: abhilash.aggarwal@christuniversity.in

M. Mehraj
Department of Business Studies, University of the People, California, USA
e-mail: mehvish.mehraj@uopeople.edu

H. Adam and F. A. Malik (eds.), *The Political Economy of Gender*,
https://doi.org/10.1007/978-981-92-2785-3_16

the recommendations supported by this study as a part of comprehensive institutional reforms.

Keywords Global capitalism · Women workers · Labor exploitation · Female Precarity · Patriarchy · India · Bangladesh · Labor reforms · Intersectionality

1 Introduction

Global capitalism with its emphasis on profiteering and global supply chain (GSC) networks, has had a dramatic impact on the job market on the labor markets growing in South Asian nations like India and Bangladesh. However, this development has opened job opportunities in export oriented sectors for women like textiles, it has also maintained a gender subordination. The accounts of gendered intersectionality with patriarchy, caste, migration status and socio-economic abuse have been documented upon female laborers in these regions since decades (Kustin et al., 2025). The economic parity of female laborers is widened by low wages and unsafe working conditions in Bangladesh's textile sector (Basirulla et al., 2024), which analogous to the textile and electronic sector of Indian sub-continent.

The labor landscape of South Asia was drastically changed in 1990's, accelerated by neoliberal reforms integrating the seeds of global capitalism. India's and Bangladesh's prominence rose as key players in GSC of textiles, garments and electronics, propelled by trade liberalization policies, prioritizing export oriented industrialization and foreign direct investments (Rahman et al., 2012). This profound transformation transitioned Bangladesh into second largest exporter of *Ready Made Garments* (RMG) manufacturing hub in South Asia (Mamun & Hoque, 2022), attracting rural women to work in formal and informal settings. In due course a "race to the bottom" approach within GSC in South Asia led to the creation of a chain of systematic exploitation resulting in suppression of wages and labor rights (Norberg, 2024). A de-liberate corporate strategy to recruit young women into low-wage, precarious jobs framed as 'suitable' for their 'nimble fingers' and perceived docility was put in action (De Neve, 2014).

The pandemic in 2019–2021 further exposed vulnerabilities, as GCS disruptions led to mass layoffs and unpaid wages, disproportionately affecting women workers (Antipova, 2021). By 2023, pandemic layoffs disproportionately targeted women as it was reported with 64% job losses in Bangladesh, bearing the brunt, they faced systematic wage discrimination, precarious contracts and hazardous conditions amplified by weak regulatory enforcement (Premji et al., 2023). This trend is not organic but engineered by global retailors and local suppliers who exploit gendered social hierarchies to depress labor costs. While in the current scenario, 'automation' now threatens 60% of female dominated apparel jobs by 2030 (Filippi et al., 2023), yet worker resistance is growing from Bangladesh's Accord on Fire Safety to India's Garment Labor Union, challenging the myth of passive feminized labor.

As per the World Bank Gender Data Portal report of 2024, women comprises 60%–80% of export manufacturing workforces, yet earning 100$ to 125$ less than men monthly (World Economic Forum, 2024). Moreover, the capitalist supply chain pressures tight deadlines and order volatility, thus intensifying workplace oppression, including overtime upto 18 hour shifts during peak seasons and sexual harassment as well. The TNCs leveraging neoliberal trade policies, deliberately target countries like India and Bangladesh for 'labor arbitrage' through outsourcing production to zones with weak regulations and abundant 'cheap' female labor (Ali et al., 2025). This profit maximization calculus intersects violently with patriarchal norms by employers who actively prefer women workers, perceiving them as 'docile', 'less unionized' and 'socially conditioned' to accept low wages, which results in a 'gendered exploitation loop'. Thus, patriarchal political economy externalizes reproductive women labor with juggling factory shifts, unpaid care work and subsiding capitalist production with their bodily exhaustion (Haque, 2025).

This Chapter aims to examine how global capitalism contributes to the gendered oppression in women workers in India and Bangladesh, using political economy lens to analyze labor conditions, intersectional dynamics and policy recommendations. The core issue this study confronts is, the triple entanglement of global capitalism, entrenched patriarchy and systemic exploitation that traps women workers in cycles of precarity across South Asia with special reference to India and Bangladesh.

2 Literature Review

This literature review synthesizes extant research to scrutinize the exploitation of female workers in India and Bangladesh within GCS. It unveils a multifaceted interplay among global capitalism, patriarchal systems and intersectional inequalities. Drawing on feminist political economy, it illuminates how global capitalism harnesses women's labor to amplify profits, thereby entrenching and perpetuating patriarchal hierarchies. *Peter Custers* (Custers, 2012) introduces the 'sectoral sexual division of labor', where women in India and Bangladesh are relegated to low-status roles in garments due to perceived docility and lower wages. Intersectionality reveals how gender intersects with class, caste and migration status, amplifying vulnerabilities. For instance, Dalit women in India face caste based exclusion (Soundararajan et al., 2024), while migrant women in Bangladesh encounter wage theft (Ahmed, 2024). Social reproduction theory underscores women's unpaid labor, such as childcare, as critical to capitalist accumulation, yet devalued by patriarchal norms argues that women's exploitation in sweatshops stems from both gender and class, with capitalist commodification facilitated by patriarchal devaluation of labor (Mezzadri, 2016).

Colonial legacies and neoliberal policies shaped gendered oppression. British colonial land policies in India created structural inequalities, confining women to low-productivity tasks (Afzal-Khan, 2022). Neoliberal reforms, driven by the World Bank and IMF, prioritize privatization, reducing public services and pushing women into informal work (Moloney, 2022). In the 1980's and 1990's, India and Bangladesh saw women enter garment industries due to lower wages, but global production shifts pushed them into precarious work (Ashraf & Prentice, 2019). In India, female labor participation dropped from 57% to 44% in rural areas from 1987–2011, reflecting patriarchal barriers (Afridi et al., 2016). As per the study of 2024, in Bangladesh, the garment sector employing 85% women, reflects 'informality precarity complex' driven by capitalist priorities, as seen from the 2013 *Rana Plaza collapse* exposing deadly exploitation, starkly highlighting ongoing unsafe conditions and with women relegate to low paying roles (Ahmed, 2024).

Furthermore, the intersection of race, gender and class further complicates the experiences of women workers in the Global South (Niumai, 2025). Women of color, particularly in post-colonial nations like India and Bangladesh, often bear the brunt of both racial and gendered oppression within global capitalist frameworks (Nazneen & Okech, 2021). In India, a 2025 study by *Dev* and *Sahay* scrutinizes India's underutilized female labor force, underscoring that notwithstanding educational and health advancements, circa 60% of working-age women persist beyond labor markets. Principal barriers encompass disproportionate unpaid care burdens and scarce formal part-time prospects. Advocating their formalization and caregiving redistribution, it forecasts *female Labour force participation* (FLFP) ascending six percentage points, from 37% to 43% (Dev & Sahay, 2025).

3 Objectives of the Study

The primary objective of this chapter is to critically analyze how capitalism's extractive architectures systematically perpetuate gendered oppression of women workers in India and Bangladesh, moving beyond isolated critiques to expose the synergy of transnational capital, state policy and patriarchal norms in sustaining exploitation. While the research is oriented towards the following specific objectives namely:

1. To examine the role of global capitalism in shaping labor conditions for women workers in India and Bangladesh.
2. To analyze the influence of colonial gendered intersectional dynamics shaping susceptibilities of female labor dynamics.
3. To compare the ramifications of global capitalism and attendant exploitative practices on female workers in India and Bangladesh.
4. To advance policy reforms designed to ameliorate gendered subjugation within labor markets.

4 Research Methodology

This study adopts a review based methodology, utilizing secondary data analysis and comparative analysis grounded in the political economy of gender and intersectionality, to examine the capitalist mechanism sustaining gendered subordination among female laborers in India and Bangladesh. This approach effectively delineates the complex realities faced by women in GCS, while balancing economic growth and protection of labor rights. Emphasis has been upon novel and regionally specific sources shedding light on the plight of female laborers. The literary synthesis incorporates a broad spectrum of authoritative sources spanning the preceding two decades, encompassing distinguished academic journals, institutional reports and pertinent digital publications.

Finding commonalities such as unsafe working conditions, low wages and gendered intersectionality are analyzed and evaluated through policy and case studies from Bangladesh and India. Thus, providing a thorough and compassionate perspective on gendered injustices entangled with socio-cultural and economic aspects, this method integrates a nuanced framework derived from feminist political economics and recent developments in GCS framework.

4.1 Limitations of Study

The study doesn't conduct its own primary empirical research and is reliant on secondary data analysis of literature. The study limits its generalizability to other geographic locations by focusing exclusively on South Asian nations of India and Bangladesh. However, the inherent bias in the selection of sources, along with the exclusion of quantitative methodology may reduce the depth and objectivity of the study.

5 Colonial Legacies and Gender Participation

The British imperialistic norms solidified patriarchal structures in its colonies, reflecting the neoliberal deregulation in contemporary economic structures of India and Bangladesh reflecting gendered exploitation in labor markets. Established through legislations (*The Permanent Settlement Act, 1793*) dominating male ownership, thereby limiting women to domestic chores or informal sectors for redundant wages in textile and agriculture sectors (Joshi, 2007). State-led industrialization in 1990's post-independence in Bangladesh, perpetuated this gender gap by assigning women to low paying, seasonal work in jute manufacturing industry, sidelined by feminized precarity where males were employed with formal education and training.

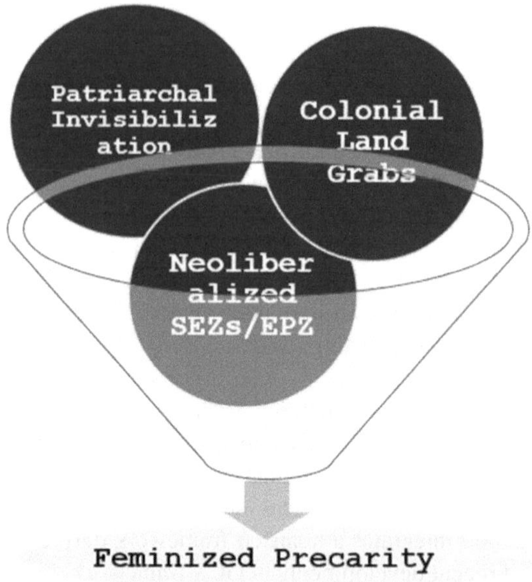

Fig. 1 The effect of unbroken Chain of colonial-capitalist ontology. *Source* Own work

Such ideology crippled mobility and access to formal work for women, a paradigm that persists even today in modern era.

The neoliberal reforms since the 1990's amplified inequalities under the guise of 'progress', as *Structural Adjustment Programs* (SAPs) imposed by World Bank of IMF dismantled labor protections and privatized public sectors. In lieu the labor markets saw a shift towards industrialization, but pushed women into informal sectors like domestic work, where they still face caste-based harassment and domestic abuse (Adnan, 2016). Further, the neoliberalism weaponized colonial patriarchy into a triple burden, by imposing 14 hour factory shifts under surveillance, unpaid care work post-shift averaging 4.5 hours/day and caste or religious exclusion limiting mobility leading to feminized precarity as analyzed in Fig. 1.

5.1 Gender Composition of India's Workforce

From the end of the colonial era to the eve of liberalization, India's labor market travelled a strikingly gender divergent path. In the 1940's the census recorded one third of adult women and well over half of men in economic activity, while the FLFP hovered in the 28–34% band through 1951 (Prasad, 1983). Virtually all of those women who were working on family fields or in home based crafts, were kept out of economic tables until 1961, when statisticians broadened their horizons resulting in an apparent rise in women employment. However, two major changes in 1960s and 1970s led towards a short decline in the FLFP. Firstly, 'factory', 'mines' and 'work restrictions' excluded women from the new *Green Revolution* and *public works jobs* that were drawing men out of farming. Secondly, the 1971 census abruptly stopped classifying many unpaid family helpers as workers, which lead to an overnight collapse to barely 12% in female *labour-force participation rate* (LFPR) while the male LFPR stayed at 45%, giving India a headline ratio of roughly five working men foe every working woman (Anshida Beevi et al., 2018).

The statistical definition was amended in 1981 and again in 1991, revealing a modest rebound to 19.7% in 1981 and 22.3% in 1991 but women still formed only about one worker to four. Spectrally the gulf was wider by 1991 as more than four-fifths of employed women were still in agriculture, while the only non-farm niche employed 5% of them in low paid services. But men by contrast were twice as likely to be in industry and three times as likely to hold a service-sector post (Misra, 2025). From 1940 to 1990, India's workforce grew larger and more modernized, yet it persisted as overwhelmingly male-dominated, with female participation rates declining mid-century before a partial recovery. This gender disparity was evident across sectors as agriculture absorbed most workers, disproportionately women; industry and services remained male-centric, confining females to undervalued rural labor, thus centering India's growth narrative on patriarchal structures upto mid-twentieth century.

The World Bank Development indicators as depicted in Fig. 2 (World Bank, 2025a), indicate early stability for female LFPR from 1990 to 2005 hovering just above 30%. A long slide is visible from 2006 to 2020 as a continuous fall to barely 19% at the pandemic trough. Although a sharp rebound in provisional data from 2022 to 2024 estimates a jump back to the low 305 range, but this relies on model projections that splice household survey signals with macro controls until verified and subject to revision when India's *National Periodic Labour Survey* (NPLS) micro data from 2023–24 become public. Comparing with the global average (~47%) and even the South-Asia average (~38%), these levels remain well below underscoring the need to raise women LFP in Indian labour force.

5.2 Gender Composition of Bangladesh's Workforce

In Bangladesh's long and uneven march from colonial Bengal to newly independent nation, the gender balance of its workforce changed more in how statisticians saw women than in how women actually worked. In the 1940's and 1950's most rural women labored as unpaid family helpers in rice and jute growing processing, yet the colonial era in 1941 and Pakistan era in 1951 censuses counted barely a silver of them because only wage earners were classed as 'workers'. It was in the 1961 census that in East Pakistan more female appeared compared to the Western wing, with women making up about 11% of the recorded labor force, which was almost double the percent (6%) due to amendment in the legal definitions of recognition (Haroon & Jan, 1964). After independence the pendulum swung back, as the first Bangladesh census in 1974, conducted amid post-war devastation and restrictive social norms,

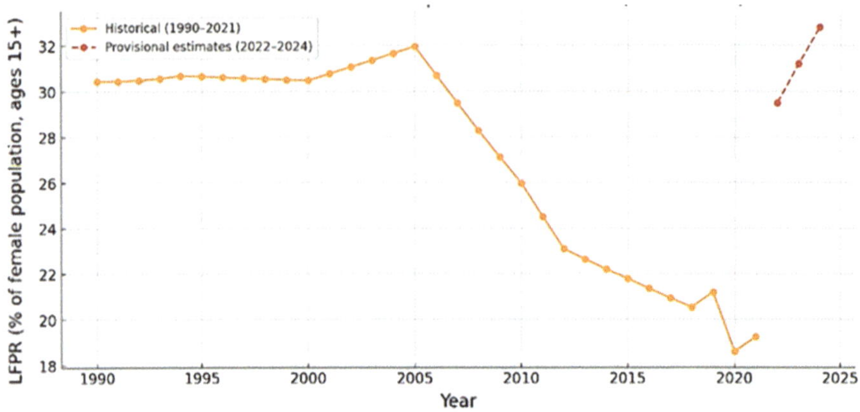

Fig. 2 Female labour force participtaion Ratio India (1990–2024). *Source* Data adapted from 'World Bank Data on modelled ILO estimates (ILOSTAT)'

attributed the female LFPR at 4%, rising only to 8% by 1984 as small scale poultry, fisheries and NGO micro-enterprises began to tug women into cash work (Heintz et al., 2018). Even the 1981 census could still find out only 4.3% working women per 100 females aged ten and over, providing how home based and an annual activity slipped through the official nets (Nabi, 1992).

The real structural break came late in the 1980s when export oriented ready-made garments exploded around *Dhaka* and *Chattogram*, as by 1990 World Bank series show female LFP leaping to 26.6% of adult women and roughly 21% of the total labor force, signaling the moment women began to occupy one job in every five and to remake Bangladesh's shop floor demography (CEIC, 2025). Thus, from 1940 to 1990, the official female proportion of Bangladesh's workforce evolved from statistical obscurity to provisional acknowledgment, approaching widespread industrial integration, an trajectory moulded not by abrupt influxes of women's labor, but by gradual recalibration of their perennial contributions and a late-decade proliferation of factory roles uniquely suited to them.

The *World Bank Development* indicators depicted in Fig. 3 (World Bank, 2025b), indicate a slow but steady climb through the 1990's and early 2000s, with female LFPR edged up from about 26% in 1990 to 30% by 2009, reflecting rising education, smaller families and early garment sector growth. Accelerated gains between 2010 and 2019 rates moved sharply higher, peaking at 36.3% in 2019, due to the RGM boom, which absorbed millions of rural women, large public health and education investments that delayed marriage and boosted secondary school completion. Although, the Covid-19 setback in 2020–21 brought lockdowns which closed factories and informal activities, pushing LFPR down to 34.6% in 2020, which recovered modestly in 2021. The post pandemic rebound figures suggest a bounce to 37% in 2022–23, while the provisional point puts 2024 much higher, at 44%. This gap signals that 2022–24 values rely heavily on short run projections as they should be treated as tentative until survey verification.

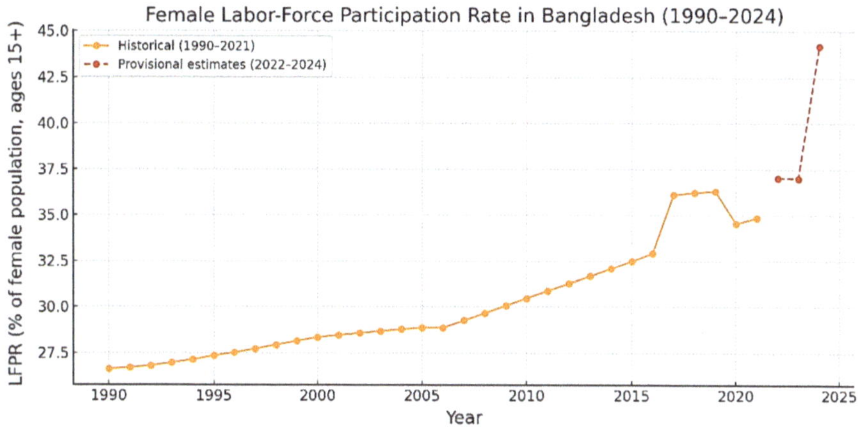

Fig. 3 Female labour force participtaion Ratio Bangladesh (1990–2024). *Source* Data adapted from 'World Bank Data on modeled ILO estimates (ILOSTAT)'

Nevertheless, Bangladesh emerges as South Asia's frontrunner in FLFP, albeit trailing the global average by 7–8%. Advances are predominantly in export-driven manufacturing and rural non-agricultural roles, with scant representation in skilled services. Sustaining this momentum hinges on job diversification beyond garments, enhanced childcare and secure urban transit to retain educated women in employment.

6 Female Precarity and Nexus of Exploitation

In the classic sense first articulated by labor economist *Guy Standing*, feminization of labor describes a two-fold shift. Firstly, a numerical rise in woman's participation in paid work, especially in labor intensive, export oriented industries and; secondly, a qualitative restructuring of work around attributes historically ascribed to women-low wages, 'flexible' hours, home or piece work, weak bargaining power and high job insecurity (Standing, 1989). In global supply chains these two trends *converge* into transnational brands fragment production, outsourcing risk and search the world for suppliers, who are able to deliver 'fast', 'flexible' and 'cheap'. South Asia has become a prime destination and within the region India and Bangladesh are the emblematic cases (Williams, 2022). South Asia's labor market is still dominated by vulnerable employment, yet export oriented manufacturing like garments, leather, electronics and tea has carved out pockets of rapid female employment growth. These pockets are where global supply chains dovetail with patriarchal social norms, caste hierarchies and neoliberal policy reforms, generating a distinct pattern of gendered precarity.

6.1 Case Studies

The intricate tapestry of global economies, women workers in India and Bangladesh often find themselves ensnared in a web of exploitation, where global supply chains, patriarchal social norms, caste hierarchies and neoliberal policy reforms converge to create a distinct pattern of gendered precarity. This perpetuating inequality caped through socio-cultural structures as discussed below.

The Age Old Exploitation and Genting Indian Textile Sector: In South India, Tamil Nadu has been a significant employer in Indian textile and clothing in the famous Tirppur District. Young women aged 18–25 years from poor rural families are recruited as apprentices for three years. These women, often migrants are promised training and accommodation but receive low wages approximately U.S. $1.50/day and minimal benefits, living in dormitories near factories. A different but equally insidious form of exploitation thrived under the guise of one such recruitment scheme, 'Sumangali Scheme' meaning 'Happy Bride' scheme, which targeted primarily impoverished Dalit adolescent girls, luring them and their families with promises of a lump sum payment upon completion of a 3–5 year contract, ostensibly for *marriage dowries* and explicitly marketed as a 'dowry fund'. The girls are treated like a *bonded labor* in isolated, prison like hostels within mill compounds, with restrictions on movement and communication with families. They endure a more than 12 hour shift, with 7 day working in hazardous conditions like extreme heat and suffocating cotton dust causing byssinosis in many. Wages during the contractual period are pitfully low, often below U.S. $1/day after deduction for food and lodging, with rampant wage theft through arbitrary fines (Jumde & Kumar, 2024).

The cheap yarn produced feeds directly into global garment chain, supplying major international brands who benefit immensely from the artificially suppressed labor costs enabled by this gendered exploitation. A study in 2024, noted that adolescent girls are particularly vulnerable with some facing risks of trafficking for sexual exploitation (Solidaridad-South & South East Asia, 2012). This scheme has elicited vehement condemnation from labor unions and NGOs in Europe and the US for contravening core labor rights, encompassing freedoms of association, mobility, and equitable compensation. Advocacy by NGO has impelled global purchasers to sever ties with recalcitrant factories or proffer admonitions. Notwithstanding India's duty to conduct stringent inspection under ILO Convention No. 81, inadequate enforcement sustains such exploitative regimes (Patel & Mondal, 2013).

Electronic Manufacturing Hub and Modern Stressors for Youth: The rapid proliferation of electronic manufacturing hubs in India have become essential to global digital economy. Though lauded as a hallmark of progress (smartphone sector), they expose a persistent pattern of gendered exploitation. Facilities supplying Multinational conglomerates like Samsung, reveal entrenched systematic deficiencies, perpetuated by deliberate neglect of contract labor, intensifying performance expectations and systematic abuse of female youth workers (Andrijasevic & Novitz, 2020). Recruited predominantly via intermediary labor contractors under transient, renewable agreements, denominated as 'trainee', 'apprentice' or 'fix-term arrangements', these female laborers are not concomitant to permanent tenure, compensatory leaves, gratuity and social security measures. Furthermore, prolonged shifts are aggravated by mandatory overtime to satisfy rigorous production limits, often extending 12-hour durations with routine threats of contract dissolution, monetary penalties, egregious verbal abuse and physical coercion. Notwithstanding corporate social responsibility mandates and audits by entities like Samsung, analyses reveal their inadequacy in apprehending the contract workforce's plight or the 'pressure cooker' milieu pervading assembly lines (Krummel & Siegfried, 2021).

The Bangladesh Garment Industry and Beyond: A 2025 study by the *Rights Lab* found that 86% of workers in the informal RMG sector met the criteria for forced labor, with women and internal migrants disproportionality affected (Kliuha et al., 2025). Young women from impoverished rural areas are actively recruited. They are valued for perceived attributes like manual dexterity, docility, acceptance of lower wages and tolerance for monotonous work. The exploitation and lethal consequences of supply chain pressures, stand monumental as a horrifying disaster unfolded on April 24, 2013. An eight story commercial building housing five garment factories supplying major Western brands like 'Primark', 'Benetton' and 'Mango' collapsed, with a death toll reaching a staggering 1134, with over 2500 injured in what was reported as 'Rana Plaza Disaster'. While brands benefited from the cheap production, the complex web of sub-contracting allowed them to deny direct responsibility for factory conditions. The physical and social distance between the gleaming retail stores and Dhaka slums enabled plausible deniability (Bossavie et al., 2023).

Less than a decade later of the Rana Plaza Disaster, another devastating fire broke out at the in Naraynganj, Bangladesh. Workers described blocked exits, inadequate fire extinguishers and lack of training as chilling echoes of pre-Rana Plaza conditions (Hossain, 2019). This fire occurred after the much lauded 'Bangladesh Accord on Fire and Building Safety', initiated post Rana Plaza disaster that had transitioned into a national body, the *Ready Made Garment Sustainability Council* (RSC). Critics argued that RSC lacked the Accords robust independence, binding enforcement power over brands and transparency. The fire exposed weaknesses in transition, suggesting oversight can regress under national pressure. Meanwhile in 2024, another RMG facility (Anzir Apparel), abruptly ceased operations without disburding owed wages to its laborers, citing declining orders and insufficient funds as justifications, owing a life debt to more than 500 workers and their families (Khaled & Ansar, 2024).

6.1.1 Comparative Analysis

The systematic subjugation of female labourers is predicated in India and Bangladesh, which are crucial nodes in the GSC. Different economic structures, social hierarchies and political determinants post-independence cause the particular expressions to differ. In contrast to India's more diverse terrain of exploitation, bolstered by contractual slavery and caste-discrimination, Bangladesh is dealing with a 'garment centric monoculture', plagued by lapses in safety protocols. With India's pervasive enforcement gaps across varied industrial sectors, Bangladesh reaps the benefits of Accord based externally imposed safety regulations. The structural foundation, however remains unaltered, sustained by feminized precarity, regional power struggles and global economic marginalization as discussed in Table 1.

7 Policy Reforms

India and Bangladesh are positioned in a significant but delicate equilibrium. Although it offers essential pathways for FDI, export-driven growth and new technological advancements, integrating the norms of global capitalism necessitates addressing significant legal and regulatory challenges that infringe on national sovereignty and restrict flexibility of domestic policy. While, India is benefiting from a more expansive economy, maintains relatively a robust legal framework, though continually struggling to reconcile global economic integration with native imperatives. Conversely, Bangladesh as a smaller economy demonstrates greater vulnerability to fluctuations in the international market, with its trade policies deeply influenced by 'least developed country' status and dependence on export focused industries. Binding international agreements, particularly *Bilateral Investment Treaties* with *Investor-State Dispute Settlement* mechanisms, expose governments to costly arbitration for enacting public welfare regulations and creating documented 'regulatory chill effect'.

In Bangladesh, the RMG sector's reliance on global supply chains creates a nexus of exploitation where the international retailors cost cutting pressures lead to compromised labor standards. The study in 2022, highlights how order cancellation during Coivd-19 by UK based TNCs triggered widespread job losses, while subcontracting to informal factories increased forced labor risks (Guedhami et al., 2022). Bangladesh's labor legislation, encompassing the 2006, 2013 and 2018 amendments, falls short of international benchmarks such as CEDAW and ILO convention 138, notably in safeguarding minimum working age. This lacuna, exacerbated by scant unionization, renders female workers susceptible to exploitation. While the *Accord on Fire and Building Safety*, a binding pact endorsed by 175 retailers has ameliorated safety in select factories, wider entitlements linger unaddressed.

While India's overall female labor force participation remains law, there is a documented shift away from formal garment factory work towards even more precarious home based or small unit work. Legally, these informal workers fall outside the

Table 1 Comparison of exploitation in India and Bangladesh

Aspect	Bangladesh	India	Shared character
Economic structure	Extreme reliance on RMG sector	Diversified economy with concentrated exploitation hotspots	Export oriented, manufacturing dependent on cheap labor
Workforce	Mass recruitment of rural women (mostly Muslim) through national rural recruitment networks	Intersectional exploitation of (Dalit/Adivasi girls) with hyper exploitative recruitment systems	Deliberate feminization, lower wage acceptance
Employment	Direct employment	Third party labor contractors (TPCs)	Rural to urban migration pipelines
Key vulnerabilities	Rural poverty, gender norms silencing dissent, safety as primary battleground	Caste discrimination, patriarchal control, contract labor traps	Intersectional marginalization and lack of worker empowerment
Key issues	Low wages, forced labor, sexual harassment, safety neglect, wage theft via deductions	Low wages, bonded labor, dowry bondages, forced pregnancy testing, wage theft via opaque pay structures	Precarity: Short-term contracts, job insecurity Gendered wage suppression: Below living wages, pay discrimination
Legal protections	Weak: Fails to meet ILO/CEDAW norms, union suppression	Weak: Limited enforcement of ILO convention 81,	Corruption, regulatory capture, ineffective CSR audits, brands influence policy
Brand accountability	Limited: Binding only for factory safety	Plausible deniability: TPLCs/subcontracting obscure responsibility	Opaque supply chains, audit failures, order cancellations without liability

Source Own Work

labor protections, however, the *Building and Other Construction Workers Welfare Board* under the 1996 Act, aims to provide welfare benefits to informal workers, but challenges towards registration, primarily limit its effectiveness. The new labor codes, including the *Occupational Safety, Health and Working Conditions Code, 2020*, have been criticized for not adequately addressing informal workers needs (Krishna, 2025). In 20,201, an effort to address these challenges was made by the Ministry of Labor and Employment, through the '*E-Shram*' portal for creating a database of the informal workers across the country and provide them access to various welfare schemes with more than 300 million registration upto December 2024(Rajput & Rajan, 2023). Similarly, the most significant among the new codes stipulating the formation of a *State Unorganized Workers Welfare Board* is the *Code on Social Security, 2020*, as are formulated in two states of India, namely; *Gujarat* and *Tamil Nadu.*

As global capitalism has propelled trade liberalization in both countries, aligning with international accords under WTO. In India, this is manifested through reduced tariffs and non-tariff barriers, encompassing 16 effective Free Trade Agreements and ongoing negotiations by August, 2025. In a similar vein, Bangladesh has implemented a rapid and forceful liberalization programme which reduced protective tariffs and import duties to boost imports. But, its economic forecast is gloomy for F.Y. 2025 affected by trade disruptions and global slowdown, necessitating competing and effective policy reforms (McPherson, 2025). While, emerging regional trends indicate friction between the two south Asian countries, with India imposing trade restrictions after Dhaka's strategic shift towards Beijing in 2024 (Huq, 2024). This shift encapsulates larger geopolitical manoeuvres inside a capitalist framework, with WTO debates about trade policies, bilateral agreements and interstate ties hinted by substantial global legal implications.

8 Conclusion and Policy Recommendations

GSC leverage established feminized precarity, limiting social, cultural and economic autonomy, thus curtailing operational cost and flexible employment structures. Manifesting significant contradiction in economic growth of women laborers driven by the intentional undervaluation, with more than 90% facing lack of social security reaping profitable ventures internationally. The scare of 'automation' and AI crossover in industrial sector hasn't stern the pillars of GCS with female laborers being devaluated in production and manufacturing hubs. To address these significant challenges posed by global capitalism in the labor markets of India and Bangladesh, the following policy recommendations are put forth to promote and protect gender equality in labor markets.

(i) *Uplifting Economic Status* of married women by expanding their access to formal education and public employment opportunities through vocational and technical training programs focused on post-training placement assistance.
(ii) *Promoting Digital Literacy and Entrepreneurship Training* in rural areas to enable flexible freelancing opportunities, thereby reducing reliance on precarious jobs.
(iii) *Reforming legal framework* to ensure equality in inheritance laws, housing and credit, digital financial services and expanding joint tilting programs to support entrepreneurship in value-added sectors.
(iv) *Strengthening Social Protection* through micro-credit schemes for female laborers, tax intensives for enterprises, community based childcare facilities in industrial sectors, integrated with parental leave policies to alleviate household burdens.

(v) *Strengthening International Labor Standards* in export sectors, through legal restrictions on anti-discriminatory and anti-harassment practices, regular audits and incentives for compliant GSC.
(vi) *Investing in Safe Public Infrastructure* to enhance women mobility through dedicated transport and access urban job market through promoting sectoral diversification with quotas for female employment.

By adopting these policy recommendations, both nation can cultivate inclusive labor environments, empower women in the workplace and encourage sustainable economic growth that aligns with international and national objectives.

Disclosure of Interest It is hereby declared that writers hold no financial or other interest that may conflict with this research.

References

Adnan, S. (2016). Alienation in neoliberal India and Bangladesh: Diversity of mechanisms and theoretical implications. *South Asia Multidisciplinary Academic Journal, 13.*

Afridi, F., Dinkelman, T., & Mahajan, K. (2016). *Why Are Fewer Married Women Joining the Work Force in India? A Decomposition Analysis over Two Decades.* IZA Discussion Paper No. 9722. IZA, Bonn. Retrieved August 16, 2025, from https://ftp.iza.org/dp9722.pdf

Afzal-Khan, F. (2022). The fundamentalist nexus of neoliberalism, rentier capitalism, religious and secular patriarchies, and south Asian feminist resistances. *Wagadu: A Journal of Transnational Women's & Gender Studies, 24*(1), 239–264.

Ahmed, S. (2024). Wage theft, secrecy, and derealization of 'ideal workers' in the Bangladesh garment industry. *Organization Studies, 45*(6), 881–901. https://doi.org/10.1177/01708406241236608

Ali, A., Ahmad, A., & Ahmad, K. (2025). Labour exploitation and wage inequality in multinational corporations: Evidence from five developing economies. *Qualitative Research Review Letter, 3*(2), 97–125.

Andrijasevic, R., & Novitz, T. (2020). Supply chains and unfree labor: Regulatory failure in the case of Samsung electronics in Slovakia. *Journal of Human Trafficking, 6*(2), 195–208.

Anshida Beevi, C. N., Wason, M., Padaria, R. N., & Singh, P. (2018). Gender sensitivity in agricultural extension. *Current Science, 115*(6), 1035–1036. https://doi.org/10.18520/cs/v115/i6/1035-1036

Antipova, A. (2021). Analysis of the COVID-19 impacts on employment and unemployment across the multi-dimensional social disadvantaged areas. *Social Sciences & Humanities Open, 4*(1), 100224. https://doi.org/10.1016/j.ssaho.2021.100224

Ashraf, H., & Prentice, R. (2019). Beyond factory safety: Labor unions, militant protest, and the accelerated ambitions of Bangladesh's export garment industry. *Dialectical Anthropology, 43*, 93–107.

Basirulla, M., Tasnim, F., & Mahmud, M. S. (2024). Female garment Workers in Bangladesh Facing Human Rights Violation; a search to find the root causes. *Cosmopolitan Civil Societies: An Interdisciplinary Journal, 16*(3), 85–103. https://doi.org/10.5130/ccs.v16.i3.9089

Bossavie, L., Cho, Y., & Heath, R. (2023). The effects of international scrutiny on manufacturing workers: Evidence from the Rana plaza collapse in Bangladesh. *Journal of Development Economics, 103107*. https://doi.org/10.1016/j.jdeveco.2023.103107

CEIC. (2025). *Bangladesh bd. Labour Force: Female: % of total labour force (2024).* Retrieved August 16, 2025, from https://www.ceicdata.com/en/bangladesh/labour-force/bd-labour-force-female%2D%2Dof-total-labour-force

Custers, P. (2012). *Capital accumulation and Women's labour in Asian economies* (Rev. ed.). Monthly Review Press.

De Neve, G. (2014). Fordism, flexible specialization and CSR: How Indian garment workers critique neoliberal labour regimes. *Ethnography, 15*(2), 184–207. https://doi.org/10.1177/1466138112463801

Dev, A., & Sahay, R. (2025). *Unlocking women's workforce potential.* Ideas For India. Retrieved July 26, 2025, from http://www.ideasforindia.in/topics/productivity-innovation/unlocking-women-s-workforce-potential.html

Filippi, E., Bannò, M., & Trento, S. (2023). Automation technologies and the risk of substitution of women: Can gender equality in the institutional context reduce the risk? *Technological Forecasting and Social Change, 191*, 122528. https://doi.org/10.1016/j.techfore.2023.122528

Guedhami, O., Knill, A., Megginson, W. L., et al. (2022). The dark side of globalization: Evidence from the impact of COVID-19 on multinational companies. *Journal of International Business Studies, 53*, 1603–1640. https://doi.org/10.1057/s41267-022-00540-8

Haque, R. (2025). *Contemporary gender transformations in South Asia: Transcending the archetype of womanhood* (pp. 43–64). Emerald Publishing Limited. https://doi.org/10.1108/978-1-83708-368-820251003

Haroon, K., & Jan, Y. A. (1964). Main economic characteristics of the people of Pakistan: Sixth release from the 1961 census. *The Pakistan Development Review, 4*(2), 314–331.

Heintz, J., Kabeer, N., & Mahmud, S. (2018). Cultural norms, economic incentives and women's labour market behaviour: Empirical insights from Bangladesh. *Oxford Development Studies, 46*(2), 266–289. https://doi.org/10.1080/13600818.2017.1382464

Hossain, N. (2019). Rana plaza, disaster politics, and the empowerment of women garment workers in Bangladesh. *Contemporary South Asia, 27*(4), 516–530.

Huq, E. (2024). China-Bangladesh strategic Alliance in the 21st century: Implications for India following of Bangladesh's recent political shift. *Journal of Indian Studies, 10*(2), 185–204.

Joshi, S. (2007). Men, women, and domestics: Articulating middle-class identity in colonial Bengal. *The Journal of Asian Studies, 66*(2), 564–566. https://doi.org/10.1017/S0021911807000769

Jumde, A., & Kumar, N. (2024). 'Mutated Sumangali scheme': Challenges in enforcement of labour Laws in spinning Mills of Tamil Nadu. *Journal of Labor and Society, 27*(2), 170–184. https://doi.org/10.1080/24730580.2024.2353529

Khaled, A. F. M., & Ansar, A. (2024). Bangladesh's ready-made garments sector rebound: Revisiting gendered labor precarity and dependency. *Asian Journal of Comparative Politics, 9*(2), 218–237.

Kliuha, A., Bosatta, L., & Schwarz, K. (2025). *Modern slavery and child labour in Bangladesh's garment sector: Documenting risks and informing solutions.* Rights Lab, University of Nottingham.

Krishna, N. R. (2025). Occupational safety, health and working conditions (Osh) code, 2020 and interstate women migrants: A gender integrative evaluation. *Indian Journal of Public Administration, 71*(2), 406–411. https://doi.org/10.1177/00195561251338111

Krummel, D., & Siegfried, P. (2021). The dark side of samsung's value chain: The human costs of cobalt mining "blood, sweat and cobalt". *Journal of Geoscience and Environment Protection, 9*(02), 182.

Kustin, B., Reinecke, J., & Donaghey, J. (2025). Transnational capitalism after Postcolonialism: Researching the interfaces in global supply chains. *Journal of Business Ethics, 202*(2), 243–261. https://doi.org/10.1007/s10551-025-05985-z

Mamun, M. A. A., & Hoque, M. M. (2022). The impact of paid employment on women's empowerment: A case study of female garment workers in Bangladesh. *World Development Sustainability, 1*, 100026. https://doi.org/10.1016/j.wds.2022.100026

McPherson, M. F. (2025). *Macroeconomic management in Bangladesh: Challenges and opportunities Bangladesh public administration project*. Policy Brief Series, Harvard Kennedy School.

Mezzadri, A. (2016). Class, gender and the sweatshop: On the nexus between labour commodification and exploitation. *Third World Quarterly, 37*(10), 1877–1900. https://doi.org/10.1080/01436597.2016.1180239

Misra, S. B. (2025). Revisiting rural non-farm sector employment in India: Trends from 1993-94 to 2023-24. *Indian Journal of Human Development*. https://doi.org/10.1177/09737030251322830

Moloney, K. (2022). *Who matters at the World Bank?: Bureaucrats, policy change, and public sector governance*. Oxford University Press.

Nabi, A. K. M. (1992). Dynamics of internal migration in Bangladesh. *Canadian Studies in Population, 19*(1), 81–98.

Nazneen, S., & Okech, A. (2021). Introduction: Feminist protests and politics in a world in crisis. *Gender and Development, 29*(2–3), 231–252. https://doi.org/10.1080/13552074.2021.2005358

Niumai, A. (2025). Intersecting inequalities: Unravelling gender and social exclusion in contemporary society. *Journal of Social and Economic Development, 27*(Suppl 1), 1–8. https://doi.org/10.1007/s40847-025-00435-y

Norberg, J. (2024). Globalization: A race to the bottom—Or to the top? 247. In S. Lincicome & C. Packard (Eds.), *Defending globalization* (2nd ed.). CATO Institute.

Patel, V., & Mondal, N. (2013). Women in the workforce where are they? *State of the Urban Youth, India, 2012*, 91.

Prasad, B. (1983). The employment strategies of the Indian five-year plans: Reasons for their failure. In *Employment policy in a developing country a case-study of India* (Vol. 2, pp. 363–395). Palgrave Macmillan. https://doi.org/10.1007/978-1-349-06646-9_1

Premji, S., Begum, M., Laila, K., Jahangir, S., & Tahsin, F. (2023). *Working and hurting in little Bangladesh: Precarious work, health and return to work*. McMaster University School of Labour Studies and South Asian Women's Rights Organization.

Rahman, S. H., Khatri, S., & Brunner, H.-P. (Eds.). (2012). *Regional integration and economic development in South Asia*. Edward Elgar Publishing.

Rajput, K., & Rajan, S. I. (2023). Visibilising invisible population: E-Shram portal and essentiality of internal migration database in India. *Journal of Social Inclusion Studies, 9*(1), 82–94.

Solidaridad-South & South East Asia. (2012). *Understanding the characteristics of the Sumangali scheme in Tamil Nadu Textile & Garment Industry and supply chain linkages*. Technical Report, Cornell University eCommons.

Soundararajan, V., Sharma, G., & Bapuji, H. (2024). Caste, social capital and Precarity of labour market intermediaries: The case of Dalit labour contractors in India. *Organization Studies, 45*(7), 961–985. https://doi.org/10.1177/01708406231175319

Standing, G. (1989). Global feminization through flexible labor. *World Development, 17*(7), 1077–1095. https://doi.org/10.1016/0305-750X(89)90170-8

Williams, E. (2022). Appalling or advantageous? Exploring the impacts of fast fashion from environmental, social, and economic perspectives. *Journal for Global Business and Community, 13*(1). https://doi.org/10.56020/001c.36873

World Bank. (2025a). *Labor force, female (% of total labor force)—India*. Retrieved August 16, 2025, from https://data.worldbank.org/indicator/SL.TLF.TOTL.FE.ZS?locations=IN

World Bank. (2025b). *Labor force, female (% of total labor force)—Bangladesh (2024)*. Retrieved August 16, 2025, from https://data.worldbank.org/indicator/SL.TLF.TOTL.FE.ZS?locations=BD

World Economic Forum. (2024).*Global gender gap report 2024*. Retrieved July 22, 2025, from https://www.weforum.org/publications/global-gender-gap-report-2024/.

Anna Bashir is currently appointed as Senior Assistant Professor at Kashmir University Law School, with prior experience in Indian Society of International Law, New Delhi. She earned her Doctorate in Private International Law from Delhi University, LL.M. in Patent & Designs Law from Ankara University, Turkey, LL.M. in Commercial Laws from Aligarh Muslim University and LL.B from Kashmir University and qualified UGC NET. She is a recipient of The Hague Academy of International Law Scholarship (Netherlands), WIPO-KIPO Fellowship (South Korea), WIPO Fellowship (Turkey) and Xiamen Academy of International Law Scholarship.

Abhilash Aggarwal is serving as an Assistant Professor at School of Law, CHRIST (Deemed to be University), Bangalore, Pune Lavasa Campus. A doctorate in law from Central University of Haryana, Mahendragarh, India with a specialisation in Gender Rights and Personal Laws. A Gold Medallist in LL.M. in Constitutional and Administrative Law from National University of Study and Research in Law, Ranchi. His research portfolio spans some of the most pressing contemporary legal questions, including the ethical and regulatory dimensions of Artificial Intelligence in judicial decision-making, cybersecurity and human rights, responsible digital governance, social media censorship, criminal justice reforms and constitutional law.

Mehvish Mehraj is serving as Assistant Professor in the Department of Management at the University of the People, California. She holds a B.A. LL.B. and an LL.M. in Constitutional Law from the Central University of Kashmir, with a doctorate in law from the University of Kashmir focusing on refugee rights and education of children, along with a Diploma in Cooperative Management from the J&K Cooperative Society. Her research primarily focuses on international refugee law, with particular emphasis on the intersection of human rights, migration and state obligations in the global legal framework.

MIX
Papier aus verantwortungsvollen Quellen
Paper from responsible sources
FSC® C105338

If you have any concerns about our products,
you can contact us on
ProductSafety@springernature.com

In case Publisher is established outside the EU,
the EU authorized representative is:
Springer Nature Customer Service Center GmbH
Europaplatz 3, 69115 Heidelberg, Germany

Printed by Libri Plureos GmbH
in Hamburg, Germany